The SS *City of Flint*

The SS *City of Flint*

An American Freighter at War, 1939–1943

M<small>AGNE</small> H<small>AUGSENG</small>

McFarland & Company, Inc., Publishers

Jefferson, North Carolina

Library of Congress Cataloguing-in-Publication Data

Names: Haugseng, Magne, 1951– author.
Title: The SS City of Flint : an American freighter at war, 1939-1943 / Magne Haugseng.
Description: Jefferson, North Carolina : McFarland & Company, Inc.,
Publishers, 2021 | Includes bibliographical references and index.
Identifiers: LCCN 2021014602 | ISBN 9781476685366 (paperback : acid free paper) ∞
ISBN 9781476643236 (ebook)
Subjects: LCSH: City of Flint (Ship) | World War, 1939-1945—Atlantic Ocean. |
World War, 1939-1945—Transportation. | Naval convoys—History—20th
century. | Cargo ships—United States—History—20th century. | Shipwrecks—North
Atlantic Ocean—History—20th century. | World War, 1939-1945—Naval
operations. | World War, 1939-1945—Naval operations—Submarine. |
BISAC: HISTORY / Military / World War II | HISTORY / Military / Naval
Classification: LCC D774.C488 H38 2021 | DDC 940.54/293—dc23
LC record available at https://lccn.loc.gov/2021014602

British Library cataloguing data are available

ISBN (print) 978-1-4766-8536-6
ISBN (ebook) 978-1-4766-4323-6

Front cover image: SS *City of Flint* the day after being liberated,
now safe in Bergen, Norway, around 5 November 1939.
She was anchored just below the Bergen Maritime Academy
(courtesy Bergen Havnekontor's Arkiv, Bergen Byarkiv)

Printed in the United States of America

McFarland & Company, Inc., Publishers
Box 611, Jefferson, North Carolina 28640
www.mcfarlandpub.com

To the memory of Al Becker

Acknowledgments

First of all I have to mention Al Becker, who survived 46 days in the lifeboat and who shared all his experiences with me, thus providing such inspiration and unstinting support. His advice and information through many, many helpful, supportive and interesting emails have been crucial in developing the final part of this story. Regrettably Al passed away before I managed to complete the manuscript. In his place, Al's son John Becker has provided generously from his family photos, for which I am very grateful.

Secondly, Günter Belling's support has been fantastic, over so many years and so many great discussions. Günter has a genuine interest in history and in the *City of Flint*. So many have helped in so many ways: Svein Aage Knudsen for information and for help to locate photos; Sivert Alme who helped sort the apples and who showed me the quay; Astrid Riddervoll, who tasted the wonderful *City of Flint* apples and who told me the story of Haugesund; Miles Tollemache, who was in Bergen at the time; Johannes Kühne for advice on the T. Vorhatr; Rudolf Gahler who was third in command in the prize crew. Günter knew Rudi and Hannes. Øivind Ask at *Bergens Tidende* helped with Norwegian information; as did the Nasjonal Bibiliotek at Oslo and the Nobel Institute, who granted me such generous access to their archives. Dr. Browning provided some very useful signposting. The Museum of the Atlantic at Halifax was very helpful as were the University Libraries at Galway and Leeds and the National Archives of America. Terje Inderhaug, whose father later saw action in the Olav Tryggvason helped greatly when the distance between England and Bergen became a problem. Jone Engelsvoll helped locate obscure legal texts; Martin Boyle advised on the official German reports from 1939 and Michael Ellstermann provided generously from his sources of information on U-575, including unpublished papers and photos from the crew members. Greg McClelland generously provided information and photographs from his archive on his grandfather's time at sea. Professor Joshua M. Smith who helped identify the young sailors from the U.S. Merchant Marine Academy at Kings Point, Averill Buchanan, the Mariners' Museum and Park, the Norwegian Naval Museum, Fred. Olsen & Co., and the Bergen Archive who helped with photographs, very valuable signposting or support. Through all of this, my wife had to put up with endless discussions and lots of papers. Without her support none of this would have happened.

Table of Contents

Section V—Postscript

Introduction

The work to chart this story has simply grown and grown in significance and in reach. It started with a few references in Norwegian newspapers from October 1939. Initially it was difficult to see from the short references why an American freighter was even mentioned once, let alone repeatedly, in provincial papers in a country seemingly far from the *City of Flint's* regular routes. The significance of the events around the ship became abundantly obvious when the headlines from *The New York Times*, also from October 1939, hove into sight. Research soon uncovered a series of voyages that set the ship apart from any other vessel the members of her crew had ever seen.

The U.S. was not involved in any wars when the *City of Flint* sailed right into a European one. Even in Britain, the Second World War was often referred to as "The Phony War" during the fall of 1939. Rest assured that there was nothing phony about the treatment this American freighter experienced.

The work to unravel the story of the *City of Flint* and those who sailed in her yielded some impressive facts. This was a ship that ended up moving through a very special combination of events. Hers was a war that did not start at the Pearl Harbor bombing in December 1941, but on the very day Britain and France declared war on Germany, 3 September 1939.

Every year in the United Kingdom, the 3rd of September is celebrated as Merchant Navy Day. The celebration is in honor of the sacrifices of the merchant navy in war. The date was picked to commemorate the very first sinking in World War II of a merchant ship, the *Athenia*. This was a large passenger liner bound for Montreal with passengers returning home to safety to escape the coming European war. She had over 1400 passengers and crew on board when she was torpedoed. The *City of Flint* was one of the first ships on the scene to help with the rescue.

The story of the *Athenia* sinking has been told elsewhere, by a number of authors. It is not a major part of the story of the *City of Flint*. It has to be included as the freighter, in one of her later experiences, sailed right in to the event, purely by chance, and then ended up playing a major role in it all.

Her story continued in this vein. The 20-year-old freighter was among the first American ships to enter the European battle zone as the Second World War ebbed and flowed. Even her sinking and the rescue of her crew were extraordinary. This is a story where personal courage, determination and endurance came to be tested by the enormous forces of nature and by self-serving politicians in Norway, the former Soviet Union and in Germany in equal measure.

Her next trip to Europe saw the *City of Flint* become front page news on both sides of the Atlantic. The capture by the German warship *Deutschland* was one of the events in the fall of 1939 that really enthralled a large international audience. Newspapers and radio brought the story right into the homes of a very receptive horde of listeners every day. Here was a freighter, from a neutral country, fully laden with goods for English and Irish ports, being taken prisoner by one of Germany's largest warships and being told to sail to a German port where the entire cargo would be unloaded and sold. Watching the American crew every step of the way was a team of German navy personnel, armed to the teeth with bombs, guns and hand grenades. They even set scuttling charges all over the ship to make sure that if they could not have her, no one else would either. As we shall see, it came close to this, very close.

There is a story to be told in this alone—but in addition, here was an American ship being ordered to sail to Murmansk in communist Soviet Union in order to avoid being cornered by the British Royal Navy. It was a diplomatic nightmare for the U.S. ambassador in Moscow who could only watch as the German and Soviet forces collaborated. For the American crew, stuck on their ship in a freezing port far beyond of the Arctic Circle as they watched their captors being allowed ashore, it was a real trial. It was not much better when the German Prize Command was put back on board and they sailed, hugging the coastline (first the Soviet one, then the Norwegian), as they proceeded south towards Germany, captive and with the threats of an attack from the British.

Could this really happen? How could the Norwegians allow an American ship with an American crew to be forced, against their will, by a German Prize Command to sail in their waters, protected by Norwegian naval vessels? Norwegian authorities mishandled the case very badly. The details of how their ministers and their advisers changed their minds and changed the story is still there to be seen at the Norwegian State Archives in Oslo. It is fascinating reading. As is the plan Lord Louis Mountbatten of the British navy developed to capture the ship; he even had two boarding parties ready, prepared to jump aboard! Documents at the British National Archives were riveting reading, describing the chase along the Norwegian coast, ending with Mountbatten miscalculating the speed and location of the *City of Flint*.

She anchored, against all Norwegian advice and warnings, at Haugesund, a small coastal city where the local German consul was doubling as the resident spymaster. That night soldiers from neutral Norway, guns at the ready, finally boarded and liberated her, interning the German Prize Command in the process.

The actions of Nazi Germany played right into President Roosevelt's hands. On the very day that the *City of Flint* was liberated by armed Norwegian marines, the Neutrality Law was changed. From that day onwards, struggling Britain and France could come and buy arms in the U.S. Without access to the vast American arsenal, the war in Europe could have been over, in Hitler's favor, in months.

It would not have been possible to piece together this story without significant input from documents from the U.S. National Archives and Records Administration. The details from the event itself have come from sources far closer to the actual action—from the young man who ended as one of the Prize Command navigators, from the son of the Prize Commander and from eyewitnesses along the coast of Norway. It is the use of such sources that makes this account so unique.

Even Hitler became personally involved in the handling of the *City of Flint*. He guaranteed her safe return to the U.S. At the political level, the aftermath of the incident on the coast of Norway caused a real high-level squabble between the German navy and her

Foreign Office. Even during our research, so many years later, the blame game surfaced again in naval circles.

Returning to Baltimore, the *City of Flint* was faced with the newly introduced American legislation that blocked her from continuing the regular run to ports in the European war zone.

Pearl Harbor changed it all. The *City of Flint* was one of the first U.S. merchant ships to be armed and a contingent from the U.S. Armed Guard joined the ship in readiness for her first convoy. She was going back to the Soviet Union, now fully laden with military aid.

The United Kingdom was again an ally and with the ban on European sailing lifted, the *City of Flint* was the first civilian U.S. ship back in British waters. From now on, the *City of Flint* would certainly "do her bit" for the war effort. Her trip to Britain was merely the first leg of a journey to provide help to the new ally, the Soviet Union. The *City of Flint* was the second U.S. merchantman to sail a war cargo to Murmansk during World War II. It was a tough stint for a crew where most of them had no experience of war. Only good luck and good shooting by the Armed Guard saved them from the dive bombers.

The reports and eyewitness accounts captured details of what must have been a terrifying attack, yet as we see, the Armed Guard never flinched. They remained at their posts throughout, firing at the enemy planes as they came screaming down towards them. To stay at their guns when they saw the bombs being released must have taken more than nerves of steel. It is this gritty determination that the story brings out again and again.

With the convoy route to Murmansk becoming far too dangerous at the onset of the Arctic summer with the lack of darkness, a new supply route had to be found. A long and far less well known route was introduced to keep Stalin's forces supplied and in the war. American merchant ships, with very little escort cover, started to sail from East Coast ports, heading south around Africa and north in the Indian Ocean and up into the Persian Gulf.

Ports with names that became notorious during the more recent Iraq wars were in the summer of 1942 at the heart of a huge freight operation. The heat, the sand and the primitive conditions exacted a heavy toll from all those who sailed there, the merchant navy crews among them. The *City of Flint* was one of these ships. Her Bridge Log reflects the arduous work at each Gulf port and the suffering of the crew.

Hardly back home, she was readied for yet another convoy, this time to help supply the Allied forces in North Africa. Such was the importance of these supplies, that when the U-boats torpedoed a number of tankers early in January 1943, Admiral Dönitz, the head of the German navy, was thanked personally by General von Armin, the army officer in charge of the German forces in North Africa.

Into this campaign sailed the *City of Flint* on what was to become her final convoy. During a terrible storm, she had to heave to in the middle of the Atlantic and secure her cargo, only to lose touch with her convoy. Stalked for hours by a U-boat, she was sunk. One of the eyewitnesses was a crew member in the U-boat. His diary has never before been published and he himself was killed when the U-boat was destroyed during a later war patrol.

The unpublished eyewitness accounts allow us unique access to experience the final convoy both from the conning tower of the U-boat that sank her and from the bridge of the *City of Flint*. The U-boat also picked up the cook, whose story is very different from that of any regular prisoner of war. His skill at bluffing saved the entire convoy.

Sadly six of the *City of Flint's* crew perished. It could easily have been 16 deaths. The skills of a young Norwegian sailor and the determination of the other nine in the final lifeboat saved all their lives. The dramatic eyewitness account, recounted here, of the 46 days they spent in an open boat before rescue is a humbling read that really serves to illustrate what sailors endured. Only one other account of survival after such a long time in a lifeboat is known, namely that of Louis Zamperini, the hero of *Unbroken*.

One eyewitness and survivor was Al Becker. During the summer of 1942, Al realized that six months after America's entry into the war, he too would soon be drafted into the armed services. As he saw it, the alternative was for him to take the initiative, which he did. He liked the navy best; that was where he decided to sign up.

Without Al, who lived to tell the story, we would never have known anything about the terrifying time of the survivors in the fourth lifeboat. There are official reports of the sinking in official archives, but they simply do not do justice to the men's endurance. Two young men from the lifeboats that were rescued early—Donald W. Summerhayes and John Corrigan—also submitted their reports of the sinking to the Merchant Marine Academy at Kings Point, New York. On placement to learn seamanship, they came to experience a dramatic torpedoing in which the ship's cargo of fuel exploded above them in a huge fireball, into which the ship sailed relentlessly. It took strong nerves not to jump overboard at that stage. Those who did were never seen again. Fortunately, the explosions did not set off the secret consignment of poison gas stored in the cargo below deck.

Al Becker watched it all; he saw the bridge-wing being blown off the side of the ship as the torpedo exploded. Much later, he told me the story, bit by bit.

Mariners everywhere brought their wartime experiences right into the homes of their families. The sailors had gone to sea to do a job of work. None of them expected or were prepared for the way the war would treat them. They suffered and endured. Tragically, far too often their sacrifices have gone unrecognized and after the war their struggles frequently met with little more than indifference. They all deserve to be heard and to have their stories told and remembered. This is one contribution to it all.

The Personalities

Al Becker—A born survivor, who sat through 46 days in the No. 4 lifeboat and lived to tell the story.

Winston Churchill—Was very keen to liberate the ship to ingratiate himself with Roosevelt.

Joseph A. Gainard—The skipper who steered the *City of Flint* and her crew to safety in 1939.

Günther Heydemann—The skipper of *U-575*, the man responsible for the sinking of the *City of Flint*.

Adolf Hitler—Promised the *City of Flint* a safe journey home.

Rohmar Johansen—The young Norwegian who looked after the No. 4 lifeboat and who saved them all.

Halvdan Koht—Norwegian foreign minister; was he merely naïve or simply pro–German?

Fritz Julius Lemp—The man who torpedoed the *Athenia*.

Louis Mountbatten—The British naval officer who gambled with his only chance to capture the ship for Churchill, and lost.

Vyacheslav Molotov—The powerful Soviet Commissar responsible for the relationship with Germany and with the USA.

Hans Pusback—Commander of the German Prize Crew on the *City of Flint*.

Franklin D. Roosevelt—The President wanted his ship back.

Axel Wenner-Gren—Swedish millionaire. His yacht was involved in the *Athenia* rescue.

The Ships

Athenia—The first British ship to be torpedoed in the Second World War, commemorated on Merchant Navy Day, 3 September each year, in Britain.

City of Flint—An ordinary American freighter, which helped rescue passengers from the *Athenia,* was captured by the Germans, chased by the British, and liberated by the Norwegians, only to be torpedoed three years later with poison gas in the cargo.

Deutschland—The large German warship that captured the *City of Flint.*

Knute Nelson—Fred Olsen Line ship, first on the scene in the *Athenia* rescue.

Lorentz W. Hansen—Norwegian freighter sunk by the *Deutschland.*

Olav Tryggvason—Norwegian warship that liberated the *City of Flint.*

Stonegate—British freighter sunk by the *Deutschland.*

Southern Cross—Swedish yacht, owned by millionaire Axel Wenner-Gren.

Abbreviations

AB—Al Becker
ADM—Admiralty, Britain
BAMA—German Federal Archive, Military Records
BBC—British Broadcasting Corporation
BdU—Befehishaber der U-boote
FO—Foreign Office (British
KTB—Kriegstagebuch (War Diary)
GFM—German Foreign Ministry
MBE—Member of the Most Excellent Order of the British Empire
PRO—Public Record Office, British National Archives, London
RA—*Riksarkivet*, Norwegian State Archive
OKM—*Oberkommando Marine*, German Naval Command
OKW—*Oberkommando Wehrmacht*, German Armed Forces Command
SKL—Seekriegsleitung, navy leadership

The Beginning

1

Preparations

Why would the political situation in Norway be the subject of one of the briefings for officers on board one of Germany's finest warships, the *Deutschland*?[1] It was the middle of August 1939 and the Peace Treaty of Versailles had not even come of age. Summer guests along Germany's North Sea beaches were only beginning to think of returning home. The contrast between the white sandy beaches and the warship wardroom might have been stark, but the topics of conversation may well have been disturbingly similar. The talk of impending war was everywhere. In the *Deutschland*, the discussion was more focused, more in line with one of the debates from naval war-gaming virtually since the end of the last war.[2] Had Germany had forward bases for U-boats and surface vessels in France and in Norway, British fleet movements could have been more easily destroyed and merchant shipping would have had a far easier route back to Germany.

The naval port of Wilhelmshaven, where the *Deutschland* was based, was becoming increasingly busy. In the case of the *Deutschland*, even extra personnel, beyond their normal complement, were now ordered aboard. Some of these were merchant navy officers. If at home and "between ships," they were now being requisitioned by the German navy.

In southwestern Norway people were enjoying a late summer, warm enough for them to be drawn to the white sandy beaches along a coast which was totally open to and unsheltered from the forces of the North Sea. These waters, protected only by Norwegian neutrality, offered German ships a safe route home from the oceans of the world. All their opponents could legally do was to stand back and watch. The Hague Convention XIII of 1907 allowed merchant navy ships belonging to belligerent nations to proceed unimpeded through territorial waters of neutral states. They could take as long as they required to reach their destination, and were allowed to stop as often as they wished. Warships, on the other hand, would, according to the Hague Convention, need to be on the move. Some countries even insisted on advance notice of any visits by warships. They would only be permitted to seek harbor in case of emergency or they would risk being interned.

In August 1939, war had yet to be declared, but alas, all over Europe, its inevitability was becoming increasingly obvious. So far, knowledge of its start date remained confined to a relatively small group. At its center, Hitler was accelerating his preparations. There were still some benefits to be had from the element of surprise. As the summer was drawing to a close, European governments were preparing for war. In early July Britain called up her reserve personnel for the navy. The official reason was that some maneuvers were planned for August, but in reality, Prime Minister Chamberlain wanted the Royal Navy as battle-ready as possible by early September.

Britain was convinced that when the war commenced, the most significant threat offered by the German navy came from their potential use of the largest ships. As commerce raiders, with high speed and long range, they could wreak great havoc and destruction for British sea-borne trade, thus making surveillance of their movements a priority. The U-boats on the other hand would be hamstrung by the German commitment to the Hague Convention and the "stop and search" requirements on U-boats before sinking any ships.[3] Such tactics would be entirely unusable against convoy traffic, as long as Hitler honored his commitment.

In Britain, "signals intelligence" from deciphered German navy radio messages was nonexistent. Over the last years before the war, German code experts had worked hard to improve on the commercially available Enigma coding machine and by 1939, they were confident of having a completely secure code system. At the British Code and Cypher School, they had a German section, which in turn had a naval unit, which by the summer of 1939 comprised only one officer and a clerk. They did not even have their own cryptanalyst to work on the German naval codes.[4]

The only solution to the information shortfall was to mount a continuous surveillance patrol across the North Sea. The patrol line ran from Montrose in Scotland to the Obrestad lighthouse south of Stavanger on the southwest coast of Norway. The job was to have been done using Anson airplanes, until someone discovered that this aircraft did not actually have the range to reach Obrestad. Instead, the task was allocated to the Second Submarine Flotilla. The five boats allocated to do the patrol left port around 24 August, but by then it was already too late.

Europe was still enjoying the fading vestiges of peace when the pocket battleship *Deutschland* slipped out into the North Sea mists. Her prime task was to prey on British shipping, once war broke out. According to the German Prize Regulations, her Master, "Kapitän zur See" Paul Wenneker, was permitted to sail home any ships, even neutral ones, carrying contraband, if he chose to do so. Alternatively he could sink them on the spot.[5] In planning commerce raiding in the waters where he was now headed, namely the North Atlantic south of Greenland, Wenneker and the German naval command must have considered the possibility of stopping neutral American ships. Nevertheless, his job was to seize every contraband-carrying ship as a prize, and send them to a German port to discharge the cargo. The fate of the ships would be settled at a Prize Court. Germany regarded this as entirely in line with the Prize Regulations. Britain and Germany seemed to agree on the interpretation at the time. Ensuring that the prize actually altered their course and headed for an alien port was more problematic and meant placing a contingent of armed soldiers on board. For any commerce raider, like the *Deutschland*, the problem was that each such Prize Command would deplete her complement, unless they actually carried extra crew for this task. Germany regarded any product that could contribute to the war effort, directly or indirectly as contraband. Effectively, there was very little chance of continuing any trade with a country at war with Germany without violating their contraband rules.

The German ship sailed prepared. On leaving port she carried five extra naval reserve officers who could serve as Prize Commanders; three B-Dienst (intelligence) personnel, experts on codes and cryptology; and four additional wireless operators to serve on these potential prizes. In addition, the *Deutschland* would benefit from the extra services provided by a weather observation technologist and a weather signal cryptologist—both seconded from the Naval Observatory in Wilhelmshaven.[6]

On the Eastern Seaboard of America, it was very much "business as usual." Captain

Joseph Gainard, now on his third journey to Europe since taking over the American freighter *City of Flint* in March that year, had on the previous two journeys visited both German and British ports. The United States Maritime Commission owned the *City of Flint*. She was on charter to the United States Lines. The *City of Flint* was a freighter with a regular route to Europe, which had altered little since the 1920s. She would bring a cargo comprising a vast range of products to European ports. As the cargo was discharged, she would pick up a batch of return cargo and move along the coast to another port for a part load, before turning back to towards the American East Coast. This routine happened again and again. With a new crew she departed Norfolk on Thursday, 10 August for New York to pick up a European cargo.

The *City of Flint* left New York for Manchester, Liverpool, Dublin and Glasgow on Monday, 14 August. This was the very day when Hitler told his assembled top military leaders that the war was coming. The German Naval leadership started recording their War Diary the following day.

As they reached the European ports, Gainard was amazed to learn that so many eager travelers would like to sail with him back to any American ports. He ran a freighter; all were politely refused passage.

In Berlin and in Moscow, diplomats were working at a near frenetic level. Over the last few weeks Foreign Minister Ribbentrop had been busy drafting a non-aggression pact with the Soviet Union. By mid–August the efforts were beginning to pay off, according to Laurence Steinhardt, the U.S. Ambassador in Moscow. He claimed that at the same time, Stalin kept a Franco-British negotiating team waiting.

Both sides in the budding conflict were wooing the Soviet Union. For Germany, such a pact would serve several purposes. It would seal the fate of Poland, which would be wedged between two allies, both of which would benefit from her demise. Second, the pact would split Stalin from British and French interests and, many hoped, prevent a two-front war if Anglo-French promises to Poland of military support in case of war were honored. Thirdly, it would perhaps pacify Stalin until Hitler was satisfied the German forces were strong enough to match anything the Soviet leadership could field.

Sir Neville Henderson, the British Ambassador to Germany at the time, described the news of the agreement as a "bombshell" when it became known on Monday, 21 August. He seemed to have been far more ill-informed than the American diplomats. The U.S. Chargé d'Affaires Kirk in Berlin did not trust the integrity of the German telegraph. He often used his colleague in Paris, Ambassador William Bullitt, as a safe route. That Monday Kirk used the Paris route to send U.S. Secretary of State Cordell Hull a message. Kirk had learned that Hitler would attack Poland on Friday the 25th. Unknown to Kirk, his prediction was merely one day wrong. By Monday evening Hitler saw Ribbentrop off at the airport as he flew off to Moscow for the signing ceremony with Stalin. Hitler was very keen to secure this agreement before he entered Polish territory.

In London the Foreign Secretary, Lord Halifax, made light of the news, describing the pact as potentially insignificant, and asked Henderson to take another personal letter from Chamberlain to Hitler. Hitler replied by return, stressing that Germany had never been seeking conflict with England and had, in fact, for years strived to win friendship.[7] As if to prove exactly the opposite, the second of his two modern pocket battleships left port as planned the day after. In the evening of Thursday, 24 August, Hitler returned to Berlin. Seventeen seagoing U-boats had started leaving their bases in Kiel and Wilhelmshaven a full week earlier, all bound for the eastern Atlantic, closest to British shores. The next day, 14 smaller U-boats headed out for positions in the North Sea.

The British meanwhile, were totally unaware of all these naval movements. The Royal Navy was, however, moving their own ships into position for war. Within a week, all the vessels allocated to the Home Fleet were either already at Scapa Flow or at the Humber, or underway to join them.

Then Hitler faltered. In Italy, Mussolini claimed he had no resources to lend Hitler in case of war with France and Britain. Hitler had relied on Italian support; now he had to go it alone. Mussolini's disastrous wars had been too costly; he required several years to rebuild his forces. Temporarily the war was off. The stay of execution, the power to stop his willing executioners, was all in Hitler's gift.

Germany had sent virtually all its major ships and U-boats to sea, and they could not be called back as easily as the land forces that were told to stand down. The U-boats had all sailed the long distance north around the British Isles to reach the open waters of the Atlantic. Bringing them back now would mean that, once back at base, each U-boat would require re-supplying, which would take time. Holding them in port temporarily only to order them back to sea later without re-bunkering would mean that they would be of use for only a limited period of time. Staying on station meant remaining surfaced, in the same position, for large parts of the time to maintain air supplies and battery charges, which risked detection. Furthermore, the longer they remained at sea in peacetime, the shorter the time they would be available for action before being forced to return to base, regardless of the fact that most captains kept their boats at sea until perilously short of fuel and provisions.

In Washington, a steady stream of increasingly alarming signals reached the desks at the State Department. Even if the mood among American politicians had yet to swing fully behind the President, his core team shared Roosevelt's view of European developments. A war in Europe would impact on America. Forewarned was forearmed; Secretary of State Cordell Hull now introduced a 24-hour work schedule for his office staff. From now on, the State Department would never close.[8]

Hitler's logic, his approach to waging war, was "landsinnig"—land-based. His strategies and plans dealt with physical gains of territory and his experts in the Operational Art were all from the army. They had learned how to conduct large-scale battles during the First World War. His opponents, Roosevelt and Churchill, on the other hand, had minds focused on a global vision of international trade and of a balance of power based on the control of oceans and of sea-borne logistics. Now, he announced the pact with the Soviet Union on the same day as the *Deutschland* went to sea. For the Poles, it was but the briefest of respites. The tension hardly lifted on the Polish border before the invading Germans overran the defenders a week later.

All over the world European ships were suddenly caught up in a war, which would make their return home infinitely more complicated. The British registered *Stonegate* had barely arrived at her destination when it all started. She was at the Chilean port of Tocopilla to pick up a cargo of saltpeter and was bound for the Clyde, where a substantial part of the British chemical industry was located.[9] The largest explosives manufacturing plant in Britain, Nobel Explosives Company Ltd.'s Ardeer factory at Stenston, together with several other similar plants nearby, all had easy rail access to associated plants around Glasgow.[10]

By Sunday, 3 September, German U-boats were ready on station around the coast of

Britain, and at 1400 they were told to commence war operations, in accordance with the Prize Regulations. The war had started.

The rules for German surface vessels meant the *Admiral Graf Spee* and the *Deutschland* were permitted to sink merchant shipping only after first stopping and searching them. The German Prize Regulation even required them to ensure the safety of the crew.

U-boats were even more disadvantaged. The Prize Regulations took the entire element of surprise away from the U-boat if they stopped any likely target, for they had to conduct a time consuming search of the ship and ensure that the crew, together with any passengers, had the opportunity to leave the ship safely. As a result, the U-boats were ordered to attack only ships which could justifiably be torpedoed without any warning— enemy warships, troop ships, ships under escort and ships that if told to stop for a search, attempted to transmit their position with a warning signal.

Northern waters and in particular Norwegian territorial waters were crucial for the safe route back to Germany in the case of war. On Friday, 25 August, Hitler approved the transmission of a series of coded messages to recall the entire German merchant fleet. It would prove to be a disaster.

To return home from South America, they all had to sail north, up the Denmark Strait, around Iceland. Then they had to skirt the ice on the Greenland side until nearly as far north as Bear Island before heading east towards the Norwegian coast where they could turn south towards German ports within the safety of neutral waters.

Against the advice of senior naval officers, Naval High Command insisted that an extra phrase be added to the final message to the German ships, namely "within four days."[11] All over the world German ships now turned tail and ran for the nearest port.[12] These were crucial days when the British navy was not yet properly deployed, the blockade of Germany was not fully operational, yet the order cost Germany dearly.

The volume of imports to Germany started to drop dramatically with so many ships tied up in foreign ports and by the middle of September even the State Ministry for Economic Affairs was voicing its concerns. German ships had sailed into neutral harbors all over the world. If they could only manage to reach Norwegian waters, they stood a great chance of making it home. Too much cargo, of value to the war effort, had still not been brought back to Germany.[13]

Berlin now felt they could draw on Soviet facilities. Having first directed some of the German merchant fleet to head for Murmansk, they now decided to ask for Soviet cooperation over the shipping issue. On Wednesday, 6 September, they informed the Soviets that from then on, German ships would be directed to Murmansk where local crews would be expected to help with unloading. The Germans wanted the Murmansk authorities to facilitate the transshipment of any cargo to the railway and then on to St. Petersburg by train. At the Baltic port, German ships would pick up the cargoes and transport them to waiting German recipients. By Friday, the Soviets had agreed to this.[14]

Britain regarded Norwegian waters as an integral part of their efforts to blockade German trade. Two days after the British declaration of war, the British ambassador in Oslo, Sir Cecil Dormer, opened negotiations with the Norwegian Minister for Foreign Affairs, Halvdan Koht, who deliberated over the agreement for seven months before finally signing it on 11 March 1940.[15] Three weeks earlier the Norwegian Government had signed an agreement with Germany, committing Norway to maintain the volume of exports to Germany at the 1938 level. Britain, on the other hand, declared in the middle of

September that she would resist violation of Norwegian territory as fiercely as if the UK itself were under attack.

As the German traffic along the Norwegian coast grew, the German Naval High Command increased their activities in the area.[16] When fully laden freighters neared home, German authorities were anxious not to see the ships sunk during the final stages of the journey. Merchant shipping was issued with a specific order not to approach the Norwegian coast south of 63° N. The ships should then proceed south along in-shore waters. Most ships stopped at Bergen where the consul provided information and instructions for the next leg of the journey home. With an increasing volume of traffic, Bergen was too far north to be able to give the real support now needed. Germany secured permission to establish a new consulate at Haugesund and the newly accredited vice consul Ewald Lanwer left Berlin on Friday, 6 October.[17] Once Lanwer was in place he would take over the crucial role of advising the ships. The waters immediately south of Haugesund were very exposed, without any islands or skerries for protection. The significance of Norwegian territorial waters was referred to on a virtually daily basis at the German Naval High Command's conferences. Their use of neutral waters was proving a reliable route.[18]

There was a very good reason for German ships to stop at Haugesund, Lanwer explained later. The German navy tried to help by providing the protection of a U-boat if at all possible. Such protection could only be possible if strict rules for reporting at Haugesund and departure from Haugesund were adhered to. They should radio for further instructions and wait for permission to leave.[19] Berlin needed to know before 1400 what a ship's departure time would be. In order to maximize the benefits of the cover of darkness the ships should leave Haugesund between 1600 and 1700. Small wonder that the Germans were so keen to open a consulate there that fall.[20]

The Norwegians would have been well aware of the actual strategic significance of their territorial waters to the survival of the German merchant fleet. It was a route, which although open to all seafarers within the rules of the new Norwegian Neutrality Regulation, offered a clear advantage to the Germans. Yet closing the coastal shipping lanes totally to all ships of belligerent nations would have been a step clearly favoring the British side. The accepted notions of neutrality as set out in Hague Convention XIII provided some measure of international support for the Norwegian government when attempting to steer a political middle course. The reality was that Foreign Minister Koht in Oslo had to avoid the wrath of Germany while attempting to please the British with whom the Norwegian Royals shared ancestry. This proved impossible. Koht was simply not up to the job. On the other hand, if the job he had been elected to do was to keep Norway out of the war, it could simply not be done with the resources he had available.

2

A Helping Hand

The sun had hardly set once on the new warring nations before the first U-boat victims were struggling to survive the waters of the Atlantic in the evening of Sunday, 3 September 1939. The Donaldson Atlantic Line's unarmed liner *Athenia* (13,581 tons), the first ship to be torpedoed, had left her last European port before war had even been declared.[1] In fact, her location should have indicated this to the U-boat. Furthermore it was a fully laden passenger liner, supposedly safe from unannounced attacks. She was Montreal bound from Glasgow, Belfast and Liverpool, but was torpedoed and sunk 250 miles west of Inistrahull in Donegal. The Cunard White Star Line operated the ship. Against Hitler's specific orders, the torpedo struck without warning. The sinking provided the banner headline for *The New York Times* the following morning: "British Liner *Athenia* torpedoed, sunk; 1,400 passengers aboard, 292 Americans; all except a few are reported saved."

By August 1939, as war in Europe seemed inevitable, numerous transatlantic sailings had been cancelled, stranding thousands of Americans at ports all over Europe. Towards the end of the month the State Department sent detailed instructions to London, Paris and Bern. The latter was to become the European clearinghouse for repatriation. All U.S. bound ships were to be used. Knowing that the *Athenia* was sticking to her sailing schedule, hers was one of the departures the diplomats were filling to capacity. The uncertainty over the looming war ushered Americans home and many Europeans abandoned their homes in the hope of a more peaceful new life in America.

The fatal torpedo hit the *Athenia* during the second seating for dinner, around 1940. From a U-boat's perspective, this is the ideal time to attack. Sunset was less than an hour away. The ship would be silhouetted against a setting sun and the onset of darkness would provide cover for the escaping U-boat. The actual sinking was slow; the ship did not disappear below the waves until around 1040 the following morning, a full 15 hours later.

As the *Athenia* started to transmit the SOS signal asking for assistance, several ships joined the dramatic radio dialogue. Stavanger-bound Swedish *Alida-Gorthon* relayed messages from a ship called the *Southern Cross* to the British Admiralty. The admiralty sent messages back to the *Southern Cross* on the position of the sinking liner.[2]

As soon as the captain of the *Southern Cross* heard the first SOS signal around 2130 he sent a telegram to the *Athenia*: "distance from you 50 steering full speed to your assistance." On the red Marconigram form the telegrapher on an unknown ship relaying the message had scribbled "*Knute Nelson* also in communication with *Athenia*."[3] Pure fate placed Wenner-Gren and his yacht the *Southern Cross* close to the very first civilian casualties of the war. Only weeks earlier he had been busy using his high-level contacts in London and Berlin in a frantic attempt to prevent the war. When he failed, Wenner-Gren

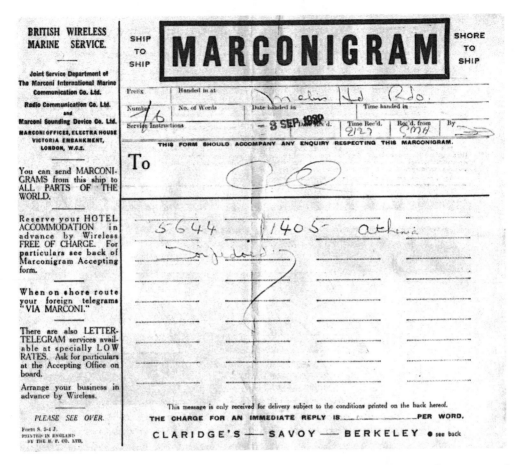

The radio signal alerting the world to the liner *Athenia* being torpedoed in the evening of 3 September 1939. She had left port in peace; now she was the first casualty of the new war (© McClelland Archive).

and his American wife decided to relocate to the Bahamas for the duration. They were actually en route to the Caribbean when, thanks to Oberleutnant zur See Fritz Julius Lemp of the *U-30*, the new war caught up with them.

Churchill was notified around 2230, that evening. *The Times*, published in London the very morning the story broke on the world stage, only managed to include a reference to the incident in some of its later editions. The rescue operation had hardly begun by the time the Fleet Street deadline for the morning edition temporarily silenced the typewriters. Because of the time difference, *The New York Times* had at least another five hours before going to print, during which they could develop the story for their front page. As expected, the story created an outcry in neutral America, where many felt they had no part in the European conflict.

Gradually, a number of ships joined in the rescue. The first on the scene was the Norwegian tanker *Knute Nelson* of the Fred Olsen Line. Panama-bound *Knute Nelson* was less than 60 nautical miles away.[4] Miraculously it took them only four hours to reach the stricken ship. When they arrived, they initially saw only the red emergency lights from the lifeboats all around them.

Shortly afterwards, around 0230 Monday morning the *Southern Cross* arrived. The

Norwegian freighter *Knute Nelson*. The ship picked up several hundred survivors from the *Athenia* sinking, transferring some to the *City of Flint* and taking the rest to Galway, at the west of Ireland (courtesy Fred. Olsen & Co.).

yacht took 370 survivors on board and later transferred them to other ships. As luck would have it, the ship was big; the *Southern Cross* had been described in the press as "one of the largest yachts in the world."

When the Swedes arrived they were met with a sight of lifeboats and their glimmering lights and life jackets dotting the heavy seas over a vast area. They used a searchlight to locate the lifeboats. The heaving swell had nearly flooded many of the boats; some were by now overfilled, as they had picked more survivors from the water. People sat in the lifeboats waist deep in water. They had spent nine hours in the lifeboats.

By 0900 Captain Joseph Gainard and the *City of Flint* had arrived on the scene and started to take on passengers from the *Southern Cross*. At that stage, none were in the water. Several more were still in their floats and lifeboats, scattered around the *Southern Cross*. On Gainard's orders, the *City of Flint* lowered her own lifeboats in order to help pick up survivors. One of these lifeboats was under the command of young Carl Ellis from Newtonville, Massachusetts.[5] Gainard had himself been torpedoed while serving on the U.S. troop ship the *President Lincoln* in May 1918. He knew the significance of gathering the survivors and the life rafts to prevent them spreading across a vast area of empty sea.

A husband and father tortured by uncertainty was Scot John Hayworth, safe in Canada. His wife and two daughters aged ten and six were returning from Scotland on the *Athenia* when the war caught up with them with such ferocity.[6] After a long and torturous wait, the news was particularly trying for any parent; his youngest daughter, Jacqueline, had been rescued, but was back in Scotland, waiting with strangers to come across to Canada on another ship. His wife and other daughter Margaret had been rescued by the *City of Flint*. There was no information on the fact that 10-year-old Margaret had sustained very serious injuries from the exploding torpedo.

The parents of three-year-old Rosemary Cass-Beggs eventually heard that she was alive and well.[7] Only, they learned of her survival on their return to Oxford in England, with little Rosemary moving farther away from them by the minute. She was safe, but heading towards the Canadian port of Halifax aboard the *City of Flint*.[8]

As the British destroyers *Escort* and *Electra* arrived that Monday morning, one of them took on board all the British survivors that remained on the *Southern Cross*. The rescued passengers were given the choice to move to the British warships and return to Britain or be transferred to American freighter the *City of Flint* and continue across the Atlantic. Many chose the American freighter even though the transfer proved to be quite a trial for them. They had to go back into lifeboats for the short journey across to the waiting ship.

Once on board, they discovered that the *City of Flint* was already carrying some passengers. All of them gave up their bunks to the *Athenia* survivors. The ship now had a great many new passengers to accommodate and some of them turned to help treat the survivors who had suffered only minor injuries, freeing up time for Dr. R.L. Jenkins and his other volunteer helper, Dr. Lulu E. Sweigard, to treat the more seriously wounded.[9] They had quite a number of patients. The *City of Flint* received 220 passengers from the *Southern Cross*.[10] In the meantime the *Alida-Gorthon* had provided blankets and provisions for the *City of Flint* for her journey to Halifax, the closest port on the western side of the Atlantic.

Merely an hour after the *Athenia* sinking, the British War Cabinet met in London. The agenda was up to date. The sinking of the *Athenia* was Item 6. The short minutes summed up the icy cold ruthlessness of the members of the Cabinet, and spoke volumes for the eagerness to bring the United States closer to the British side in the conflict: "The occurrence should have helpful effect as regards public opinion in the United States."

Officially, Germany never did take responsibility for the sinking and the Americans remained neutral. President Roosevelt did, however, continue proceedings to lift the export ban on war materiel, as set out in the Neutrality Act. The subsequent actions of the German navy against the *City of Flint* kept degrading their standing in American public opinion. As we shall see, the Neutrality Act was changed in early November 1939, much to the delight of the French and British governments. It provided a real boost to their ability to fight the war. European democracies really needed access to American weapons and military equipment to show the world that Britain and France could and would fight Hitler's Germany. Secretary of State Hull had in January 1939 agreed that the Neutrality Act in reality prevented Britain and France from buying weaponry to defend themselves. The embargo might actually encourage Hitler to go to war. The U.S. Ambassador to France William C. Bullitt advised President Roosevelt that the Neutrality Act, as it stood, would contribute to the actual defeat of Britain and France.

It was reported from Washington that the U.S. Maritime Commission's ship the *City of Flint* had notified them that she had picked up 236 survivors from the stricken liner. According to Joseph A. Gainard, the Master of the *City of Flint*, he knew when the *Athenia* actually went down.[11] The *Athenia* radio operator had tied his Morse key down before leaving the ship. This was standard practice; it made the radio transmit a steady signal which could be used to locate the stricken vessel. When silence again prevailed on the international emergency frequency, the ship had gone. Gainard's ship had been moored alongside the *Athenia* in Glasgow and left on a similar course 36 hours later. Although a freighter that normally could take only a few passengers, the *City of Flint* left with half of a party of schoolgirls as only half of them could be accommodated in the liner. Such was the pressure to bring home as many Americans as possible as Europe descended into the terrifying fog of war once more. The American ambassador, Joseph P. Kennedy, had been personally involved in persuading Gainard to take any passengers at all. In the end Gainard accepted 28 passengers. He explained later that he conceded only as a favor to his friend.[12] Kennedy would most likely have known Gainard from his time as chairman of the U.S. Maritime Commission.

As the *City of Flint* approached the North American coast, two of their patients who had sustained serious injuries were transferred to the U.S. Coast Guard cutter *Bibb*. Sadly, the Coast Guard cutter was not in time; one of their patients, little Margaret Hayworth, died that Saturday night. Hers was the first Canadian life to be taken by the war. The *City of Flint* reached Halifax the following Wednesday. For privacy, Dr. Jenkins and Lulu had moved her to an empty lifeboat where she was embalmed. Canadian soil would be her final resting place, not the cruel North Atlantic.[13]

The survivors included eight so severely wounded that they had to be taken off the ship in Halifax on stretchers. The scene on the quay at Halifax was described by the arriving survivors as "very sad." People had travelled up to Halifax to meet their loved ones, some only to be totally grief stricken by the lack of news.

On 8 September 1939, Mrs. J. Borden Harriman, head of the American Legation in Oslo, received a telegram from her State Department, instructing her to thank the Norwegian government for their assistance during the *Athenia* rescue. Unknown to her, Mrs. Harriman was less than two months away from working very closely with a second ship from that operation, namely the *City of Flint*.

The news of the *Athenia* sinking flashed around the world in hours. Berlin was suddenly worried that the impact of the *Athenia* sinking would be as bad as when the *Lusitania* was torpedoed by a German U-boat off the coast of Ireland during the First World War. Within days of the *Athenia* sinking, Hitler repeated his orders for the navy not to attack ships carrying passengers, even if part of a convoy, and regardless of nationality. Although front page news in American papers, the sinking was soon to be overtaken by news from the war in Europe.

Events started by a German dictator had lifted the name of an American freighter from quiet anonymity to front page news. The *City of Flint* had been elevated to celebrity status. Captain Gainard's sure and steady handling of the rescue introduced him and his ship to an impressive audience on both sides of the Atlantic.

The war was still in its first week.

Section II

The Prize

3

Trapped

Kapitän zur See Paul Wenneker took the *Deutschland* to sea from Wilhelmshaven under the cover of thick mists in the afternoon of Thursday, 24 August 1939, before hostilities broke out. The plan was to hide in the North Atlantic.[1] The orders for the ship to prepare for departure had actually been issued three weeks earlier. They were to follow the Prize Ordinance strictly when attacking British merchant shipping.[2] As luck would have it, the ship slipped out just as the Royal Air Force's general reconnaissance squadrons were grounded.

Wenneker took the ship slowly past the swing bridge and out the Jade, watching the sandbanks carefully until he was clear of Roter Sand before setting a course directly up the middle of the North Sea. Obersteuermann Rudolf (Rudi) Gahler, who kept the ship's War Diary, later explained that as they reached Dogger Bank, Wenneker assembled all available crew members at the rear deck. Addressing them below the reassuring gun barrels of their main stern battery, he told the nervous crew that although war had not yet been declared, they were on their way to take up waiting positions to start sinking enemy ships once they received the signal to do so.[3]

By 0915 the next morning they were just off the Utsira lighthouse, west of Stavanger on the south-western coast of Norway. It was a tense time, trying to sneak out of the North Sea past the British, when suddenly a lookout spotted a light aircraft. In his War Diary Wenneker noted that it could belong to an aircraft carrier.[4] Some tense waiting followed until they concluded that they had actually not been spotted. In fact, the British did not spot the ship until November, by which time she was back in the Baltic.

By Saturday, as he looked at the weather forecasts, the cautious Wenneker decided to go north, around Iceland and enter the Atlantic through the Denmark Strait, running between Iceland and Greenland. The weather system south of Iceland promised good visibility, which meant that any of the many fishing vessels expected in those waters might easily spot the warship trying to sneak past.

Early Monday, 28 August, they saw the first icebergs. At the time, they were running on only one engine because the starboard one had to be stopped due to an overheating bearing. Wenneker decided to call in his supply ship, the *Westerwald*, to practice the transfer of supplies. On Wednesday morning they spent three hours transferring oil from the vast tanks of the freighter.

So far it was still peacetime and life in the ship was relaxed. By the afternoon of Thursday, 31 August, the reality of it all started to hit home. At 1800 hours Wenneker received a general broadcast message from the German Admiralty, the Seekriegsleitung: German naval units were to commence war operations against Poland at 0445 hours on

***Westerwald*, heading south past Bergen, toward Germany, 29 November 1939. She had been acting as the supply ship for the *Deutschland*, the ship that captured the *City of Flint* a month earlier (CC Riksarkivet, Norway).**

the following morning, Friday, 1 September, but in home waters only. Units in the Atlantic were to remain passive. Even in the event of a declaration of war by Western Powers, force should only be used in self-defense, or on specific orders.

Wenneker was still moving away from the conflict zone and he considered his options carefully. As Rudi typed the War Diary, he saw that within three days they would be on station off the east coast of Greenland. He could not escape the war, however. At 1945 hours he learned that England and France were mobilizing all their forces. Italy, on the other hand, declared her intentions to remain neutral. By Sunday morning, 3 September, the weather was closing in. A biting force 7 wind was building from the north-northeast and the seas were heavy. At 1100 hours ship's time, a signal came in over the radio: "To all units in the Atlantic. Commence war with England immediately."[5]

In Berlin, they were starting to put in place the relevant paperwork for the war. In order to introduce a trade war, where the taking of ships under Prize Regulations was allowed, the start of such a regime had to be founded in law. Germany now formally did this. The Prize Regulation came into force at 1200 hours that Sunday.[6] The actual procedure to take over a neutral or enemy merchant vessel was basically state sponsored piracy. The fate of the ship and the cargo would be decided in a special court established solely to deal with such cases. The ship would be referred to as a Prize, the court as a Prize Court. There were Prize Courts established in several harbor cities, including Hamburg. They were all controlled from the German Reich's Prize Court, located two blocks away from the American embassy in Berlin.

Britain operated a Prize Court at the London Law Courts. They did not pretend to grant independence to the process. The British Prize Department was located in Houghton Street in London, at the Ministry of Economic Warfare.[7] Britain had used the Prize mechanism successfully for centuries. The sharing out of the value of a Prize was dealt with in some detail as early as in the "Black Book of the Admiralty" of around 1351.

The *Athenia* sinking was a particularly belligerent breach of all conventions for naval warfare. The man in charge of the German navy, Grand Admiral Erich Raeder, wanted to wage a trade war, a "Handelskrieg," on Britain, basically in order to choke off all supply lines to the island kingdom. That was why he had sent two pocket battleships to sea and that was why scores of U-boats took up positions around the British Isles. They were, however, supposed to follow the rules.

Throughout the next day the *Deutschland's* lookouts spotted several ships passing on the horizon. Wenneker had obviously placed himself in a key position for waging his trade war and early on Tuesday morning he sent up his airplane. The pilot headed south, looking for likely targets. By 0900 hours, three hours had passed and the plane had not returned. The plane had been forced to land on the sea. It took Wenneker until 1600 hours to locate the plane and bring it back on board.

An hour later they received a message sent to the *Admiral Graf Spee* and the *Deutschland*. They were to break off offensive operations and hide away from their areas of operation. As a result, Wenneker now headed back north towards the Denmark Strait.

At the end of September, Raeder travelled all the way to the newly conquered Polish territories for a meeting with Hitler. Raeder argued that the initial phase of the U-boat war in the Atlantic was now at an end. He therefore wanted to expand the war. Hitler finally agreed to Raeder's request to be allowed to "sink on sight," but not quite.

Any merchant ship, whether belonging to the enemy or to a neutral country, could only be sunk if they attempted to use their radio once asked to heave to for a document and contraband inspection. As a rule, however, Hitler wanted neutral merchant shipping treated well. Furthermore, no action was permitted against passenger liners.

Having won this concession from Hitler, Raeder excitedly went on to argue that it was becoming increasingly important to use the pocket battleships actively in this war. They had been deployed so long that their provisions were diminishing, thus very soon forcing them to return to port without having seen any action. October was to be the beginning of the second wave of U-boat action and it would make sense to coordinate the deployments. Hitler agreed.

That Sunday, in Norfolk, Virginia, Captain Joseph Gainard made the first entry in the new Bridge Log for his next journey in the *City of Flint*. The ship was docked at the Norfolk army base. It would be the job of the deck officer on duty to maintain the log. Each day of the journey had a double-page spread and the entries had to be signed off on a daily basis by Chief Officer Warren Rhoads and countersigned by Gainard, the Master. It was a quiet day, overcast, but still, the log had one brief entry: "no work this day, the Sabbath observed."[8]

As the stevedores started work in the morning of Monday, 24 September, it was still overcast, but the grey weather was forgotten when they discovered that a case of Ballantine's Scotch Whisky bound for Richmond, Virginia, was empty. The log offered no explanation as to where the whisky had gone.

All Norfolk cargo was quickly loaded, there being only 12 consignees.[9] Since Norfolk was regarded as the start of the new journey, the crew had to be reassigned. Before they departed, they were offered the opportunity to be paid off, or re-engaged for the new sailing. Those of the crew that remained with the ship complained that after the *Athenia* rescue they had had only six hours at home before sailing again, but others did what sailors the world over often did; they stayed in port until they felt like picking up a ship again.

Just before 2230, the pilot came aboard and they cast off. He did not stay long, as leaving the inshore waters at Norfolk was quickly achieved. They were heading north along the coast towards New York, pushed by a gentle southwesterly.

In Germany, Raeder was back at his desk. He spent Monday translating Hitler's agreements into a plan of action. Via a radio transmission he placed the *Deutschland* under starter's orders: "Assume that imminent reintroduction of trade war is likely."[10]

During the night Wenneker took his ship towards a pre-arranged spot in the Denmark Strait for a final transfer of oil, provisions and ammunition. They were lucky; the wind dropped to a gentle breeze from east-southeast and by lunchtime the job was done.

Admiral Raeder had let them off the leash. Wenneker now sat down to assess the situation. Rudi had to type a long entry in the War Diary. Wenneker wanted posterity to know the reasons for his actions. During the early part of the cruise he had taken his ship on a southeasterly course from the southern coast of Greenland, cutting across the area which would be traversed so frequently by Atlantic convoys over the next few years. At that stage, Wenneker had seen nothing of interest. He decided to head further south in order to hit the tanker routes from the Caribbean.

The British freighter *Stonegate* had sailed from Panama to Kingston without any escort at all, a journey of some 4 to 5 days. She had a cargo of 8600 tons of saltpeter. They therefore willingly waited for 24 hours when they arrived in Kingston to be able to join the next convoy north, even if the escort was a single light cruiser and a French submarine, the *Surcouf*.[11]

In the 1920s the *City of Flint* had a regular circle route between Philadelphia and Baltimore on the American East Coast and ports in Britain, Ireland and Germany. At each port she would discharge or pick up cargo, sometimes both, but sailing empty between ports made the owners no money at all.

The routes and ports of call for the *City of Flint* during the 1930s were not logged anywhere systematically, but her operators had an interest in Trans-Atlantic trade and she continued to make regular calls to ports in and around the British Isles, such as Hull, Bristol, Dundee, Belfast, Dublin and Hamburg. Gainard took over the *City of Flint* in March 1939 as she was loading at Norfolk, Virginia, at the time on charter to the Southgate Nelson Lines; Gainard had the ship on another round trip to Germany during the summer and would probably have continued similar runs had the geopolitics permitted. Her presence in a British port at the end of August 1939 was due merely to the latest part of such a sailing schedule.

The freighter's roots stretched back into the final months of the First World War. As part of the war effort, the U.S. administration organized a series of Liberty Loans and as towns and cities all over America struggled to raise support for the fight for world liberty, some were rewarded for their effort by being given an opportunity to name a ship. These new ships were built to replace those sunk by German U-boats and to expand the reach of the American merchant navy once the war was over. In the state of Michigan, only two cities were invited to name such ships; one was Detroit, the other was Flint.

It was regarded as a privilege to receive such an offer and great care was taken to ensure that the ship's name met with as wide popular support as possible. In the case of Flint, the Genesee (County) War Board therefore asked the local newspaper, the *Flint Journal*, to help. During early February 1918, each edition of the *Journal* included a blank coupon, inviting the readers to suggest a name for "their" ship, before returning the completed entry to the War Board. In the *Journal's* Friday, 18 January 1918 edition, the name chosen by popular vote was announced to be *City of Flint*.[12]

The ship was included in an order for 60 Type A freighters awarded to the American Internal Shipbuilding Company on 7 May 1918. The yard had by then enough orders to build 180 freighters and the first one was named on 5 August 1918 with President Woodrow Wilson and his wife in attendance. When the *City of Flint* was launched 16 months later, she was the 74th freighter to be completed by this huge shipyard. She was a 4,963-ton oil burning "Hog Islander" named after the location of the yard at Hog Island, Pennsylvania. (Today the Philadelphia International Airport covers the site.) The yard was created specifically to manufacture ships, as fast and cheaply as possible to a standard size.

All parts and components used in the construction of the ships could be swapped for similar parts from other ships being built at one of the slipways around them. The width of a U.S. flatbed rail freight car determined the maximum width of any part used. This process allowed parts to be sourced anywhere and then moved in by rail. The ship had originally been laid down as the *Collingdale*, but her name was switched to the *City of Flint* during the construction. Mrs. J.W. Fenton, the wife of an official from the United States Shipping Board, the owners, launched the ship on Saturday, 27 December 1919.

Two months later, the completed ship was handed over to the Board, who immediately put her to work on the Trans-Atlantic European routes. Later, the lease was formally transferred to the American Hampton Roads Line. As the U.S. Maritime Commission superseded the American Shipping Board, so did the control of the *City of Flint* and her crew. On 2 March 1937 Joseph P. Kennedy wrote to President Roosevelt accepting the invitation to become the first chairman of the new Commission. As war broke out in Europe in September 1939, the *City of Flint* was sailing for the United States Lines and Kennedy was the American ambassador in London. In February 1939 he had been sworn in.

For the *City of Flint*, New York was the final stop before crossing the Atlantic, bound for European ports. During the afternoon, as they came up the coast, Gainard wasted no time in trying to develop the efficiency of the crew. He let them undergo fire and lifeboat drills. "Efficiency of crew poor," Gainard noted.[13]

Two hours after midnight they passed the Ambrose Light Vessel just off Long Island and picked up pilot E. Brown for the trip into New York harbor. Looking east at West 13th Street, they passed Pier 54. The *Carpathia* landed her *Titanic* survivors here in April 1912. Later, the *Lusitania* left from the same pier, never to return.

This time the destination was Pier 58, the first of the four piers used by United States Lines. These were the original Chelsey piers, build for Cunard and the White Star Line's majestic liners such as the *Olympic* or the *Titanic*. The *Titanic* would have docked at Pier 60, had she ever made it to New York.

They docked early in the morning of Wednesday, 27 September; loading started immediately. For a ship, any time spent loading or unloading was time wasted. The quicker the turnaround between sailings, the more money the ship generated. There was always time pressure.

The weather cleared during the night and as the stevedores returned early Thursday, the clouds were broken. It was to be a fine, clear fall day. During the afternoon they had a stark reminder of the distant war in Europe. Four men from the U.S. Army spent over two hours carefully fitting out and instructing the uneasy members of the crew how to use gas masks.

German Intelligence decided to warn the two warships in the Atlantic, the *Admiral Graf Spee* to the south and the *Deutschland* in the North Atlantic, that superior forces could be expected in the shipping lanes and it might be necessary for the two to pull back to "emptier" parts of the ocean. The broadcast added that newspapers in America were now talking about the new convoy system which had been introduced between Halifax in Nova Scotia, Canada, and England.

At the Hudson River, early Friday morning, a gang of riggers came aboard the *City of Flint*. They rigged out stages, which they used to paint large American flags on the sides of the ship. Painting the ship was a job that sailors at times had to do at sea. In comparison, this was easy, but it did reinforce the image of a European war zone awaiting them.

Loading was still continuing, although again, no work took place during Sunday. On Tuesday, 3 October, the loading gangs had to forego lunch. Having sealed the hatches, they had to stow the deck cargo. The pilot was actually already aboard before the loading was finally completed at 1700 hours, and an hour later they were underway.

By following the Eastern Seaboard northwards they were heading directly into a strong northeasterly wind, with a heavy swell. The crew trimmed the vents to prevent water coming in and prepared for the first night "under sail" as the ship settled in to the rhythm of the sea. This was the Atlantic after all; nobody expected a totally smooth crossing to England.

It was cloudy and overcast off the coast of Maine the following day, with a fairly rough sea. The *City of Flint* was experiencing some pitching and rolling, but was still managing an average speed of 9 knots. As they passed the Nantucket Light Vessel at 1800, the duty officer, Lewis, would have been pleased to note that the wind and the sea were easing a little. For the Americans, it would be an easy night.

In the German vessel, Wenneker was determined to capture or sink ships. At 0600 the following morning, on Thursday, 5 October, he ordered a westerly course: 270°. He had decided to stay on this course for a full day before turning north. It meant that he was cutting across any likely route of merchant shipping moving eastwards from the coast of America. By 1110 the ship went to action stations as Wenneker ordered the Prize Alarm to be sounded. His new course had finally yielded a victim.

The *Stonegate* had been proceeding on course until around 1100 that morning when the third mate, on bridge duty, suddenly alerted the captain to a trail of smoke that he had spotted on the horizon. The unknown ship had obviously seen the British freighter. By the time the Master, Frederick G. Randall from Robin Hood's Bay in England, managed to get to the bridge the ship was bearing down on them. It did not take the British long to identify the approaching vessel as the *Deutschland*. Her intentions were made abundantly clear as she fired a shot across their bows and ordered the unarmed freighter to stop. The Germans followed procedures. The next step was the formal warning, by signal flags, for the British not to use the radio. That signal did, however, come too late to stop the *Stonegate*'s wireless operator's first attempt to transmit; Randall had been quicker than the Germans with their signal, and his radio operator was already transmitting. But he had not been quicker than the German wireless operators. They were already monitoring the international emergency frequency and promptly jammed the British signal. As a result, nobody could hear them.[14] The German War Diary, however, did not even refer to their own efficient procedures, it only claimed that the *Deutschland*'s radio operator had been monitoring the emergency frequency, only to hear his English counterpart tap out a message, warning others and giving their position: "Danger. Unknown warship. 31N15, 53W10."[15]

When the German man of war stopped the *Stonegate*, little did they know that on board was not only the ship's own crew of 22, but also 15 survivors from the crew of another sunken British ship. These had transferred to the *Stonegate* in Panama. The *Stonegate* was owned by the Turnbull Scott Shipping Company of Whitby and was registered in London. The majority of the crew came from the Whitby area.[16] Now they were all transferred to the warship as prisoners.

The Germans used gunfire to sink the freighter.[17] While aboard the German ship the British crews apparently received the best of treatment and were given both plenty of food and cigarettes. Wenneker had been a British prisoner during the First World War, and been well treated; now he treated his captives in a similar manner. Not all of the imprisoned crew members were equally clear as to the identity of the German raider, but when debriefed in Britain later, it became clear that certain telltale signs had been noticed. On her mess deck, for example, they had spotted the plaques commemorating the losses from the air attack off Majorca during her brief spell in the Spanish Civil War.[18]

That night a German broadcast informed their forces that three British cruisers had joined the hunt for the German warship in the South Atlantic. These were thought to be the *York*, the *Berwick* and the *Exeter*. This particular choice of ships pleased Wenneker who was to the north, looking even further north for his safe haven. According to his latest information, the *Berwick* and the *Exeter* both belonged to the so-called "Canada Station," watching the traffic in the Northern Atlantic.[19] Their removal strengthened Wenneker's hand, as he noted in his War Diary that evening. The British were still unaware of his presence in the North Atlantic. According to his note, the information had reached Germany from London via Rome.

Friday, 6 October provided yet another example of the value of information picked up in neutral countries; the German naval broadcast noted that American naval bombers now patrolled the entire route from the southern tip of Florida to the northern edge of South America. Wenneker felt that this reinforced his view that his ship was not suitable for waging war along the coasts of the West Indies so he withdrew on a northerly course.

In the afternoon Gainard called another fire and lifeboat drill. This time the crew acquitted themselves better in the fire drill. "Fair" was the skipper's summary of their efforts. In the lifeboat drills however, he was still not too pleased. This time they even swung out the lifeboats, as the ship was continuing at full speed. Gainard was a hard taskmaster, but knew that their lives depended on the speed and proficiency of lowering the lifeboats. Ultimately, he alone had the responsibility for his crew and the ship. He had survived a sinking during the previous war and had just experienced the *Athenia* rescue first hand. Gainard knew how a well-trained crew could save lives in an emergency.

The success of one sinking reinforced Wenneker's determination. During the morning they were sailing into better weather and by Saturday afternoon Wenneker had sent off his spotter plane to look for likely targets. The *City of Flint,* however, remained unseen.[20] The two ships were at that stage around 200 km apart and closing, but the reconnaissance sortie covered only half of that distance. To make matters worse for Wenneker, during recovery the aircraft was damaged and put out of commission yet again.

The *City of Flint* was around 120 km south of the tail of the Grand Banks. The sea moderated and the waves stretched to a longer northeasterly swell. Until the afternoon they enjoyed a nice fall day, but by evening the wind was building rapidly and the ship was pitching heavily as she continued to force her way through the head sea. The fo'c'sle was continuously awash as the waves broke.

A further 150 km to their south was the *Deutschland,* sailing a course virtually parallel to that of the *City of Flint.* Neither ship was aware of the other. While Gainard had no interest in meeting any ships during his crossing, Wenneker was determined to find as many as possible. During the day the German warship gradually slipped ahead of the *City of Flint.* Wenneker's normal cruising speed was at least one and a half times that of the freighter.

Monday, 9 October, brought no change in the weather or in the *City of Flint's* routine. The rough sea south of the Flemish Cap made the ship pitch and roll heavily, but all they could do was to keep heading east. Wenneker ordered another substantial course change for the *Deutschland.* He went back on a straight westerly route, 270°, while keeping a relatively high speed of 18 knots. Once more, his tactic was to steer a westerly course by day and an easterly one at night, hoping to cut across the shipping lanes at very sharp angles. Within hours he should cut across the course of the *City of Flint,* but would his lookouts spot the Americans on such a cloudy, overcast day?

By lunchtime, the two ships were only around 50 km apart, still sailing on courses which would cross, but still undetected by each other.

Then, at 1459 hours the German lookouts spotted the smoke from an unknown ship. The *Deutschland* saw another chance and closed at high speed.[21]

At 1510 hours the Prize Alarm was sounded. Wenneker was facing what was to become his most famous prize, the American *City of Flint,* bound for Manchester, Liverpool, Dublin and Glasgow. She carried a cargo of tractors, grain, apples, hides and wax—in total about 4000 tons. Captain Gainard later claimed that they had taken all reasonable precautions to show the world that the *City of Flint* was indeed a neutral ship, which should be granted free passage. Six days out into the Atlantic she was at 43° 44' North: 43° 01' West when they were hailed by signal flags from the warship. The Germans were far better at spotting the U.S. freighter than vice versa; the Americans only spotted the ship on the horizon to the southeast—three points on the starboard bow—a mere eight minutes before they were told to stop.

Gainard had initially hoped that the light grey paint on the forward part of the warship indicated that she was French, but alas, they decided she was too heavily armed. Now they were looking down the wrong end of a menacing series of eleven-inch German naval guns.

According to Gainard, the Germans had already lined up the main batteries to open fire. By the time they had closed to a mile, all main and secondary batteries were swung inboard simultaneously. Gainard recognized the artillery drill; he had retired from the U.S. Navy with the rank of Lieutenant Commander due to injuries sustained in an explosion in a gun turret. All his experience was simply transferred to the merchant navy. He had been a merchant mariner ever since.[22] He knew when to heave to and offer no opposition. In his Bergen statement to the State Department, Captain Gainard, the veteran from the First World War, added that the speed of the *Deutschland* when she closed on them was approximately 25 knots.

As the *Deutschland* came closer, the Americans soon spotted the swastika flying above the ship. Suddenly a flag hoist appeared on the signal flag line above the bridge, comprising the letters LUU—"Do not use your radio." This was quickly followed by a second hoist: CFM—"I am sending a boat." On this trip, the *City of Flint* was bound for several destinations in countries at war with Germany; consequently Gainard would have known all too well what was likely to happen next. Just 23 years earlier he had served in a converted German blockade-runner, then sailing as a U.S. merchant vessel, the *Willehad*. When America was still neutral during the early part of the First World War, Gainard had been serving on a ship, which was busy avoiding British contraband controls. Then like now, if stopped, arrest of ship and cargo was the likely outcome.

The *Deutschland*'s radio station monitored the airwaves for any attempt from the *City of Flint* to transmit warning signals. None were attempted. Fortunately for the Americans, Gainard complied with the German order not to use the radio to signal that a raider had stopped him. The routine would normally have been to attempt to transmit "RRRR RRRR RRRR," the position and the ship's call sign KUCV (for the *City of Flint*).

Curiously, Wenneker, in the *Deutschland*, seemed to know exactly where the *City of Flint*'s radio room was located and as the ship stopped, the German warship maneuvered around her stern and stayed off the stern port quarter. From his position, Wenneker could fire directly at the American radio room, which was located on their port side. At that distance, the explosion from a single shell of the German secondary artillery would have devastated the U.S. radio room.[23] When their motor tender came across, this was the first place the Germans posted armed guards, beside the American radio. Neither Schuss nor Faust, the two American radio officers, had any chance of surreptitiously transmitting a warning signal.

To Gainard, the experienced American, it was quite obvious that the Germans had been at sea for some time. The battleship's sides were badly fouled and rust was breaking out all over the ship. Although he did not make clear his reasons, Gainard suggested in his report that the ship was based somewhere in Spain, although he doubted that they had official Spanish government support. His instincts were correct. The *Deutschland* had indeed been to Spain, but for an earlier mission: to provide support for Franco during the Civil War, although her role had been rather ignominious. On 29 May 1937 she had been attacked by a flight of bombers as she was sailing off Ibiza. The ship sustained substantial damages to one of the gun turrets and saw more than 20 crew members killed and 73 injured from the two bombs that hit the ship. She had to retire to Wilhelmshaven for repairs. In retaliation, the German cruiser *Leipzig* later bombarded the town of Almeira.[24]

Judging from his War Diary, it appeared as if Wenneker regarded the task of bringing the prize home as a relatively easy one. The *Deutschland* had six Prize Crews on board. After all the time at sea, this was his first opportunity to deploy any of them and he also planned to transfer the crew from the sunken *Stonegate* to bring them back to Germany. Nevertheless, all Wenneker thought was required in terms of German forces was, as he referred to it, "a small Prize Command" comprising three officers and 14 men, 17 men in total.

Over the next few weeks, several assumptions were made in Washington and in

London as to why the *City of Flint* was not sunk like the *Stonegate*, but in his War Diary, Wenneker made clear his reasoning:

1. The steamer is useful due to fuel and provision and suitable captain.
2. The cargo is valuable.
3. The necessity of testing the possibility of sailing a Prize through Norwegian territorial waters.
4. Opportunity to get rid of the prisoners.

Then added later in longhand between the typed paragraphs:

5. The unsuitability of sinking an American steamer during the time when the American Neutrality Act is being debated.[25]

This line of thinking is interesting for several reasons, not least because it illustrated how aware Wenneker was of the American neutrality debate and of its potentially damaging outcome. U.S. Secretary of State Hull, and his ambassador to France, Bullitt, had both argued that an early lifting of the ban on arms trade with Britain and France would have delayed Hitler's start of the war. Germany did not want to intentionally do anything which might increase the war-fighting capabilities of her opponents and thus prolong the war. Although Germany too would have been able to purchase arms in America, the route home with each cargo was far more difficult and perilous than for a British ship. In fact it was this very route which Wenneker wanted to test with the *City of Flint*, namely through Norwegian inshore waters.

Wenneker did not, at this stage, seem to be aware of the true value or the significance of the cargo. In one of the holds Gainard had a large quantity of nickel. Nickel was a particularly useful metal in times of war and Germany was so keen to increase its stocks that I.G. Farben wanted to take over the only European mine, at Petsamo in Finland.[26]

The *Stonegate* crew-members were, according to Wenneker's statement, prisoners of war. They had been the crew of an enemy ship, sunk in accordance with the Hague Convention, and their status was quite different from that of the Americans. Although Wenneker was already at sea at the time of the *Athenia* disaster, he would have been well aware of American sentiments over this sinking and would not have wanted to contribute further to any anti–German sentiments in U.S. policy formation.

It took less than an hour for the German boarding party to examine the *City of Flint's* papers and cargo manifest, which did not include the nickel. Following the inspection, there was a prolonged exchange of signals between the German inspection detail and the *Deutschland*. For a brief moment it was thought that if the quantity of flour carried in the cargo could have been reached and offloaded, the ship would have been released, but this was not possible considering the location of that part of the cargo, deep in the No. 4 hold and hampered by a deck cargo of metal barrels. In terms of the right to declare "a good Prize," the actual share or proportion of the total value of the cargo, which constituted contraband, was immaterial under German Prize Regulations.[27] As the cargo manifest revealed more of the true content of the holds of the American freighter, their chances of escape vanished.

The *Stonegate's* crew knew the Germans were hunting for another ship, but as they had to stay below decks, they did not see the *City of Flint*. Early in the afternoon on Monday, 9 October, Captain Wenneker informed Randall that he hoped to get the British crew transferred off his ship that evening. The crew comprised 25 British and 11 Arab sailors and in addition, the ship carried one unfortunate Chilean passenger. They were told that they would be joining an American freighter, which was to be taken to Hamburg under German command as she had been found to be carrying contraband. Later, Captain Randall compared the friendly treatment they received on the German ship in the Second World War with having been torpedoed without warning only a good 20 years earlier. Wenneker's respect for the lives of his prisoners was much appreciated.[28] He visited his British captives daily to ensure that their lives were as comfortable as possible.

Wenneker removed the initial inspection party from the *City of Flint* and replaced them with a Prize Command. They all wore German navy uniforms, but the officers referred to them as soldiers—and they seemed to have been gathered from a wide range of postings—torpedo boats, cruisers, training stations etc. They had 14 different cap ribbons, some of them from the *Emden*.[29]

It took an hour to transfer the prisoners and the Prize Crew under the command of 48-year-old Leutnant zur See Hans Wilhelm Franz Peter Pusback. Once he was aboard, at 1740 hours, he informed Gainard that he had been ordered to take the ship to Germany. In the Bridge Log, Gainard recorded his protest: "It may be true that belligerents may consider cargo as contraband, but my country does not, so I protest the seizure of the vessel."

Pusback's reply was also recorded: "This is a case of war, captain, and it is a question for higher officials to settle."[30]

Facing an armed group of Germans, Gainard had little choice but to comply. Within twenty minutes the Prize Crew was installed, in control and ready to sail. Their leader was an effective and experienced seaman; he knew how to establish his authority.

Pusback came from Bremerhaven. Together with his family he had lived at 37 Grüne Strasse for more than five years.[31] They were three, Pusback, his wife, Tony Adele Elisabeth (née Dreyer), and their 16-year-old son, Hans Holger.[32] By 1939, Pusback was the captain of a fruit carrier called the *Brake*. The ship belonged to the newly created Union Trading and Shipping Company.[33]

According to his service record he was recalled to the colors on 15 August 1939 with the same rank as he left the Imperial Navy 20 years earlier, but now as a reservist. We know he reported to the *Deutschland* only a week later, wearing the uniform of the Kriegsmarine. The next day, his new ship sailed.

His transfer to the *Deutschland* owed more to bad timing than to commitment. With his experience, Pusback would be valuable to the navy and his ship was discharging in a German port at the end of July merely days before the *Deutschland* received her orders to prepare to sail to commence the trade war.

There were some intriguing similarities between Pusback's ship and the *City of Flint*. At 5400 tons, the *Brake* was only slightly larger than the *City of Flint* and she was of the same age. Under her new master, that fall she was making her way back to Germany from Vigo around the British Isles, south of Iceland, towards the Norwegian coast. They reached Norway less than a week ahead of the *City of Flint* and following the same route along the coast as the *City of Flint* would do; the *Brake* was back in Bremerhaven on 23 October.[34] In 1945, the *Brake* was transferred to the U.S. Maritime Commission, the owners of the *City of Flint*, as a prize.[35]

On his return, Gainard claimed not to remember the name of his German Prize Commander. Gainard hoped to protect Pusback. The American's description of Pusback throughout the event suggests that he wanted to shield the German from the adverse publicity his actions might otherwise earn him in America. Equally, he may well have wanted to help Pusback avoid any recriminations from his masters once he returned to Germany. He feared Pusback's family were potential hostages for the Nazi rulers. Gainard would have acted like this only if he felt Pusback deserved support. The two skippers probably had more in common than what actually set them apart. It was this commonality that made the battle of wills of the next few weeks such an even fight. The mutual respect, earned only gradually, was nevertheless there by the time they came to part.

Stonegate's Captain Randall later claimed that Pusback had told him that his own ship had been in Hamburg ready to sail when he had been transferred to the *Deutschland*. Pusback had also told him that the only serving naval officer in the Prize Command was the engineer. The others, himself included, came from the Naval Reserve.[36] That was not entirely true as Rudi Gahler, the navigator, was serving in the navy. He was on placement in the *Deutschland* to gain experience between navigation courses.[37] He had actually served in the *Deutschland* since Hitler sailed with them to Norway in 1934.

At first the Germans were unsure if the *City of Flint* really could accommodate them all. When asked about the ship's capacity to carry extra passengers, Gainard told them about his last trip, the *Athenia* and the unexpected number of passengers he ended up having to accommodate. Even before the *Stonegate* crew was brought on board, the crew was told to muster on the forward hatch. Pusback wanted to warn the Americans that if they did not accept his authority and if they caused any trouble he would put them in the lifeboats and sink the ship. His command of the English language was perfectly adequate for the purpose and the Americans were left with no doubt about who really was in charge from then on.

The British prisoners aboard the *City of Flint* were told in no uncertain terms by Pusback that they would do as the Americans said and that his German soldiers would reinforce any orders given if necessary. He actually promised to set them free once they reached a German port, but if they caused any trouble, he would have them shot.

Initially, Wenneker was reluctant to let the captain of the *Stonegate*, Captain Randall, join the rest of his crew on the American ship. Wenneker thought of keeping the Master and his Chief Engineer on the warship. Fortunately he relented and let them all go.[38] They departed at 1805 hours. The *City of Flint* saluted the *Deutschland* with three blasts on her whistle. Wenneker replied in kind.

From the time that Pusback took command of the *City of Flint*, no positions and no latitudinal or longitudinal readings were recorded in the ship's log. Gainard made sure his Bridge Log was kept as up to date as possible under the circumstances. Although he no longer entered the exact position, the courses steered were recorded with the times of alteration. They also recorded the engine speed. All in all, they had enough information to be able to reconstruct the route later. (No explanation is available as to why the method of recording the course was changed. The circumstances around this change remain a real mystery to the present.)

The German Prize instructions actually told them to keep their own navigational log.[39] The navigation was to a large extent done by Rudi, Wenneker's supernumerary navigator. Now, he found himself third in command of a Prize Crew.[40]

In worsening weather the *City of Flint* was shipping significant amounts of water forward of the bridge. The sea spray washed over them as the rough seas continued to break across the fo'c'sle. Under German command, it was hardly a great day to celebrate a birthday. Gainard was 50 years old on Wednesday, 11 October. He was born in Chelsea, Massachusetts. Nobody knew. "Rough sea, pitching" his Bridge Log reads.

The bad weather continued unabated and did not improve for several days. By Thursday afternoon they were enduring a rough beam sea and heavy pitching and by evening they were shipping water everywhere. The decks disappeared under the seas when the largest waves broke over them.

On Sunday, 15 October, Wenneker sent a message to the German Naval Command, informing them of the sinking of the *Lorentz W. Hansen* and of the captured Prize the *City of Flint*, which he had sent home via "territorial waters" as he put it. Significantly, he also informed them of a new radio call sign, which he had ordered his Prize Crew to use when communicating with Germany, EANL instead of the *City of Flint*'s official one, which was KUCV.[41]

Something happened to the radio aboard the *City of Flint*. From the moment they stopped for the German ship, the transmitter ceased functioning. It remained out of action, for transmissions, as long as the Germans were on the scene. Gainard was a shrewd man and a worthy opponent for Pusback. In his book, he did not explain what happened to the radio; only that he observed that one of the German Prize Crew members, Funk-Gefreiter Cornelius Stöhr, a radio operator, never succeeded in making the radio operational. Any members of the ship's own radio crew, on the other hand, were not permitted to enter the radio room. As the *Deutschland* had used a combination of signal flags to get them to stop and to order them not to use the radio, it is not known exactly when the radio started to malfunction. As a matter of routine on any merchant ship of his day, the radio would have been used to transmit regular control messages back to the shipping line's office. Without this reassurance the office would post the ship missing, which they had not done until now.

Had the ship been sinking during this period, without any means of effective communications, the person who damaged the radio could have been held responsible for the lack of contact during such an emergency. Gainard, out of loyalty, obviously was not going to leave any of the members of his crew or himself open to this sort of liability even after their successful return. The lack of communications with German naval command came to impact crucially on Pusback's actions over the next couple of weeks. According to the *City of Flint*'s Scottish supernumerary radio operator James MacConnachie, the Germans inquired as to whether the *City of Flint* had a radio direction finder, which would have helped them locate positions ashore. Several of the Norwegian lighthouses used radio beacons to aid navigation. He added that the Germans never sent a single message during the time he saw them on the ship.[42]

The United States Lines should have had a control message, a position report, on Thursday, 12 October; it was never sent. Nor did they receive one on the 14th, the day before she was to have docked at Manchester. By now the shipping line staff were worried and on the advice of another of the Line's captains they acted as if their ship had been captured. Although no display of concern was made public, the State Department started working to contact the ship. On the *City of Flint*, however, they heard nothing other than regular public radio broadcasts.

Much later, as the ship was riding at anchor in Bergen harbor, John Edgar Hoover, Director of the Federal Bureau of Investigation (FBI), sent a letter to American Secretary of State Cordell Hull warning him of a potential leak that had come about on the *City of Flint*. Hoover claimed to have information from a confidential source, alleging that one of the members of the ship's crew was a communist.[43] This communist had, according to the information, been in radio contact with the German warship before she stopped the *City of Flint*. The individual named in this intelligence report was in fact on the ship, but no further reference can be found for this allegation. Hoover attempted to apportion some of the blame for the ship's fate to communism, to which he was clearly opposed. Although Hoover named the crew member, it does not seem fair in the present analysis of the events to expose the man to a totally unfounded allegation.

Pusback left Gainard in charge, while he himself looked after security. A German Prize Court, he explained, would decide the fate of the ship. During this first meeting, both men were clearly testing each other. As they discussed the journey ahead, the German suggested a course and looked at Gainard, who told him he would not have chosen such a route. Once the American had explained his own choice, Pusback admitted that that was really his own choice too, but he wanted to see how cooperative the skipper would be and was testing him. Gainard had won his confidence: "So we proceed by various courses, finally arriving at Tromsø."

MacConnachie in his radio interview explained that Rudi, the German navigator, had told him that as long as they could reach the Norwegian coast far enough north, he was confident that they could reach Germany. During one of their discussions, Pusback confidently dismissed any concerns they had about British patrols in northern waters and around the Shetland Islands.

The German's plan was a simple one. He hoped to skirt the coast of Greenland, heading north up the Denmark Strait until he reached 70° N. At that stage he would be north of Iceland and by turning to an easterly course, he would sooner or later reach the northern Norwegian coast.[44] Gainard was apparently the only member of the crew who actually knew the course or the location of the ship at any one time. Ellis, the fourth mate, argued that although the officers of the *City of Flint* stood their watches as normal, they felt powerless. The German navigated, checked the course, and steered.

A series of secret radio messages, which the German naval command had issued to their merchant navy early in the war, were effective. German freighters started to sail north, continuing through the Denmark Strait and just avoiding the edge of the ice belt east of Greenland. They like Pusback, turned east towards the coast of Norway. Once in Norwegian waters, they were safe from any pursuing British ships.

As the volume of German ships grew, however, the Royal Navy's so-called Northern Patrol got wise to the actual route. The British placed their ships at two key locations, one to the south-east of Iceland, the other between Greenland and Iceland in the Denmark Strait.

Then, the Denmark Strait became the "eye" in a very large low-pressure zone. As the barometer readings continued to drop, formidable gales were building from the south-east.[45] By the time the *City of Flint* appeared on the scene, the weather must have been fierce, yet neither Pusback nor Gainard and his officers mentioned it when recounting the journey. The Northern Patrol's War Diary, however, described how the sailors slept in hammocks covered in oilskins. Their old C and D class cruisers proved to be "very wet" and not up to the challenges of the North Atlantic's winter storms.[46] They lost equipment overboard; even depth charges disappeared over the side in the heavy seas. The weather substantially reduced visibility, and made it far more difficult for the ships to maintain their stations in the patrol lines. The result of this was that the Germans slipped through the net quite easily.

As Pusback headed north, the British commander-in-chief of the Home Fleet released a larger ship to join the Northern Patrol. The *Sheffield* was nearly twice the size of the smaller cruisers struggling with the mountainous seas. Finally, after six weeks of ineffective patrols, the gap would be plugged. Again, the German timing could hardly have been better. The *Sheffield* was re-routed from operations in the North Sea to join the Northern Patrol after a brief stop at Scapa Flow. During the morning of Thursday, 5 October she played host to King George VI as he spent a couple of days visiting his ships. Early Sunday she weighed and slipped quietly out through the boom defenses.[47] By Tuesday, 10 October she was on station. Pusback unknowingly was heading towards a ship he would not be able to avoid very easily and their meeting was at most just five days away.

MacConnachie later remembered how the Germans grew increasingly anxious. The tension seemed to grow as the temperature dropped. They were aware of the British patrols and were desperate to avoid being spotted. Wednesday saw them still on the northerly course. The next day came and went as the weather was deteriorating rapidly. Superstitious or not, the inopportune date/day combination, Friday, 13 October, added to the stress among the Prize Crew. In the meantime they were continuing towards the narrowest part of the Denmark Strait, with the solid Greenland pack ice to the west and the very north-western corner of Iceland to the east. Somewhere in between the British patrols were constantly on the move searching for returning German freighters.

During Saturday, 14 October, the course was changed towards east-north-east, but it was not until Sunday lunchtime that the courses changed to an easterly direction. There was a dramatic change in the temperature over this period. Within 24 hours the temperature plummeted. It went from 11° C (52° F) at lunchtime Saturday to 0° C (32° F) by Sunday lunchtime. Similarly, the water temperature dropped too; by Sunday evening it was at 0° C, the temperature at which fresh water would freeze.[48]

Early Sunday, they had their first warning of things to come, passing two large icebergs and within an hour and a half they had spotted two more. They were close to the edge of the polar ice. The wind was building again, the sea was rough and they were sailing through passing snow flurries. It was miserably cold; they were all growing tense, hoping to avoid the ice.

It was Gainard's next log entry, more than the actual course, that provided the final proof of the *City of Flint* course mystery. In Gainard's own account, he refers to "passing the east coast of Greenland." In the rest of his book of the incident Gainard is vague about the course, apart from a map which indicates that they sailed to the east of Iceland, on a far more easterly course, between Iceland and the Faeroes and northwards through the Norwegian Sea to reach the Norwegian coast north of the Arctic Circle. Yet, this is an area where floating icebergs in October are extremely unlikely. The area is simply too far from the ice and currents are completely wrong for carrying the ice this way. So why would Gainard hide the real course? It adds to the mystery of the missing coordinates in the Bridge Log.

We have recreated the real course. Using his knowledge, skills and experience in navigation, a Master from the German merchant navy went over the Bridge Log and re-calculated the course using compass course readings and engine revolutions. Rudi, the Prize Crew navigator, said many years later that they sailed close to Jan Mayen, but he had at that stage no data to support his memory. Now we have learned that he was right. As the log talks about "a northerly course" they would not be heading east to the south of

Iceland, they simply had to be sailing north up the Denmark Strait. By midday Sunday 15 October they were heading nearly due east on a course which would take them directly towards the Norwegian islands of Lofoten.

A further clue to the true course comes from Pusback. In his report on the trip, written later when interned in Norway, he made the course abundantly clear: "…then navigating along the coast of Greenland always near the ice edge through the Denmark Strait to Norway."[49] This also fits with the map produced in the *Life Magazine* article two months after the ship's return to Baltimore, yet by September when Gainard's own book was published, his map suggested the other route.

Incredibly, on Friday the 13th, with the German Prize probably less than a two-days sail away from the *Sheffield*, the British ship had to run for port. Just at the critical time, she needed refueling.[50] In fact, she was probably just docked by the time the *City of Flint* slipped unseen past the other patrolling ships. The temperature dropped, ice started to form along the decks and drifting snow was by now clinging to the cold steel hull. Without proper charts, the course took them ever closer to the edge of the pack ice, which by mid–October was starting to grow eastwards into the Denmark Strait and the Norwegian Sea further to the north-east. So much so, that all day Tuesday and the following night was spent avoiding drifting ice.

It was Ellis' job to keep an eye on the water temperature as it dropped. From early morning they had taken hourly temperature readings of the water, which at one stage in the afternoon dropped below freezing. They were certainly inside the iceberg zone, to the north of Iceland, but none of the Americans knew where they were, apart from Gainard. Warren Rhoads, the First Mate, acting on instinct, felt sure he had known when they had reached the southern end of the Denmark Strait.

All day they spotted icebergs and after dark they sailed into thick fog patches and sleet. Visibility was so bad that from around 2100 they spent the next three hours merely creeping slowly ahead at much reduced speeds.[51] They even had to stop at times. Pusback would not allow them to use a searchlight to spot icebergs. He was determined not to give the British any help locating them. Finally, just before midnight, visibility improved and they could speed up again. That night few of them slept, MacConnachie claimed. A sheet of ice could easily rip through the side of the *City of Flint*, sending them all to a cold grave. The freezing water would have killed them in minutes.

Pusback must have known they were closing on the Norwegian coast as he now sent men over the sides to paint out the U.S. flags, the ship's name and the name of the shipping line. The vessel was still pitching heavily as the painting progressed. All traces of the original identity were removed. Even the shipping line's coloring on the smoke stack was painted over. The two large flag-covered tarpaulins covering the forward hatches were removed. Instead, two Danish flags were painted on canvas and suspended either side of the ship. The new name for the ship, *Alf*, was painted on the bows and stern, as well as on all of the four lifeboats.[52]

The Danish flag comprises a white cross on a red background. At the time, the press somehow picked up a rumor that the Prize Crew had cut to pieces an American flag to make the Danish one. (A comparison of the two proud flags soon makes clear how difficult such a task would be.) The German contingent included two signals personnel, Signal Ober-Gefreiter Karl Gutheil and Signal-Gefreiter Otto Pawlowsky; they used the tools of their trade in a very inventive manner. The international signals flag for "R" comprises a yellow cross on a red background. The yellow was covered using the white area of the flag for "S." Unfortunately for the Germans, the positioning of the cross was entirely wrong, thus ensuring that the flag would fail all but the most cursory of inspections.[53]

The *Sheffield* was back on station in the Denmark Strait on Thursday, 19 October, and the next day she seized the German freighter *Gloria* as a prize.[54] The *City of Flint* on the other hand, was within hours of the Norwegian port of Tromsø.[55] That week, as Pusback closed on the Norwegian coast, the Northern Patrol captured a ship virtually every day in the Denmark Strait.[56]

That Thursday and for the next couple of days, the *Sheffield* was within a good day's sailing of a target far bigger than anything they had seen so far in the war. Off the south-eastern coast of Greenland, was something more valuable than any prize, namely the *Deutschland*. Wenneker had pulled back to his waiting position of a month earlier. He was totally unaware of the location of the *Sheffield* and her supporting vessels in the Northern Patrol.[57] Had he known, the western coast of Greenland, spurned a month earlier, would have been far safer. If he had stopped to fight however, the *Sheffield* would have faced near certain destruction, even before she would have been able to bring her own guns to bear on the enemy.

Virtually all the Americans were barred from the bridge, only those on duty in the wheelhouse were allowed access. The chart room became the German arsenal. It was the German officers who regularly would visit the bridge and direct the navigation. Rudi and engineer Fritz Futterlieb actually bunked in the chart room while the other two, Pusback and Grasshoff used the first mate's room. Some of the German ratings even slept in the linen locker. Rhoads, on the other hand, spent the nights on the captain's settee. The British and American officers shared the ship's hospital.

In fairness to the Hog Islanders, they provided decent accommodation for their crews, in roomy ships. The full width of the ship remained beyond number five hatch, providing for a very wide "rear end" and a relatively large poop deck. This extra width improved rear end buoyancy which if the sea was running up behind provided for a dry ship. Unfortunately for the *City of Flint*, the opposite was the case for the bow. The design had raised the forecastle significantly in front of number one hatch, but the actual stem was a straight vertical cut, which if sailing into heavy seas, would make this part of the ship very wet indeed.

With three crews on board, accommodation had to be basic. They all messed together. The officers were to eat in turn in the forward saloon, but sometimes they just all joined in. The rest had to eat in shifts. Fortunately food was plentiful, but preparing it was not always that easy. Pusback was clearly on edge, he did not want the ship to be seen.

In the galley, he insisted they worked with only one light burning. This meant that baking, which had to be done at night was done virtually blindfolded. Nevertheless, the Germans claimed the food on the American ship was the best they had had in months. The regular crew noted their appetite. One of the German officers would even come between meals brandishing his gun to have more food when he felt like it. The Americans felt that their captors frequently ate so much they were forced to rest to avoid being sick.

Baltimorean Joe Freer, the chief steward, who had received so much praise for his catering skills by the *Athenia* survivors, certainly took pride in his work. His stores had just been replenished so Joe could handle the extra mouths to feed; they posed no real problem. The only added dimension to the catering on this trip proved to be the Muslim members of the *Stonegate*'s crew.

Pusback was nervous; during the day he demanded that the ship would have a totally smokeless run. Normally she would sail with the black smoke pouring from her stack, now they had to operate two large blowers to dissipate the smoke continuously during daylight hours. At night the ship was forced to sail with a total blackout, not even navigational lights were permitted as she continued undetected by the British navy.

Although the Germans left the American crew to sail the ship, Gainard was under no illusion as to who he felt would be first in line for a bullet if anything went wrong. He was the liaison, the go-between and the skipper all at the same time, 24 hours a day. As the German warship disappeared over the horizon, his crew was very keen "to have a go" and jump their captors, but Gainard, knowing more of their ruthless nature from his close contacts, repeatedly pulled his crew back from the brink of what would have been a bloodbath. Furthermore, the Americans had absolutely no firearms. Gainard also argued that an attack on the Germans was likely to make their case far more difficult to handle in the diplomatic arena where Gainard, quite correctly, assumed the main battle over his ship would be fought. The Prize Commander mounted guards at critical points on the ship. They even stood alongside the American crew at times, the entrance to the engine room, on the bridge, by the seacocks and in the radio room.[58]

Mostly, they were not threatening, they conducted themselves like sailors, and they mingled with the Americans without any disturbances or friction. Nevertheless the shrewd U.S. skipper warned his men to be on their guard and assume that their captors probably understood more than they were prepared to let on. As it turned out, several of the Germans understood English and they overheard American crew members discuss attacks on the Prize Commander. What none of them knew, was that as Pusback received each tip-off, he told Gainard. 'You'll need to be on your guard tonight,' he would say, "they are planning something." The skipper knew there were some hotheads among the crew and controlling them was the only way of keeping all of them safe.

The only arms referred to by the Americans were side arms, a machine pistol, bayonets and hand grenades. Gainard later referred to some charges for measuring the water depth. Only later did First Mate Rhoads realize that further equipment and explosives could have been hidden in what seemed to have been the Prize Commander's personal kit bags when they came aboard. Rhoads never knew how right he was.

One of the first tasks of the German crew had been to search the ship for arms. According to Gainard, they were very surprised when they found none; not even a personal sidearm for the captain. Neither did any of the other officers have any arms for the purposes of maintaining order. Gainard's nickname from former days may hold part of the answer to this lack of weaponry. He was once called "Slugger Gainard" for his ability to look after himself.[59] He remained calm, setting a great example for the crew.

In his account of the journey, Pusback admitted that for 11 days, he had had an opportunity to take adequate astronomical readings on only one occasion. This was the only hint that they experienced some very bad weather during the trip. To Pusback it meant that he felt he could only determine their location to within the nearest three kilometers. After all that time at sea without any sight of land, sailing across the Atlantic, and the Norwegian Sea, such a narrow margin of error illustrated the skills Pusback had as a mariner.[60]

The skipper claimed the ship's evaporator did not have the capacity to produce enough water for so many people over such a long period of time.[61] They needed fresh supplies from ashore, Gainard argued. His concern and the discussions with the crew reached the ears of the Germans, as Gainard hoped it would. Lieutenant Pusback was becoming increasingly worried the ship was about to run out of fresh water when he ordered the helmsman to make for Tromsø. Unbeknownst to him, this was a plot hatched by the shrewd Captain Gainard and members of his crew to ensure that the whereabouts of his ship became known.

Thursday, October 19, was a miserable day with clouds and snow and a large swell. The ship was rolling heavily. In the morning the Germans raised the flag of the Kriegsmarine on the aft flagstaff. They did not know exactly where they were, but by evening Gainard ordered them to cast a lead line to check the depth. Wet snow and rain soaked them as they kept up the hourly controls. At midnight they stopped. Pusback decided to ride the weather until daybreak before approaching the coast. He did not have any charts for the waters he was about to enter. They did not anchor; they merely let the ship drift while waiting for daylight. Rhoads was delighted. The stop allowed him the best night's sleep since leaving New York.

Norway of 1939 was a country where the old Viking saying still held true—"the mountains divided and the sea united." Travel was time consuming, communications slow. Bergen, the country's second city was a full night's railway journey from the capital Oslo.

Along the coast, however, travelling by sea was the only option. By the time the *City of Flint* appeared, the coastal steamer was a daily occurrence in each direction, each ship running the entire 1,100 nautical mile stretch from Kirkenes on the Soviet border to Bergen. Due to the Gulf Stream, these harbors were ice free all year, offering safety for ships seeking shelter from storms or predators. As tension grew in the Baltic, the sea-lanes around the north of Norway became even more significant to the Soviet Union, and once war broke out in Europe, the islands, fjords and skerries became the ideal shelter for returning or outward bound German merchant shipping. In addition, both sides in the conflict had their eyes on the international trade in Swedish iron ore from the Norwegian port of Narvik.

Such activity could not be watched by staff at embassies or legations in the capital. The fall of 1939 saw both the United Kingdom and Germany with a well-developed network of consulates along the west Norwegian coast; all of them to gather intelligence. They all seemed to be in the same locations; both had consulates in Tromsø, Narvik, Trondheim, Bergen, Haugesund and Stavanger. The Americans, on the other hand, were limited to their legation in Oslo and a consulate in Bergen. In 2021 consular activities are often looked after by "honorary consuls," locals with a connection to the country they represent, normally business interests. The consulates of 1939 had staff from their own countries. The number of staff seemed to indicate the level of significance accorded to the location. In March 1940, for example, the German consulate in Haugesund, a small but strategically important town in southwestern Norway, had a staff of seven.[62]

That fall, there were a great many tourists along the Norwegian coast. In October, just as the world was wondering where the *City of Flint* actually was, Norwegian police arrested two Germans for spying. The BBC, reporting on this incident, claimed that one of the arrested men reportedly kept sending picture postcards home to Germany with marks and notes saying, "This is where I live."[63]

During the First World War Norway had remained neutral. The government was determined to continue that neutrality during the new crisis of 1939. At the time, Norway was, in military terms, one of the weakest and most ill-equipped countries in Europe. Yet the government declared that rather than joining other neutral European countries,

Norway would now act independently and rely solely on their own forces, to defend neutrality and integrity.

Neutrality was, for the merchant navies involved in this, very complicated. During the first weeks of the war, there was confusion over the Regulations. The Norwegian ones included an export ban on navigation charts. Yet one of the frequent problems was the lack of adequate charts over the long and often treacherous Norwegian coast. As a Hamburg-bound ship reached Ålesund on the western coast of Norway during the very first days of the war, the German consul offered to procure for her captain the maps he needed. At the next port a well-known Bergen company, at midnight sold the skipper the relevant maps. The Norwegian pilot even had to pay as the company would not accept payment in Canadian dollars, the only currency the Germans had.[64] The fact that the pilots were employed by the Norwegian State and belonged to the Ministry of Defense must have further confounded the visitors.

Over the next few weeks, as more German ships started to reach Norway, the actual lack of charts would have become noticeable. In some cases, the local consuls must have quietly secured sets of maps; in others the agents of the shipping lines would have been doing the same.

The authorities routinely inspected the German merchant vessels as they arrived in Norwegian waters. Their radio equipment was sealed in accordance with the Neutrality Regulations. The use of radio transmitters while in Norwegian ports was prohibited. Similarly, German ships were prevented from sailing through the port of Bergen during the hours of darkness. The port had been defined as a war harbor. As a consequence, ships sailing past Bergen would have to anchor to the north or the south of the blocked area until daybreak. Without the appropriate charts, the skippers would be totally dependent upon the skills and the availability of Norwegian pilots.

On the other hand, as the German consul at Trondheim argued, the Norwegian pilots were duty-bound to be absolutely neutral and to observe total secrecy over German shipping movements. After all, it was in their own best financial interests that German traffic through Norwegian waters continued.[65]

This was the Norway where the *City of Flint* arrived late in the evening on Friday, 20 October 1939.

4

Politics of Neutrality

Very early next morning Pusback decided to proceed slowly, checking the depth every 30 minutes. They now knew they were close to the coast somewhere in northern Norway. As they thought themselves close to a pilot station, Pusback ordered a change of flag.[1] The official naval flag was removed and the flag of the German merchant fleet was hoisted in its place. This consisted of a large, black swastika on a white circular background at the center of a plain red rectangle. The *City of Flint* was to appear as a civilian vessel.

During the night a frustrated Pusback repeatedly tried to use the radio, hoping to send a telegram to Naval High Command in Berlin, but failed miserably. Somehow the *City of Flint*'s radio did not have enough power to transmit a signal strong enough to reach the German station.[2]

The combined navigational skills on the *City of Flint* were so good that when they closed on the Norwegian coast, they were just over 30 nautical miles north of 70° N. The three skippers knew how to navigate. In fact, Rudi Gahler thought that Captain Randall could have taken a star fix visually anywhere along the route and provided them with an estimated position.[3] Nevertheless, that morning, not even Randall could see anything due to a thick snowfall.

The snowstorm frustrated them. It was not until it cleared that they dared approach the coast. Finally at mid-morning they stopped at a pilot station. They nearly lost the Norwegian pilot overboard as he boarded the ship.[4] The man expected a merchant ship, not a prize travelling with an armed guard. When he spotted the uniformed and armed Germans, he nearly fell back down the ladder.[5] The cover was now well and truly blown. The pilot was a civil servant who later informed the authorities that the ship purporting to be the *Alf* really was the American *City of Flint*.

They were at the southern tip of the island of Sørøya. Pusback now had a choice, he could head north in the lee of the island and reach the town of Hammerfest in three hours. The ship could do 10–12 knots; Hammerfest was 32 nautical miles away (59 km). The alternative was to head south to Tromsø, which was at least eight hours away. Gambling on a clear run to a German port, Pusback went south. The first part of this route, approximately three hours, was across the open sea at Lopphavet, where he could easily be spotted, and the rest through some very narrow fjords. When passing through these fjords, Warren Rhoads felt they were so close to the shoreline that they could have hit anyone there with a stone, thrown from the bridge.

Reaching Tromsø took all day. It was early evening, when they finally approached the town. According to Gainard, the starboard anchor was dropped at 1845. Before reaching the town, the Germans apparently threw all the 12 bombs overboard together with

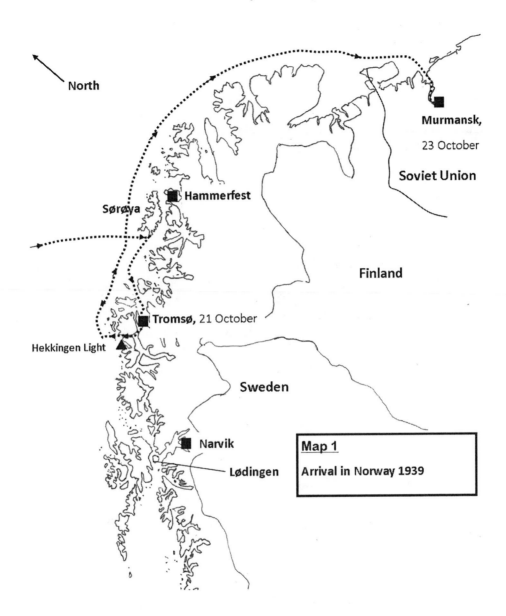

North

Murmansk,
23 October

Soviet Union

Hammerfest

Sørøya

Finland

Tromsø, 21 October

Hekkingen Light

Sweden

Narvik

Lødingen

Map 1

Arrival in Norway 1939

the only machine gun they had.[6] Gainard, however, thought they had at least 60 hand grenades left and, unbeknownst to the American, several ready-made explosive scuttling charges remained on board, primed and ready.

Within half an hour of stopping, they were visited by an officer from the Norwegian Navy's fishery protection vessel *Heimdal*, based at Tromsø.

According to Pusback, the Norwegians informed him that it was not allowed under Norwegian neutrality legislation to bring a prize to port. Pusback replied that he was not technically bringing the prize to port; he merely wanted to purchase the relevant charts and take on water for the journey to Germany as the shortage of water constituted an emergency under the Hague Convention. He added that the *City of Flint* was not a warship, merely a merchant freighter, sailed by its own crew under military supervision. The ship belonged to the German Reich because of its contraband cargo. In fact, the soldiers merely carried arms for self-protection. Once he arrived in Germany Pusback claimed, the Prize Court would determine what should actually happen to the ship. The Norwegian official relayed the story to his commanding officer, who after an hour's worth of thinking time, accepted Pusback's arguments.

Just before 2000 a water tender came alongside, followed shortly afterwards by the German consul in Tromsø, Conrad Rye-Holmboe, and his German colleague Wussow. They were expecting Pusback. Once in port, they provided Pusback with orders to proceed southwards inside Norwegian territorial waters and through The Belts to Germany.[7]

The visitors did not stay long, but the guards posted on board remained. By then, Gainard had, according to his log entries, protested formally to the Norwegian authorities. First he argued that once in a neutral port, the German Prize Crew should be removed. Later he added that he felt the ship should not be sent out of a neutral port with the German Prize Crew still on board. No reactions were recorded to his protests.[8]

At the same time the naval officer in charge of Naval District North, District 3, Hagerup, requested advice from the Norwegian Navy's High Command at Oslo. He had no problem with the request for drinking water, but he wanted his boss, Admiral Henry Diesen's advice on the requested access to Norwegian territory. Pusback wanted permission to shelter in Norwegian waters while heading south towards Germany, just like any other German merchant ship returning home. Hagerup was clearly not entirely convinced of Pusback's right to do this.

In Oslo, alarm bells were ringing. Within half an hour, the naval staff contacted Tromsø, requesting confirmation that the ship's visit really was due to an emergency. The issue in Oslo was: did the visit violate the two months' old Neutrality Regulation? In the meantime, Third District was instructed not to allow the ship to depart until Diesen had decided how to proceed.

To Hagerup in Tromsø, this meant that he had to increase his level of readiness. A couple of unarmed personnel would not be able to prevent a fully armed Prize Crew from leaving port if they wanted. Within 15 minutes he ordered one of his most modern ships, the two-year-old *Sleipner*, to prepare for immediate departure. He posted a new guard detail from the *Heimdal* comprised of two officers and two ratings on board the *City of Flint*. Only then did Hagerup grant permission to replenish 60 tons of water, but added that they were not allowed to sail without further instructions.[9]

The Norwegian guards ended up spending the entire evening on board the American ship. During this time they checked the cargo manifest and had a quick look over the ship. They quickly spotted the false nameplates and ordered them painted over. The Norwegian officials ordered the original American names be re-painted on all lifeboats, life rings, bow and stern of the *City of Flint*. Pusback had broken international law by covering up the actual identity of the ship. Curiously, they also ordered the Germans to paint over the American flag, which had pride of place on the wall on the upper bridge deck.

Pusback immediately informed the German consul, who in turn, by telephone, informed the German embassy in Oslo. At this stage the crew had not yet completed replenishing the water tank and the British prisoners were still all aboard the ship.[10]

From Hagerup came the order to change out the German merchant fleet flag for the flag of the German Kriegsmarine. At least the Norwegian authorities had recognized the strategic significance of the flag. They regarded the ship as under German naval control. It was a warship. If under a civilian merchant navy flag, the ship would be subject to customs and all the protection afforded to civilian ships on Norwegian territory. Germany, on the other hand, had a third flag used by non-warships that belonged to the state and were crewed by the navy. Norwegian legislation did not recognize this distinction. Pusback tried to use whichever flag gave him the status he saw as most beneficial at any one time.

In the meantime, the Norwegian inspection team reported that the Germans were armed. They even did a brief inventory of the arms on board.

Once Diesen was in his office, it did not take him long to realize that the *City of Flint* represented less of a threat to Norwegian assets than to the actual integrity of Norwegian neutrality. This was an issue for the Foreign Affairs Ministry. He telephoned the Foreign Ministry's top adviser at home to inform him of the ship's arrival. All that the two of them were concerned about at this stage was, quite correctly, whether the visit was permissible under the Norwegian Neutrality Regulations. The ship was told to remain at Tromsø.

At the Admiral's office in Oslo, the issues were becoming clearer. Diesen decided to act. He telephoned Hagerup and instructed him to permit just enough water to be filled for them to reach a German port. Once that was completed, the *City of Flint* was to depart. Under Norwegian Neutrality Regulations, which did not cover the eventuality of a prize entering their waters, the *City of Flint* was granted the status of a warship. They had to be out of Norwegian territorial waters within 24 hours of leaving Tromsø. Diesen even demanded to know how much water they took on board to ensure that it was intended purely for drinking. The water was quickly replenished and the tender left.

The arrival at Tromsø could hardly have been better timed by Pusback if he had planned it. The top tier at the Norwegian Foreign Ministry was just returning from Sweden, accompanying King Haakon VII and the Minister Halvdan Koht. Together with the other Nordic heads of state and their foreign affairs ministers, they had attended a meeting at Stockholm Castle. The Swedish King, Gustav, had called them together to discuss the threatening international situation.

Almost exactly one hour after Diesen ordered Hagerup to let the ship go once the water had been filled, Hagerup telephoned him back. The time was 2232 hours exactly. We know this, as Diesen had a member of his staff make a note of the conversation.[11] Hagerup dropped a bombshell, telling Diesen that the *City of Flint* actually had 37extra men on board as prisoners of war. The Norwegians assumed the prisoners were from a ship sunk by the same warship that had taken the *City of Flint*. Interestingly, the note does not record Diesen's reaction to learning of the extra men. For now it seemed he was prepared to ignore their existence.

Pusback was told to make sure that they were outside Norwegian territorial waters within 24 hours. Furthermore, the Norwegians confiscated the maps provided by the German consul the night before. At the same time, the Norwegians informed them that they no longer insisted on the ship flying the official flag of the German navy. Pusback immediately changed to the flag of the merchant navy. To him, this change must have appeared as a sign of uncertainty, even weakness. He pushed for further concessions.

Close to midnight Diesen needed reassuring. He phoned the Norwegian Foreign Ministry. It seemed that the enormity of the decision, for which he had volunteered to take sole responsibility, had started to sink in. Whether left to his own devices or through conversations with members of the naval staff, Diesen had concluded that there was more to this than just allowing a group of German soldiers to sail their prize home. The contours of the geopolitics were beginning to appear to him.

Diesen now explained that from his perspective, the case was more complicated than originally thought. He had just learned (he claimed) that the ship had British citizens on board. These had probably come from other ships sunk by German warships. It was unclear under the law, Diesen explained, whether the British should be released and put ashore. He added that local naval units had been ordered to detain the ship until further notice. For now the situation seemed to be contained.

In Tromsø, Pusback argued that he had far too many people on board: a crew of 42 neutrals and 37 non-combatants from an enemy nation. He felt that this should justify special treatment in terms of access to Norwegian territorial waters.[12] Interestingly, it seemed that the local navy units were prepared to concede. They had probably seen so many German freighters sailing south over the last couple of weeks that they did not think one more would make any difference. The one proviso they made, according to Pusback, was that he had to wait for final confirmation from Oslo. This bought Norway time. The one condition with which Pusback had to comply was not to contact land. He was to remain isolated at anchor in the harbor.[13]

Seemingly unbeknownst to the Norwegians, Pusback's chat with the German consulate in Tromsø had started a chain of events all of its own. A coded telegram, marked "Secret," was sent to Berlin to update the Foreign Ministry of the situation. The Oslo Legation did not even know the name of the American ship at this stage, but they did know Pusback had only 24 hours sailing time before he had to leave the safety of Norwegian territorial waters. They also knew that the charts provided by the Tromsø consul had been confiscated. The German consul in Narvik was ordered out into the islands where the ship would pass on its way south, to be ready to offer assistance.[14] It was Berlin's first move in the strategic game that now commenced over the American freighter.

Norwegian Foreign Minister Halvdan Koht had by now been briefed on the prize issues. He alone decided what should be done. Advised by his legal team, he told Admiral Diesen that (a) nothing was to be done regarding the ship's British prisoners and (b) the admiral's decision on the 24-hour rule remained in force. Diesen was asked to telephone this order to Tromsø immediately.

Diesen clearly wanted the sequence of events and the origin of the decision to be recorded for posterity. He sent a formal record to the Norwegian Ministry of Defense, secure in the knowledge that bureaucracy would safeguard his account.[15]

Saturday, 21 October, in London, the British War Cabinet was told that one of the Northern Patrol ships, the *Colombo*, had picked up some interesting intelligence from a Norwegian ship they had inspected. They had learned from the captain that the ship had been stopped nine days earlier by "a warship of the *Deutschland* class" east of Newfoundland.[16] He described the ship well. Only two such ships could be at sea at the time: the *Admiral Graf Spee* and the *Deutschland*. The information was significant, as this was the first warning that there was a German warship operating as a commerce raider in the North Atlantic.

It took until Saturday lunchtime before Pusback's answer came back from Oslo. The captain of the *Sleipner* was instructed to inform him that not only did the original order to leave Norwegian territorial waters within 24 hours stand, but the newly acquired set of charts of the Norwegian coast were to remain locked up somewhere ashore. The German consul in Tromsø had purchased a complete set of 27 charts for Pusback. If he still planned to sail southwards in Norwegian waters for 24 hours, he would be escorted by a torpedo boat.

The punctilious Norwegians still wanted their paperwork in order. At lunchtime, customs officials came aboard to seal the hatches. A pilot followed them soon after and at 1400 hours the German consul turned up again, but he only stayed half an hour. Nevertheless, it was a clear breach of the Neutrality Regulations.

Koht's integrity was saved by the German Prize Commander, Pusback, who having won all the concessions he wanted, requested permission to disembark the British prisoners. Pusback turned to Hagerup for permission and he in turn quickly telephoned Diesen who, acting on his own authority, accepted Pusback's offer.

The Tromsø chief of police would receive the British sailors and ensure they saw the British consul. Koht's inept actions were defused by his own staff who, no longer bound by his orders, saved the British sailors from German prison camps and possibly worse.

It was confirmed in the Norwegian press statement issued by the Norwegian Ministry for Foreign Affairs two weeks later that the prisoners were released at the request of the Prize Commander and not due to Norwegian pressure or insistence.[17] Pusback would have been well aware of the fate awaiting the British crew once they set foot on German soil. He could justifiably argue that he expected to improve his standing with the Norwegian authorities if he set the British civilians free. In his mind, Pusback may well have differentiated between the "International Estate of Merchant Mariners" and the true members of Hitler's war machine, and in Tromsø he saw a chance to serve his true allegiance without upsetting the militarists at home.

On arrival the *City of Flint* had an assortment of people on board: 17 German Prize Crew; 37 who had been taken off the British merchantman *Stonegate* and transferred from the *Deutschland*; and the American crew of 41. The actual crew of the *City of Flint* was six below the normal complement for the ship. Unbeknownst to Pusback, they also had one passenger, namely the Scottish telegraphist James MacConnachie, who had served the ship well during the *Athenia* rescue mission.

Without an extra telegraphist the ship would not have complied with regulations for carrying passengers during the previous journey. Normally they would not have carried any, but on the previous trip, when they left Glasgow just a day behind the *Athenia*, the American Ambassador had himself persuaded Gainard to help repatriate stranded Americans wanting to escape the war. Gainard enlisted the young Scot, who had been promised free passage home on the ship's next trip. So far the Prize Crew had not discovered him.

Having successfully engineered the ship's entry to a neutral port, Gainard was plotting his next little victory over the Germans. He now planned to smuggle James ashore as part of the *Stonegate*'s crew, fearing that if the ship ever reached Germany, he would be put in a prisoner of war camp. The ploy worked: 37 British sailors were transferred from the German ship and 38 men left the ship in Tromsø. James was free to travel home to Scotland. Even the Norwegian authorities did not know that the Scot did not belong to the *Stonegate* crew.

The plan was not without its element of near comedy. The young Scot was returning from America in a style befitting a returning adventurer. James planned to leave the ship in his best clothes, with shiny new shoes and a gleaming suitcase. His "shipmates" of the sunken British freighter barely owned the clothes on their backs. In his book, Gainard recounts how the departure was "toned down" and the American suitcase left behind. Gainard promised to send it on to Scotland as soon as possible and, it was sent from Bergen a few weeks later.

As it became known on board that the British crew was to be released, a frantic spate of letter and telegram writing beset the American crew. No one in the outside world knew where the ship was and certainly not where they would end up. Pusback must have picked up on all this activity and let it be known that each man to be released would be searched when disembarking. This in turn caused most of the messages to be destroyed. He did not, however, consider the shrewdness of the English Captain Randall. The messages he carried were never detected.

Telegrams to let their wives know " All well" went to Mrs. Gainard at Melrose, Massachusetts; Mrs. Rhoads at York, Pennsylvania; Mrs. MacFarland, Dundalk, Maryland; and Mrs. Faust, Baltimore Maryland. Three telegrams telling their wives "All well, don't worry" went to Mrs. Robertson at Norfolk, Virginia; Mrs. Kebler at Mattapan, Boston, Massachusetts; and Miss Cyvilla Trump at Baltimore, Maryland. All of the telegrams were passed on to Mrs. J. Borden Harriman, the U.S. Minister to Norway, head of the U.S. Legation in Oslo. They were included in her report to the State Department for them to notify the anxious relatives, who until now, had heard nothing from their loved ones.

At lunchtime on Saturday, 21 October the British captain was informed that he and his crew would be put ashore instead of being brought back to Hamburg as Pusback apparently had originally planned.[18] This was the Prize Commander's first encounter with the political battle which was to engulf his command from now on. Nothing in his previous career could possibly have prepared him for what was to come.

Pusback had stayed long enough to repeatedly contact the German Embassy in Oslo by telegram. Once he agreed to comply with the Norwegian 24-hour rule, it seemed that the authorities relaxed. He was allowed to contact the German consulate in Tromsø, telling them to pass on the news of the imposed time limit and also that from now on, he would act at his own discretion. He acknowledged that he was on his own.[19] The consulate learned that under Norwegian rules he would leave Tromsø by 1700 hours that afternoon for his journey south and that upon departure he was allowed to remain for only a further 24 hours within Norwegian territorial waters. Pusback added that the charts the Tromsø consul had helped him acquire had been impounded on behalf of the Norwegian Government.[20]

Just before Captain Randall was disembarked, Pusback had hinted that he expected to be met outside Norwegian territorial waters by an escort of destroyers. In fact, it turned out that he actually received a secret telegram while in Tromsø and it was this telegram which instructed Pusback to head north, towards Murmansk.[21] There is, however, no record of such a telegram in the Naval High Command's appropriate file, which also does not include the telegram Pusback sent that day, nor did he refer to it later in his account of the episode.[22]

The transfer of the British prisoners was being supervised by the British vice-consul, and closely watched by local police and customs authorities. The British had posted an officer from the Royal Navy to work alongside the local man. The Germans had boosted their consulate by installing a German national as vice-consul. Tromsø was becoming a strategic port in northern Norway. Mid-afternoon a Norwegian navy launch came alongside to take off the British crew from the *Stonegate* and under armed guard the American crew had to stand by and watch the British civilians being moved to safety. Fifteen minutes later the *City of Flint* weighed anchor and departed.[23]

Norway was treating the ship in accordance with rules for warships. They did not accept the German excuses. Little did Koht know that a couple of weeks earlier, on 3 October and 9 October, Hitler had actually discussed the possibility of occupying Norway.[24]

The *Sleipner* accompanied them, just to ensure that they did leave Norwegian waters. On the *City of Flint* the helmsman was young Willy Neher, who had been joined in the wheel house by a Norwegian pilot. They sailed southwards through the islands towards the open sea. The pilot later transferred to the *Sleipner* and the navy led the way out past Hekkingen. The *City of Flint* was escorted to the edge of Norwegian territorial waters, where they arrived at 2020 hours that evening, well within their allotted time. The weather was overcast and raining. As they proceeded out to open waters, the weather thickened. They met a heavy south-westerly sea and a large swell and as a result, were occasionally shipping large amounts of water.

Moving out from the port, Gainard saw firsthand what other Europeans thought of their German guards as the *City of Flint* was still flying the swastika. They passed close by a group of Polish fishing vessels that had obviously managed to escape the Nazi annihilation of their country six weeks earlier. Their insulting gestures could not be mistaken, regardless of the nationality of the spectator.[25]

There were two serious issues to be considered before deciding whether to set a southerly course or to head further north. Gainard's plan to break cover had worked. The world now knew where the *City of Flint* was and this fact was bound to make warships from each side head northwards towards the area. The captain had firmly placed the innocents between a rock and a hard place—both sides in the deadly conflict would watch Pusback's every step, eager to exploit any mistake to their own advantage. In the middle was a neutral ship from the most powerful nation in the world, being temporarily escorted by a ship from one of the weakest neutral nations caught up in the conflict. As if to add to the German officer's problems, the weather was deteriorating fast. This was, after all, well into the season of fall storms, and in the waters to the south there were mines that could be torn lose and set adrift by the swelling seas. Furthermore, Pusback had no charts for any parts of the Norwegian coastline. The night they left, Gainard later claimed, mines sank five ships in areas they would have been going through if they went south.

Before turning back, the Norwegian escort watched the *City of Flint* continue on a north-westerly course. On leaving Tromsø, Pusback informed the *Sleipner* of his plan to head for open waters outside Norwegian territory and make his way southwards out at sea. At this stage they lowered the German flag they had been required to fly within Norwegian waters.[26] Norwegian Neutrality Regulations insisted on all ships flying the appropriate national flag when not at anchor or in port. The *Sleipner* was back in Tromsø before midnight. Their problem had gone away, they thought.

On the bridge of the *City of Flint*, Pusback kept a close eye on the *Sleipner's* navigational lights and on the lights from the coast. Once they were around 10 kilometers out, they hit a snowstorm. Immediately the ship was enveloped in a thick shower of snow and hail. Under cover of the snow and the darkness, Pusback ordered a northerly course towards Murmansk. He did not plan any stops on the way. The sea remained rough and the wind stayed with them from the west. Unbeknownst to the American crew, at 1800

Sunday afternoon, they passed the North Cape to starboard, still sailing east, towards Soviet waters.

The events that unfurled in Tromsø harbor that Saturday seemed to have been very low key. The local press did not react in any way.

Incredibly, no one in official Norwegian circles in Oslo had thought of alerting the U.S. Ambassador, Mrs. Harriman, of the fact that the ship was in a Norwegian port, but under German command. It was the American ambassador in Stockholm who telephoned her to say that through newspaper circles he had heard that the *City of Flint* had called at the Norwegian port, but had sailed again. Harriman then phoned the journalist the next morning, only to be told that the ship had indeed left the previous day on a northerly course.

When the southbound steamer came through Tromsø that Saturday night, 21 October, the *Stonegate*'s crew was dispatched south. According to the timetable, the steamer arrived at midnight on Saturday evening and left again about three hours later.[27] The British crew had spent the day relaxing at a local hotel where the British vice-consul had managed to secure accommodations for all of them. Once aboard, the crew would basically be out of reach of everyone. They were the only ones that could provide the Americans or the British with any information at all on the behavior and plans of the German captors, but nobody had thought of asking them.

At the German Embassy in Oslo, on the other hand, they were working overtime that evening trying to locate the *City of Flint*. Ambassador Werner Von Neuhaus was deploying all his resources to try and find her. Instead of going back to Wussow and Rye-Holmboe at Tromsø, he delegated some of the task to their vice-consul in Trondheim.[28] By the evening he contacted Wussow by telephone with a mission. Wussow was to travel to Lødingen immediately. All foreign ships sailing south would be expected to change pilots at Lødingen. If the *City of Flint* was heading south, Pusback would be quite justified in calling in. That was where he could be given new orders for the journey south.

As the crow flies, Lødingen was 200 km, around 12 hours' sailing time, from Tromsø. It was Saturday night, several hundred kilometers north of the Arctic Circle, at the end of October, and the cold Norwegian winter had started. According to the weather forecast, there was a storm brewing. Wussow could not find a single boat owner willing to make the journey, which could easily last 15 hours, each way. He knew the *City of Flint* had left ahead of him as he had received the order and he knew its optimal speed was 10.5 knots. Only a limited number of options now presented themselves. The best one was actually the coastal steamer, even if the ship called at various small towns on the way south. He would travel in the same ship as Captain Randall and his crew, whom the Germans had just released.

Norwegian officials escorted the British crew on board. After all, they had not been processed via normal immigration procedures. It is unlikely that this transfer would have happened without a member of staff from the British consulate being present. Any of the consular staff would have known Wussow, at least well enough to spot him on sight, but none of the British sailors would have known who he was. As long as he could manage to steal past the British consul, Wussow would be able to remain incognito for the duration of the ten-hour journey. There are no records of his having been spotted. According to his own report, this part of the journey was uneventful and Captain Randall's report did not refer to any encounters with Germans on the way along the Norwegian coast.[29]

On Sunday, 22 October at 1315 hours Oslo time, the German Embassy received a telephone call from Berlin. News of the American prize had reached the Foreign Ministry.

More than 20 hours after her departure, through primitive communications or ineptitude, the news of her departure from Tromsø had only just reached Berlin. The German Foreign Office was aware of the frailty of the regulatory protection afforded to a prize when sailing in territorial waters of a neutral state. They stressed that the ship should endeavor to remain in Norwegian waters as long as possible. In fact, Pusback was ordered to do so, but he should not stop. The German-controlled ship would be permitted to remain in territorial waters only if she kept on the move, Berlin thought.

According to Wussow, he arrived at Lødingen on Sunday at 1345 and the timetable confirmed that the coastal steamer was indeed due in at 1400.[30] It is unlikely that he would have been able to locate anybody else who could have brought him that distance in such a time. As he checked with the pilot station, he discovered that the *City of Flint* had not passed through the narrow sound on its way south. An hour later, he was talking to his embassy in Oslo by telephone, no small feat in a village where each telephone call had to be pre-ordered via the switchboard and manually connected. Entirely without a grasp of the real situation, one of the embassy's senior advisors now ordered him to get in touch with the ship.[31] Wussow was told to stress the German view of the Norwegian 24-hour rule and the need to keep on the move. The problem was, there was simply no way of telling Pusback.

In the fall of 1939, Lødingen would have been no more than a tiny hamlet built around the bunkering facilities and the pilot station. As the *City of Flint* was clearly not about to turn up, Wussow did not stand much of a chance of fulfilling his orders. He did not give up. Ever the resourceful agent, Wussow decided to pay a visit to a Norwegian patrol boat which just happened to be at quay.

Finally he had some luck. Wussow seems to have put his cards on the table and explained to the Norwegian naval officers that he was trying to catch up with the *City of Flint,* which was a German prize. One of them explained that the *City of Flint* had passed Hekkingen at 2100 the previous evening. He added that the ship had been escorted out of Norwegian waters by a torpedo boat. The Norwegian was very well informed of the *City of Flint*'s passage, and he could even provide Wussow with the ship's official call-sign KUCV. At this stage Wussow must have felt himself among friends; he asked if they could help him transmit his message to Pusback. This was clearly more than the Norwegian's job was worth. He now decided to defer to the Commanding Officer, none other than Commander Hagerup back in Tromsø. Hagerup declined to help, quoting the relevant parts of the Norwegian Neutrality Regulations as the reason for his decision.

Regardless of the precarious nature of communications within Norway in 1939, by Sunday afternoon, the Chargé d'Affaires at the German Embassy in Oslo had been sufficiently briefed on the situation. Von Neuhaus lodged a protest with the Norwegian authorities, arguing that he considered it wrong to withdraw the charts and to limit the ship's stay in territorial waters.[32] They argued that the ship was not a warship, but a ship merely taken over by a foreign power and as such did not have to leave Norwegian territorial waters once departed from the port of call.

Although he had placed himself out of reach of telephones during all of Sunday night, Norwegian Foreign Minister Koht must have been really concerned over this German protest. When he finally saw it Monday morning, he actually sent a copy to His

Majesty Haakon VII, the King. Three days later the Norwegians replied, only to reject the German protest.[33] It was a brief and robust rebuttal, which referred to the Norwegian Neutrality Regulations as the basis for the 24-hour rule. Perhaps even more significant, it also pointed out that the same Regulations actually made the export of Norwegian maps illegal. Diesen was only given a chance to agree to the text via the telephone before the statement was submitted to Koht for approval. Koht, on his part, even sent the King a copy of the proposed response.

The same regulation made it quite clear that any warships belonging to a belligerent nation could not remain in "inner territorial waters," i.e., in inshore waters, in the fjords, within the range of islands and skerries, etc., for more than 24 hours.[34] Only if expressly allowed to do so in an emergency, could ships deviate from these rules. They defined a warship as, "a ship under the command of the military."[35]

By Monday, 23 October, at the meeting of the British War Cabinet, Churchill had the bit firmly between his teeth. The report on the deeds of the *Deutschland*, the second item on their agenda, triggered far more detailed conclusions. They now had some brief intelligence from vice-consul Sæter in Tromsø. The Cabinet was informed that the *City of Flint* was heading south, towards Hamburg and that the Royal Navy was out to stop her.

Rosyth was ordered to send the destroyer *Jersey* up to the Norwegian coast off Bergen. She was to head for Marsteinen Lighthouse, and had to be there by 0800 hours the following morning to commence a sweep northward along the coast. The aim was to capture the prize.[36] It was a tight schedule, but with such a brand new vessel capable of 36 knots, it would be possible to reach the destination on time.

While in Tromsø, Pusback had taken the opportunity to use the German consul to contact his minister in Oslo, requesting further instructions. Judging from the subsequent choice of action, he now had to fall back on earlier instructions, namely to head for the Soviet Union if Norwegian territorial waters were denied him. Before he ever set foot on the deck of the *City of Flint*, Pusback knew from discussions with Wenneker, that if Norwegian waters were closed to him, Murmansk would have to be his alternative destination.[37]

Pusback asked Gainard what he thought of the idea of heading for Murmansk. Hoping to be one step ahead of the German in the strategy game, Gainard agreed, claiming that this would be a good idea; he was banking on the Soviets giving him his ship back. Czarist Russia was a signatory to the Hague Conventions of 1907.[38] While Gainard may well have hoped for some moral support under the notion of international laws of the sea, Pusback on his part may not have known of the existence of the Non-Aggression Pact negotiated by Molotov and Ribbentrop. It had been signed the day before the *Deutschland* had put to sea. The Pact even included secret protocols on how the two powers should share territory between them. The Soviet leadership had in fact twice offered the German navy suitable sites for a complete German naval base at Kola. Murmansk was a logical option for Pusback as it had been for countless other German skippers that fall.[39]

The German was still winning.

The departure from the Norwegian port of Tromsø was the last anyone knew of the *City of Flint* for the next 48 hours. The ship had still not appeared on the world's media stage. Pusback did not have the appropriate charts for the journey to Murmansk.[40] He had to navigate on compass bearings around the northern part of Norway, past the large

Varanger Peninsula and continue around Rybachiy Peninsula. The final leg was merely steering a straight southerly course towards the mouth of the wide Kola Bay.

On the morning of Monday, 23 October, Pusback ordered the official flag of the German navy to be flown.[41] He knew that by claiming military status, he would avoid all civilian immigration and customs procedures. At that stage they were coming around the Rybachiy Peninsula. At 0930 hours they entered Kola Bight and within half an hour they were ordered to stop, only to wait nearly until midday for permission to enter Kola Fjord itself.

Stalin's war with Finland had not yet started. The lighthouse at Set Navolok would still have been lit, marking the western tip of the bay. Directly to the south was the mouth of the fjord. At the opening was the Letinsky Pilot Station. Civilian ships would be expected to stop here to request pilotage for the rest of the journey in to Murmansk. When the *City of Flint* arrived, they were totally unannounced.

They were permitted to proceed on their own until 1330, when two pilots came aboard from the pilot station. Just beyond the pilot station was the entrance of the fjord, which led to the naval base at Polyarnoe. This was a military zone, blocked to outsiders. Even when leaving Murmansk, ships had to take on pilots at Salny Island for the brief journey to the mouth of Kola Bay.

Pusback explained later that once the Soviet authorities realized the status of the ship, they disappeared. Gainard dropped the anchor at Murmansk at 1500 hours. Just before midnight a group of Soviet naval officers, together with some customs officials, came on board. They checked the ship's papers and sealed the radio room. No transmissions were permitted while in port. All formalities were quickly dealt with. The Soviets could not speak German; they used an English-speaking translator who informed Pusback that he should expect further instructions from the Soviet government during his stay.

Gainard saw an opportunity to request permission to contact the U.S. Embassy in Moscow. While this was not refused, nothing was actually ever done to effect his request. According to his log, the Soviet officials asked Gainard if he had anything to say to them. Gainard recorded his reply in the log: "The German officers claim us as Prize to be brought to Germany. Before doing anything I respectfully ask for an opportunity to ask advice from my Embassy."[42]

As Pusback and his men arrived in Murmansk, the town could boast only two paved streets.[43] Walking along any of the other heavily used roads meant plunging into ankle-deep, semi-frozen mud. Sturdy, well-built stone houses were outnumbered by anonymous-looking wooden buildings, built in a hurry to accommodate the influx of workers as the town had grown quickly during the previous two decades.

At the center of town, two large hotels had pride of place. The more modern of the two, Hotel Arctic, was the focal point for any visitors. It was the regular meeting place for those of the locals who could afford it. Murmansk was a town in a hurry. Around town, work on building sites or in factories continued throughout the night. The streets were brightly lit and everywhere loud music blared from large loudspeakers, only to be interrupted by the occasional political message. The hotels sprang into life every sixth evening. In Murmansk, every sixth day was a day for resting, and resting normally meant drinking.[44]

At midnight, Soviet press agency Tass, suddenly issued a press release, informing the world of the *City of Flint*'s whereabouts. For two days the world's press had been quiet on the issue of the *City of Flint*. The brief interlude at Tromsø had attracted both American and British attention to the drama.

Suddenly, after a good two days' sailing, an American ship, which had been lost to the world, with German soldiers in charge on board, arrived in Communist Soviet Union. For the Royal Navy the chase was off, for the time being.

5

Americans in Communist
Soviet Union

The *City of Flint* had appeared in the northern port of Murmansk in the Soviet Union. To the average American, such a development was less likely than just about anything else that could have happened to the ship. No neutral power had the right to become the custodian of another neutral nation's ship, which had originally been taken over by force by a third country at war. Consequently, it was expected that the Soviet Union would hand the ship back to the American crew. Many were actually surprised that the Soviet Union even admitted to playing host to the German prize. The press argued that rather than admitting to such unconventional actions, the Soviets could merely have kept the ship's arrival at Murmansk secret.[1]

The customs officials did not leave the ship until 0200. Yet within three hours they were back on board.[2] One of the Soviet naval port officers informed them that the *City of Flint* was free to sail as soon as their papers were returned. The official also assured Gainard that he would return later in order to help the American contact his Embassy. He even enquired about how soon they could be ready to leave port. Gainard had decided to do some maintenance work on one of the ship's boilers. Being justifiably anxious to get underway, Gainard assured him that the ship could sail at once on two boilers, cutting in the third boiler, which was being serviced, at sea. If he could help it, nothing was going to prevent Gainard making a run for it—once he got his papers.

Pusback, on the other hand, was advised to stand down his Prize Crew and remove them from the ship. Once the Soviets had explained the situation to Pusback and assured him that the Soviet Union was definitely a friendly neutral power, he agreed. The Soviets argued it was in the interest of an early solution and easier settlement if the Germans were to come off the ship for some time.[3] The Soviet Neutrality Regulations of October 1939 were not well known outside Moscow. Not even authoritative American sources were aware of the Soviet laws on this point.[4] The world really did not know what the Soviet Union would permit under its current rules. Alternatively, they could turn their alleged neutrality to fit any given situation which, in reality, is what they did.

That morning the German Prize Crew disembarked with all their belongings and kit. They were interned at the naval station. One of them, a German radio operator, was rushed off to a Soviet hospital with diagnosed appendicitis.

In New York, where it was still only late afternoon, the press immediately picked up on the announcement from Moscow. It was even the newsmen who broke the news of the *City of Flint*'s whereabouts to Mr. A.J. McCarthy, Vice President of the United States

Lines, and the man in charge of the Line's operations. When they contacted him at home on Monday evening he could only express his surprise at the news.[5]

It had been a brilliant diplomatic coup for Germany when the Soviet Union signed the Non-Aggression Pact only two months earlier. The incredulity now caused by the *City of Flint's* visit to Murmansk illustrated a lack of appreciation of the closeness of the two countries at that time in history.

Foreign Minister Koht, in Oslo, must have expected that the American ship would come back to haunt him. The majority of German ships bound for a home port came through Norwegian waters when sailing from Murmansk. The Norwegian experts on neutrality now knew that it was only a question of time before their reasoning would be put to the test by some of the sharpest legal brains in three different, large and powerful countries.

In the morning of Tuesday, 24 October, the *City of Flint* was again in the newspapers on either side of the Atlantic. *The New York Times* had the time to prepare a front page banner headline for its Tuesday edition. As in the case of the *Athenia* sinking only a month earlier, the Germans were portrayed as attacking neutral Americans, which could only drive a wedge between the public and anything Germany might try to do. In Washington, the Maritime Commission released the names of all the members of the crew to the press. In New Orleans, as Mrs. Ellis Long scanned the list she discovered to her horror that her son Percy McHaffie was among them. She had lost touch with Percy when he signed on his first ship four years earlier.

In London, the *City of Flint's* arrival at Murmansk was the lead item of the BBC's first radio news bulletin of the day.[6] In Berlin the German Admiralty claimed to have absolutely no knowledge of the seizure. Perhaps more worryingly for the German Naval High Command was that they only now learned that the *City of Flint* was at Murmansk, and that the Prize Commander had been interned, and this concerned them.

The affair was bound to impact on the U.S. neutrality debate. One of the Senate's leading advocates of changes to the neutrality laws, Senator James P. Byrnes, immediately predicted a political impact as a result of the German seizure. Within hours Byrnes was proven right. Later that day the Senate voted to reduce the debating time on the proposed legislation. The seizure of the *City of Flint* had injected an element of urgency into the debate.

Hitler had withdrawn his Ambassador to the U.S. a year earlier, fearing his expulsion after the Kristallnacht riots in Germany. The Embassy was under the control of Hans Thomsen during the *City of Flint* affair. He had to deal with an increasingly inquisitive press and a hostile Secretary of State, Cordell Hull. Thomsen totally misread the situation.

Hull was being quite frank with the press, admitting that they had heard nothing concerning the German seizure of the American freighter, and adding that his Chargé d'Affaires was effectively being stonewalled in Berlin. The Germans were saying nothing.

Although it was not yet Tuesday lunchtime in Washington when Thomsen sent Berlin a telegram, it was already early evening in Berlin. He was keen to explain the American reaction to the capture of one of their ships. Incredibly, he claimed that the news had been received calmly, as an unavoidable measure of war. There was a strong wish to keep American ships away from the European war zone altogether, he argued. The capture had also renewed doubts about the effectiveness of the British blockade of German warships, according to Thomsen.[7] Very few of the sentiments in Thomsen's telegram could have been inspired by actual articles in the press. To make matters worse,

Thomsen did not seem to have waited to hear the outcome of President Roosevelt's press conference that morning. It was probably just as well. The President lambasted the Germans for taking the American ship, which he argued had been on a perfectly legal voyage. If British bureaucrats had wondered about the President's views, they had now had them confirmed.[8] Even the Norwegian press claimed that Washington saw the seizure of the American ship as a "psychological mistake," which was bound to influence the Senate's treatment of the neutrality debate.[9]

The only country apart from Germany who may have had the opportunity to gather any sort of information on this affair was Britain, who had actually had one of her representatives meeting the *City of Flint* at Tromsø. The British consul and his naval attaché had ample time to interview the *Stonegate* Master before he joined the others on the coastal steamer south. It is difficult to understand why this did not happen. It was only when Captain Randall reached Bergen several days later that the British consul had the presence of mind to interview him in some detail about the affair, but by then the *City of Flint* was already on its way back from Murmansk.

To the German Ministry of Foreign Affairs, the internment of the German Prize Crew was a violation of the Hague Conventions' definition of the right to seek port due to distress or problems. The lack of charts qualified as a problem, they argued.[10] In sum, the prize had only called at Murmansk due to distress, as would be permissible under the Conventions. Naval High Command discussed the problem during the day, and later their Naval Attaché in Moscow was ordered, by telegram, to effect the lifting of the internment and to ensure that the re-equipment of the Prize Crew was done quickly. He was also to provide orders for Pusback's return journey to Germany.[11] Berlin's view of Soviet reality and German influence was staggeringly different from the reality in Moscow.

As soon as the Prize Crew had been removed from the ship, the Murmansk harbor authority notified the German Embassy in Moscow. Surprisingly it became clear that even after Pusback's meetings with the German consulate staff at Tromsø, the navy's leadership were still not aware that the *City of Flint's* radio was out of commission. They ordered the Prize Commander to maintain a listening watch on the radio and to transmit only in emergencies.[12] The navy now requested instructions to support the prize in any form to be issued to the German consulates at Narvik, Trondheim, Bergen, Haugesund and Gothenburg. The navy administrators did not issue any advice with this order to explain the tricky nature of the various Hague Conventions from 1907, nor did they make clear what was regarded as acceptable behavior for Prize Commanders when in neutral waters. They were all expected to act as they saw fit.

All they knew in Washington at this stage was that the ship had arrived in Kola Bay, north of Murmansk and that "the crew" had been interned. The sketchy information had come from the Soviet news releases; no official statement was forthcoming. The question was: were the Germans interned or was it the U.S. crew they had locked up? In Oslo, the U.S. Ambassador Harriman approached the Norwegian authorities for information. All Ambassador Laurence Steinhardt could do in Moscow was to read the newspapers and request a meeting with Potemkin, the Soviet's vice-commissar for foreign affairs. To add to his frustration, Tuesday, 24 October was an official day of rest in Moscow. Nonetheless, it turned out that Potemkin was prepared to see the American and they met that afternoon. Steinhardt was invited to the Foreign Affairs Commissariat, which was located opposite the infamous Lubyanka Prison. In fact, every time Steinhardt went anywhere near them on official business, he had an escort of U.S. secret service men. Potemkin continued to play for time, as he claimed that the official Soviet line was still unclear. In Moscow they knew too little about the American ship.[13]

According to Steinhardt, the meeting had been perfectly cordial with Potemkin promising further details. This would normally take a few days, as there were no consulates at Murmansk, which in effect was a closed city to foreigners. All Steinhardt's own attempts to reach Gainard by telephone came to nothing. As if the Murmansk end was not difficult enough, he soon learned that telephone calls like his were now to be accepted only during certain hours each day, normally around lunchtime in Moscow.

Berlin was next. Head of the U.S. Legation Alexander Kirk, having been alerted the previous evening, now set off to the German Ministry of the Navy. He continued to the Ministry of Foreign Affairs and ordered some tentative enquiries in Hamburg at the Prize Commission. The story Kirk was being told in Berlin was rather different from the version Steinhardt had learned in Moscow. According to the Germans, the Tass story was basically untrue. They could not, however, tell Kirk anything more substantive about the real story behind the *City of Flint's* sudden appearance in Northern Russia.[14] Neither Göbbels' Propaganda Ministry, nor Raeder's Admiralty could offer any information as to a German raider taking the *City of Flint* as a prize. The truth was that captain Wenneker had already told the authorities nine days earlier, but the Admiralty spokesman denied all knowledge of the affair.[15] Even the Naval High Command's War Diary entry for the 15 October 1939 acknowledged that Wenneker had captured the *City of Flint* and sent her "home."[16]

It is unclear where Kirk's actual office was at this time. The United States had purchased the Palais Blücher at Pariser Platz 2 in 1931, hoping to turn it into a real showpiece among Berlin embassies. It was not to be. A fire destroyed virtually the entire building and it was not until 1939 that some of the Embassy functions were moved into the restored building. The location could not have been better—at the top of the promenade Unter den Linden, in the shadow of the Brandenburg Gate, minutes away from the centers of the German administration and half way between the Reichstag and the government ministries in Wilhelmstrasse.[17]

In the fall of 1939, the majority of the U.S. diplomatic functions remained at 39 Bendlerstrasse. When facing the Tiergarten Park, the Embassy was at the top end of the street, on the right. At the bottom of the street, on the opposite side, were offices belonging to the German military.[18]

Graf von der Schulenburg, the German Ambassador in Moscow, had no problems reaching Molotov, who actually invited the German diplomat to a meeting over the *City of Flint*. Molotov seemed to want to let von Schulenburg know that the internment of the Prize Crew was a mere formality. The Soviets would naturally accommodate the German prize in any way they could, he assured von Schulenburg. On the other hand, he added, Molotov felt that the Soviet Union as a neutral power had been placed in an embarrassing position vis-à-vis the American government.[19] Since American Ambassador Steinhardt had tried to intervene twice the day before and the U.S. press was creating a lot of fuss, the Soviets did not like it. There were obviously limits to Soviet accommodation, regardless of the fine words of the Friendship Pact.

Von Schulenburg tried to reassure Molotov that as the U.S. too had signed the relevant Hague Convention, they had to accept what was happening as part of approved procedures. Molotov replied, however, that although he would look at the legal situation, he would request that the German government in the future avoid cases like this one. In diplomatic terms, this would have been equal to a major dressing down. The Germans had better move the offending ship rather quickly.

As Tuesday, 24 October was coming to an end for busy American diplomats and agents, Harriman in Oslo finally had the actual numbers of people on board the U.S. ship but alas, no information about the American crew.[20] In Moscow, the German's initial claim that the ship had somehow lost all its charts apart from the Murmansk one was rejected by the Murmansk authorities, hence the internment of the Prize Crew.

Captain Gainard, on his return to Baltimore, denied this version of events. He argued that the ship had never been that far north, and as Tromsø was far outside his "regular" run to England and Germany, he had never needed and therefore never acquired charts for those waters. The American Chargé d'Affaires in Berlin, Mr. Kirk, received a memorandum from the German Ministry for Foreign Affairs stating that the ship sailed to Murmansk due to the lack of charts and this in turn had constituted an emergency. An emergency would again justify the prize calling at a port to deal with the situation. In Britain the reason was seen as one of necessity, preferring Soviet assistance to Norwegian internment.

In its Tuesday editions, a Norwegian paper quoted the Soviet news agency Tass as stating that the ship had been held back and the Prize Crew arrested, which would have been entirely in keeping with neutrality rules and international law.[21] Both President Roosevelt and Secretary of State Hull issued statements on the *City of Flint* to the press. The President stressed the perfectly legal voyage, while Hull, in his briefing, focused on the lack of information and stressed that American diplomats in Moscow and Berlin had been promised more information as soon as it became available. At this early stage Roosevelt did not know that the Soviet administration was withholding information.

The American draft Neutrality Bill moved to the next stage in the proceedings, and supporters hoped for a decisive vote in favor within the next couple days. This bullish line was also reflected in a later telegram from Cordell Hull, to Ambassador Steinhardt in Moscow. Hull pointed to Articles 21 and 22 of the relevant Hague Convention and argued that if the ship had not already been released, it most certainly should be. Failure to do so would compromise Soviet neutrality.[22] In a statement later that night, Hull accepted that a small part of the cargo of the *City of Flint* probably could be regarded as "absolute contraband." He also stressed that one of their chief interests was to find out what had happened to the American crew.

By Tuesday evening the Soviet naval authority officials had not returned to the *City of Flint*. It was still not possible for Gainard to send a telegram to the Embassy in Moscow.[23] On Wednesday, 25 October at 1130, the British War Cabinet met in London. With Churchill present, the *City of Flint* had crept up the agenda. The discussion, which was becoming a daily occurrence, seemed to have taken on a rather perfunctory appearance that morning. They merely noted the arrival at Murmansk and that the Germans had been interned. All they had to go on was a report from the Soviet news agency Tass.[24]

In London as the afternoon wore on, more news on the capture of the *City of Flint* was reaching the media. The BBC featured the ship and the public was able to follow the story as it unfolded. The pressure to act was therefore building in step with the expectations. The German warship was identified for the first time. The *Deutschland* was blamed for the sinking of the *Stonegate* and for providing the Prize Crew to the *City of Flint*. The public even knew that the reason for the calling at Tromsø was a shortage of water and they had heard that the *City of Flint* lacked the appropriate charts for sailing to Germany.[25] This information came from the German Admiralty in Berlin which was smarting over the Norwegian handling of this issue. All sides were obviously well aware of the power of the media in a game over a prize. No one in Washington or in London could get hold of any information from those involved.

The American ship was incommunicado in Murmansk and the crew of the *Stonegate* was out of reach on the coastal steamer on the way south to Bergen. On Wednesday, 25 October, when the coastal steamer arrived at Trondheim on her way south, the Norwegian authorities posted police guards on the gangway, apparently to prevent illegal entry to Norway by any members of the British crew. The *Stonegate*'s Captain Randall denied the crew permission to be interviewed or photographed and they were confined to their cabins during the brief stop. The skipper later stressed the embargo in his affidavit to the U.S. consul and added that he was forbidden from giving any interviews. The British consul in Trondheim used the stop to call on Randall, but even after a lengthy discussion they declined to provide the press with any information. The trouble was, the consul did not pass anything to anybody else either!

One member of the group did, however, tell the press that it was indeed the *Deutschland* that had seized the England-bound *Stonegate* six days out of Panama. James MacConnachie, the erstwhile *City of Flint* radio operator, did not feel obliged to remain silent. He had not been part of the *Stonegate*'s crew. James was between jobs and obviously felt that publicity would not hinder his chances of finding work once back in Britain.

On Wednesday, 25 October the Murmansk naval authorities cancelled the internment of the German Prize Crew. The cancellation was made because it had now been discovered that the ship had called in Murmansk in need of emergency repairs, the Soviets observed.

The American Chargé d'Affaires in Berlin, Alexander Kirk, had been informed that the German Prize Crew had declared "Havarie" as the reason for heading for Murmansk. This term, recognized in international shipping, indicated that some sort of emergency had caused the detour around the northern part of Norway. It could cover a multitude of excuses, but the German Ministry of Foreign Affairs explained that the cause for this emergency was the lack of charts for the route south to Germany. The British and the Americans were less sympathetic. The lack of charts aboard the *City of Flint* was hardly surprising seeing that the ship was bound for Liverpool. If the Prize Crew had not been furnished with adequate maps before starting their part of the journey then it was a German problem, not a "Havarie."

The German Ambassador von Schulenburg had different issues with Molotov. First of all Schulenburg was invited to meet with Molotov to explain the reasons behind the prize entering Murmansk. The Soviet Minister pointed out at that the American Ambassador had twice tried to contact him since the day before and the American press was now making "an awful lot of noise." Schulenburg tried to hide behind The Hague Convention XIII and the rights it granted to the captor, but Molotov brushed him off, asking that the German Government ensure any future such cases be avoided. The Soviets were clearly not too worried about upsetting the Germans over the prize.

In Murmansk, Gainard spent the better part of Wednesday, 25 October attempting to secure permission to go ashore to contact the U.S. Embassy. Finally at 1910 hours a group of Soviet officials turned up, but their task was merely to examine cargo manifests and bill of lading. As they left twenty minutes later, Gainard managed to persuade one of them to accept a telegram for onward transmission to the Moscow Embassy. He requested that the Maritime Commission in Washington and the U.S. Lines office in London be notified of their situation.[26]

That Wednesday evening Secretary Hull must have been close to losing his patience with the Soviet authorities. Wherever he was at the time, he insisted on phoning in a further telegram for Steinhardt in Moscow. Hull was determined to learn the fate of the American crew. He now suggested the Embassy send a member of staff to Murmansk by plane if need be. He added:

> "If there continues to be evident a pre-disposition to avoid giving you adequate information, you might wish to throw out a hint, of course without commitment, to the effect that there is after all some relationship between the treatment accorded our vessels in a foreign port and the treatment to be expected for foreign vessels in our ports."[27]

The contrast with the treatment received by Pusback and his men could hardly have been greater. He had been in contact with the German Embassy in Moscow and was satisfied that he had received all the information he required to sail the *City of Flint* home.[28] After the three days ashore, he was asked to take his men back on board the *City of Flint* and prepare to sail within 24 hours.

In a further twist that brought a "human interest" dimension to the story, Mrs. Gainard now entered the drama. She sent off identical telegrams to the German Foreign Minister Joachim von Ribbentrop and to his Soviet counterpart, Vyacheslaff M. Molotov, pleading for clemency for her husband and the rest of the crew.[29] Mrs. Gainard was desperately seeking information concerning their safety.

When the Soviets actually slept seems entirely unclear. Thus, the German envoy had to be equally nocturnal in his ways. In the middle of the night a note arrived, this time from Potemkin. The message was being relayed from Molotov informing Schulenburg that the Murmansk internment of the *City of Flint* had been lifted. Only a verification of the cargo now kept the U.S. freighter in port. The reason for the call at Murmansk was now put down to "sea damage."[30]

During the night, the Soviet news agency Tass suddenly announced that they had released the interned Germans. Naval authorities in Murmansk, not civilian authorities, had taken the decision.

The news agency explained that a mistake had been made in interning the Germans. It was now clear that the *City of Flint* had sought entry to Murmansk to carry out emergency repairs. Incredibly, the American Ambassador, at that late hour, managed to reach Potemkin by telephone. Potemkin confirmed the release of the Germans, but stressed that the Prize Crew was not back on board the *City of Flint*. He would not confirm if the ship was free to leave port under its American crew.[31] In Moscow, the nature of the repairs had not been specified.

The German Naval High Command was growing increasingly concerned. They felt that an excuse had now been provided for the visit to Murmansk, but only as long as the status of the ship had not been changed. If she was in Murmansk due to engine trouble, they argued, it would be different from being brought in as a prize. Seemingly, the Soviets, although treaty-bound to Germany, were also worried about their relationship with America. If the status of the ship changed it could work against the Germans regaining control. Berlin claimed this would be counter to international law.

This line of argument did show that the German Ministry of Foreign Affairs was aware of the fact that a prize could not go to port in a neutral country without a reason.[32] The rule was set out in the Hague Convention XIII's Article 21. This explained that if no justification existed, the Soviet Union as a signatory to the Convention, would be obliged to invoke Article 22 and set the prize free. In reality only Tsarist Russia had acceded to the Convention.

Although the Hague Convention may have been clear enough, it was the status of the ship that would be the deciding factor. The Germans wanted her accepted as one of their warships, seeking a safe harbor for repairs. This would be acceptable under Article 17.

The trouble was, the ship was not German; she was American, and she was in Murmansk against the will of her lawful captain. The Germans knew this full well. Their own instructions for taking a prize included a set form to the completed by the commanding officer of the warship that captured a prize. The form was then issued to the officer in charge of the Prize Crew. It was a delegation of power. If Wenneker and Pusback acted according to their instructions, the *City of Flint* was indeed a prize and she would have the right to fly the flag of the German navy.

The Soviets had so far acted in accordance with Article 21. They had released the ship to the original officers and crew and had interned the Prize Crew. The only problem was, Gainard was stuck in port. This guaranteed the Soviets the opportunity to change their minds if they wanted to side with the Germans after all.

It was not lost on Gainard that all the German crews in Murmansk were allowed free movement to shore while the American crew remained isolated aboard their ship.[33]

Gainard's papers never turned up and on Thursday, 26 October he ordered a flag hoist signaling a request for permission to go ashore, presumably to look for the missing documents.[34] At this point a Soviet neutrality patrol vessel came up behind the *City of Flint*, blocked her escape route, and dropped anchor under the stern. The patrol vessel also replied to the signals, denying permission to go ashore. All the Americans could do was continue to wait.

In Norway, the press was now reporting from the Moscow Bureau of United Press that the interned *City of Flint* had been released, but to the German Prize Crew.

Mrs. Gainard's telegram was receiving attention in Berlin; she had after all, gone "straight to the top" and addressed it to "Ribbentrop Foreign Ministry Berlin."[35] They fired off a telegram marked "very urgent" to the embassy in Moscow demanding to know if the crew was "complete and safe and sound on board." It took a day for the reply to come back, but by Friday morning the German Embassy in Washington was instructed to inform Mrs. Gainard that the "captain and crew of the *City of Flint* are not injured and well treated in Murmansk." Ribbentrop himself wanted to be informed when the reply had gone.

As Gainard awaited permission to leave, the customs crew returned. The cargo inspection was proving to be a particularly elaborate process. All day Gainard had to use his own crew to shift cargo. After lunch six Soviet customs officials turned up with a gang of 11 men. They spent the entire afternoon examining the ship and its cargo. One by one, all five hatches had to be opened and the inspectors proceeded to open cases of cargo for inspection. To have some measure of control over this process, the captain insisted that his crew open and close the hatches; he was obviously not comfortable with the work of the inspection crew.[36]

By midnight Gainard noted that it had still not been possible to communicate with his embassy.[37] Finally the Americans had some luck. Although the official report to the Norwegian Ministry of Foreign Affairs of the *City of Flint*'s visit to Tromsø the previous Saturday was still in the post, the U.S. Embassy's own contacts in Oslo located some information. A source reported that some of those landed at Tromsø had arrived by coastal steamer at the West Norwegian port of Bergen. The Ambassador, Mrs. Harriman, immediately asked her consul in Bergen to contact them. Back came a report by telephone—the U.S. crew were all well. The source of this information was Randall, the *Stonegate* skipper, who was now in Bergen with his crew awaiting passage to Britain.[38]

The British had no proper detailed account of the situation until Captain Randall finally disembarked at Bergen. One Bergen news photographer managed to catch Randall on camera as he came ashore. When he was approached for an interview he declined the invitation rather brusquely. The pressure of having to look after his crew and fend off the press was obviously taking its toll, even after this short time.

The U.S. consul at Bergen, Maurice Pratt Dunlap, wasted no time when Randall arrived. He persuaded the Englishman to visit the American consulate and give them a written statement as to how they had all been treated and how the Americans accepted the military takeover. The following afternoon, American Eastern Standard Time, Washington finally had more details on the event. Once in Bergen, the crew members were taken to a hotel, and they all left for England at the first opportunity on the Norwegian steamer *Mira* bound from Bergen for the Tyne, where they arrived on Monday, 30 October.

Randall did not have much of an opportunity, however, to travel home to Robin Hood's Bay. The British authorities were very keen to learn first-hand, at last, what the conditions had been like on the *City of Flint*. He had to jump straight on the train for London. His interview with the Admiralty took place the following day.[39] Although the *Deutschland* had sunk his ship, Randall claimed that her captain Paul Wenneker was a perfect gentleman. He had even given the English mariner a signed photograph of the German warship. The behavior of the German captain had so impressed even Gainard that Randall had promised to have 40 copies of the photograph made for the captain of the *City of Flint* at his request.[40] It was this photograph First Mate Warren Rhoads later referred to in his radio interview in Baltimore when he was asked how he knew which ship had captured them.[41]

Randall added that Wenneker had been in a British prisoner of war camp in Wales during the First World War. He had not forgotten the fine treatment he had received at the hands of his British guards barely 20 years earlier.[42]

The indecisiveness of the Murmansk port authorities had so far kept around 20 freighters blocked in at the Kola Bay port for long periods of time. To make matters worse, several of these were by now running short of basic food due to the prolonged stay. A Swedish ship had however left port earlier that week. This was due, it was thought, to intense diplomatic pressure from the Swedish Government, who threatened to hold back a Soviet ship in return. In the case of the *City of Flint*, pressure was being applied from at least two very different sources: Washington and Berlin. Some news reached Norway about conditions in Murmansk when the released Swedes called at Lødingen Pilot Station on their way south.

As the Americans were stuck on their ship with no papers, they could see German ships move in and out of the port. Gainard reported several interned German ships at Murmansk; the liners *Bremen, New York, St. Louis* and *Hamburg* were all there, together with at least six tankers, including the *William Riedemann* and the *Hart* and four cargo ships.[43] One of these tankers was loaded to the gunwales with oil. Gainard suspected it was on the way out to replenish the *Deutschland* or to replenish other German ships that called at Murmansk. All of these would either need to rely on their superior speed, as in the case of the *Bremen,* or use Norwegian territorial waters to move into and out of German waters safely. Their crews could move freely between their ships and the shore using their own boats. German ships clearly had more freedom of movement than neutral ones.

It was as if Thomsen, the German Chargé d'Affaires in Washington, had listened to CBS that evening before he sent a brief telegram to Berlin. Even he was beginning to see where Roosevelt was going with his policies. Thomsen pointed out that the American government was endeavoring to portray the seizure of the *City of Flint* as an "unfriendly German act."[44] Thomsen claimed that the President wanted to use the story to swing Congress around in favor of lifting the embargo on weapons exports to countries at war. The awareness of the American separation of power between the Executive and Congress, a democratic process that was no longer in existence in Germany, is noteworthy.

On Thursday, 26 October, when the Murmansk authorities completed their examination of the *City of Flint's* cargo and ordered the release of the ship, the vessel was requested to leave port immediately.

Again, the good news was accompanied by some bad. Early Friday morning, the tug *Debotin* came alongside with some Soviet officials on board. They proceeded to transfer the German Prize Crew, who came back on board accompanied by a group of Soviet naval officers, minus one man who remained in hospital with appendicitis. Their Soviet escort explained again that the ship was a German prize and that it was free to leave immediately. An hour later the Soviets returned to the tug and departed, leaving the Prize Crew in charge of the *City of Flint* once again.[45] They had now well and truly violated American neutrality and, by reinstating German control over the Prize, they had also ignored the Hague Conventions.

Diplomatic pressure was building on Moscow. The Soviets clearly wanted to be rid of the troublesome ship fast. Ideally they wanted the ship away before they had to provide an official explanation to the Americans, who they did not want to upset. Gainard, the naval veteran from the previous war, had other plans. He decided to leave in his own good time. Besides, enemy ships might now be looking for them. He heard the news nearly at the same time as Schulenburg—by listening to American shortwave radio.[46] According to a German news agency dispatch from Moscow, quoted by Reuters, Pusback and the German Prize Crew were again on board and in charge of the *City of Flint.*

The German press was confident enough to publish the story, quoting a telegram from Washington as the source. They even claimed that U.S. legal experts regarded the German action as acceptable under international law. "Sources in Berlin" added that all German naval units had strict instructions to act within the Prize Regulations. "There is no doubt that the seizure of the steamer is correct," Berlin claimed.[47] The article went on to describe how such cases were being brought before the special court for a final ruling on how the German navy had acted. It was made abundantly clear that the reason for the *City of Flint* calling at Murmansk was a "Havarie" under the Hague Convention, i.e., an emergency. There were no hints as to what that actually meant.

In the meantime, there was only frustration for the American diplomats in Moscow, nearly 1000 miles from the actual site of this international tug of war. They were unable to learn anything about the ship's crew. The Murmansk port authority refused to answer calls and the port itself was located inside the large northern exclusion zone, closed to all foreigners. They had no more than "unconfirmed reports from the Kremlin" to rely on for news that the American crew was indeed still on board the ship.

In Murmansk, just after lunch on Friday, 27 October, a tender carrying port authority officials came alongside the *City of Flint*. This time they returned the identification certificates. They left within 15 minutes. Two hours later, another four Soviet officials came on board, this time spending an hour on the ship before leaving.[48] None of them seemed to be sufficiently senior to be able to make any real decisions. They merely kept checking papers.

By the end of that Friday, frustration at the U.S. Embassy was running even higher. Although Steinhardt had been able to reach the actual port of Murmansk by telephone twice, he had failed to reach Gainard. Unbeknownst to the Ambassador, Gainard was having the same experience. He made repeated requests for an opportunity to contact his Ambassador in Moscow. By the time he finally left Murmansk, Gainard was furious with the treatment he had experienced from the Soviets. The entire visit to Murmansk filled him with disgust.[49]

The Soviet Union claimed to be acting in accordance with the Hague Conventions of 1907. U.S. Secretary of State Cordell Hull used the same basis for his argument that no justifiable cause or emergency existed. The Prize Crew should therefore be arrested and the command of the ship handed back to its American captain, Steinhardt argued, but in vain. Potemkin argued that this merchant ship had arrived at Murmansk with declaring "Havarie" and was therefore not seaworthy. Once the Soviet authorities had convinced themselves that the ship was again fit to sail, they had insisted on her departure but under the exact same conditions as when she came in to Murmansk. That meant with both the German and the American crews on board. Altering this fact, Potemkin pointed out, would violate well-recognized principles of international law.[50]

"Customary" law, not written law, was in 1939, a significant aspect of both international law and the Law of War. Thus the fact that the Soviet Union had not acceded to the Hague Conventions of 1907 was less significant. The Conventions were, after all, a codification of norms. Universally accepted traditional rules of warfare and the codified norms, such as the Hague Conventions, were observed in parallel, and this continues to be the case.[51] It has, however, been pointed out that in 1935, "Soviet legal material on naval warfare was extremely limited."[52] It was this principle of generally accepted customary law which the Soviet Union used when stating their case at the Nuremberg War Crimes Tribunal.

In the case of the *City of Flint*, the Soviet lawyers looked to Hague XIII's Articles 21 and 22 for how to treat a prize in neutral waters. Ginsburgs argues that these two had over the years gradually been accepted internationally. Article 23, however, had seemingly been left behind. This article would have justified setting free the Prize Crew and allowing them to sail the prize to another port. Doing so would open up Soviet ports to a dangerous precedent that would clearly be of huge potential advantage to Germany but to no one else. It would ultimately make the U.S. question the Soviet Union's claim to neutrality.

Instead the Soviets initially rejected the German claim of right to entry due to an emergency, e.g., a "Havarie," a recognized international concept. Hence the internment of the Prize Crew. At this stage the Soviets should have handed the ship back to Gainard. Such a move would have been very strange, considering the dozen or so German ships sheltering in the same port and the ink hardly dry on the Molotov-Ribbentrop Pact. In addition, the Soviet Union had offered the German navy a secret location known as Basis Nord for their ships to refuel, etc.

The Soviets, most likely the Narkomindel (their foreign office) who would have been dealing with this issue, discovered their own reason for calling the ship a "Havarie." If they regarded the ship merely as a merchant vessel with an emergency, even if this was simply a shortage of relevant charts, the Soviet Union would not need to take a view of the status as a prize.

There is no evidence in relevant German files of any collaboration between Narkomindel and the German Foreign Office on this issue. The Soviet Union had made a mistake, now they had decided on a way out of it. The solution had to be implemented quickly, before the U.S. added any more pressure on them or started to threaten sanctions.

Finally, Steinhardt penned a personal and strictly confidential report for the U.S. president, the Secretary of State, and the Under Secretary. He explained his concerns that the Soviet Government actually had withheld information deliberately, and that there was a genuine conspiracy between the Soviet authorities and the German government over the ship.

Gainard later confirmed in his affidavit that the charts were one of the main reasons for going north, and at Murmansk they were provided with a set by other German ships anchored in the port.

A German wireless signal stated in the evening of Friday, 27 October that the release of the *City of Flint* to its Prize Crew was in accordance with the Hague Convention. It would have been entitled to seek shelter until any emergency repairs were carried out. Speaking later on his return to Baltimore, Gainard denied point blank any suggestions that the ship had ever been in need of repairs, but at the time he was effectively silenced, unable to contact his government.[53] Berlin obviously felt that they had won another round.

The British evening news bulletin, broadcast by the BBC, announced that the U.S. Senate, within the last half hour, had voted 67 to 22 to repeal the embargo on exporting arms to Britain and France. Formally, the House of Representatives could still scupper the President's plan, but this seemed increasingly unlikely. For Roosevelt, the case of the *City of Flint* had virtually outstayed its usefulness. The ship's capture had so spectacularly enhanced what the sinking of the *Athenia* had highlighted a month earlier, namely the menace of Hitler's regime.

The Norwegian leadership had far more imminent issues to resolve. Admiral Diesen knew that it was only a question of time before a very political issue arrived at a quay under his responsibility. As long as any visit complied with the Neutrality Regulations, Pusback would be OK to proceed, otherwise, the Prize Crew should be interned and the ship liberated. Similarly, Diesen doubted that the ship could be denied access to Norwegian territorial waters. Interestingly, it seemed that an advisory note outlining the interpretation of the Neutrality Regulations had been shown to Koht before being conveyed to Admiral Diesen. The file version carried Koht's amendments concerning access to Norwegian waters in his own hand: "But only for 24 hours!"[54]

This amendment caused some consternation in the Foreign Ministry. The original advice was typed on Friday and Koht's amended version was finally telephoned to the Admiral the following evening. The Minister's prerogative, to make policy decisions "on the hoof," had prevailed, but the limitation was only legal under the Neutrality

Regulations when Norway regarded the prize as a German warship. The decision was in line with the limit placed on their stay a week earlier, when the ship had been regarded as of equal status to a warship. On the other hand, the order to fly the German merchant fleet flag and to concurrently set time limits similar to those imposed only on war ships, had been wrong a week ago and it was still not correct. To do so was a politician's decision, which if exposed as incorrect in negotiations could be altered either way, depending on the circumstances.

In London, the Admiralty started to prepare for their part in this cat and mouse game. They notified the Navy's commander-in-chief at Rosyth that it was now probable that the Norwegians would deny the *City of Flint* permission to use the territorial waters during their sail south. It might also mean that the German navy would dispatch either surface vessels or submarines to escort home the prize, which by now was rapidly becoming a celebrity in the world's media. The Admiralty suggested that two destroyers should be sailed to the vicinity of Utvær Lighthouse. This location was the northernmost of two lighthouses marking the entrance to the Sognefjord, around 50 nautical miles (ca. 90 km) north of Bergen. Even if the *City of Flint* tried to make a run for territorial waters from this location, the superior speed of the destroyers could quickly head them off.

Around 2300 on 27 October 1939, two Soviet officials came aboard on the *City of Flint*. Incredibly, they were there to return three containers holding the Prize Crew's arsenal.[55] Pusback was now handed a signal received by the shore-based telegraph office. All the German consulates along the Norwegian coast were standing by to help. He was to keep radio watch permanently, but not use the transmitter unless he was responding to a call from Germany or it was an emergency. The German Naval High Command still did not know that the *City of Flint's* radio was out of commission. The message added that the Haugesund consul, Lanwer, had charts available and he had two skilled pilots ready to help them along the coast. Most significantly, Pusback was told he had unlimited access to Norwegian territorial waters. Whatever Norwegian Foreign Minister Koht had scribbled on the decision a day earlier, German pressure in Oslo had now clearly undone.[56] There were no warnings attached to this message, saying that Pusback could not stop while in Norwegian waters.

In the early hours of Saturday, the British Admiralty started moving destroyers to the Humber in readiness for a dash across the North Sea to somewhere on the Norwegian coast. Later that day they added: "Great importance is attached to the interception of *City of Flint*." So much importance was attached that as many of Home Fleet's destroyers as required could be used for this operation, but the signal also warned that the prize was escorted by no less than two German submarines.[57] The stakes were high and going higher. British authorities saw the *City of Flint* as an opportunity to prove their pro–American stance to Congress as well as to the American media. Britain needed help, hence the decision to use such extensive naval power to liberate the freighter.

Among the inner circle of advisers available to Secretary of State Hull, the pressure was clearly building. The ship had seemingly disappeared. For them, a weekend break seemed out of the question. Twice during Saturday Hull called in his advisers for "closed door" sessions. The perceived lack of clarity surrounding The Hague Conventions and the Prize Law must have been high on the agenda.

Without any armed German guards, Gainard had probably been very keen to get away from Murmansk as quickly as possible, but with them back on board, knowing that the U.S. was doing its best to free him and his crew, why should he rush to sail the ship to Germany? The longer he stalled the better for any navy looking for them on the Norwegian coast. By now he had two boilers out of commission and could not go anywhere for quite some time. The Soviets were stuck with their problem until Gainard was good and ready.

The Soviet authorities kept on sending various officials on board. Another two turned up in a tug at 0230, only to spend 20 minutes aboard before leaving. Then at 0400 the water barge returned. At 0815 a naval tender came alongside and two Soviets came aboard. After half an hour they left with Pusback and his deputy. At 0955 the water barge departed. Half an hour later the two Germans returned to the *City of Flint* and the naval vessel left.[58]

The excuse for the change from Gainard's original plan was that he was a free, neutral ship in a neutral port, as the Soviets themselves had told him he was; he decided to clean the boilers. He argued that he knew there was another long sail ahead and he wanted his ship to be ready for it. Consequently he had cut out a second boiler and neither would be back on line in less than 24 hours. Regardless of Moscow's impatience, they could do nothing to speed up the process. No wonder Gainard observed his relationship with the Soviets deteriorate by the hour as that of the Germans improved.

Traditionally the relationship between Norway and Britain had always been very cordial. The then Norwegian crown prince, later King Olav, was born at Sandringham, a property in England that belonged to the British royal family. In Bergen, the British consulate had established a new section in the fall of 1939 to organize the Norwegian area of convoys of merchant shipping between Methill in Scotland and Bergen. The Royal Navy provided escort services for these convoys. Rear-Admiral Karsten Tank-Nielsen was responsible for naval operations in the entire West-Norwegian sector from Jæren to the southern border of the County of Nordland. Had the American ship headed south, virtually the entire journey in Norwegian waters would have been in his Second Sea Defense District.

Sometime over the previous three days Tank-Nielsen discussed the situation with the British consul in Bergen, Mr. C.A. Edmund. It transpired that the Norwegian was secretly relieved that the prize had turned north to Murmansk. Had she sailed south, the Admiral felt he would have had to take action. He was convinced that had he done so, the Government would not have had the courage to accept responsibility. Instead Tank-Nielsen thought it likely that the Norwegian Government would have distanced themselves from him and informed Berlin that the regional naval authority had exceeded its power and had done so without support or approval of the Norwegian government.[59]

Ultimately, if the *City of Flint* came south and if she was not captured, she could spell the end to a great and distinguished naval career. It also spoke volumes about the lack of decisiveness in the Norwegian government, particularly on the part of Minister for Foreign Affairs Mr. Halvdan Koht and Prime Minister Johan Nygaardsvold. The special Investigating Committee established by the Norwegian Parliament after the war reported in April 1947 that the two, Koht and Nygaardsvold, worked to maintain a pacifist approach to neutrality. Koht admitted in the report that he, before the invasion of Norway, had thought the Germans would respect Norwegian neutrality and that he had feared an attack by the Allies more than an attack by Germany.[60]

Finally, Tass announced the departure to have taken place in the evening of Saturday, 28 October by which time a cloak of darkness provided the ideal cover for the departure.[61] Even the departure was not without drama. At precisely 1638, the *City of Flint* started to weigh anchor, only to be stopped at 1650 by a patrol boat. They brought their guns to bear on the Americans as they drew alongside and signaled the ship to stop. Only after a second patrol vessel intervened and some intense exchange of signaling between the two did the Soviet ship permit their exit.[62] At 1750 they received new orders to proceed and at 1755 the anchor was away. They proceeded at full speed down the Kola Bight. The *City of Flint* had spent four days 23 hours and 10 minutes in Murmansk.[63] As they finally left, the German merchant fleet flag was flown; it remained aloft for the remainder of the Prize Crew's time aboard the ship.[64]

According to the German press the *City of Flint* had only called at Murmansk on the previous Wednesday, 25 October because of engine problems. By Friday, the Soviet authorities had checked the cargo and accepted the German position on the contraband. One German newspaper held that it was entirely in line with the Hague Convention of 1907 for the Soviets to release the ship to the German Prize Crew.[65]

By mid-afternoon on Saturday, the British Home Fleet commander-in-chief was continuing his preparations. Whatever the two destroyers *Fearless* and *Foxhound* had been told to do previously was now cancelled. They were the chosen ones to make a run for the Norwegian lighthouse at Utvær. The time scale was now more realistic; they had to be on station by 0600 Monday morning. Once there, they were to commence a sweep to the north to intercept the *City of Flint*. Although the weather was turning colder, the forecast predicted a light breeze instead of the previous week's storms. It should be an easy sail.

For the British, the plan of attack was now becoming more detailed. The commander-in-chief suggested that regardless of whether the ship was using the inner channel or not, by the time she reached Stadlandet she would have to tackle open waters. This particularly open stretch of the coast was notorious. There was no shelter to hide behind. The two ships were to patrol in this vicinity for 48 hours before returning to base. If they did succeed, the *City of Flint* should be taken to the British contraband control harbor at Kirkwall in the Orkneys. The Prize Crew should, however, be removed first.[66]

In the middle of all of this turmoil and diplomatic point scoring sat the German Prize Crew under the 48-year-old Lieutenant Pusback. Pusback's background and experience was becoming an increasingly interesting part of the drama. In Berlin, they asked: Why did Captain Wenneker of the *Deutschland* entrust the command of the prize to one of the lowest ranking officers on his ship when he at this stage had several officers to choose from? This prize was his first after all.

One of the strengths of the *Deutschland* was its vast cruising range. By mid–October Wenneker still planned several more months of raiding. His ability to bring up more ships carrying contraband would be a reasonable assumption and each would require a Prize Crew being drawn from his original complement of surplus crew. Pusback represented a good solution to Wenneker's dilemma. The Lieutenant was older than the average officer at that level; he had more all-round experience and could therefore be assumed to be far more likely to be able to improvise whatever necessary to see the prize safely home to a German port. Perhaps even more important to Wenneker, himself an officer of the former Imperial German Navy of the First World War Pusback too had served in the "old" navy.[67] After unemployment as a result of the peacetime reductions, Pusback had found himself a job in the merchant navy, where he had done well for himself before being called up as an officer of the naval reserve.

Wenneker would know soon enough how the journey was progressing. He received a radio message explaining that the prize's visit to the Soviet Union had triggered an American objection to the treatment of the ship and that the Soviets now wanted to ensure that this would not be repeated. Molotov had made his position clear. The message added that future prize ships should use neutral territorial waters to reach Kiel. They did not want to upset the Soviets. It also stressed that any ports could be visited only in accordance with the Hague Convention XIII's Article 21. At that stage the Germans knew exactly what a prize would be permitted to do while in territorial waters of neutral states.[68]

As they left the Kola Bay, Gainard was wary of what might happen if they met any British warships. From Murmansk, Pusback ordered the ship to stay well within territorial waters, even if it meant hugging the contours of the coastline. This was in strict adherence with German procedures. At night, when he would not be spotted, Pusback moved out into deeper waters, only to return to a coastal course during the day.[69] The German Prize Instructions for the navy, a secret manual, stressed that for their own purposes, Germany only recognized territorial waters as being up to 3 nautical miles out from the coast.[70]

Little did Pusback know of how close to a new and particularly fierce war he really was when in Murmansk. The outbreak of the Finno-Soviet winter War was a week off. The Soviets were particularly determined to retake the land-bridge the Finns had taken a few years earlier, which linked them to the sea in a narrow bridgehead running along the Norwegian border and which effectively cut the Soviet Union off from that western country. The Petsamo corridor was a mere 30–40 kilometers wide. The tension was running very high in the entire region.

The Norwegians were becoming increasingly aware that they could in fact be next. If the Soviets overran the Finns, why should they stop before they reached the natural year-round ice-free harbors of northern Norway? On Tuesday evening, 10 October, northern Norway had actually been placed on a war footing.[71]

6

Back to Norway

Even the short journey across to Norwegian waters had its moments of drama. Neither Pusback nor Gainard ever seemed to have much time to relax. As the *City of Flint* sailed out of the wide Kola Bay, passing the Set Navolok lighthouse, they needed a northerly course before turning more westerly to skirt around the vast Rybachiy peninsula. Upon leaving Soviet territory, they crossed briefly into Finnish waters. The north-westernmost point on the peninsula, Mys Nemetskiy, was in Finnish hands.

Willy Neher was helmsman that evening of 28 October 1939; his watch was from ten until midnight. But just as he was about to be relieved, Pusback suddenly found himself between the coast and a blacked-out vessel that suddenly appeared to starboard.[1] He ordered Willy to alter the course and head in closer to shore. As the *City of Flint* turned, so did the blacked-out pursuer and Pusback quickly decided to call out all of his Prize Crew. He was not about to let anybody take his command away from him without a fight. Fortunately, as the *City of Flint* increased her speed, the unknown threat seemed to have been left behind.

An hour later though, she was back on their tail. The blacked-out pursuer had not abandoned them just yet. This time Willy was ordered to take the ship further away from the shore, out into international waters. As they again picked up speed, the off-duty members of the Prize Crew were ordered to stand to, armed and ready to fight. At this stage they even thought the unknown ship might have been a Soviet trawler intent on bringing the *City of Flint* back into port under protective custody. Finally, by daybreak, they could relax; she was gone.

Young Willy Neher was born in Germany and had immigrated to America as a child. During the journey he had understood every word of what the Prize Crew had been talking about. In fact, when on duty in the wheelhouse at night, alone with Pusback, the two spoke German together. Pusback was therefore totally aware that his conversations were understood and the content passed on to Gainard.

At daybreak they were off the Norwegian coast to the west of the Varanger fjord. Late that afternoon they rounded North Cape and by early evening they called at Honningsvåg to pick up two pilots for the inshore journey south.

In Berlin, they knew when the *City of Flint* had left Murmansk and could therefore calculate where on the Norwegian coast Pusback would be. That information was treated as a military secret at the Ministry of Foreign Affairs in Wilhelmstrasse. American diplomats in Berlin tried twice on Sunday, 29 October to telephone the Ministry seeking any news. On each occasion they were blocked. The lack of fresh information was blamed on the *City of Flint*'s radio silence. A feature, the Germans claimed, which was due to the fear of being located by the British navy as she came down the Norwegian coast.

Already as Pusback headed north from Tromsø on his first visit, German diplomats

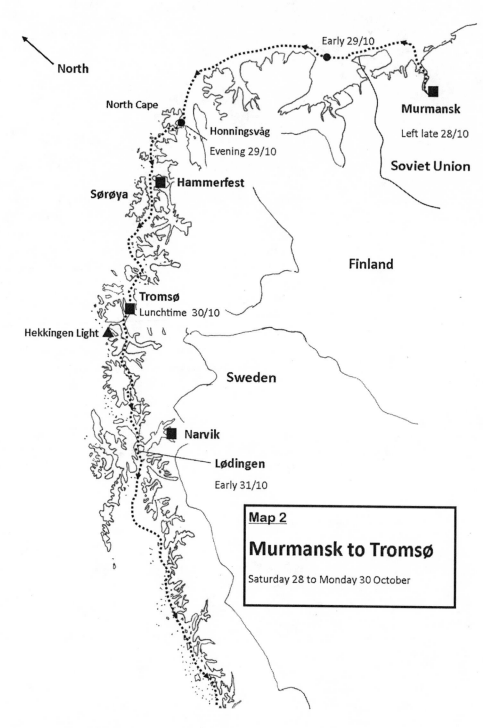

North

Early 29/10

Murmansk

Left late 28/10

North Cape

Honningsvåg

Evening 29/10

Soviet Union

Sørøya

Hammerfest

Finland

Tromsø

Lunchtime 30/10

Hekkingen Light

Sweden

Narvik

Lødingen

Early 31/10

Map 2

Murmansk to Tromsø

Saturday 28 to Monday 30 October

in Oslo had protested over the 24 hour ruling. They asked that the ship be permitted to proceed in Norwegian territorial waters. The detour to Murmansk had merely provided the Norwegians with more thinking time. At the time, Norwegian authorities turned down the request, referring to their Neutrality Regulations.

In Wilhelmstrasse, staff had been re-examining their case in the light of Koht's latest refusal. On Saturday they sent a long telegram to their legation in Oslo.[2] The German government did not share the view of the Norwegian government. Their priority was to see the prize safely home and now their main obstacle appeared to be the Norwegian interpretation of the Hague Convention. The Ministry were annoyed that the Norwegian government saw it as their preserve as an independent neutral nation-state to maintain the integrity of Norwegian territory.[3]

The Germans also argued that it was totally unfounded for Norway to ban exports of maps. The Norwegian export ban was in fact a violation of human rights, they argued. This case was merely related to the safety of human life at sea, which all civilized peoples should appreciate, said the Germans.

By the time the *City of Flint* returned to Norwegian waters, Koht needed a solution, a politically expedient reason for his choice of bedfellows, the British or the Germans. As part of his personal approach to the Germans, Koht invited the German ambassador to his office for an informal briefing around the official Norwegian reply to his request. The meeting was scheduled for Monday afternoon.

The Norwegian naval staff's daily intelligence reports, issued at noon, covered the previous 24 hours. Monday's report included all the flying activity of the previous day and added that Monday morning saw five naval vessels, assumed British, heading north. At 1100 they were located off Stad. All along the coast, from Stad to Stavanger, five to ten foreign airplanes were active throughout the morning.[4]

By lunchtime that Monday, October 30, 1939, the *City of Flint* was back in Tromsø where the Prize Commander hoped to break his journey. In a statement issued by the Norwegians later, they denied the very act they now allowed, namely a stop. The apparent duplicity seemed particularly significant. The ship had technically not stopped, they argued, but merely proceeded very slowly south down the fjord past Tromsø. Pusback on the other hand, remembered it differently. His own report of the matter was written later, at leisure, in internment without the concern of being reprimanded by history. He was able to state quite categorically that as he arrived at Tromsø around midday on Monday, 30 October, the patrol boat had specifically ordered him to anchor.[5] The Norwegian Navy's Intelligence Report for that day confirmed Pusback's statement: 1210—The American merchant vessel *City of Flint*, which was taken as a prize by Germany arrived at Tromsø. 1600—*City of Flint* departed Tromsø.[6]

At 1240 Commander Hagerup telephoned Diesen to let him know the *City of Flint* had returned half an hour earlier. At 1310, a mere 30 minutes after the first call, Hagerup had made up his mind. He telephoned Diesen to say that there was no legal reason for the stop. Pusback only wanted passage south. Consequently, the stop was illegal and the ship should be escorted out of Norwegian territorial waters.

The first notification of the return of the American ship reached the Norwegian Foreign Ministry in Oslo at 1245. They then received a second call from Diesen an hour later confirming that the ship remained at the port. This was serious. They knew that technically the *City of Flint* was in breach of the Hague Convention and of the Norwegian Neutrality Regulations; therefore, they had due cause to liberate the ship. The time was now nearly 1400 and Ambassador von Neuhaus was due at the Ministry at 1430. Koht decided not to act, although he knew that whatever way he looked at this he would be wrong to permit this stop. It was a clear violation of Norwegian neutrality.[7]

Shortly after arriving at the port of Tromsø, an officer from the patrol boat came across to the *City of Flint*. Pusback was again requested to leave Norwegian waters by the route past Hekkingen. This time, however, the German was more confident of his facts and refused to comply, arguing that he had been given specific information which actually granted him leave to remain in Norwegian waters for the duration of his journey south along the coast. The Norwegian would not back down and left to check his facts with the admiralty in Oslo.[8]

In the afternoon, a mere 10 minutes after Koht's meeting with von Neuhaus had started, the Ministry received a telephone call from Admiral Diesen. It had taken less than five minutes for Diesen, after Hagerup at Tromsø telephoned him, to decide that this issue required some high-level action rather quickly. Pusback had shown the Norwegian authorities a telegram ordering him to use Norwegian territorial waters. While at Murmansk he had received the order from the German Embassy in Moscow. The telegram stated categorically that neutral states like Norway or Sweden did not have any time limits on the use of their territorial waters.

Diesen now wanted to know how to respond. Since Koht had spent the morning working on the reply, which von Neuhaus by then had received, Diesen was told the same story. The visit was different this time; there were no stops, merely sailing and therefore, no limit. The Germans had achieved what they wanted exactly at the time when they needed it.

The far more serious reason for the telephone call, hidden behind this discussion over the 24-hour rule, was that Admiral Diesen too was aware of the ship's clear breach of the Neutrality Regulations. Diesen knew that Koht was meeting von Neuhaus and the Admiral backed away from taking the responsibility for ordering the release of the prize on his own. Von Neuhaus' meeting was perfectly timed.

The ship even took on board some supplies before leaving. German bullying in Oslo had clearly paid off. This was another clear breach of the Hague Convention and as it was noted by a local journalist working with the United Press, the violation quickly came to be reported quite widely.

At 1457 Diesen telephoned his order to Tromsø: "If so wished, *City of Flint* may use Norwegian territorial waters when passing through."[9]

All this took time and it was not until nearly an hour later on that Monday afternoon the *City of Flint* put to sea, heading south escorted by two Norwegian naval vessels.[10] The 18-year-old, 220-ton torpedo boat *Stegg* was joined by *Ægir*, a modern two-year-old destroyer. Norway clearly meant to ensure that neither Pusback nor anybody else violated Norwegian neutrality.

At their informal meeting, Koht went on to tell von Neuhaus that the *City of Flint* had in fact returned to Tromsø two hours earlier, but departed after about an hour accompanied by a Norwegian naval vessel. If the prize had hoped to go into port in Tromsø, it would have been the duty of the Norwegian authorities to take the ship into custody, intern the Prize Crew and subsequently declare the ship free. This scenario was outlined to the German as a hypothetical one. It had not been the case, Koht claimed, as the ship merely used the inner route through the area, sailing south via the Tromsø Sound. He even showed the German on the map the route of the ship over the last few hours.[11] Therefore, in terms of pure transit through Norwegian territory, the Norwegian minister stated that he agreed with the German interpretation of the regulations.

Koht admitted that there would be a difference between an actual stop in a Norwegian port and a mere passage through Norwegian waters. The first time the *City of Flint* visited, she had actually stopped, hence the use of the 24-hour rule. Now all the German Prize Commander wanted was permission to sail unopposed through Norwegian territorial waters without any stops.

In Koht's way of solving the problem over the right of passage in Norwegian territorial waters, he could not allow himself to acknowledge that the ship had stopped at Tromsø with no reason at all. Like Stalin had done the previous week, Koht avoided issuing any statement to anybody until the issue had passed—i.e., the troublesome ship was again at sea.

Nevertheless a dangerous precedent had just been created. A ship sailing under the command of the German armed forces, carrying people who were not at liberty to decide freely where to sail or where to disembark, was granted official permission by a member of the Norwegian Government to proceed unencumbered in Norwegian waters for as long as they needed. The Hague Convention of 1907 had recognized the special status of a prize, but the participating heads of state had not agreed over how to tackle such special cases. That part of the Convention was never ratified. The concept of a prize was ignored in the Norwegian Neutrality Regulation of 1938; instead they had defined a warship as any ship under the command of the armed forces.

When she first arrived, the *City of Flint* was escorted out of Norwegian waters, subject to the 24-hour rule. Now the same ship, still under German command, was treated as a civilian vessel and therefore granted permission to enjoy the protection offered by Norwegian territorial waters. Koht even sent King Haakon an advance copy of this curious decision.[12]

Halvdan Koht had, at this point, totally surrendered to German pressure. His own regulation, as signed into law by the Norwegian king a year earlier, clearly defined the prize as a warship, as it was under military control. Pusback had even used this fact himself as he entered Murmansk flying the flag of the German Kriegsmarine

The real reasons for Koht caving in to the German will never be known. His own file-notes of the encounter with von Neuhaus describe a meeting where the Norwegian went to great lengths to explain the reasons for his concession.

Even after World War II, the Tromsø incident was covered up. When the official Norwegian history of the war was written, the *City of Flint*'s second visit was not described correctly. As if in some perverse loyalty to the past, the author of Norway's *Naval War 1940–1945*, volume 1, Commander E.A. Steen, claimed that the ship merely sailed slowly through the port without anchoring or stopping at a quay.[13] Curiously, it was the Germans who were credited by Steen with ensuring compliance with all international and Norwegian regulations. His was a very simplistic and shallow description of the *City of Flint* incident, concluded with two further factual errors that reading even the press coverage would have prevented, namely that the ship later discharged its cargo in Bergen and that it subsequently returned home in ballast.

In light of the Norwegian attitude to the status of the *City of Flint*, it was not surprising that less than four months later the Germans tried again to use Norwegian territorial waters. This time to move a naval supply ship, the *Altmark*, along the same route as the one planned for the *City of Flint*. The *Altmark* had acted as the supply ship for the *Admiral Graf Spee* as she was conducting her commerce raiding in the South Atlantic. When the raider was scuttled at Montevideo, the *Altmark* made her way back to Germany with 299 British crew members from the sunken ships, now as prisoners of war. By the 16th of February the Royal Navy was on her tail and the destroyer *Cossack* broke

Norwegian neutrality rules to chase the *Altmark* in to the bottom of the Jøssingfjord in southwestern Norway. The British boarded the Altmark, defeated German opposition, released the prisoners and returned jubilant to Britain.

Had the *City of Flint* been forced out into international waters, there was every likelihood that the Royal Navy would have denied Berlin the prestige victory they so badly wanted. The ultimate outcome for Gainard may not have been that different, but Koht's international standing may well have been less devalued.

In Tromsø, Hagerup arranged for escort duties southwards. He contacted Sea Defense District 2, based in Bergen, under the responsibility of Rear Admiral Carsten Tank-Nielsen, requesting that one of his ships take over the escort duties at the boundary between the two districts. Diesen on his part claimed to have contacted Bergen ordering them to dispatch the *Olav Tryggvason* to relieve *Ægir*. In addition to issuing the orders to deploy the relevant ships, Diesen specified the duties of the escort: "(1.) To ensure that the *City of Flint* does not break off her journey without legal reason. If so she is to be denied leave to continue. (2.)To ensure that the *City of Flint* is not called, stopped or attacked in Norwegian territorial waters. The escort should not interfere in the navigation of the *City of Flint* and should follow behind the *City of Flint*."[14]

By 2000 on Monday evening, Lieutenant Cowell took his submarine *L-27* in to the very edge of Norwegian waters, as close to shore as international law permitted. They were just to the south of the island of Stord, at the mouth of the Hardanger Fjord. Unbeknownst to them, they were, at that stage, less than 30 km from a German U-boat. Östen had started his patrol with *U-61* in this area only a day earlier and because of all the aerial activity, Östen noted that he was located between Selbjørnsfjord and Korsfjord—well inside Norwegian territory and very close to *L-27*.

As the German boat sailed northwards to the Utvær lighthouse north of the Sognefjord, the British continued south, heading back to base. Östen proceeded to move away from the Norwegian coast. The *City of Flint* was at sea on a southerly course and it was only a question of time before she would reach Östen's allocated patrol zone.

That evening at 2200 an unofficial embargo was issued to all news desks in Norway: "The Foreign Ministry requests that the press does not refer to the movements of the *City of Flint* along the Norwegian coast."[15]

It is quite difficult to understand why none of the Norwegian officials involved in the *City of Flint* affair in Tromsø thought of informing the head of the American Legation in Oslo of the fact that the *City of Flint* had returned. The blatant lack of cooperation is hard to comprehend and very difficult to explain.

The incredulity does not stop there. When American Ambassador Mrs. Harriman finally learned of the ship's return, it was actually from the same journalist who had confirmed the *City of Flint*'s first visit. He had promised to keep her informed of developments. Mrs. Harriman immediately contacted the Foreign Ministry only to be told that, since it was so late (around 1800) the office was closed for the day. On the previous day (Sunday), however, the same office had been sufficiently staffed to deal with the latest German protest about the *City of Flint* and pass it on to Admiral Diesen at 2000.

Harriman was not going to be silenced however. She sent a message to the American State Department in Washington Monday night telling them that the *City of Flint* had returned to Norwegian waters, flying the swastika. Her telegram added that the story had not yet been officially confirmed in Oslo. By 0140 Tuesday morning, a press agency was distributing this story from Washington to "all takers." There was nothing Oslo could do to stop it. The Norwegian press, closer to the action than all others, was therefore quoting Washington as the source of their stories on the *City of Flint* that Tuesday morning.[16] At the same time, Harriman was finally informed that the ship had indeed called at Tromsø, but had only stayed for a few minutes. The Norwegian Foreign Office had come dangerously close to lying to the United States.

In fact, the Associated Press' contact in Stockholm talked to the German consul at Tromsø that Monday evening. The consul confirmed that he had indeed been aboard the ship during her stay. The subsequent article, which was published that afternoon thanks to the six-hour time difference, pointed out that the ship had arrived at Tromsø at 1300 local time and departed around 1600, a full three hours later. The international press knew what had happened.

The official Norwegian attempt at managing the access to information concerning the *City of Flint* had overtones of naïve ideas of superiority. The BBC's news bulletin at 2100 announced that the *City of Flint* had visited Tromsø, but left at 1600.[17] Within 10 minutes the young Bergen journalist Egil Tresselt had contacted the Norwegian Admiralty asking for comments. To add gravitas to his role, Tresselt claimed to be representing the London paper the *Daily Mail*. Yet no official statement was issued.[18]

The next morning in London, the BBC even added that the German consul had been on board the ship. Meanwhile, in Oslo, Foreign Secretary Halvdan Koht seemed determined to ignore the incident, seemingly hoping it would go away.

At 0500 in the morning of Tuesday, 31 October, Admiral Tank-Nielsen personally telephoned the naval staff in Oslo. He knew his superior officer Diesen well from their days as fellow submarine officers. Six British warships had been spotted at Stad; one of them even entered the Vågsfjord, well inside Norwegian territorial waters. When challenged by *Draug*, the foreign warship curiously requested a greeting be passed on to Crown Prince Olav from his cousin and seemed rather unconcerned over their location. The British captain added that *Draug* could easily guess why they were there, but that they would prefer to take the *City of Flint* while outside Norwegian waters.[19]

As Harriman's meeting was taking place in the Norwegian Foreign Office, the *City of Flint* had finally arrived at Lødingen on the south side of the Lofoten islands, exactly where the German vice-consul Wussow had been looking for them just over a week earlier. It was time to swap pilots. Unfortunately neither Pusback nor any of his soldiers had any money in an acceptable currency. Gainard had to step in and cover the costs of the pilotage in U.S. dollars.

The British Ambassador to Norway, Sir Cecil Dormer, was obviously quite pleased with the information flow from his own sources in Tromsø and, locally, the British vice-consuls. The differences in Dormer's account of what happened, from the official Norwegian version provided to Mrs. Harriman, would give serious cause for concern. The ship had stopped at Tromsø. Furthermore, no one was allowed on board apart from the relevant Norwegian authorities and perhaps most crucially, the German vice-consul, who went out to the ship in his own boat. The Norwegians did not even consider it necessary to quarantine the prize during the stay.

That evening it was known, at least in the British Foreign Office, that the *City of Flint* had left Tromsø. The message they received also added that a German ship, *Schwaben*, sailed south from Tromsø around an hour before the *City of Flint*.[20] The 13-year-old German freighter from Norddeutscher Lloyd was on its way back to Germany with a 10,000-ton cargo of wheat from Buenos Aires.

Having outsmarted the Americans again, the Germans felt confident of success. A Norwegian paper reported German glee over the complicated legal issues facing the British navy should they wish to sink the *City of Flint*. It did not seem, however, that anybody in Germany had worked out a way of communicating this optimism to the man at the middle of the crisis. Hans Pusback had to keep his own counsel, supported only by what he could pick up on regular civilian radio broadcasts. Although Pusback had some contacts with Germans while in port, he was effectively isolated at sea. Somehow, Berlin had not yet understood the communications problems. His radio watch did, however, pick up an important message broadcast over the Norddeich transmitter that day.

At this stage the German naval leadership was actually being unwittingly misled. From Narvik, their new consul, Edholm, who had only been in the post a few weeks, reported that the *City of Flint* had left Norwegian territorial waters. It was this erroneous information that made the Germans decide to send Pusback a radio message.

Amazingly, Pusback did indeed receive the message. On Tuesday, 31 October, they must have decided to gamble on Pusback listening to the same frequency they had used for the secret messages at the start of the war. That day the Norddeich transmitter sent a message to a seemingly fictitious call sign—OHYL. It did not fit with the false call sign assigned by Wenneker in the *Deutschland*, nor did it fit the genuine one. The message, though, was clear enough; it explained that the Norwegian Government had conceded on their 24-hour rule and that he was ordered to report his departure time from Skudesnes-fjord to the consul at Haugesund.[21] Pusback told Lanwer about the message when they finally met that Friday night. In fact, this telegram confirmed the secret message he had received from the German Embassy in Moscow while in Murmansk, namely that he could use Norwegian territorial waters for as long as he needed to. Nobody, Pusback claimed, had ever mentioned the fact that he could not anchor; how else could he report to the Haugesund consul?[22]

In his report to the State Department, Gainard explained that during the stop at Tromsø, the Norwegians took the time to seal his hatches and put the German Prize Crew in touch with their own consul.[23] The captain noticed too, that a German freighter, the *Schwaben*, had also put into Tromsø, for fuel for the final lap of her journey from South America to Germany. As a civilian ship she was accorded the right to proceed unattended down the coast, unencumbered by the careful scrutiny that the Prize Crew on the *City of Flint* had to endure.

In New York the papers noted that MacConnachie had advised them that the Prize Crew had planted several scuttling charges aboard the *City of Flint*. Pusback was determined to sink the ship rather than lose command of the ship before he could sail her to a German port.

In Haugesund on the other hand, Lanwer received a telegram from Pusback on Tuesday, 31 October. Pusback wanted to let Lanwer know when to expect him. The intriguing question was: How was the telegram sent? The *City of Flint* had left Tromsø the night before and the German vice-consul had visited the ship during the Monday afternoon. Pusback could have asked him to send the telegram, which Lanwer received the day after.

Berlin most certainly did not seem to be aware of Pusback's message. In it he notified Lanwer of an estimated time of arrival at Haugesund of around 0300 in the morning of Friday, 3 November. Pusback clearly had a schedule to stick to for his journey. Perhaps most importantly for Lanwer, Pusback requested a visit from the consul. This made Lanwer conclude that the *City of Flint* actually required assistance.[24] In Lanwer's later defense of his actions, this was significant. Pusback had given him just cause, which would fit with the Berlin bureaucrat's order to help, but only in case of need. In German, the insertion of the word "gegebenenfalls" into the text of the order to Lanwer allowed Berlin to give an order, but at the same time leave the decision as to whether to act on it or not entirely up to the recipient.

A British plan to intercept and capture the *City of Flint* was under development and a formidable force was being dispatched to achieve the objective. Heading up the force was the "Fighting Fifth," the Fifth Destroyer Flotilla, D5. Its commanding officer was none other than Lord Louis Mountbatten. His ship was the destroyer *Kelly*, and in his flotilla were also the *Fearless, Foxhound, Bedouin, Eskimo* and *Matabele*.

The plan was based on a blatant violation of Norwegian neutrality, resting on the assumption that the Norwegians would not be providing any escort for the prize as she sailed through Norwegian waters. It is important to stress that his plan, which he developed for the mission, was dated Tuesday, 31 October, before he ever left British waters. Mountbatten cannot have been under any illusions over the legality of what he planned to do: "rather than to allow her to escape altogether, she is to be boarded inside territorial waters."[25]

Strangely he felt he could justify such action under the Hague Convention XIII, which only covered the case when a ship had actually been captured within the territorial waters of a neutral Power. While he used Article 3 to justify his plan, Article 2, had he read it, forbade it: "Any act of hostility, including capture and the exercise of right of search, committed by belligerent warships in the territorial waters of a neutral power, constitutes a violation of neutrality and is strictly forbidden."[26]

Regardless of Britain being a signatory, the perceived benefits of helping America must have far outweighed the sanctions little Norway was considered to be able to mount against powerful Britain, which she normally regarded as an ally.

Attacking at Stad was not necessarily that straightforward. Although the protection afforded by islands, rocks and outcrops was nonexistent, these were deep waters, perfectly navigable as much as 2½ miles inside territorial limits. The window of opportunity to mount an attack would be very narrow. If they were spotted, the *City of Flint* could either make a run for more sheltered waters further inside Norwegian territory, or the Prize Crew might simply decide to scuttle the ship. Either way, it was imperative to place a substantial British force on board the American ship as fast as possible.

They were not relying on their own ships' complements to achieve this. The British had actually borrowed two boarding parties from the battle cruiser *Hood* and from the battleship *Nelson*. The 24 men from *Hood* were on *Kelly* and the 24 from *Nelson* were on *Bedouin*. The two destroyers were to move in fast, one on either side of the freighter, with the men jumping across as soon as the sides of the ships closed. *Kelly* was going to the ship's starboard side and *Bedouin* to port. For the members of the boarding party, this would be an extremely hazardous maneuver. If they jumped too soon, or the defenders threw them off, and they ended in the sea between the two ships they would almost certainly be squashed to death. There had been absolutely no opportunity for the helm crews on either ship to practice; they had to make this work the first time. They had already rigged up extra gangplanks, which were to act as drawbridges when the ships closed in.

In his plan, Mountbatten makes a chilling point about the German Prize Crew, namely that their contact with other German surface vessels might well mean that their firepower could have been augmented. Nobody on the Allied side knew what the canvas bags really contained when they were carried on board by the Prize Crew as they transferred from the *Deutschland*. Nor did they know what Pusback had been provided with in Murmansk, but they did know that other German ships had been hiding at the same Soviet port.

Should they need more force, a further 22 of each of their own two ships' crews were to be ready to follow the first wave in. This would place a total of 92 armed British service personnel on the *City of Flint*.

The weather forecast was good; there was to be a full moon, making a night attack entirely possible. Mountbatten still wanted to make sure he did not board the wrong ship and before he left Sullom Voe, he asked for more detailed information on the *City of Flint*. He also wanted confirmation that there were no Americans on the ship, yet all signals to date had assumed that the original crew was still there. While he wished to avoid killing anyone, he was ready for a firefight. It was even specified in the plan that no weapons heavier than 0.5 inch caliber should be fired at the ship. The American property was to be handed back to them without any damage.

Only the *Kelly* had any medical personnel and they would take on any casualties, but the German prisoners would be split between the two attacking ships in order to reduce their chances of rebelling. Once liberated, the *City of Flint* was to be escorted to the British contraband inspection harbor at Kirkwall on Orkney.

They were concerned over the prestige the Germans placed upon this prize. Would they actually let the ship go without a fight? Or would they, in this final battle over her, set off scuttling charges and go down fighting? As the ship was fully laden, the easiest access to the bottom of the ship was likely to be via the engine room. A special attack group was picked to head for the engine room, grab any German Prize Crew members they could find and force them to return down into the bottom of the ship with them. If any explosions were to go off, these prisoners would die with their captors—unless they identified the charges in advance. If need be, force could be used to bring the prisoners back down, they were all too aware of the dangers of being on board if the charges went off and the search-time might well be defined by burning fuses.

The briefing was thorough enough to include the phonetic spelling for the required order for the removal of any charges: "BOAMBER WECKNAYMEN SO—FORT" [Remove the bombs immediately].[27]

As earlier signals had suggested that the prize might be accompanied by two German submarines, the remaining four destroyers were split into two anti-submarine groups. They also had the interesting task of fighting off any other enemy escorts. Captain Mountbatten did still not know that the ship was escorted by the Norwegian navy.

After a commanding officers' conference aboard *Kelly*, the Fighting Fifth sailed at dusk on Sunday night, 29 October, and was on station at Utvær Light at 0600 the next morning. The ships spread out across a line stretching 22 miles out to sea from the edge of Norwegian territorial waters. The force now swept north, arriving at Stadlandet four hours later, but they met a problem. The Norwegian navy had placed their destroyer *Draug* on guard duty. As the Fifth's position was still on the 22-mile line stretched away from the Norwegian patrol boat, they assumed that the *Draug* would only have seen the ship closest to its own position. Unfortunately, there was also a Norwegian seaplane overhead. The pilot could not have avoided spotting all the other ships not yet discovered by the Norwegians on the ship below. For Mountbatten, this was hardly going to be the ideal spot for an attack. As the boarding parties were ordered to stand down, the first of only two shots to be fired during the entire episode, neither of them at the enemy, rang out! One of the crew had dropped the butt of his loaded rifle down a bit too hard, with the safety catch off.

Mountbatten decided that as they were already spotted, he might as well have a friendly exchange with the Norwegian ship and closed to greet them by megaphone. As the *Draug* approached, they kept their forward gun on the British intruder. The problem was, the British quickly saw this for what it was, empty posturing. They could see down the barrel of the gun pointed at them and right through it. Not only was the gun not loaded, but the Norwegians had not even closed the breech. It transpired from the exchange that although the Norwegian skipper did not mind them being there, it was quite clear that his role was to see that the British ships did not violate Norwegian neutrality.[28] As if he wanted to pull rank on the Norwegian captain in his own waters, Mountbatten apparently replied: "Please give my compliments to my cousin, Crown Prince Olav."[29]

The first part of the plan was not going to work. The British task force would not be able to snatch the prize from the jaws of neutrality without anybody spotting them and matters were about to deteriorate further. An hour before midnight they heard from the Admiralty that the British vice-consul in Haugesund had reported some unidentified warships moving north. They had been so far out to sea that identification had not been possible. They had moved at intervals, the first one sailing past at 0900, the second at 1200 and the last one an hour later.[30] Mountbatten assumed that these might well be German surface vessels moving north to rendezvous with the *City of Flint* at Stad.

By now it was dark and Mountbatten had to make up his mind as to how to tackle the unspecified threat. He decided to let one of the lighter destroyers, *Foxhound*, remain immediately to the south of the Stadlandet. The real reason for this was that they would be close enough to board the *City of Flint* if *Kelly* and *Bedouin* were engaged with enemy action. The larger of the destroyers was moved slightly further out to sea, with *Fearless* to act as decoy to draw any German forces towards the guns of the Tribal class ships.

The ships were hardly on station before the next message from the Admiralty ticked in. London had heard from the now very alert British consulate in Tromsø. The *City of Flint* had left at 1700, under escort of a Norwegian torpedo boat. This meant that they were still around 48 hours' sailing away to the north. Mountbatten pulled out. He took his force back to Sullom Voe in the Shetland Islands for bunkering. Staying any longer at Stad might have drawn in enemy forces in submarines, ships or even aircraft. Apart from the danger this would have represented to the British force, it would also have alerted the Germans to the British plan.

Specific times start to become significant to the story at this stage. The ships were back at Sullom Voe on Tuesday, 31 October by 1330. They were all refueled and ordered to return at 0530 next morning. This would take them back to Stad by 1600, which Mountbatten calculated would be at least four hours before the *City of Flint* could reach the area, even if she was sailing at maximum speed, which he had been informed was 12 knots.

During the evening as his ships were preparing to leave, Mountbatten reassessed the situation. He knew it was not going to be quite as straightforward to take over the prize as he had thought originally. Not only was the *City of Flint* under escort, but the escort was even sailing under a neutral flag. The message was clear; Norway was not going to let anyone violate their neutrality without opposition. They were even deploying air reconnaissance to stay on top of the situation. The element of surprise was of the essence. If spotted, the British force would either merely see the *City of Flint* be escorted so close to land as to make any rescue attempt impossible, or they might not see the ship at all as the Norwegians could hold the ship back until the threat had gone.

7

The Chase

As the escorted freighter faded out of sight that Monday afternoon, heading south down the intricate patterns of fjords south of Tromsø, she effectively disappeared from the public eye. *The Times* (London), for example, did not receive any more news of the ship until the end of the week. The Saturday edition reprinted the official British Admiralty view that the *City of Flint* could now seek refuge in Norwegian and Swedish waters until she reached the Baltic. They added a clear warning: Should the ship emerge from inside the territorial limits for whatever reason, matters would change. The Germans knew they were being followed.

In London, the War Cabinet held that as the ship was American, any political initiative towards the Norwegians ought to come from Washington. They had to move quickly, however, and Foreign Secretary Halifax was asked to contact Ambassador Kennedy urgently. If in time, the British might prevent the ship from entering German waters through third-party political interventions. While there seemed to be adequate precedence for removing the Prize Crew, Norway might welcome American diplomatic support for wanting to force the ship out of Norwegian territorial waters. The British navy would then be on hand to remove the Prize Crew and release the ship.[1]

The Norwegian government was about to endure a diplomatic pincer movement. The British and the Americans felt that the *City of Flint* should basically be ordered out of Norwegian waters or in to a Norwegian port where the Prize Command might be interned and the ship liberated. The justification for such action would be the irregularity committed by Pusback in calling three times at neutral ports.[2]

On Wednesday, 1 November, *The New York Times* published a map of the route it was thought the *City of Flint* had sailed. They claimed she would have passed Lødingen by then. Lødingen was in a central position on the crossroads of the two main coastal sea-lanes at the Lofoten Islands, north-south and east-west. The little hamlet had a pilot station and could provide bunkering facilities. From Tromsø, the lighthouse was about 100 nautical miles away. If the *City of Flint* was doing ten knots, the distance would have taken them around ten hours to cover. She should have passed Lødingen during the very early hours of Tuesday, 31 October, as reported the day after. A sharp-eyed reporter had spotted them accompanied by the Norwegian destroyer *Sleipner*.

The British Admiralty, on the other hand, thought they knew better and Tuesday night sent Mountbatten a message informing him at Sullom Voe that the freighter had only passed Lødingen Lighthouse at 1100 that morning.[3] That gave the ship an average speed of a mere 6¼ knots—nearly half her real speed. If that speed were maintained, the *City of Flint* would not make an appearance within reach of Mountbatten's force at Stad for nearly another two days. Sailing directly for the point on the Norwegian coast

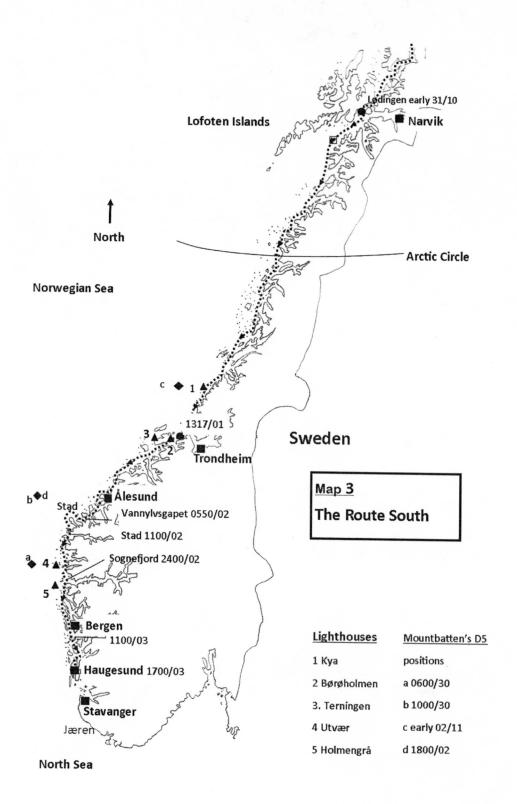

Lofoten Islands

Lødingen early 31/10

■ Narvik

↑

North

Arctic Circle

Norwegian Sea

c ◆ 1 ▲

· 1317/01

Sweden

3 ▲ ◆ ▲
    2 ▲ ■
    ■ Trondheim

Map 3

The Route South

b ◆ d
  ■ Ålesund
Stad
    Vannylvsgapet 0550/02

    Stad 1100/02

a ◆ 4 ▲   Sognefjord 2400/02

5 ▲

■ Bergen
  1100/03

■ Haugesund 1700/03

■ Stavanger

Jæren

North Sea

Lighthouses	Mountbatten's D5
1 Kya	positions
2 Børøholmen	a 0600/30
3. Terningen	b 1000/30
4 Utvær	c early 02/11
5 Holmengrå	d 1800/02

as agreed earlier would now mean waiting for two periods of daylight, where the force would be vulnerable to enemy attacks and to detection by the Norwegians.

Faced with this new information, Mountbatten reasoned that any daytime attacks would need to take place outside territorial waters. The only alternative was to determine an alternative attack zone, where the seizure could take place during the night, and where the Norwegians were less likely to suspect such an incident and therefore would not have mounted any patrols.

The Americans worried. Their ship had become the very sought-after prize in a deadly game of hide and seek along the Norwegian coast. If British naval units engaged the Germans, American lives could be lost. There were realistic fears that the Germans would set off charges to sink the ship below them, rather than let the ship be taken by the British. The *City of Flint* could even become the target for an ill-considered barrage of artillery in a duel between warring naval units. Washington now wanted to ask both sides in the conflict to consider the rights of the innocents. These sentiments were clearly expressed in Norwegian papers and were probably not lost on the British nor the Germans either.

In the meantime, on board the *City of Flint*, it seemed to be steady sailing southwards. The Norwegian coast was a long one and the freighter, although moving through narrow fjords where they had never been before, made steady progress. The coast was a labyrinth of small islands and skerries, making navigation difficult for mariners not familiar with local tides and currents.

At Sullom Voe, Mountbatten was reworking his plans. He had decided on an alternative approach for an attack. Thankfully the Norwegian coast was full of irregularities. The edge of territorial waters followed an equally irregular line. Across all these twists and turns shone the reassuring beams of the chain of lighthouses. By sailing directly on a line-of-sight course between lighthouses, the ship would, in theory, at times be outside Norwegian territorial waters. Mountbatten had spotted just one such location—he thought. That was where the attack would be mounted.

As so often, the plan was based on a series of assumptions and second-hand information. Most significant was the intelligence offered by an old Admiralty message actually sent out even before the *City of Flint* had left Murmansk.[4] This message claimed that the *City of Flint* was most likely proceeding south outside territorial waters. For now it clearly suited Mountbatten to accept this, although it would be contradictory to the message stating that the ship had passed Lødingen, a message which he had also accepted because of what it said about the *City of Flint*'s sailing speed. Pusback would not have passed Lødingen had he stayed outside territorial waters.

Coming south along the Norwegian coast from those latitudes, a natural barrier exists, the island of Vikna, which blocks easy passage along the coast. If the *City of Flint* was moving south in inshore waters, she would appear through a narrow sound between the island and the mainland, called Nærøysund. From there they would appear into open sea across the Folda. If, as the British Admiralty believed, the ship moved seaward of the Vikna, they would be even easier to stop in this area. As they came across the stretch of open waters, they might be navigating by the lighthouse, Kya Light, which was coming up on their bow to the south. A straight course for the lighthouse would actually take them across a stretch of international waters as the edge of territorial waters bent away to the east, following the actual coastline.

Experience from convoy activity in the Western Approaches had taught

Mountbatten that few of the freighters that claimed to be able to do ten knots could actually do so. In this case, fully laden, with, he thought, a barnacled and fouled skin, coupled with a reluctant crew, her actual top speed was likely to be far less than her theoretical maximum. He decided to deploy his destroyers accordingly. At no point did his account of his planning refer to the fact that the two cruisers *Glasgow* and *Newcastle* were on station off Stadlandet in support of his action. He never shared the plan with them. The Fighting Fifth would patrol north at 24 knots and sweep south to be back on station at Stadlandet by early Thursday evening, where the prey was to be theirs. The role of *Glasgow* and *Newcastle* was reduced to that of the beaters. Two of Mountbatten's own officers apparently disagreed with the captain's obvious gamble and made their views known. They were overruled.

When the British War Cabinet met on Wednesday, 1 November, Halifax reported back from his conversation with the American ambassador regarding the view that Norway should liberate the American ship.[5] Kennedy had agreed to urge the U.S. Government to agree with the UK. Virtually at the same time as they were meeting, Commander Tryggve Briseid, the commanding officer of the Norwegian minelayer *Olav Tryggvason*, took charge over the escort duties of the *City of Flint*. This meant that the ship was now in the area controlled by Rear-Admiral Tank-Nielsen in Bergen. He, at least, knew exactly where the *City of Flint* was.

The rendezvous point for the new escort to meet the prize was at Børøholm Lighthouse at 1400. As the *City of Flint* headed towards the light from the north, they would have passed the mouth of the fjord in to Trondheim. The torpedo boat *Trygg* was still in attendance. The small convoy continued south for nearly an hour, past Terningen lighthouse, the next marker on the way. These lighthouses were a crucial part of the route. The plan was that in clear weather it should always be possible to see at least one light anywhere on the entire coast. Without them, the complex network of fjords would only have been navigable during daylight hours. Pusback could have avoided it all by heading west, out into the open sea, but then he would have had to forego the safety of the Norwegian escort and the laws protecting those sailing in Norwegian territorial waters. Little did he know that his main antagonist, Mountbatten, was too far north to ever see the *City of Flint*; Mountbatten did not know this either.

Before continuing southwards, Commander Briseid's second in command, Captain Dingsør, signaled the *City of Flint* to stop. A Norwegian naval officer was sent over to provide the German commanding officer a copy of a document called "An Announcement from the Norwegian Ministry of Defense."[6] The brand new document set out the Regulations for naval movements in Norwegian territorial waters. The Norwegians were not taking any chances that the Germans would at some stage in the future claim ignorance of the document. It was even provided both in English and German translation.

At the beginning of September, Norwegian authorities decided the time had come to highlight their status as a neutral nation. Each port authority received copies of the new Neutrality Regulations, in Norwegian, German, English and French, 200 in each language. They were to be handed out as required to ships whose masters claimed not to be aware of the Regulations. Norwegian pilots had also been supplied with the leaflet for distribution. Yet, so far it did not seem that Norwegian port authorities at Tromsø or at Lødingen or any of the pilots had given Pusback or Gainard any copies, regardless of the relevance to their situation.

Aboard the *Olav Tryggvason*, Dingsør added one very important additional piece of information: under no circumstances would the ship be allowed to move through any areas defined as "war harbors" during the hours of darkness.

The report submitted later by the officer in charge of the *Olav Tryggvason* is very specific on this point. It was noted that the Prize Commander asked if they could anchor at such ports. The answer was an emphatic "no."[7]

As they sailed past the Kvitholmen Lighthouse, to their right, they were about to enter the unprotected waters of Hustadviken, one of the more notorious stretches of open waters on the entire coast. No islands sheltered this part of the route from the heavy seas of the North Atlantic, nor was there anywhere to hide from prying British warships. The Norwegians were obviously well aware of the opportunities; a further torpedo boat, *Snøgg*, was waiting for them. As the convoy again reached safer waters, the *Snøgg* was ordered to return to base.

Sailing through these waters had several advantages: it was easy, the fjords were wider and the light was still good. They were making around 10 knots, close to the maximum for the *City of Flint*, but barely cruising speed for the two naval vessels following in its wake. The timing seemed rather good. They enjoyed sheltered waters during the night, and came up to Vanylvsgapet around 0550 the following morning. They were about to enter another notorious stretch of open sea: Stad. The British force was nowhere to be seen as Mountbatten had ordered them to rendezvous there 12 hours later. Mountbatten was still steaming north. The daily Norwegian intelligence report noted that he was nearly 24 hours late.[8]

Pusback was probably very relieved to learn that again, the Norwegians had more ships on hand. Two ships from the 3rd. Naval District's First Destroyer Division, *Garm* and *Draug*, had moved in advance to take up their positions; now they too joined the escort. Rear Admiral Tank-Nielsen knew perfectly well how exposed this particular area was and he did not want any later recriminations. The extra ships were, however, around 30 years old with armaments limited to six 3-inch guns.

In London, the Admiralty was determined to put on a good show, clearly without thinking of the cost of it all. The cruisers *Newcastle* and *Glasgow* had been en route from Spithead bound for Rosyth, having left Spithead at 1915 on Tuesday evening. Just over three hours later the Admiralty ordered them to proceed directly to a position well out to sea, and slightly to the south of the previous patrol's area at Stad on the West-Norwegian coast. They were to act in support of Mountbatten's operation.

During the night, the Royal Air Force's Coastal Command received a signal from the Admiralty. The signal included the likely position of the *City of Flint* although it was thought to be too far to the north of their northernmost patrols.[9] The Admiralty duty captain still pleaded with the RAF to continue looking. They also passed on information on the navy's ships operating on or near the Norwegian cost. This information was immediately forwarded to the relevant Groups within Coastal Command.

By daylight on Wednesday, 1 November, three different patrol beats were to be flown as part of the search. The first one, comprising four Saro Londons took off from the Shetlands, heading directly eastwards towards the Norwegian coast at Bergen. Flying in a formation covering a 40-mile wide track they were to sweep north following the coast until level with Trondheim before turning home.

The second beat was covered by a single Sunderland Flying Boat from Invergordon. This plane was to head directly towards Stadlandet. This was the most exposed part of the Norwegian coast, where the *City of Flint* was most likely to move out beyond the territorial limit so as to remain in safe waters. From there, the plane was to sweep north to 65° 20' N, before flying six miles directly westwards out into the Norwegian Sea and then turn back. This was a very interesting route which illustrated where the British forces thought their naval units might have a chance to take over the prize. Like the open sea at Stad, the Norwegian coast, just short of 65° N, offered another navigational obstacle for Pusback, namely a group of islands. If the *City of Flint* sailed around the islands, she might move so far from the coast as to possibly leave Norwegian waters in order to avoid the myriad of rocks and skerries in that area.

The third patrol was to head for the Norwegian coast further south and then turn north, thus covering the southernmost segment of the coast from Stavanger to Bergen.

On Wednesday all the patrols were flown as directed and all planes returned safely, without having spotted the ship. That evening, Coastal Command HQ received a description of the *City of Flint* from the Admiralty as noted by the British consular staff at Tromsø. At least they would know what to look for when repeating the patrols the following day.

In Haugesund, Lanwer received another telegram concerning the *City of Flint*, again from the Foreign Ministry in Berlin, addressed to him personally. By now he had received at least three such telegrams concerning the ability to be ready to provide help and assistance to the prize. He was ordered to tell Pusback to leave Skudesnesfjord at dusk and maximize the use of territorial waters on his journey south through the Belts. Berlin also wanted Lanwer to let them know when Pusback would be leaving. The consul clearly needed to speak to Pusback in order to convey all this information as well as the actual reason for the strict scheduling of departures from Skudesnes.[10]

The British consulate in Haugesund was monitoring when southbound German ships departed. On Monday, 30 October, they sent a telegram to the Admiralty in London explaining that, as a rule, the German ships left Haugesund late in the afternoon. The assumption was that the German merchantmen would stay inside Norwegian territorial waters until they reached the open, unprotected coast at Jæren, before changing to a southerly course directly towards Germany. The consular staff felt that at this point of the journey, the ships were being met by an escort and that the rendezvous was arranged in advance.[11] Conditions in a small town like Haugesund were clearly rather transparent. It was difficult to keep anything secret. The Norwegian telegraph office in Haugesund later discovered an inappropriate relationship between one of their female operators and a member of the German consular staff. The British consulate generally held that their telephone conversations were listened to by "third parties."[12] The telegraph office manager now suggested to her that she would need to choose "between God and Mammon."

Lanwer's report would make it abundantly clear what his primary role really was, namely to call up U-boat escorts to meet German ships heading south to Germany. The German merchant fleet had already seen significant losses since the beginning of the war and many of their ships were scattered in ports around the world. Those that made it as far as Haugesund were to be given the best chance possible to make it home. All German ships were to anchor at Haugesund and wait for permission to depart, and the departure was not allowed until after 1600. Berlin had to be informed of any departures two hours earlier.[13]

On Thursday, 2 November at 0715, *Glasgow* spotted her first darkened ship. They increased speed to take a closer look.[14] They were virtually halfway between the Shetlands and the Norwegian coast, at the Tampen fishing grounds. Just as the patrol was satisfied that the first ship was not the *City of Flint*, a second ship was spotted and they raced off at 25 knots to see who the darkened merchantman was. They had to circle the ship to learn her identity. When *Glasgow*, using a flag hoist, requested her name, the ship's reply in international flags was completely unintelligible. When they got close enough they could however, see the name *Gunny—Panama* painted on her sides along with the Panamanian colors. When *Glasgow* checked the on board copy of Lloyds Register, they found her port of registration to be Bergen. The *City of Flint* was still as elusive as ever.

Flight Lieutenant Thomas and Pilot Officer Porteous, together with a crew of four, took off from the Shetland Islands at the same time as Captain Frank H. Pegram in *Glasgow* was checking his first ship. They were flying a Saro London, with the identification K-5910, from the 240 Squadron. As they reached the Norwegian coast, they turned north.

The two cruisers maintained the course for the patrol area for three hours before breaking off in response to a report from the aircraft of an enemy merchantman near the entrance to Nordfjord, slightly further south. They were still intent on providing back-up to any action in which Mountbatten would engage the Prize Crew. Now they moved south to remain on station to the west of the target. At noon they were in an ideal position as back-up for any action launched by Mountbatten's force at Stad. The two cruisers were 85 km directly west of Stad, well over the horizon, yet close enough to move in quickly if any action was about to commence.

Less than an hour later, at 1259, Flight Lieutenant Thomas informed *Glasgow* directly that the ship resembling the *City of Flint* was in the company of two other merchant ships. She was spotted coming around the inside of Bremanger island around 25 nautical miles (ca. 45 km) to the south of Stadlandet. A little earlier, at 1245, the Coastal Command aircraft had reported the sighting to the Admiralty.[15]

One ship was identified as the Finnish vessel *Canopus*, another bore the name *Kiel*. Bringing up the rear were two unidentified armed British ships. According to the report, Thomas and Porteous both claimed to recognize the *Kiel* as the camouflaged *City of Flint*.[16] They even took photographs of the ship, which meant that the plane was well inside Norwegian territory, but it was the wrong ship.

At this stage Pusback was being very cautious. He took the *City of Flint* very close to the shore. The Norwegian navy's report noted that he actually took the ship in the shore side of a group of skerries—Bukketyvene—while the entire escort passed on the seaward side. His caution was about to pay off as they spotted two blacked-out hunters just outside the four-mile territorial limit, with possibly two more standing off further out. If these were Royal Navy units, they did not recognize the *City of Flint*. It is far more likely that these ships were other merchant vessels, blacked out in order to avoid detection.

Stad is a notorious stretch of water which sailors unfamiliar with the area would want to avoid without help from pilots. Pusback had to rely on the skills of his Norwegian pilot. The *City of Flint* and its escort continued in the Vågsfjord, past Måløy and remained seemingly unseen in sheltered waters. At Måløy, *Olav Tryggvason* stood down the two torpedo boats as the *City of Flint* continued in the lead, picking its course carefully and with a constant variation in the speed, which was mainly very slow.

Even if no one else could find the *City of Flint*, the press could. An Associated Press contact spotted her as she passed Måløy, and so by the time America had woken up, the location was already in their papers. Their press was not bound by Norwegian embargo rules. At that time, Pusback and Gainard had an escort comprising two naval vessels and the journalist expected her to pass Bergen that evening.

In Melrose, Massachusetts that Thursday, 2 November, Mrs. Gainard was at home anxiously waiting for any news of her husband, his crew and the ship. Since sending her telegrams to the Soviet and German foreign offices, she had a reply from Berlin via the American diplomatic bag to Secretary Hull, but she had heard nothing from Moscow. As a follow-up to the message from Berlin, she had a phone call from the German consul at Boston. He wanted to stress the fact that in Berlin, individuals in the Foreign Ministry were confident that the American Master and his crew were all safe and well aboard the ship. The message may not have satisfied Mrs. Gainard, but it did achieve its second goal: it was reported in the American press. It helped keeping the story alive and in front of the American public and members of Congress.

The *Glasgow's* commanding officer found it difficult to believe that the *City of Flint* had actually made it so far south already. His reasoning seemed fairly logical. He had assumed that Mountbatten had planned to sweep in towards the coast at the most southerly point she could have reached at her best speed. As he had underestimated her speed, Mountbatten was still to the north of it all. To make matters worse for Pegram, he had not received an earlier Admiralty signal, which in fact had stated the maximum speed of the American ship to be 10–12 knots. He also believed the destroyers were only around an hour's sailing to his north.

Flight Lieutenant Thomas had already reported his first sighting by the time a second patrol took off from Invergordon. The aircraft was N-9025 from 228 Squadron, flown by pilot officers L.L. Jones and Le Maistre. They were flying a Shorts S25 Sunderland and were cleared for takeoff at 1140.[17]

Since Mountbatten was in charge of the operation, Pegram in the *Glasgow* did not even know the details of his plan. It was broad daylight and had he tried to intercept the *City of Flint*, he was justifiably concerned that he would achieve little other than compromise Mountbatten's plan and violate Norwegian territorial waters in the process. Consequently he did not close in on the coast at that time. As he was contemplating launching his own aircraft to clarify the situation, N-9025 appeared to continue the patrol. It was this plane which was credited with spotting the *City of Flint* that afternoon, but the exact location has not been recorded. Pegram was now very anxious that both London and Mountbatten learned what the real situation actually was. He asked N-9025 to report the location of the American ship to London, and also to include the exact location of the two cruisers in the message. Pegram must have felt tantalizingly close to being able to finish the chase. The pilot made his report, but did not inform the destroyers of the actual positions of the cruisers. The forces were still unable to pin down the location of the opposition, but the seriousness of the situation was becoming horribly clear to Pegram. There was every likelihood that the second ship, which had now been reported to them, was actually the missing freighter. The destroyers were, however, entirely in the wrong place to stop her. It must have been particularly bitter to realize what was in the process of happening—when the *Glasgow* could so easily have been off Stadlandet in time to block her passage. If only Pegram had known her top speed and had been given the opportunity to act as a fail-safe to Mountbatten's plan.

It was time to improvise. They now knew Pusback's best speed, they knew where he was heading and, best of all, Pegram knew exactly where he was. Between them, the two British cruisers planned to cover each of the possible exits from the fjords where the *City of Flint* might come out to avoid islands or skerries during the night. The stakes were high, the crews were keen and the trap was set.

They even got a trial run. At dusk, a ship of approximately the same size as the *City of Flint* was spotted—she was just outside territorial waters. At 1736 Pegram went to full speed, 30 knots, and signaled "Battle Stations"—the order to place the entire ship's complement on the highest state of alert, ready to fire or be fired on. The next log entry read, "1749 warning shot across her bows."[18] Then "1750 go as required, 20 knots, *Newcastle* ordered to board." The *Glasgow* circled both ships. The victim should never have turned to make a run for the coast. She turned out to be the Norwegian *Ringulv*, America-bound with wood pulp whose captain probably thought he was about to be sunk by German raiders. In his report of the incident Pegram did not actually say they fired the warning shot across the bows of a neutral merchant vessel going about her normal business. He merely stated that she was "stopped and boarded."[19]

Pegram was being watched. As his log made no reference to it, he may not have seen the Norwegian airplane high above, but the incident was included in the naval intelligence report delivered the following morning. In fact, the operation had taken place well within Norwegian territorial waters according to the report.[20]

Mountbatten tried desperately to regain the initiative. Only an hour earlier the Admiralty had warned him of the true speed of the American freighter. Virtually at the same time as Pegram was preparing to board the wrong ship, the Admiralty sent Mountbatten a further signal confirming that the *City of Flint* had been spotted off Stadlandet at 1100 that morning. He needed a new plan. Later that night he offered up a suggestion to back off until the *City of Flint* had reached the unprotected open waters off Obrestad at Jæren, south of Stavanger. He felt that such an operation as the one he had originally planned could be executed there, in broad daylight. Pegram now finally broke radio silence to disagree. He could not see why the *City of Flint* should leave Norwegian territorial waters during daytime—particularly if she knew she was being followed. The only outcome he saw was that the regular German air reconnaissance of the area would spot the British units. This could trigger either bombing or submarine attacks, or both.

The distance from Stad to Obrestad is around 230 nautical miles (ca. 420 km). This represented nearly 24 hours sailing for the *City of Flint*. Even the British cruisers moving at twice the speed would take ten hours to cover the distance. The plan just did not seem realistic. The Bergen area had been designated as a "war harbor" by the Norwegians. Pusback was not allowed to move through any such area during the hours of darkness. He had to slow down to avoid anchoring, which further delayed the arrival time at Obrestad.

Gainard was concerned that as they were moving ever closer to Germany, an excuse to stop was becoming increasingly important. The slight injury one of his wipers, Sellars, incurred as he left the engine room might provide an excuse. He later argued that Pusback either did not know the extent of the injury or chose to ignore it.

At 2000 in the evening of Thursday, 2 November 1939, they had passed through a narrow channel which opened onto the outer parts of the longest fjord in Norway, the Sognefjord. The route the *City of Flint* now followed was well known. The ship headed towards the open sea again, steaming down the Sognesjø, a widening part of the fjord, stretching between islands directly out into open waters.

A mere 35 km to the west of Pusback's position at that time were the two British cruisers. They were only just outside the Norwegian territorial limit. At that stage neither side was aware of the position of the other. Pusback, however, must have been very aware of the opportunities for a British surprise attack as he faced open waters, which he was about to enter. The freighter was just to the south of the light at Kråkenes on the island of Sula when the *Olav Tryggvason* received a signal from them by "blinker" (the Aldis Lamp): "We want to anchor Haugesund. See my consul. Need doctor ill American."[21]

Pusback needed to buy time, at this rate he would reach Stavanger in southwestern Norway early the following day, which did not fit. Stavanger overlooks the start of a very open and particularly exposed part of the Norwegian coast, Jæren. There are no islands or skerries for a distance longer than a day's daylight sailing. The ship would be particularly vulnerable to British attacks over this part of the coast and tactically it was a stretch of water best crossed in the dark of night. The Prize Commander had no valid reason under international law to stop. He had to keep moving if he wanted to avoid the threat of internment. Haugesund was about 24 hours sailing away and clearly the sick American was in no danger, so they continued southwards. There was, though, no reason for Pusback to be complacent.

Two hours later, Diesen in Oslo received a telephone message from Rear Admiral Carsten Tank-Nielsen to relay the request for a doctor and seeking advice for the escort. Diesen was clearly wary of another stop at a port, advising that Dingsør in the *Olav Tryggvason* should stop the ship at sea to check on the health of the sailor. Only in the case of an emergency would he accept a call at Haugesund. In such a case, he would be justified in accepting the stop under the Norwegian Neutrality Regulations.[22]

In Haugesund, Consul Lanwer had received his orders for the *City of Flint*, again. The Foreign Ministry in Berlin sent him a telegram, addressed to his "office" at Hotel Bristol. His post was so new he had not yet had the opportunity to rent an office. Berlin now explained that the Prize Commander on the *City of Flint* had orders to call at Haugesund if required. In other words, the decision to call was entirely Pusback's—if he made the wrong decision, he could always be blamed for it later.

Lanwer was asked to wire Berlin any further developments as soon as possible. It was particularly important, the telegram said, to make all possible arrangements required to ensure a safe arrival for the prize at a German port. The consul was requested to provide the Prize Commander with all support and assistance. This was no blanket request to all consulates along the coast. The German Foreign Ministry had ordered Lanwer to help, and to be ready for action.[23]

At this stage the route Pusback had chosen nearly sealed their fate. As he kept a course running approximately west-south-west out of the Sognefjord, he chose to avoid some of the narrow inlets immediately to the south of the long fjord. He would have remained unseen from the sea had he chosen the inner route on this stretch too, as he had done consistently until now. Instead they went far enough west to reach the northern approaches to Bergen, the Hjeltefjord, which would see them all the way to the city.

The British warships were running with their navigational light blacked out at this stage in order to avoid detection.[24] They were inside Norwegian territorial waters. People on the island, clearly aware of the issues surrounding the *City of Flint*, had seen the silhouettes of the large warships as they moved into position.[25]

The area the *City of Flint* was sailing through was quite wide and widening further still towards the ocean to the west. At 2330 Glasgow spotted the navigational lights of the *City of Flint* and her escorts. Twelve minutes later Pegram ordered "Battle Stations" again. The ship's crew must have been rather jumpy by now, sensing that they were close to achieving something. The duty radio operator sent off a quick report to London, notifying them of the sighting. Then, his log noted, Pegram closed on the ship, ready for action.

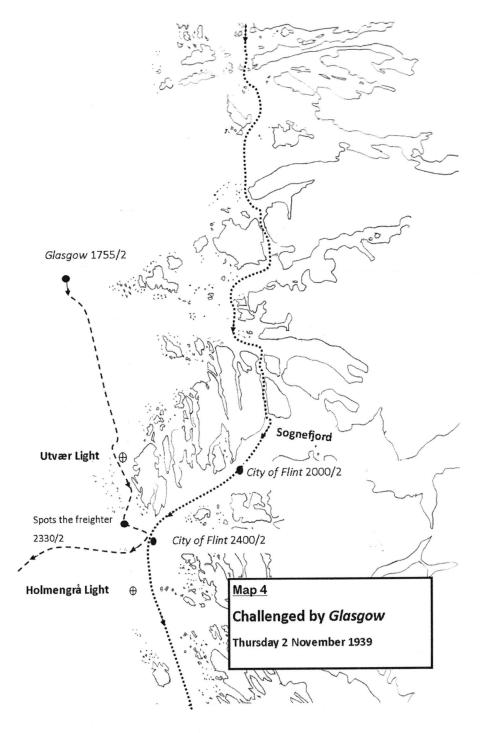

Glasgow 1755/2

Utvær Light ⊕

Spots the freighter
2330/2

Holmengrå Light ⊕

Sognefjord

City of Flint 2000/2

City of Flint 2400/2

Map 4

Challenged by *Glasgow*

Thursday 2 November 1939

At five minutes to midnight the *City of Flint's* wheelhouse was suddenly lit up by a bright searchlight being played along the ship. They were 4.5 nautical miles northeast of Holmengrå lighthouse, which placed them right in the middle of the open waters at the mouth of the long Sognefjord (at N 60°, 55', E 4°, 40'3, according to Dingsør). All Pusback saw was that a blacked out warship suddenly raced towards them at high speed. They seemed to have been waiting, hidden from the fjord by one of the nearby islands.[26] The duty officer on the *Olav Tryggvason* could see a blacked-out ship, possibly as large as a cruiser at 212° W. The *City of Flint* was at this stage around 700–800 meters ahead of the *Olav Tryggvason*, heading south. The unidentified ship used its blinker to flash two letters from the international communications code towards the *City of Flint*: "SC—Sierra Charley (What is your name?)"

The Norwegian escort, behind the prize and slightly further out to the *City of Flint*'s starboard, was still virtually shrouded in darkness when Dingsør decided to intervene. After all, they were well inside Norwegian territorial waters. His searchlight suddenly cut through the black night onto the dark intruder before he flashed a terse response: "*Olav Tryggvason*. You are in Norwegian territorial waters."

The *City of Flint* continued south without responding.

Pusback had no weapons for any offensive action against the Royal Navy. But he had demolition charges ready. On his orders German soldiers now raced to agreed locations at the bottom of the ship—seeking out its weakest spots. He had three charges, each of them a German pre-packed charge containing 2 kg of high explosives.[27] Backed by a timer and placed in the right location, any one of these charges would have been enough to scuttle the ship. The water depth where they were was around 500 m. None of these charges had been detected at Tromsø a week earlier. Within minutes, all Pusback had left to do was to order the timers started. He would only just have allowed enough time to get everybody off the ship before the explosions, but not long enough for a British anti-demolition team racing against the clock to find them.

The intruder tried to position his ship across the bow of the *City of Flint* in such a way that Pusback needed to maneuver around him to starboard to avoid collision. If this happened it would mean the *City of Flint* moving further seawards—closer to international waters and the ship being "fair game" to the enemy. Pusback kept a steady course, not moving. He knew what was at stake. He also knew they were less than 3 km inside the territorial limits.[28] The ship was prepared for demolition. Now, he waited. It was Pegram's move.

The unidentified ship backed off. There was no time to relax—only minutes later she was spotted again at 241° W of them at a distance measured to 3600 meters. The Norwegian naval vessel retained its position as before—off the *City of Flint*'s stern to starboard. When challenged by the Norwegian naval blinker, the unidentified stranger replied[29]: "I will not infringe your rights. I hoped your friend was coming out. Good night."

At that she disappeared, heading west into the dark waters. No identification had been provided, but the close encounter could hardly have eased Pusback's mind; he too had understood the British message.[30] He had to continue, no stops were allowed.

In his account of the event, Pusback referred to this as an enemy cruiser, "probably Arethusa Class." The Arethusa Class of cruisers were a relatively small type of light cruisers, weighing in at around 5,220 tons. They only had six guns in the main armory, each at 6", configured in three twin turrets. The absence of the fourth turret from the stern section, together with the clear gap between the forward superstructure and the fore funnel, would be two of the most distinguishing parts of the profile of an Arethusa Class vessel.

The *Glasgow*, a Town Class cruiser, was substantially larger at around 9,300 tons and had significantly heavier armament with her twelve 6" guns configured in four triple turrets.[31]

Having quickly assessed the situation and pulled the *Glasgow* back from the tense moment, the crew went on stand down and Pegram sent an immediate update to London. He did not give up the hope of still finding an opportunity to catch Pusback off guard. The *Glasgow*, unbeknownst to Pusback or his Norwegian escort, actually kept the *City of Flint* in their sights for the next two hours. Pegram commented that the *City of Flint*, in the capable hands of a Norwegian pilot, who must have been terrified, was consistently well out ahead of the escort who followed around 700 meters behind. The Norwegian navy was most certainly not aiding or abetting. They merely followed, and escorted where the Germans decided to take the ship, but their duties only lasted as long as the ship remained in Norwegian territorial waters. Judging from the Norwegian report of the escort duties, they knew exactly where they were at any time during the journey. Dingsør's use of lights and lighthouses as navigational points in his report made the route very clear.

The Germans clearly did not want to find another stretch of open waters again soon, and certainly not in the dark. At 0320 that morning, Pusback tried another approach: "The pilot is asking may we proceed Kalvanes."[32] The Norwegians were in no mood to compromise and kept up the pressure; the blinker flashed back a curt reply: "No, you are not permitted to enter the war port before sunrise."

Bergen was a Norwegian war port and as such foreign ships were not allowed to enter or exit during the hours of darkness. Pusback was on the very edge of the prohibited area and had to spend the rest of the night virtually stationary in the fjord, waiting for daylight. They were nearing Bergen from the northern end of the Hjeltefjord. In truth, they halted here, although no one actually acknowledged it. The *City of Flint* had to wait for daylight. They could not continue and did not want to turn north back towards the unknown British intruders.

More or less at the same time, Pegram called off his attempt. At 0345 Friday, 3 November, he pulled back to the west and disappeared. He reported his actions to the Admiralty and was given a new objective. An hour later he spotted Mountbatten's *Kelly* before continuing north. The *Glasgow* was off the case and no longer in support of the failed operation. Instead she was sent back to Stadlandet to hunt for the large and very fast German liner, the SS *New York*, which the Admiralty thought might make a run for it to get home from Murmansk.

Friday morning the Admiralty knew exactly where the *City of Flint* was. They even told the press, in time for the BBC to feature the news in its lunchtime bulletin.[33] Interestingly, the way the press statement was worded said absolutely nothing about the Royal Navy having given up the chase. The radio bulletin, like the newspapers, alerted its audience to the fact that "light forces" had spotted the *City of Flint* heading south along the Norwegian coast. The Admiralty was probably not very enthusiastic about admitting that two heavy cruisers and an entire destroyer division of five ships had so far failed to prevent the American ship from reaching German waters.

The tone at the meeting of the British War cabinet that morning was subdued. They were informed that the *City of Flint* had been spotted the day before and that two cruisers had been dispatched. Interestingly, no reference was made to Mountbatten's force.[34]

The chief of the Naval staff, Sir Dudley Pound, explained their strategy. They had dispatched naval units to the points on the Norwegian coast where the *City of Flint* might need to move outside territorial waters. This had proven not to be the case. The *Glasgow* had located her at midnight inside Norwegian waters, under escort by a Norwegian minelayer. Politically it would not have been advisable to take action to liberate the ship under such circumstances. Furthermore, the *City of Flint* had, by then, reached a point on the coast from where it would be perfectly feasible to continue the voyage to a German port without ever having to leave territorial waters. Consequently, the Admiralty had called off the operation. At the Foreign Office the view was that it was up to the U.S. government to deal with the problem via diplomatic channels.

As soon as Churchill heard the news, he insisted that the Foreign Office notify Joseph Kennedy, the U.S. Ambassador, immediately. The British were admitting privately that one of their ships had "signed" the *City of Flint* early that morning. In other words, they must have been well inside Norwegian territorial limits. They did also admit to having been "warned off" by a Norwegian Man of War.[35] The rules of the game were being upheld, but only just. That Friday morning Kennedy sent a brief but telling message to Hull at the State Department, informing him of the approximate location of the *City of Flint* (she was proceeding south in the inner channel escorted by the Norwegian ship *Olav Tryggvason*) and adding that the British Royal Navy was very frustrated that they were unable to take any action. There was very little chance of the prize coming outside Norwegian territorial waters.

Later that day, the Foreign Office sent a hand-delivered note to Kennedy where they explained the circumstances around the hunt for the *City of Flint*. They argued that the Admiralty had considered it "most improper" that Norwegian forces provided the German controlled vessel with an escort.[36] As if all the British efforts did not speak for themselves, the letter added: "In the circumstances the US Government can have no cause to complain at our action, and every reason to feel aggrieved with the Soviet and Norwegian Governments."

Perhaps the way the British absolved themselves of any blame was more telling about their own attitude toward recriminations than about the real political perspective. On the other hand, the Foreign Office felt that Norway had not acted in accordance with the rules. Their file copy of the note to Ambassador Kennedy has a very telling addition, written in the hand of an unknown official: "Norwegians should not have allowed ship into Tromsø for the second time." Regardless of Mountbatten's miscalculation, Norwegian Foreign Minister Koht was not covering himself with glory over this.

In Washington they were not in a position to add anything to the story at this stage. Had the British force tried to board, the outcome could have been less certain than the Admiralty assumed. A report from Sir Cecil Dormer, the British ambassador in Oslo, dated a few weeks later, added a very sobering postscript. Had an attempt to board been executed, the Germans would have set off explosive charges to sink the ship. Pusback's own statement written while in Norwegian captivity confirms this.

In his report of the patrol, Pegram made it clear that at no time did he envisage pursuing the *City of Flint* through territorial waters, particularly as a Norwegian warship was present.[37] He did, however, add a very telling comment, namely that he had not been party to any special instructions from Mountbatten, which might entertain any departure from "normal international law." In other words, if they were to have violated Norwegian rights, he should have been told.

Pusback, who knew nothing of his good fortune, still felt the pressure. He had no option but to continue if he wanted to avoid internment, and as light improved, the *City of Flint* picked up speed to around 10 knots. It was not until 0700 that they were permitted to enter the Bergen harbor zone. There was a continuous line of small islands to the right, sheltering them from the open sea and any British warships. For the next few hours

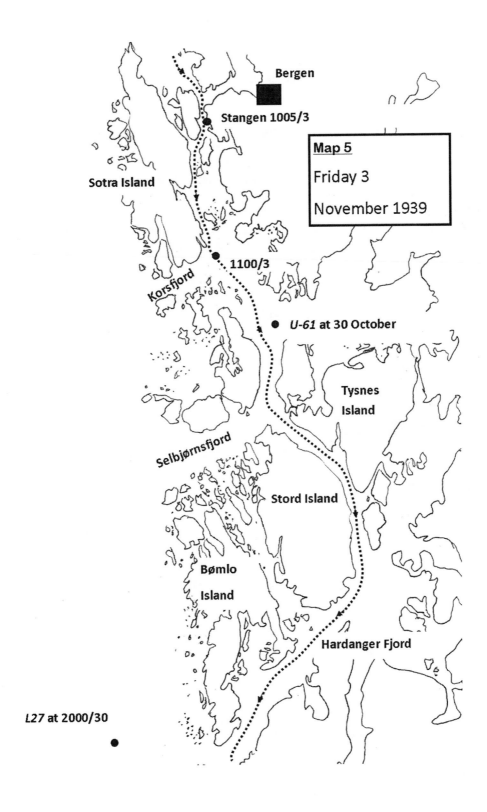

Bergen

Stangen 1005/3

Map 5

Friday 3

November 1939

Sotra Island

1100/3

U-61 at 30 October

Korsfjord

Tysnes
Island

Selbjørnsfjord

Stord Island

Bømlo

Island

Hardanger Fjord

L27 at 2000/30

they still made slow progress, finally passing Stangen Light (now known as Stongi)—at 1005.[38] Pusback had made it past the City of Bergen. Briseid made a point of noting the time they passed various lights or navigational points as they went.

The Norwegians had decided to check out the story of the sick American that Pusback had reported the previous evening. As Briseid logged them passing the next light at 1100 that morning, he signaled the *City of Flint* to stop.

The *Olav Tryggvason* sent the ship's own doctor over. Captain Lowzow accompanied him. Not one for missing an opportunity, Gainard showed the officer around the entire ship—including where the Germans were quartered. When the doctor reported a patient with a slight leg injury, the Prize Commander was informed that he could not go to port, but had to continue his journey. The doctor had only been on board for half an hour to dress the bruised ankle of Allison Sellars, a wiper from Wilmington, North Carolina, using medicaments requisitioned from his own ship's first aid supplies. Sellars had stumbled and fallen over some drums in the deck cargo and injured his shins. His injuries did not prevent him being one of the first off the ship in Bergen when the crew was granted shore leave a few days later. As Gainard pointed out in one of his interviews in Bergen, the injuries had been sustained nearly three weeks earlier.

Pusback argued, however, that he really needed to talk to the German consul at Haugesund. Again Captain Lowzow stressed that this was not a valid reason for anchoring. He added that if the *City of Flint* did so regardless of this advice, the ship would be stopped and the issue of internment would need to be examined. On learning the severity with which the Norwegians would treat such a violation, Pusback confirmed that he would not anchor at Haugesund, but would proceed to Kopervik where he would halt only long enough to change pilots.[39] Nevertheless, he did discuss this again with Gainard. The American, probably sensing an opportunity, reassured Pusback that the Norwegians would not dare to take any action against him, even if he did stop. Pusback knew he needed to buy time. He did not want to pass the long stretch of open waters from Jæren to Lista at Norway's southernmost point in daylight.

Once Lowzow conveyed the doctor's conclusion to Briseid, the captain sent a message to Tank-Nielsen in Bergen. Around 1300 Tank-Nielsen phoned Oslo to pass on the results of the medical examination and inform the Admiral that the request to anchor at Haugesund had been denied.[40] All morning, the average speed had been no more than around four knots. Pusback was very determined indeed to buy time now that he was in inshore waters.

The torpedo boat *Stegg* joined the escort at this stage. The Norwegians may well have expected further British interest once the waters opened up to the south of Stord island. In fact, the layout of the fjords was very similar to the area where the British flotilla had closed in the previous night. The mouth of the Bømlafjord was completely open to the sea beyond. The area, Sletta was one of the notorious stretches of the coast—and there was more to come. To the south of Haugesund the coastline was completely open; there would be no more natural protection until the ship reached German waters. If the British navy had failed before, this time they had plenty of open waters to catch their prey. Mountbatten was right in planning his next attempt for this area in terms of cover, but wrong in his estimate of the *City of Flint*'s sailing time and wrong to disregard the escort. Small wonder then that Pusback seemed to regard Haugesund as such an important point in his journey.

The problem was that Pusback was by now more than 12 hours behind the arrival time he had passed to Lanwer, who did not know that night-time passage through the war harbor at Bergen was prohibited.[41] Any of his seniors—the consul general at Bergen, the embassy in Oslo, or the Foreign Ministry in Berlin—should have told him about the delays. As it was, the long delay remained unexplained to him.

Consequently the consul was growing increasingly anxious and the pressure from Berlin was piling up. On Friday, 3 November, he received yet another telegram from them, urging him to support the *City of Flint*. Lanwer was convinced of the need for U-boat cover for the ship, particularly as he had heard new confirmation of British naval units operating along the coast. Each of the BBC news bulletins from Friday lunchtime onwards claimed that the British navy had the *City of Flint* in their sights as she headed south. Their transmissions were listened to daily on the West Coast of Norway.[42] It was imperative, Lanwer thought, that Pusback did not depart from Kopervik at the wrong time, without any support on his flank. In addition, Lanwer had procured the required charts as well as a lighthouse book. He had also lined up two particularly reliable pilots.[43]

That morning Lanwer got hold of a motorboat and sailed out into the shipping lanes where they passed Haugesund. All day he was out looking for the *City of Flint*. In the end he concluded that Pusback had probably been delayed overnight north of Bergen. As the *City of Flint* was likely to be running with minimal (if any) lights showing, Lanwer reasoned that after darkness he would not be able to spot the ship, let alone see the German flag. Like Pusback, he had no radio. Lanwer was alone. He had no support and he could not afford to fail.

The Norwegian press, who ought to have been able to track the journey had, as requested, abstained from printing anything on the *City of Flint* during its journey south. In the northern approaches to Bergen, however, a local photographer in Hjeltefjord caught the ship on camera as she came south on Friday, 3 November, five days after they had left Tromsø. This was front-page news the following day. The paper quoted a Berlin source as explaining that the German navy expected to see the ship reach the port of Stettin some time during the night of Saturday/Sunday. Alternatively, the source said, the ship might dock in Rostock or Kiel. They had also granted permission to a number of American journalists to be present. Only the ship hitting a mine could now prevent the Germans from triumphantly parading their catch to the world. In London, *The Times* explained that the ship would be able to reach her destination by merely exploiting the contiguous Norwegian and Swedish territorial waters all the way to German ports on the Baltic.

In Norway, an international press corps was now gathering. They all thought the chase was nearing a crucial phase. If the press knew that the stretch of sea south of Haugesund was wide open, unprotected and easily within reach of British naval bases, then Pusback knew it too. Furthermore, the press pack could see it with their own eyes. Feeling they had second-guessed the Germans, the journalists had established themselves with a real grandstand view of the stage where they thought the drama would be played out. They had descended on Kvitsøy Lighthouse, on a small exposed island facing the open sea, halfway between Haugesund and Stavanger. The lighthouse keeper and his assistant could only watch as the journalists started arriving.[44] Ever practical, the lighthouse team had seen the weather close in and wondered how long they might be stuck with all the extra mouths to feed.

Rumors were circulating easily among the journalists. The *City of Flint* had already been spotted in three different locations that morning. The journalists stayed put however. The ship was expected to be clearly visible sailing south towards them by lunchtime, but they could still see nothing. Frantic phone calls were made from the island. Nothing new was forthcoming and one enterprising journalist, Egil Tresselt, left the island by motorboat heading north towards Haugesund, where the ship was most liable to be found. The coastal town had, because of its strategic location, both British and German consuls. The British consulate under Johannes Sundfør M.B.E., had been in existence since before the last war.

In Oslo, Ambassador Harriman's peace was thoroughly shattered by the press that afternoon around 1500. Even in 1939 the press was using available technology to their best advantage. Copenhagen-based United Press International correspondent Ralph Peters called her, enquiring about the ship as his latest information placed the *City of Flint* somewhere off Bergen. When contacted, her consul at Bergen, Dunlap, spent an hour checking, only to report back with no news at all. He even ventured that it was unlikely that the ship had made such good progress on its way south.

8

Turning Point

When the *City of Flint* approached Haugesund, the *Olaf Tryggvason* was in the lead. Behind them the German freighter *Schwaben* was about to catch up with them again. The German vice-consul at Haugesund, Lanwer, had briefed her Master, Paulsen.[1] The ship also picked up two *Kraft durch Freude* (KdF) pilots, who were to take them to the Swedish border. The German welfare organization ran regular cruise ships along the Norwegian coast; having their own German pilots instead of relying on Norwegian ones seemed convenient. It also meant that German sailors came to know in detail how to navigate Norwegian waters.

The *Schwaben* had left Tromsø ahead of the *City of Flint* bound for Germany with a valuable South American grain cargo. As per instructions by radio broadcast, Paulsen had taken his ship into Haugesund awaiting orders of when to leave Skudesnes. His was a civilian merchant vessel allowed to do so according to the Hague Conventions. During his discussion with Lanwer, the consul mentioned the problem of how to communicate with the *City of Flint*. This was significant. Lanwer was one of the few who knew that the *City of Flint*'s radio transmitter did not work. He had received a telegram sent the day after the ship left Tromsø, which he knew someone else had sent on Pusback's behalf, hence the discussion with Paulsen, who just happened to be in the right place at the right time.

Between them they decided on one final attempt to stop the ship and prevent Pusback from departing Skudesnesfjord at the wrong time, as Lanwer felt he had been instructed to do. Lanwer later argued that they did not have much choice by way of flag hoists. Paulsen offered to use a combination of signal flags and Morse light signals to ensure that Pusback understood that he should contact Lanwer at Haugesund. In order to achieve this, he would turn his ship around and sail back northwards until he came face to face with the *City of Flint*.

Around 6 km north of Haugesund, they met.[2] It was still daylight. Paulsen in *Schwaben* ordered a flag hoist comprising the flags D and G, a combination with a very clear message: "Anchor soonest."[3] He followed that up with a message on the blinker to anchor at Haugesund and contact the consul at Hotel Bristol.

At Haugesund the *Olav Tryggvason* stopped briefly off the new Garpeskjær quay to pick up mail. Around 15 minutes later the *City of Flint*, followed by *Stegg*, appeared in the harbor at very low speed. Shortly after, the *Schwaben* closed on them from astern, passing the *City of Flint* to its starboard, but running very close to the American ship before continuing its journey south—at least that was the view from the Norwegian escort. From the bridge of the *City of Flint* it was far more dramatic. As the bridge wings of the two ships drew level, Paulsen shouted a message to the leader of the Prize Crew, Lieutenant

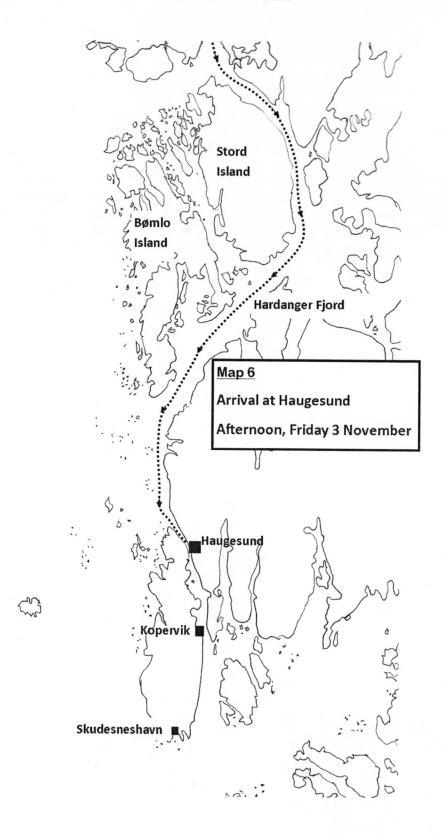

Pusback: "Anchor at Haugesund and get in touch with Bristol Hotel."[4] Pusback chose to interpret the message as a direct order. He later argued that he considered this order to take priority over the one issued by the captain of the *Olav Tryggvason*.[5] Although the message had been relayed in German, it was not only the German Prize Commander and his fellow soldiers on the bridge of the *City of Flint* who had picked up the message. Willy Neher heard it too. Suddenly the young American knew that things were about to change. Pusback was planning to stop.

The German consul at Tromsø had reported the two ships heading south at virtually the same time. The publicity gain of outsmarting the British Royal navy would be great if the prize could be brought safely back to Germany. Lanwer actually took advantage of a ship with a valuable cargo on her final leg of a journey all the way from South America to relay the message. Pusback could hardly have missed the significance of it all. He was now searching for a viable excuse to anchor. The chief engineer was asked if his engines did not need any repairs. He rejected the question. Gainard reminded Pusback of the secret telegram and its usefulness in Murmansk and later in Tromsø, wondering if it would not help him out of yet another tight corner.[6] He had obviously told Gainard that he had received the telegram, but had not let him in on the secret of the actual text, namely that he should push for permission to use Norwegian territorial waters as long as he required.[7]

Pusback did not know what to do. The maneuver would have reminded him of the vulnerable position of his ship, with no means of communicating with the outside world, without permission to stop and with no knowledge of the enemy forces sent out to capture him. The British monitored his movements. Even the BBC's radio broadcast made that clear. Yet, as he later explained to the German consul general in Bergen, the two Norwegian pilots he had on board warned him repeatedly against stopping in a Norwegian port. In internment, Pusback later argued that, from his perspective, the order passed to him in such a dramatic manner clearly took precedence over any other order he might have had.[8]

In Berlin, the Naval High Command had now learned of the enemy air reconnaissance of the previous day. They had also heard that further south in the North Sea, the *Newcastle* was waiting, supported by a naval unit. It was clearly not going to be easy for Pusback to break through to Germany via international waters.[9]

As the British were closing in (or so Berlin assumed) the American government asked the Germans for caution. They feared for the American crew. The Americans anticipated two equally dangerous outcomes from this problem: either the ship would be blown up by the Prize Crew or it would be sunk as a result of a fight with British naval units.[10]

Meanwhile, Rear Admiral Fricke, at the German Naval High Command, decided that it was time to start planning the arrival of the *City of Flint* at Hamburg. After all, he had just been promoted; he did not want anything to go wrong. On Friday he fired off an urgent note to the Reichskommisar in charge of the prize process.[11] He stressed that the *City of Flint*'s arrival time at Hamburg was not yet known. The American consulate should be advised of the arrival as soon as this was confirmed. Fricke went on to remind the Reichskommisar that in accordance with the Prize Regulations, the Prize Court was open to the public. The American Board of Shipping could participate and the owners of the cargo could hire a German lawyer to start preparing their case.

Fricke told the Prize Official that as soon as the ship was in German waters an officer representing the navy would go on board to explain the situation to Pusback. The navy obviously did not want Pusback to say the wrong things in Court, neither did they seem to recognize the concept of fair play. The Americans had to prepare their case without any contact with Gainard and his crew.

When the ship would sail through the Kiel Canal, no contact with the ship was to be permitted. Once in port at Hamburg, the American crew would need to decide who they wanted to act as witnesses for their case. Fricke claimed that he would not even allow the Americans ashore before they picked their witnesses—which he claimed the German Prize Regulations allowed for. In fact he conveniently ignored the paragraphs which argued that the Master, the officers and all the crew of a prize were free once in port if citizens of a neutral country.[12] Finally, Fricke added that no American journalists were to be permitted onto the ship.

The Berlin Prize Court was located at Matthäikircheplatz 12.[13] The majority of the American diplomatic functions in Berlin were still based at Bendlerstrasse 39, a mere two blocks away.

Haugesund was in 1939 a small shipping town in southwestern Norway with several international shipping lines to its name. That Friday afternoon it suddenly found itself center stage in the big power game of international politics. As people headed home after a day's work, those who paid any attention while walking along the quays would have seen a large ship accompanied by a smaller one, approaching the town from the north. The obvious intention seemed to be to pass down the narrow fjord separating the town from the island of Karmøy. At 1730 the *City of Flint* moved at very low speed across the harbor basin before making a turn. With a roar from the chain, the anchor suddenly ran out. As always, Gainard executed the actual maneuver to drop anchor because the ship was apparently not easy to bring to a halt this way.[14]

The persistence of Egil Tresselt, the young Bergen journalist, was finally rewarded. He had left the rest of the press corps by the island lighthouse and gambled on Haugesund to be the site where the *City of Flint* would see its luck change. Although it was dark by the time he arrived, there was a large black-painted vessel riding at anchor in the harbor, off the new Garpeskjær quay. This was the only quay in Haugesund where large ships had enough depth to be berthed. As his little motorboat approached the ship, the slow chugging noise of the ship's engine was heard. An official denied him permission to board. Along the railings several crew members were silhouetted against the lights on deck. The lights were positioned to illuminate the water all around the ship. No one could approach unnoticed.

Passing along the side of the ship, just below the American crew members, Tresselt could make out the blackened faces of engine crew watching the lights from the houses dotted along the seashore. A German guard on deck prevented him from talking to the Americans and the journalist ordered his boatman to take the boat around the stern and along the other side of the ship. Being so close, he was determined to attempt a conversation with them. The problem was the lights hanging from the masts. Again an eager German guard spotted him and stopped any Americans from replying to his shouted questions. As they headed back to shore empty handed they noticed the torpedo boat *Stegg* moored nearby. They were building up steam in the boilers. With a displacement of 220 tons, *Stegg* was one of the three largest torpedo boats in the Norwegian navy. Although 18 years old, it was still one of the more modern vessels available.

The local press, now with a world exclusive in sight, was quick to head for the ship, only to be denied access by the Norwegian escort. The following afternoon all the local paper could legally do in their measured front page reporting was to point to the contemporary legislation preventing journalists from speculating and developing independent lines of enquiry. They were still gagged.

Roosevelt's attempt to overturn the neutrality policy was proving successful. The U.S. Congress voted 243 to 181 in favor of lifting the embargo on exporting arms to countries at war. According to the Norwegian press, Western European nations had at that stage a total of 880 planes on order in the U.S. Orders to an estimated value of $1 billion (1939 value) were expected within the next few weeks.

The fate of the *City of Flint* was followed very closely in America; its impact on popular opinion contributed to the size of the majority of this crucial vote. Hull, in his memoirs, was quite clear on this. The *City of Flint* incident had helped supporters change the legislation. He also argued that it illustrated where Soviet sympathies lay, namely, with Hitler.[15]

At the port of Haugesund the *Olaf Tryggvason* immediately dispatched Captain Lowzow to check on the reason for the sudden change of plan. In reply to direct questioning by the Norwegian naval officer, who also outranked Pusback in seniority, the German replied that he had received orders from his government to talk to his consul in Haugesund and he regarded it as his duty as an officer to obey. Regardless of the threat of internment, Pusback had decided to anchor at Haugesund. Perhaps the final clue to his decision is to be found in the town's local paper the following morning. They reported that the ship's movement southwards had been broadcast on British radio. The arrival was not unexpected in the town and if Pusback could not talk to the world, it is more than likely that he listened to what the world had to say about him. The BBC's bulletins even mentioned an injured sailor and they also noted that "several British vessels" had been seen on the Norwegian coast.[16] They were watching the *City of Flint's* progress. Pusback had followed orders, but he did not achieve the objective, namely to go ashore to seek out the German consul. Dingsør used his own initiative and refused to let him go.

The timing of the events as they now began to unfurl is particularly interesting. The ship had hardly come to a halt at Haugesund before the American ambassador had been tipped off by Peters, the United Press International man in Copenhagen, who clearly had a stringer in Haugesund who informed him that the ship had arrived and anchored there. Harriman herself then managed to contact the Norwegian port officer at Haugesund, but he merely referred her back to the person in charge in Oslo, Admiral Diesen. Diesen probably knew no more than the American and was, as Harriman described him, "very reticent."[17] He tried to persuade Harriman to talk to the Foreign Ministry although she told him the office was closed for the weekend. At that point, fortunately for the Admiral, he was saved from further embarrassing stonewalling by an urgent telephone call from Bergen and Harriman had to let him go.

The time was 1840 and it was Tank-Nielsen who wanted to talk to Diesen. Pusback wanted to see his consul, which Dingsør had denied. Now Tank-Nielsen urgently wanted instructions for what to do next.[18]

At 1900 he returned Tank-Nielsen's call, ordering him to keep the ship at Haugesund. A meeting with the German consul was not an acceptable reason for stopping, but even so, Diesen was not prepared to order any further action on his own initiative other than to prevent the ship from leaving.

One of the Norwegian newspapers made a different point: If they had anchored at

Haugesund to provide medical assistance to the injured sailor, they should have brought him ashore to the local hospital. Instead the ship rode at anchor for hours without any such effort, thus raising suspicions and making those watching assume that the medical condition was not the primary reason for the stop.[19] At the same time the paper reported that preparations were underway in Germany to receive the prize.

Lowzow, who had to make up the rules as he went at this stage, told Pusback not to have any contact with the shore for the time being. Pusback promised to comply, although this prevented his deputy from reaching Lanwer as Pusback had asked him to do only minutes earlier.[20] *Olaf Tryggvason's* commanding officer, Briseid, now went ashore to use more effective means of communications with his superiors. He telephoned Tank-Nielsen from a public telephone. At this stage, Lowzow again advised Pusback that he had to remain where he was and that any contact ashore was denied. Pusback accepted this.

In Oslo, a decision to act was slowly coming. Diesen had pointed out to an official at the Foreign Ministry that he could not see any alternatives to actually liberate the ship and intern the Prize Crew. This time the Ministry agreed, but they still felt the issue should be presented both to the Foreign Minister and to the Minister for Defense, who had so far not been involved at all. They were determined to let Foreign Minister Koht front the decision. It was up to Diesen whether he consulted his boss.[21]

They then both started looking for their respective ministers. When the Foreign Ministry telephoned Koht's home in an Oslo suburb, they were advised that the minister was actually in the city—somewhere. They discovered that the Minister was not at the Ministry, nor did his office know of his whereabouts. The man at the center of the affair had disappeared. An exasperated official telephoned Diesen, only to be met with a similar story. Defense Minister Monsen could not be found either. Both ministers would have been aware of the gravity of situation, before literally going to ground somewhere in Oslo. The question still remains: were they deliberate in their efforts not to be available when decisions would be needed over the possible use of Norwegian forces?

At that point the Admiral actually rose to the occasion and decided to order the liberation and the internment. Nevertheless, the enormity of his decision must have hit Diesen once he replaced the receiver. He ordered one last attempt to locate his minister. Meanwhile, the Foreign Ministry telephoned Koht's home again, leaving a message, which summarized Diesen's decision.

To Diesen's great relief, he now finally managed to track down Monsen, who turned out to be "in conference" somewhere with Koht. Conspiracy theorists could easily question their willingness to be found. Both now agreed with the Admiral's decision. Diesen finally telephoned Tank-Nielsen in Bergen to order the necessary action. It would be up to Tank-Nielsen how he executed the order. At that stage the Foreign Ministry seemed to have closed down for the night, leaving the navy to deal with the problem.

In the meantime Briseid had received a crucial order by telephone from the officer in charge of the Second Sea Defense District: "Liberate the Prize. Intern the crew. KA."

"Kommanderende Admiral, Admiral Commanding." This was Tank-Nielsen in Bergen. The Admiral had made up his mind relatively early that evening that under existing legislation he could liberate the *City of Flint*. He was very much in agreement with the officers on the *Olav Tryggvason*. Their report referred to the rules as set out in The Hague

Convention XIII, Article 22. The right to take over a prize which contravened the Convention by anchoring without valid reason. Regardless of the subsequent overtures from Oslo, the Americans later gave Tank-Nielsen all the credit for having decided to free the ship.

Diesen had already demonstrated his "belt and braces" approach to decision making. After he had talked to his man in Bergen, he proceeded to send him a telegram confirming the order. His contribution to the action was to advise Tank-Nielsen, when they discussed the order over the telephone, that it might "cause difficulties from the German side." Tank-Nielsen ought to "be prepared for anything."[22]

When Tank-Nielsen gave the order to take over the ship it was still early in the evening. Haugesund was brimming with scoop-hungry journalists. His action would be analyzed very carefully by strategists in capitals all over the world. The more he could keep under wraps, the more room to maneuver he would have later. He waited until literally the last journalist was seen leaving the pier. This also provided some indication of how close to shore the ships were at this crucial stage in the operation. One journalist, Egil Tresselt, was actually named in this consideration. Tresselt had been particularly persistent and inventive in his pursuit of the *City of Flint*, using his own hired boats along the coast and telephoning Tank-Nielsen for news from various ports as he went.

In the Norwegian navy's file covering the *City of Flint* episode, someone who probably understood the true significance of "being prepared for anything" quickly produced a hand-written note entitled "Precautionary Military Action Regarding the *City of Flint*." Tank-Nielsen had addressed the significance of Diesen's words. At 2100 that evening, Dingsør was preparing the *Olav Tryggvason* to board what was to all intents a hostile warship protected by armed soldiers. In support of the operation, Tank-Nielsen ordered an increase in the level of readiness at all his installations and ships from the southern point of Norway to Trondheim. To the outside world, Tank-Nielsen was placing his forces on a war footing. Although he stopped short of mobilizing more troops, he specified that all should be prepared to set out mines, to prepare the many forts along the coast and to ready all vessels.[23]

As the Norwegian admiral spoke, Oberleutnant zur See Jürgen Östen in U-boat U-61 was on the Norwegian coast just south of Haugesund. It was his first war patrol. He had left Kiel a good week earlier for a patrol along the West Coast of Norway. The *U-61* had been patrolling on a direct southerly course until daybreak Thursday, when he altered his course and headed straight for Skudesnes. Now he could help if needed.

It is not known what Pusback actually thought or did during the hours after the ship came to a shuddering halt in Haugesund harbor. German honor depended upon his decision. He would have known about Hitler's success in Poland. He had heard of the sinking of British naval vessels at Scapa Flow before he left the *Deutschland*. He knew the British Royal Navy was on his tail; even the BBC had said so. That day they kept on saying so in every news bulletin from lunchtime onwards. He knew of the immense American pressure to regain control of the ship from his visit to Murmansk and he had experienced Soviet support for his cause, all without any opportunity to discuss his options with his superiors. What Pusback did not know was how much of an embarrassment the *City of Flint* was becoming for Germany. Was this the real reason for Berlin's effort to stop the ship?

The following Monday, 6 November, *The Times* (London) offered another even more sinister reason for his decision. Rather than continuing to embarrass the powerful neutral United States, an intervention by the Norwegians would provide Hitler with a substantial grievance against Norway, should he ever want to exploit it.

The November nights are dark in Norway; light fades from 1600 in the afternoon. By the time the Admiral ordered the attack, it was pitch black. Briseid took his ship away from the quay and dropped anchor very close to the *City of Flint*'s starboard side. The official American report of the incident stated that the ship was a mere 50 feet away. From there the *Olaf Tryggvason* could keep the *City of Flint*'s bridge illuminated and lay covering fire across her decks and catwalks if a firefight started. Earlier, *Stegg* had dropped anchor to her port side.

Pusback must have watched the ships take up their positions. From their anchorage they could sweep the decks of the *City of Flint* with a lethal field of crossfire, should the need arise. In his report, Pusback noted that the moves happened just before 2300. Yet he did nothing to prepare a resistance.

As the lights gradually went out in the houses along the shore, and the evening drew to a close, Pusback's mind seemed to have been made up. Without posting any guards, he simply went to bed. A good portion of Nazi arrogance may have helped if Pusback simply believed that little Norway was far too weak both militarily and politically to take on the might of the German Reich. On the other hand, Norway was neutral in 1939, struggling to steer a middle course in an international conflict which threatened to engulf the country. Ignoring the provocation meant giving in to German intimidation. Interning the German crew meant maintaining international law and siding with neutral, but far more powerful, America, while at the same time upsetting Adolf Hitler.

The scuttling charges remained in place. Would an ardent Nazi at this stage not want to make the ultimate sacrifice? Instead we see Pusback's genuine colors shine through. If he detonated the charges, he later argued, he would also have damaged at least one of the Norwegian warships. In addition, the wreck of the *City of Flint* would have become a significant obstacle for merchant shipping movements in the harbor basin. This would, per se, have caused wider implications.[24] By accepting his position with honor, he also saved numerous American, Norwegian as well as German lives. Sacrificing lives on the altar of political incompetence was well and truly beyond the call of duty and Pusback was clever enough to see how he could exploit that incompetence in the interest of the common good.

The crew on the *Olaf Tryggvason* prepared for what could turn out to be a very dangerous mission. They knew the Germans were armed, and that they were professional soldiers. The Norwegian crew was mostly comprised of young men drafted into the navy to do their national service. By 2330 all preparations were complete and the *Olaf Tryggvason*'s second-in-command, Captain Dingsør, accompanied by three officers and 22 men, all heavily armed, quickly boarded the *City of Flint*.[25] Both of the Norwegian warships had prepared their artillery and all guns were turned towards the decks of the *City of Flint*. Only when the Norwegian boarding party was aboard the *City of Flint* did the Norwegian ships turn on their large searchlights, suddenly illuminating the freighter in harsh white light from stem to stern.

In the American ship, Chief Logan and his engine crew were quickly sent down to the engine room with express orders not to allow any Germans access. Similarly, the ship's officers were posted at positions where they could watch the rest of the Prize Crew. In the written version of events, Gainard noted that Pusback took plenty of time before he finally received the Norwegian officers.[26] Logan, on the other hand, praised the speed of the Norwegian operation. The Prize Crew had set scuttling charges virtually as soon as they came aboard the ship. Given time, Logan was convinced they would have blown up the *City of Flint*. German skippers actually had standing orders to scuttle their ships rather than to permit them to fall into the hands of the enemy.[27] Others present at the time thought that perhaps Pusback and Gainard had an understanding not to destroy the *City of Flint* if it could be avoided.[28]

Captain Dingsør informed Pusback that the Norwegian authorities had decided to intern the Prize Crew and liberate the ship. He also requested assurances that the Germans would not act in any way that could endanger people or the ship. Pusback shook his hand as to confirm that he promised to abstain from any wrongdoing. At that stage Dingsør left it to Pusback to order his crew to hand over arms and ammunition, pack their belongings and be ready to disembark within 30 minutes. It was all executed calmly and in good order. According to Tank-Nielsen, the Norwegians boarded the *City of Flint* as gentlemen and the officers of the Prize Crew behaved in a similar manner.

At 10 minutes past midnight the German Prize Crew were transferred to the *Olaf Tryggvason*. Arms and ammunition were taken care of and the Germans were allocated the cadets' mess and quarters.

On request from Pusback, Briseid did allow a brief meeting with German vice-consul Lanwer, who was now contacted. Lanwer must have been waiting for the call. It took him less than half an hour to reach the ship. This was hardly the meeting the Germans had envisaged after such a long and successful journey, with Pusback in custody and Briseid present for the entire meeting. Pusback claimed that he really did not know that he was not permitted to anchor. He only knew that the time limit on his stay in Norwegian waters had been lifted.

As he returned to Hotel Bristol, Lanwer made at least two telephone calls. The first was more than likely to the German embassy in Oslo. What was said remains unknown. He then rang the consul general in Bergen, Dr. Bischoff. Tank-Nielsen had planned his operation well. Not only did he succeed in taking the ship back without spilling any blood, but he also deployed staff to listen in on the German consul's telephone calls. Lanwer was brief and to the point. He merely informed Bischoff of what had happened and that the Prize Crew would be moved to Bergen. Oslo had no similar listening operation in place at that stage.[29]

Once Commander Briseid had informed his admiral of the successful outcome it was time to formally break the news to the Americans. Tank-Nielsen called the American consul at Bergen and told him to contact Ambassador Harriman immediately with the news that the job was done. According to Mrs. Harriman, Tank-Nielsen had at that stage not yet even informed Admiral Diesen at Naval Headquarters in Oslo. It was around 0100 before Tank-Nielsen telephoned to inform him of the latest developments. By the time Dunlap managed to get through to Oslo on the telephone it was around 0130. The Americans were asked not to make the news public until the Norwegian authorities had formally endorsed the Rear Admiral's actions.

The naval staff did endorse Tank-Nielsen's liberation of the American ship rather quickly; they could hardly have done anything else. The decision-making process at Oslo HQ was apparently sped up by the fact that it was the weekend and a number of those who might have procrastinated or even objected to his actions were not around. Tank-Nielsen had achieved the perfect timing for his actions; he had conducted the entire operation from the comfort of his own home, using a normal telephone line.[30]

A launch was dispatched from the *Olav Tryggvason* to bring Captain Gainard over for a brief conference with the Norwegians. Briseid suggested that as he was shortly to take his ship north to Bergen, Gainard might want to accompany him.

As soon as Admiral Diesen knew the operation had been successfully completed, he tried to contact the Foreign Ministry to give them the news. Bearing in mind that the Admiral had repeatedly managed to reach Foreign Ministry staff over the previous few days, it was nothing short of astounding that his report of the event admits to failure on this point. It was the weekend and the offices were empty. The first official Norwegian statement on the liberation, issued to the Norwegian press agency NTB and flashed around the world, was therefore issued not with ministerial approval, but on the newly discovered authority of Admiral Diesen. Then caution prevailed once more and he marked the written report on the final part of the saga "SECRET."[31]

The Norwegians, keen to move the ship to a safer location, further from the open sea, strongly encouraged Gainard to sail with them north to Bergen as soon as possible. The two Norwegian pilots who had been stuck on board during this tense exchange were now asked to take the ship on one final journey before disembarking.[32] At 0230 the two ships weighed anchor, heading north. Briseid's report stated that the *Olaf Tryggvason* anchored in Bergen at 0745 that morning. According to local papers, the *City of Flint* dropped anchor at Puddefjorden.[33] By chance the anchorage was just below the windows of the local merchant navy training college and within sight of their liberators, the *Olav Tryggvason*, which was riding at anchor a little further up the fjord, close to the naval headquarters at Marineholmen. At that stage it was far from clear where the Prize Crew would be interned.

The telephone lines out of Bergen were humming during the night. It is a fair guess that the German consul general in Bergen, Dr. Bischoff, was briefing their side as

City of Flint the day after being liberated, now safe in Bergen, Norway, about 5 November 1939. She was anchored just below the Bergen Maritime Academy (courtesy Bergen Havnekontor's Arkiv, Bergen Byarkiv).

American Consul Dunlap was on the phone to Oslo to brief the head of the American Legation, Florence Harriman. She had the first coded telegram to Hull on the wire by 0200 that morning, merely an hour after the actual handover of the ship.[34] Tank-Nielsen had even furnished some extra details to the report himself when he briefed Harriman of the lucky conclusion of the affair. She, in turn, could not praise Tank-Nielsen enough for his support and assistance over the incident and the Admiral continued to provide substantial support and assistance to the Americans over the next few days. The Admiral was also playing fair by the Germans. Just after 0400 that eventful morning, Tank-Nielsen telephoned Dr. Bischoff to explain to him, personally, what had transpired.

The British vice-consul in Haugesund was equally quick to report to London. Already the next day, Saturday, 4 November, His Majesty's consul in Bergen had an Admiralty signal offering a specific "indirect" convoy route for the *City of Flint*, should her Master choose to continue his journey. The trouble was how to convey the offer to the Americans. Members of the international press corps had descended on Bergen. Now they were laying siege on the American Consulate.[35] Dunlap had disconnected his telephone and actually left his house to stay with friends that Saturday night. The winning side needed time to consolidate and plan the next move.

In England, the *North East Gazette's* Saturday edition announced on the front page that the *City of Flint* was expected to dock in Glasgow four days later. According to the paper's sources, on arrival at Clydeside, representatives from the United States Lines would be effecting the discharge of the cargo.

At this stage in the war, the Norwegian Department of Trade introduced a form of censorship, but one that made perfect sense. By Monday, 6 November, the Board of the Norwegian Telephone and Telegraph Company circulated a note informing their staff of the fact that no one was allowed to disclose any type of shipping or air traffic information. Disclosure of departures, arrivals, cargo or destinations could result in imprisonment. Telegrams intended for publication in the press were included in this ban, thus making life more difficult for any foreign journalists reporting on the *City of Flint* from now on. On the other hand, it helped protect the crews of all ships moving along the Norwegian coast at the time. Britain had already introduced convoys from Norway to offer some protection across the North Sea.

With the benefit of the time lag, American papers had the chance to recast their front pages. Saturday morning, the *New York Daily News* filled their tabloid-sized front page with the following message:

> NORSE HOLD
> NAZIS; FLINT
> FREE, SAILS

At a cost of 2 cents for the newspaper, few would have resisted such a lead story.[36]

The official German news agency also published the news of the *City of Flint's* release, together with the report from the Norwegian Admiralty, but there was no official German statement available. That did not, however, mean that Berlin had settled down for a quiet weekend. By midday the Naval High Command knew that the *City of Flint* had been moved to Bergen. From their perspective, the main issue was that continued German access to the ship now seemed particularly unlikely.[37] Nevertheless they were not giving up. At their Saturday meeting they stressed that a forceful and responsible effort was now required by "*everybody*" who could possibly help.

Regardless of the planned actions, in Berlin the Navy had already started their post-mortem on the situation, and they clearly wanted to find someone to blame. Near the top of the list was the new vice-consul Lanwer at Haugesund. After such a short time in post, he had clearly failed to recognize the importance of this ship. Lanwer had also suffered from the misconception that he should order the ship in to Haugesund. This order had caused the problem. The Navy did not leave all the blame with the Foreign Ministry. The Prize Commander, Pusback, was now, according to the High Command, found not to have been up to the task expected of him, but this begged the question as to what type of training or experience could possibly prepare future Prize Commanders for such events.[38]

Dönitz, in his role as the officer in charge of the U-boats (BdU), also attended the meeting and suggested a more aggressive approach. He suggested that *U-61*, supported by other U-boats, should attack the *City of Flint* again in order to re-take the prize and bring her into a German port. The meeting seemed to have accepted Dönitz's proposal, but unfortunately he returned the next day, on Sunday, to declare defeat. The bad weather forecasts coupled with fuel shortage in the returning boats made his plan impossible to implement.

This only left Östen in *U-61*, which presently was standing by off Korsfjorden near Marsteinen Lighthouse. The first 14 km of the fjord from the mouth are over 600 meters deep, in fact far deeper than the North Sea itself. On its way north, back to Bergen, the *City of Flint* crossed the fjord escorted by *Olav Tryggvason*, both of them totally unaware of the presence of a U-boat. Nevertheless, the U-boat skipper did not seem unduly worried about the existence of Norwegian territorial waters and potential violation of the Norwegian Neutrality Regulations.[39] The original plan had been for the U-boats to be waiting at a traditional exit/entry points for the supposedly "secret" shipping movements between Britain and Norway. By Sunday, Östen was patrolling the coast, well inside Norwegian territorial waters. In the early evening he entered the fjord itself and he remained there until the next morning. He would have been at least 10 km inside Norwegian territorial waters and he was less than 40 km from the port of Bergen.

9

Pawn

Ambassador Harriman wasted no time in grasping the seriousness of the situation. Her brief telegrams to Washington early that Saturday illustrated well how she now used her contacts to unravel the whole story and prepare to take control as soon as possible. By 1000 that morning she had arranged to catch the Sunday night train which left Oslo at 2230 arriving in Bergen around 0900 the following morning. Ironically, Rear Admiral Stephan, the German naval attaché, followed her across the mountains. The two adversaries were actually on the same train and did not know until breakfast.

As soon as the *City of Flint* anchored in Bergen Harbor, U.S. consul Dunlap came on board. During their meeting, Gainard explained that he had actually heard the order to anchor at Haugesund being shouted across from the *Schwaben* as she passed.[1] In her fourth dispatch to Hull that morning, Harriman could confirm that the American crew was well and that the captain was at the consulate giving his report.[2]

At the German consulate in Bergen, life was more difficult. Early on Saturday morning, Dr. Bischoff had managed to contact Rear Admiral Tank-Nielsen to learn more about the fate of the American ship. To his surprise, the Prize Commander was already in Bergen, on board the Norwegian naval ship *Olav Tryggvason*, where they were held pending a more appropriate place to intern them. The Admiral was very cautious at this early stage and he would not permit Bischoff to see any of the internees. Tank-Nielsen pointed out that he had not yet seen them himself and until he was satisfied, he was not allowing any outsiders access.

Tank-Nielsen went directly from Bischoff's telephone call to the anchored *Olav Tryggvason*. During the morning he talked to Pusback before returning to his office. Again Bischoff was on the telephone and this time, the Admiral invited him to meet Pusback. The invitation came, according to Bischoff, around 1100 and shortly after he was being ferried out to the ship where he first had a brief meeting with Tank-Nielsen. The Admiral then actually granted him the meeting with Pusback "under four eyes" as Dr. Bischoff put it.[3] During this private conversation Pusback explained how he felt that he had not considered himself sufficiently senior to have the authority not to comply with Lanwer's orders. In his note to von Neuhaus in Oslo, the consul added that in Lanwer's view, the German State Transport Ministry had issued sufficient standing orders for him to act as he did. They were all passing the blame along to somebody else.

The ship owners too, moved very quickly. By lunchtime, the United States Lines of New York had persuaded Cordell Hull to send a telegram to the consulate in Bergen. They wanted a full Hold Survey and assurances that the ship had ample supplies of food and water on board before leaving port. They knew the ship was center stage in a big and very public power game in a neutral country where all sides in the conflict could deploy their agents and diplomatic staff. All the Americans could do was to keep their fingers crossed and hope that Captain Gainard used his discretion. The pressure of world publicity was now added to all his concerns, just as he had regained his ship and his freedom. The owners indicated that they "desired" that the captain avoided any controversial publicity, especially any comments related to various governments.[4]

At the German Embassy, von Neuhaus must have been at his desk early, nearly as early as Lanwer in Haugesund. By the time Lanwer spoke to von Neuhaus that morning, he had spent a substantial amount of time preparing for what was to be a difficult exchange.[5] According to von Neuhaus' record, he talked to Lanwer at 0930, by which time he would also have been expecting a call from Consul General Bischoff in Bergen.

According to Norwegian records, the conversation took place around 0900. At the Foreign Ministry, they had acted quickly and ordered a listening watch to be mounted by the State Telephone Company. The Listening Control Unit, the Norwegian State's secret eavesdropping operation, located at room 416 at the main telephone exchange in Oslo, was ready. The man in charge, Captain Andvord,

Rear-Admiral Carsten Tank-Nielsen, the man in charge of naval operations in Western Norway, including the successful armed operation to liberate the *City of Flint* (courtesy FMU 11, Marinemuseet, Norway).

used an expert stenographer, Ms. Skavang, to capture the conversation between the German diplomat in Oslo and the Haugesund consulate.

According to Andvord, von Neuhaus was so angry that his voice was shaking as he spoke to the consul.[6]

Pusback, on his part, claimed not to have been aware of the ban on anchoring or stopping of any sort. Lanwer argued that the naval leadership, by telegram, had ordered the consulates in Narvik, Trondheim, Bergen and Haugesund to provide support for the *City of Flint* prior to departure, or as the order put it: "vor Auslaufen zu unterstützen."

When Pusback had raised the issue of anchoring at Haugesund with the Norwegian officer in charge, he had unambiguously refused the request. Lanwer claimed that he had followed the case of the *City of Flint* closely and was well aware of the prestige associated with the prize, and all the orders he had received left him in no doubt as to the importance of his own role in it all. He acted accordingly to ensure that the correct message would be provided. From his perspective, he had achieved what he set out to do.

There was little Lanwer could do at this stage to deflect the blame and the accusations hurled at him. The naval leadership in Berlin noted that he had only recently taken up his position. He had basically misunderstood the significance of the ship and of how to respond to an order to support its journey.[7] To make matters worse, Paulsen, the Master of the *Schwaben*, described Lanwer as a young country lad from Kattowitz who had never had any experience with the ocean, and who "did not have a clue" ("hatte keine Ahnung").[8]

For von Neuhaus personally, there was a lot at stake. As far as his career was concerned, the timing of the *City of Flint* affair was perfect. Only a week earlier, the German ambassador to Norway, Dr. Salm, had died, leaving the 52-year-old career diplomat temporarily in charge. Although Dr. Salm's replacement would be announced shortly, von Neuhaus' prospects could hardly be damaged by a successful outcome regarding the issues around the American prize.

The Germans immediately objected to the Norwegian treatment of the prize, and were rebuffed by Koht, who argued that Norway had acted in accordance with the Hague Conventions of 1907. Von Neuhaus arrived at Koht's office Saturday morning to lodge yet another complaint. The letter, which von Neuhaus handed Koht during this meeting, was less than a page long. Germany threatened the worst possible consequences if the *City of Flint* was permitted to leave Haugesund. At that stage, however, the ship was already at anchor in Bergen.

The manner, in which the protest was delivered, however, left Koht incandescent with rage. He had not thought it possible that a foreign diplomat could use such offensive language.[9] The American Minister to Norway later claimed she had never seen Koht so disturbed.[10] Together with the tone of the letter, this was bullying of the purest form.

Koht's own notes from this strained meeting have survived.[11] He claimed to have told von Neuhaus that, under the circumstances, this must surely have been the best outcome for Germany. In fact, Koht added, he even believed that Germany had been actively seeking to achieve just such a solution. It would have been regrettable if this prize, with so many Americans on board, had become embroiled in fighting with British warships.

In the middle of all the political battles, a representative for Norwegian radio telephoned Koht. The Columbia Broadcasting Corporation, which would like to arrange an interview with Captain Gainard, had approached them. It would be for only 10 minutes but would be broadcast live to America. Koht was against the interview and said so. Then he added that his decision had only been made orally and that radio staff were not permitted to admit that the Foreign Ministry had been consulted.[12] The unseen hand of the untrained media manipulator again.

By Sunday morning, the loss of the prize was included in the daily situation report to Adolf Hitler himself. The vice-consul at Haugesund was being blamed for it all.[13] Hitler was in Berlin, at his office at the Reich Chancellery, grappling with far more serious issues than a single neutral freighter. By 1300 he had to decide whether to give the order to proceed to final preparations for the invasion of France, or stand down his forces. Just before lunch his shouted abuse crushed Field Marshall Brauchitsch, head of the armed forces, who wanted to put off the invasion. At 1330 Hitler gave the go-ahead for the invasion to take place a week later. In the event, after two days, he was forced to postpone the operation due to weather problems.

Mr. C.A. Edmond, the British consul in Bergen, met the Americans at their offices on Sunday morning. For the first time he was face to face with the man at the center of the drama, Captain Joseph Gainard. In fact, Edmond managed to sneak him past the waiting journalists without them spotting him. They travelled across town to the British consulate down at the harbor for a meeting with the British shipping adviser. Behind this innocuous title was the person who actually organized the convoys between Bergen and Methill in Scotland; all were escorted by the British navy. At this meeting Gainard told them categorically that the ship that captured them was the *Deutschland* and that she had been operating remarkably far north—as high as 79° N.[14] The British also learned the names of the various ships Gainard had seen while in port in Murmansk. It was perhaps symptomatic for the unease Gainard felt with it all that he was most anxious that his American compatriots never learned what information he had shared with the British diplomats. None of the personnel from the American Embassy had formally debriefed him yet, and by providing information to British officers, he, a neutral American, was providing direct support to a nation at war.

In Oslo, there was no restful weekend for the Norwegian Foreign Minister. Since seeing the German diplomat the day before, he and his team of advisers had produced an official Norwegian reply. Von Neuhaus was summoned back to the Foreign Office on Sunday afternoon at 1800 for a further rebuttal of his country's belligerent and bellicose accusations. The Norwegian pointed out that all Germany actually achieved by using such "grand phrases for such small incidents" was to damage the relationship between two friendly powers.[15]

Koht also informed von Neuhaus that a purely factual account of the incident would be issued to the press later that evening. The Norwegian naively felt the need to attempt to repair relations, which he had not planned to damage in the first place. Koht explained that he had, in fact, not included anything in this statement about the actual threats issued by the German government. After all, it was a German Prize Commander who had brought the ship into Norwegian waters. He did not, however, admit to having provided copies of Germany's threats to American Ambassador Harriman whom he had invited in for a meeting a couple of hours earlier. In fact, he had provided Mrs. Harriman with all the relevant papers in the case.

This had been a multi-layered affair from the beginning. By the time of his meeting with the American, Koht merely continued the behind-the-scenes part. In his discussion with Mrs. Harriman, Koht attempted to secure some extra measure of public support from the Americans. The two discussed a planned radio broadcast from Bergen, which was to let the captain tell his fellow Americans at home of his experience under German command. According to Koht's own brief note of the meeting, he merely expressed his full confidence in Harriman's ability to handle the interview as she had been invited to participate. Her version of events is interesting and different. According to the Ambassador, Koht not only encouraged her to do the interview; he actually gave her "a set of words," which he would be particularly pleased if she used: "The *City of Flint* case has been handled absolutely perfectly by Norway in accordance with the Hague Convention concerning the rights and duties of neutrals in sea warfare which was signed by both Germany and Norway."[16]

It was hardly surprising that Harriman sent the text in an urgent telegram to the American Secretary of State, Cordell Hull, as soon as she got out of the meeting. It was not an everyday event to experience such blatant attempts to influence the views of another country's diplomats. Hull's reply was waiting for her in Bergen by the time she arrived the next morning. Washington wanted to decide what was to be issued in terms of official publicity, and they would do it themselves, in their own good time. In other words, Koht had to mind his own business.

The ship was riding at anchor in Bergen harbor in order to remain out of reach from the news hungry media. Nonetheless, by Monday afternoon, her story graced the front page of a local paper. Egil Tressel, the journalist the navy had wanted out of the way before they boarded in Haugesund, had just learned what he later came to see as the scoop of his career.[17] He had called on the crew on Sunday afternoon, bringing them Norwegian and English language magazines and in return, he received a very detailed account of the journey as the sailors had experienced it. Even some off the sailors' own notes were made available to the enterprising young journalist. Small wonder his paper turned over the entire front page to the story. That morning they alone had the detailed account of one of the biggest selling stories of the Western world.[18] Young Tresselt had been aboard the ship disguised as a newspaper boy. United Press accredited Tresselt as a "staff correspondent" and syndicated the story in the U.S. and Canada. The crew was confined to the ship while Gainard was ashore. None of them had seen the inside of a bar since they left America and they were growing increasingly restless. They too wanted to go ashore, to feel solid ground under their feet and to escape from the inevitable smell of "ship," a mixture of fuel-oil and sea, which permeated their confined little world. It was to prove a volatile blend.

The Norwegians had clearly judged the situation right when they requested that Gainard keep his crew on board during the first few days after the rescue. Any wrong statement to the press could have complicated matters enormously for the Norwegians. When finally "let loose," the majority of the crew basically just disappeared, clearly determined to let off steam and to recover from the incredibly tense and stressful time they had just been through. On average they went absent without leave for nine days each. The worst offender was not seen for 17 days. Yet Gainard, who knew all too well what stress they had been under, dealt with the violations in a mild manner without any unnecessary restrictions being imposed.

There was no way of reaching Ambassador Harriman while she was on the train travelling across the mountains accompanied only by her two secretaries. Instead they routed her messages via the Bergen consulate, including one instructing her to stay well clear of the captain's planned radio broadcast from Bergen![19] Washington argued that the official publicity around the case should be orchestrated and managed from the American capital where they could see the "whole picture." The *City of Flint* had now become a political issue, which was far greater than just the fate of the cargo or perhaps even the wellbeing of the crew.

The plans for the broadcast from Bergen were progressing jointly by National and Columbia broadcasting companies. This was in the age of great broadcasters like Eric Sevareid broadcasting live from Paris, and William Shirer from Berlin. These pioneering journalists used the radio to reach their American audiences and to provide some snapshots of the life under the Swastika or in the countries struggling to avoid being covered by this menacing cloak. The broadcast would transport images from a west Norwegian town and the dramatic rescue of young Americans right onto the breakfast tables of East Coast America.

In Washington, Roosevelt wasted no time in pursuing his new neutrality policy. At precisely four minutes past midday, he lifted the arms embargo, and within minutes of this signing ceremony the President proceeded to establish a war zone from 60° N, just south of Bergen, to south of Spain. American ships were now forbidden to sail into this area to the east of Ireland, which covered some of their most lucrative markets. The Norwegian suggestion to Gainard to move his ship north to Bergen as the diplomatic storm broke around the ship was particularly useful. In Bergen, they would be at a port with an American consulate. As it turned out, they were also outside the new U.S. exclusion zone.

The American ambassador stepped from the train at 0900 Monday morning and was immediately faced with the international press corps. Fortunately her local consul, Dunlap, had his car and drove her across the compact center of the city to Hotel Bristol where rooms had been reserved for her and her staff. She was hardly installed in her quarters before the British consul came to pay his respects.

At a lunch, given by Mrs. Harriman, Norwegian Admiral Tank-Nielsen was one of the guests. It was far more a council of war than a social affair. The Admiral advised Mrs. Harriman to seek to have the cargo discharged at Bergen. Tank-Nielsen felt that such an action would allow the Germans a measure of "saving face." Furthermore they might well decide to leave the ship alone if she departed from Bergen, were she in ballast.[20] Leaving laden with the original cargo, German pride was far more likely to push them to attempt to sink the ship. Even if it was known that she was bringing the cargo directly back to an American port, the threat of sinking might prevail. Thinking of the value to British industry of the cargo, Edmond agreed.

To the British it seemed that to have the cargo on a Norwegian quayside would be far more attractive than to see it return all the way across the Atlantic. These were dangerous times for shipping in the North Sea. Hardly a day passed without reports in the newspapers in western Norway of wreckage, of lifeboats with dead sailors drifting ashore, of ships being torpedoed or of mysterious planes. All seen by fishermen, who could tell stories of the sharp sound of gunfire or the dull thud of explosions reaching them from over the horizon.

Edmond mentioned again that the offer which he had made to Gainard the previous morning still stood. They could attempt to sail the ship to a British port via an "indirect" convoy route. In order to discuss the convoy proposal in detail, Harriman agreed to meet the British shipping adviser the following morning.[21]

The British consulate's office in Bergen overlooked the harbor. On the floor below them were the offices of the owner of the building, Thorvald Halvorsen, who had very strong pro–German sympathies and after the war was one of the first to be prosecuted for his activities.[22] At this stage though, these activities were limited to attempting to import goods into Norway for re-export to Germany, much to the chagrin of Miles Tollemache, the young export officer at the British consulate whose job it was to stop this very activity. Halvorsen even reported Miles to his Minister in Oslo for harassment. [23]

Harriman soon heard how vulnerable individual ships would be when sailing between Norway and Britain. Norwegian authorities encouraged her to advise the American owners to unload in Bergen and either sell or transfer the cargo quietly to other ships. The *City of Flint* would become a real prestige target for every German submariner operating in the North Sea. Although this was likely to prolong the involuntary stay in Bergen by a further week to ten days, it was preferable to taking the cargo into the war zone, which would violate President Roosevelt's recently introduced regulation.

Working on a merchant navy ship at sea provides routine and predictability for the crew. Normally such a period would be "topped and tailed" by periods on shore. For the *City of Flint*, this was just not the case. They had left New York on Tuesday, 3 October. A full month later, the crew was still stuck on the ship even though they had been told they were free. This was really starting to rankle.

With so much media interest, the State Department was not of a mind to allow the crew out of their isolation just yet. Gainard and his officers had to ease most of the media pressure first; only then would the rest of the crew be allowed ashore. In fairness, there was simply no way the crew could possibly know that they were in the middle of an international political storm where a wrong word could have untold consequences. They were nevertheless becoming increasingly restless and uncooperative.

The American crew now met Mrs. Harriman in freedom and on their own ship. She came on board to congratulate the crew and to thank them for the effort to bring the tense episode to such a successful conclusion. At the same time, Mrs. Harriman wanted to help Gainard assure the crew that they would be granted shore leave as soon as the U.S. State Department had sorted out their rights and that of the ship and her cargo. They had been away for a long time. Like many of his fellow sailors, Rhoads, the first mate, felt he looked like a wild man; they were badly in need of haircuts.

Pusback had explained to his vice-consul that in his view, the greatest dangers had actually disappeared by the time the ship reached Haugesund. Berlin should re-think their line of argument and, the German consul in Bergen now felt, they should focus on an early release of the Prize Crew and camouflage the change of heart as a gesture of goodwill towards the United States.[24]

While all this was happening around him, Gainard was finally able to report to his country's authorities on the ordeal with which he had been struggling so successfully for the last three weeks. And while he was doing that, his Ambassador, Mrs. Harriman was busy behind the scenes sorting out the fate of the cargo. The Norwegians had by now formally released the ship. But it was not over yet. In glorious isolation the press was trying to work out the story. Gainard was busy providing the authorities with his perspective. Harriman was feeding Cordell Hull her observations and the intelligence she was gleaning from her informants and from Norwegian Government sources. The Germans all the while were fighting their rear-guard action to minimize the political impact.

One of several points in Gainard's lengthy report, which triggered a virtually immediate response, was that the ship had no engine trouble when at Murmansk, but had undergone regular boiler overhaul during her stay there. His report was sent telegraphically to Washington very late on Monday, 6 November. After Gainard finished his report and it had been typed, checked and coded prior to transmission. At the American consulate, it took the vice-consul 14 hours to prepare and code the entire statement. Harriman had only arrived in Bergen at 0900 that Monday morning to receive the report. We know from the report of her escape from Norway in April 1940 that she always carried embassy codes with her.[25]

The Americans were working to maintain a neutral line to all sides over the *City of Flint*. Gainard was deservedly praised repeatedly by Dunlap and by Harriman for his role. In the time honored tradition of the chase for a "scoop" he received several offers for cash payments ranging from $200 to $1000 for an interview, all of which he rejected. When he finally made his speech to the assembled press corps, he later repeated it all in a live broadcast to the U.S. via a link provided by NRK, the Norwegian broadcasting company.[26]

The broadcast was a triumph for the American network NBC, who dispatched their European correspondent, Max Jordan, to do the interview.[27]

Gainard knew he was on his own; Harriman and Dunlap had declined invitations to participate. The pressure was on the captain alone to pitch the interview at the correct level and to avoid insulting any of the powers with an interest in this affair. The speech had been repeated by Gainard several times; it was a carefully edited version of his official statement. He knew his speech would be discussed in Berlin, in London and in Washington as well as in Moscow. A sobering thought for any spokesman in 1939. The delivery was confident, fluent and his diction was clear. The speaker came across as alert and experienced in his craft. It was a well-honed and competent speech. Gainard spoke slowly, well aware of the immense audience he had at home and the impact his words could have on public opinion.[28]

Members of the Scandinavian press were delighted to observe that the broadcast went part of the way to America on a German cable.[29] Max Jordan later admitted to some trepidation over the use of this link. During a recent speech by Finnish President Erkko, the same cross–German link suffered from sudden technical problems. This time everything "went over splendidly in every way."[30]

The unrelenting pressures of being constantly watched by the German captors was one of the points highlighted by the NBC reporter at the end of his interview. Armed with pistols, hand grenades and bayonets, they never eased off their roles as guards. The captives did not know what orders Pusback had, where he received them or why he took the ship seemingly aimlessly across the icy waters of the North Atlantic or the Barents Sea. Without being able to tell the world where they were, what they were doing or even that they were still alive, all they could do was listen to the radio learning of the increasingly hectic search for them executed by the British navy.

Following the radio interview, Gainard returned to the American consulate where he briefly faced the assembled press corps. Again, he had to run through the story of the journey to Bergen. He evaded any questions on the fate of the cargo, which triggered a range of rumors about sales or auctions. Once away from the press, he joined Dunlap and Mrs. Harriman for an evening of discussion over the way to handle the ship.

On the Tuesday, 7 November, Tank-Nielsen received a detailed report of the inventory of the German arms as surrendered by the Prize Crew when the Norwegian soldiers took over. All the equipment was deposited at the naval base that afternoon.[31]

German weapons[32]

	At surrender	Tromsø Report
Hand grenades	35	12
Rifles	4	4
Rifle ammunition (rounds)	150	0
Pistols	17	17
Pistol ammunition (rounds)	387	0
Detonators	14	0
Explosive charges	3	0
Zeitzünder (Timer)	4	0
Signal pistols	2	2
Signal ammunition (rounds)	100	0

According to Pusback, the Zeitzünders, the timing devices for the explosive charges, should be destroyed as soon as possible as they were very dangerous to handle, which made their absence from the earlier report even more serious.

The list of equipment is very close to the suggestions actually detailed in the German Prize Instructions.[33] The Tromsø inventory, on the other hand, was clearly wrong. It was impossible to determine whether this was due to incompetence, design or deception. Alternatively, the Prize Crew arsenal could have been augmented while at Murmansk. The German ships there had supplied Pusback with a complete set of charts for the Norwegian coast southwards from Tromsø. In fact, the Norwegians discovered a total of 73 charts on board the *City of Flint*.[34]

Amidst all the wrangling over the ship, the cargo, the location of the ship or the status and fate of the German Prize Crew, the Norwegian authorities threw yet another stone into this political pond. With a superb sense of timing, it was announced from Kongsvinger in southeastern Norway that their ancient fortress would from now on play host to the interned German Prize Crew. Guards had already been called up and the new inhabitants were expected to arrive on Wednesday. The Norwegians were clearly planning to play this by the book.

It sent a very clear message to Germany that their prisoners were not likely to be set free in the foreseeable future. Norwegian preparations were far too elaborate for a mere short-term solution.

That morning the German consul in Bergen summarized his report of the meetings in a coded telegram sent to the Embassy in Oslo, to Naval High Command, and to the Foreign Ministry in Berlin. He and the visiting naval attaché certainly felt that Admiral Tank-Nielsen had done what he could to see the prize safely into Swedish waters. The Admiral had even posted patrol vessels at exposed positions and seen off an English attempt to contact the *City of Flint*. The Germans felt that the misfortune could be traced back to overzealous and false orders from the vice-consul at Haugesund.[35]

As the Germans went on the offensive in the press, complaining over the Norwegian action, Koht had to respond. In his new rebuttal, the diplomat claimed that Norway had acted in accordance with the Hague Conventions. In the media, it appeared as if the *City of Flint* had only called at Tromsø once. The second time, according to Koht, the ship merely passed through the Tromsø Sound. Norwegian intelligence reports, on the other hand, confirm that the ship stopped.[36]

British sources had already informed the Americans that the ship anchored on its way south, in Norwegian territorial waters, that the German consul in Tromsø had been on board for the second time in less than two weeks. This actually constituted a breach of The Hague Convention XIII. There was no emergency justifying the stop let alone allowing a German diplomat on board for advice and support. The Norwegians had told the Americans at the time that the ship had not stopped, so they could hardly admit to any falsehood at this stage.

By now the German attempts to free their soldiers and the cargo via diplomatic means started to change. The U.S. Neutrality Act had been passed a few days earlier. Arms sales to nations at war were now allowed. Although no such cargo could be carried on a U.S. keel, British ships could now come to the U.S. to bring home badly needed supplies of arms and ammunition. Germany itself might even want to seek to top up their stockpiles from American sources, so a favorable image in U.S. media was more important than ever. The navy was keen to be seen not to hinder the *City of Flint* from returning home.

That did not mean, however, that they stopped watching the cargo or the ship.

10

Cargo

Instead of visiting the British shipping adviser in Bergen, Mrs. Harriman postponed the meeting until the following morning and went off to the *City of Flint* with a Paramount film crew, who had been sent all the way from Stockholm—a journey which would have taken nearly 24 hours to complete. They spent several hours on the ship, creating substantial footage for American newsreels.[1] This proved to be particularly trying for Gainard.

The Paramount journalist had originally planned to use only a minute and a half of Gainard talking, but when he saw Gainard's draft, he increased the speaking time to six minutes. The film company expected to earn between $15,000 and $20,000 on the piece, without paying Gainard anything.

On the return from the ship, they were landed at the naval base by a barge from the Norwegian navy and they started to film Gainard's actual speech. The long and demanding filming on board the ship had brought the memories flooding back to Gainard: the armed guards, the warship, the explosive charges in the middle of the night. He simply broke down; it was all too much for him. Admiral Tank-Nielsen quickly intervened and gently led Gainard to his own private quarters at the base, where he lay down for a rest. The others simply waited. He turned down the Admiral's offer of a whisky to fortify himself; Gainard did not touch alcohol. Once recovered, he easily completed his speech.[2]

The British were still very eager to please. Captain St. John suggested that the offer of protection might stand, even if the ship was to return directly to an American port. Britain would provide escort at least part of the way.

In Washington, the U.S. State Department made it clear to the United States Lines that the Department would prefer to see the ship unloaded at Bergen and returned empty by a safe route as soon as possible. If not, they would prefer to see the entire cargo returned to the U.S.[3] The same message was also passed to Harriman in Bergen.

As the office closed, the Americans had not yet responded to the British offer of an escort. The British consul on the other hand knew that he was entertaining Mrs. Harriman the following evening and hoped that by then she would be able to bring him up to date on American plans.

Lanwer was recalled for consultation and he spent some time in Berlin producing a detailed five-page memorandum on his view of the incident. It was a robust defense of his actions. He even quoted the number of telegraphic orders issued to him regarding the fact that he had been ordered to communicate with the *City of Flint* over her departure time from Kopervik.[4] Lanwer was convincing, and was soon to be back at Haugesund. By Christmas he was involved in planning the breakthrough to Germany for the passenger liner *St. Louis*.

Unbeknownst to them, German Naval High Command had, at least internally, conceded defeat. They had heard that the *City of Flint* cargo was being unloaded at Bergen, which meant that it was finally placed beyond their control. They also noted the American no-go zone for U.S. shipping. As European waters were declared a war zone, the German navy saw this as an advantage. There was no longer any danger of upsetting the neutral Americans as long as any ship the German navy attacked was within the closed zone. Crucially, it also meant that Britain would no longer be able to benefit from American shipping capacity in maintaining the war effort.

The Germans now wanted to inform the Americans that Germany accepted the return of the *City of Flint* to America. The Foreign Ministry had even been in touch with the Naval High Command over this and Dönitz had been told to order his U-boats to leave the *City of Flint* alone.[5]

On Wednesday, 8 November, Mrs. Harriman had contacted Hull in Washington. The Ambassador was concerned that an official American statement would need to be released to the press with details of the actual cargo. She added that she would like to make public the neutral destination of the ship.[6] This was a very interesting approach, bearing in mind that the ship had been seized while in transit between the U.S. and England. The majority of the cargo was destined for British companies, although some belonged to companies in neutral Ireland. The cargo actually had a total of 206 consignees, not an unusual number for a freighter like the *City of Flint*.

The U.S. State Department insisted that they needed a signed statement confirming the seaworthiness of the ship, the safety of the cargo and the wellbeing of the crew. They also asked that each and every one of the crew members signed this, which was under normal circumstances not an unreasonable request. For the *City of Flint*, there was very little normality right then. When asked, some of the crew refused to sign anything at this stage and actively tried to convince their colleagues to follow suit. Fortunately they did not succeed, and Gainard knew well who the culprits were. He had repeatedly had to calm hotheads during the protracted crossing or Pusback's men would have had good reason for using their arms. Nevertheless, gathering the signatures was very challenging.

Ambassador Harriman's presence had a great effect. She proved to be a very calming influence, which secured the majority of the signatures while she was in Bergen. One by one the crew were called in to the captain's room where the Ambassador sat together with Gainard. Even then some of the men sent word to the captain that they would not sign, but when invited in for a quiet chat, they all added their names. The crew had found the voyage extremely trying and when they were brought in to the captain's room, the tension over what was asked of them made many agitated to the verge of tears. As Mrs. Harriman spoke to the men, they calmed down and seemed to be satisfied with her explanation as to why they had to sign the statement. The added prospect of shore leave once the owners were satisfied that they were all of good health and that they had no problems with the ship, provided substantial incentives for them to sign.

The final two signatures were secured from crew members admitted to the local hospital. Dunlap stressed in his accompanying statement that in his opinion, the problems the crew had experienced had more to do with a lack of consideration for Norwegian seasonal weather, which in mid–November was particularly cold that year. They had ventured out in Bergen with what he described as light underwear and silk socks. It seemed to be part of the consul's pastoral role to ensure that the crew switched to woolen underwear and woolen socks, which they duly did.

After considering reports from her contacts in Bergen, Harriman was growing increasingly worried over the actual secrecy surrounding the *City of Flint*. At this stage, none of the crew had been allowed ashore; no journalists were permitted on board and the ship was isolated, riding at anchor outside the main commercial harbor; the captain, a former U.S. Navy officer, was making all the statements.

They called a press conference for the next day. Judging from the reporting in the press in Sweden, Norway and Britain, Captain Gainard provided a briefing similar to the earlier broadcast to America. In an attempt to yet again deny any allegations of contraband or ammunition in the cargo, the Master appeared to have gone to some length to provide a list of the type of goods included in the cargo. He claimed the cargo contained no dynamite, no gunpowder or any raw materials for the manufacture of ammunition. Nor did it include anything else directly related to war.

German authorities in Wilhelmstrasse in Berlin were, on their part, now brushing off any approaches from the press, arguing that the issues surrounding the American ship "constituted a case for jurists not for journalists."

The press conference removed some of the pressure from the members of the crew. They were still newsworthy, but the main headlines had all been written the day before. Confirmation of all their signatures satisfied Washington. On Friday, 10 November, the U.S. State Department finally agreed that they could be granted shore leave.

The issue over the cargo, meanwhile, was becoming increasingly complicated. In London, staff in the Foreign Office, who decided they had to assert Britain's rights, sent a coded telegram to their top man in Oslo, Sir Cecil Dormer. In Britain, companies were waiting for what was rightfully theirs, and through no fault of their own they were now about to see their goods being sold by the Norwegian State. In fact, the cargo was not Gainard's to unload and sell, but he knew how far he could go and he was far more interested in safe storage for the cargo than in generating new business.

Britain wanted their ambassador to argue that the Hague Convention XIII's article 21 should be taken to mean that, when a prize was released, this release also included her cargo. London argued that even under Norwegian Export Prohibition legislation, Norway had no case. The cargo had never been imported into Norway. The cargo on the ship had not been voluntarily surrendered to Norwegian authorities. Force majeure would be the only concept coming even close to covering the fate of this cargo.

The published list did not include any references to the nickel, which was included in the cargo, nor did it mention that Nobel Explosives were among the companies who owned parts of the cargo.

The *City of Flint* carried in her cargo just over 70,000 pounds of loose nickel chromium billets and around 330,000 pounds of loose nickel copper billets. The International Nickel Company of Wall Street, New York, had sold all to Henry Wiggin & Co. of Manchester and to Mond Nickel Co. of Millbank, London. The British owners were now in the process of instructing their agent in Bergen to instigate legal proceedings against the Norwegian State and to secure trans-shipment to Britain for the nickel. They were also warning the American ship owners of their responsibilities under the contract of shipment. Sir Cecil was advised to inform the Norwegian government of the pending legal action and to request cooperation over the trans-shipment issue.[7]

The British view, which had been set out by the Cabinet no less, was that the Norwegians had no rights at all over the cargo.

The nickel was part of a far larger issue. Mixed with iron it would help create corrosion-proof steel, crucial to armaments production. In Europe, nickel was scarce. There was only one operational nickel mine in Europe at the time, at Petsamo in northern Finland.[8]

That Friday, 10 November, Grand Admiral Eric Raeder, commander-in-chief of the German Navy, had one of his regular meetings with Adolf Hitler. Der Führer was informed that the case of the *City of Flint* had gone wrong. Raeder blamed it partly on the Prize Commander for calling at Tromsø and Murmansk, but most of the blame was laid at the door of the Haugesund vice-consul Lanwer. As the U.S. now had promised to keep its ships away from Europe and away from any future entanglements, there seemed to be little to gain from a renewed takeover of the ship, Raeder, argued. U-boats were, however, on station he added, should Hitler wish to do so. Suddenly Dönitz' earlier concerns had been papered over, seemingly in a gamble that Hitler would indeed spot the political dangers of any further attempts to bring the *City of Flint* to Germany; the case in favor of letting the ship go was played up in his report. It worked.

Hitler concurred: "Nichts mehr gegen *City of Flint* zu unternehmen," he ordered.[9] No further action against the *City of Flint*. Such a decision did not take long in being translated into practical action by the Foreign Ministry and the naval leadership in Berlin.

On Saturday morning, Hitler's orders were being acted on, but they had become part of a grander, more opportune diplomatic maneuver. The Germans were on the offensive, clearly trying hard to repair the damage the *City of Flint* incident had caused them in the United States. Saturday morning, one week after the release of the ship, a member of Kirk's diplomatic staff in Berlin was invited to call at the Foreign Ministry. The briefing, which the Germans proceeded to provide, informed the Americans of what the Norwegians were about to be told about the *City of Flint* affair. The Germans had realized that they were not likely to see the freighter enter their territorial waters under Pusback's command. They would relinquish all claims on the ship and on its cargo. In Berlin, Kirk was told that as they now assumed that the ship had discharged its cargo, the German navy had been ordered to take no further action on her return journey.

The German official relayed assurances from the naval command that all German naval units had been ordered not to interfere in any way with the *City of Flint* during her return journey to its home port in the U.S.

Although the Germans first gave categorical assurances that their naval forces would not touch the *City of Flint*, they later added a proviso. Late that Saturday afternoon an official from the German Foreign Ministry telephoned the U.S. Embassy. The promise not to touch the ship still stood, but now the German official explained that it would only be honored as long as the ship discharged its cargo which, the official stressed, Berlin regarded as contraband. Secondly, the ship had to return to the United States.[10]

In Bergen, the *City of Flint* was becoming part of the social scene. In the evening of Monday, 13 November, the ship's officers were the guests of honor at a dinner dance at the American Club of Bergen. According to First Officer Rhoads, they all had a great night, feeling that they were among friends, who had virtually all been to America at some time or other.

The German propaganda ministry, however, had still not given up the fight. On 20 November 1939, Dienst aus Deutschland, the German Press Agency, claimed that the American sailor for whom the Prize Crew wanted medical assistance had since been admitted to hospital in Bergen suffering from cancer. The agency added that it should be remembered that Norwegian authorities consulted at the time had rejected the illness as negligible and that this had been the reason for the Norwegian forces taking the ship from the Prize Crew. The Norwegian Press Agency, NTB, which picked up the story, decided to consult Mr. Dunlap, the American Consul in Bergen, on this matter. Dunlap confirmed that one of the crew members remained in hospital, but added that this was not Sillars, the sailor in question. In reality Sellars had been one of the first off the ship once restrictions were lifted! Furthermore, the sailor in hospital was not suffering from any serious illness and could be discharged at any time.[11] German care for a terminally ill sailor would surely have generated much empathy had the story been true, while attributing such a fate to an otherwise healthy man in the interest of Nazi Germany's honor was a particularly ghastly attempt in media manipulation.

Compare therefore the above sick attempt to "spin" a story with the reluctance to use Gainard's visit to the German consulate in Bergen. Before the ship returned south to Haugesund to discharge her cargo, the U.S. skipper called on the German Consul to ask him to pass on to the Prize Commander the thanks of the American crew for their true spirit of seamanship displayed during the crossing to Norway. The humanity shown by the German crew had been much appreciated according to Gainard. The new German head of Legation in Oslo, Curt Bräuer was quick to inform Berlin of this, requesting advice on how to pass this nugget to the press at the best possible time.[12] He must have been not a little surprised when the reply arrived for them "not to utilize the thanks given by the captain of the *City of Flint* to the German consul in any way."

As the story of the *City of Flint*'s journey gradually became known, the restrictions on the crew were removed. At Thanksgiving, Thursday, 23 November, the American consulate entertained the officers with a special party. Kebler, Ellis, Cordoner and Rhoads had been invited to join U.S. Consul Dunlap that evening. According to Rhoads, the evening was a great success, during which they drank Dunlap's bar dry.

On the ship, their renowned steward Joe Freer was far from letting his fans down. The crew was in for a real feast according to Joe. His planning saw them through the *Athenia* rescue without going short, his astute provisioning before they left in October, together with his catering skills, saved the celebration in Norway.

Gainard, meanwhile, had jumped on a train to Oslo the previous day. Already a celebrity, he had been invited to honor the American contingent in Oslo with his presence during their Thanksgiving celebrations. Mrs. Harriman herself played hostess to Gainard while he was in Oslo. Inviting the captain of the liberated American ship to a few parties for Oslo's relatively modest circle of diplomats must have been a subtle, but effective way of reinforcing the winning side in the political tug-of-war.

When the decision was finally made to offload the cargo and offer it for sale, Gainard discovered there was no suitable warehouse space available in Bergen. Haugesund could, however, accommodate them. On Saturday they received firm orders to sail to Haugesund two days later. The tension with some of the crew was now coming to the surface. It did not help that they had to make the trip down the coast during daylight hours because of the mine danger, a point that was hardly lost on the nervous crew. After a final weekend in Bergen, they sailed during the morning of Monday, 27 November. The seven-hour journey must have been a real trial, at least some reliving their fears of a journey to Germany and imprisonment. Fortunately, the port duty log recorded their safe arrival at 1830 that evening.[13] Just over three weeks after its first visit, the *City of Flint* was back in town. Incredibly, some of the crew responsible for the ropes during docking refused to cooperate. They had decided to get their own back on somebody; Gainard was the one authority they could reach. It took several attempts to get the ropes ashore and pull the ship in properly.

As the ship was moved south, she violated Roosevelt's war zone exclusion, but the restrictions were ignored and the ship moored quietly at the new Garpaskjær quay and no questions were asked. This was the closest quay to where the *City of Flint* had anchored during her first visit. It was as far as Gainard was prepared to sail because the crew had no insurance coverage for sailing into war zones, nor had they been hired to do so. The United States Lines backed Gainard's view on this; the ship would not sail on to Britain.

It is not known how the decision to unload the cargo at Haugesund was reached. The reliable British representative there, vice-consul Johannes Sundfør OBE, was well aware of British concerns over the cargo and he knew that in Haugesund, a large privately owned warehouse was empty. The building, Staalehuset, still has pride of place on the western side of Hasseløy, immediately to the north of the bay where the *City of Flint* had anchored during its first visit. It remains an imposing five-story, whitewashed property with a grey slate roof, built in the 1920s. The rent was rumored to be 5000 Norwegian Crowns (or around £280 or $1130) per month and the owners had secured a contract for at least 6 months.[14]

A ship smaller than the *City of Flint* could be unloaded directly to the building's seaward doors, or via the adjacent quay. Such transfers could have been undertaken relatively discreetly due to the location. In the case of the *City of Flint*, the new Garpaskjær quay was the only one where the ship could be moored without any danger of grounding.[15] The quay was brand new, it would not be completed until several months later, and as a result the quay area had no storage facilities, only a small one-storey shed and no shore-based cranes. In this location it was estimated it would take around 14 days to unload a ship the size of the *City of Flint*.[16] Nevertheless, it already serviced four sailings a week to England.

The next day, on Tuesday, 28 November, Gainard telephoned Dunlap in Bergen, warning him of the problems. The tensions were by then well known to Dunlap, but he had not expected the crew to basically sabotage the docking at Haugesund.

Before leaving Bergen, one of the troublemakers had been refused re-admittance to the local hospital over his behavior. He had caused substantial disturbance while in the hospital. Dunlap made the point in his report to Hull, that some of the crew seemed determined to behave in as much an embarrassing way for the captain as possible. Even Pusback had warned Gainard that he had some very unruly elements among the crew and their behavior now certainly proved him right. Mrs. Harriman judged the situation as very serious. Over Christmas she penned a report to Rear Admiral Emory S. Land, voicing her worries. Land was chairman of the U.S. Maritime Commission, the ship's owners. The Ambassador was actually concerned that some of the crew members would put their threats into action once home and create a real disturbance over their alleged treatment.[17]

Once at quay in Haugesund several of the crew claimed to be sick in order to avoid having to give the ship a badly needed facelift after all the recent arduous journeys.[18] While all the tension was washing over the ship, Norwegian stevedores were working away, steadily emptying the ship of its contentious cargo. The Haugesund stevedores and dockers came with the reputation for being among the best. Ship-owners preferred therefore to discharge there, rather than at larger Norwegian ports. They were well paid and well treated.[19] Using the ship's own cranes, they had to unload all the cargo onto barges, which were moored alongside the ship.[20] The barges were then, one by one, towed across the harbor to the Staalehuset for storage. Once safely inside, the cargo was carefully assessed and catalogued. The British consul's instruction from London was to first and foremost locate secure storage for the cargo and then to seek to re-export as much as possible to Britain. Finally, the British consul should advice Gainard to seek to sell off as much of the remaining goods as he could.

The British consul, whose company is still trading on the same quay, had an agency agreement with Wilhelmsen Lines and with Fred Olsen Shipping. Using all his contacts, he now had to set about securing the covert transfer of parts of the cargo to any British port he could reach.

First they had to deal with the perishable part of the cargo. The *City of Flint* had around 1,600 barrels of first quality American apples in the holds. In the period before Christmas, this was a popular addition to the normal local fare. It was quickly decided to sell this part of the cargo at auction as soon as possible.

The consulate all the while was busy providing doctors and dentists for the crew members. One of the crew even contacted them from Haugesund to inform them of his recent engagement to a Norwegian girl, for whom he was now seeking an entry permit to the United States.[21]

The apples were to be sold in one of Norway's fruit growing areas where people appreciated good quality. The fruit was still remembered 65 years later. The quality of the apples varied and because of this, the barrels were sold at auction in Haugesund. All 1600 barrels sold in an hour.[22] One of the local Haugesund business people, Mr. Spesvik, bought one of the lots of apples, which he planned to sell on to the local shops once the inferior fruit had been discarded. Mr. Sivert Alme, then a young college student, financed his Christmas presents helping to pick out the rotten apples. In many cases, Sivert remembered, only part of the apples were rotten, and then the kids working there would be allowed to cut off the rotten parts and eat the rest.[23]

The cargo also contained a quantity of tinned fruit, pineapples and peaches. Mrs. Astrid Riddervoll, the consul's daughter, remembered well how the fruit was the talk of the town for weeks afterwards. The tinned fruit soon found its way into local shops. During the early part of the war, American tinned fruit still remained for sale in Nazi-occupied Norway.[24]

Another consignment from the *City of Flint*'s cargo later turned out to be of particular interest in Norway because it included a consignment of good American radios. They were unloaded and stored for sale locally, but few actually reached the shops because radios required a registration procedure and the payment of an annual listener's fee. Shortly after the occupation of Norway in April 1940, the Germans started to impound all known radios and it was no longer legal to own one. That was when the radios from the *City of Flint* came in to their own. Distributed in the greatest secrecy, they helped numerous Norwegians stay in touch, illegally, with Norwegian news programs broadcast for them by the BBC.[25]

The American ship became part of the local scene during the six-week stay in Haugesund. To the majority of the locals, however, the often inebriated camelhair-coated sailors were a breed apart. The morals of the West Norwegian Bible belt did not appreciate such wanton use of alcohol, or such conspicuous consumption as seen on behalf of their new neighbors. Nevertheless, a more commercial approach gradually prevailed and the ship's popularity grew. In the end, it was suggested the town be renamed City of Flint in acknowledgment of all the money spent by the U.S. crew.

On the first Sunday in Advent, Gainard opened his ship to all comers. Little did he know that virtually the entire town made it their business to come on board and take a closer look at this famous ship.

At the same time, the ship's radio helped keep them in touch with life in America via shortwave broadcasts. They were all aware of the Soviet invasion of Finland and as all Finnish Americans staged a Finland Day on Sunday, 17 December, so did the crew of the *City of Flint*. This group of Americans, who felt they had experienced war at first hand and been under Soviet control, donated 134.50 Kroner to the local Finland Aid collection. Regional newspapers all over Norway had similar collections running throughout the month of December 1939.

That was to be the closing of the *City of Flint*'s Haugesund chapter. On Wednesday morning they cast off again bound for Bergen. They were leaving the prohibited European war zone. It was the first short leg of the long journey home.[26]

Ironically, the ill-fated support ship the *Altmark* that had served the *Admiral Graf Spee* used the same quay after hitting a mine less than a year later.[27] The Garpaskjær quay held no favors for Hitler's navy.

11

Going Home

Two days before Christmas, as the local people sat huddled around their radios, listening for news of the war, the *City of Flint* finally weighed anchor and left Bergen, heading north, the same course as she had been forced to sail only a couple of months before. This time, however, she was in ballast. A midwinter crossing of the Atlantic with totally empty holds would be uncomfortable as the ship would float like a cork. In order to avoid just such a journey, a cargo of Swedish iron ore was to be loaded in Narvik. The price of the cargo would not cover the cost of the return journey, but would at least make it less torturous.

The Norwegians were determined to ensure that the *City of Flint* had a safe passage along the coast and Rear Admiral Tank-Nielsen had again used his good offices to secure an escort for the ship. In fact, the fierce storm, which blew up as the ships neared the wide-open ocean at Stad, made the navy advise the Americans to seek shelter for the duration. At daybreak on Christmas Eve, the weather improved and the ships headed for

City of Flint (left) back at Bergen, just before Christmas in December 1939. At anchor with other ships in the port just before heading north to Narvik to pick up a cargo of iron ore for the trip home (courtesy Bergen Havnekontor's Arkiv, Bergen Byarkiv).

Ålesund where they were due to halt for a few hours to celebrate Christmas. Now feted as celebrities, the ship's progress was watched and reported.

Two patrol planes took off from the navy's air station at Flatøy outside Bergen that morning. They were flying their regular daily reconnaissance routes. At the lighthouse, one plane turned south, the other north.[1]

The north-bound plane was headed towards a point just east of Stad which he reached at midday, only to spot a British flying boat, on a northerly course. They were less than three kilometers apart. The British plane was flying low. They undoubtedly knew from their people in Bergen when the *City of Flint* had sailed.

Half an hour later, the pilot spotted the *City of Flint* heading north. The Norwegian navy's small destroyer *Troll* escorted her.[2] They were accompanied by an unknown whaler and as the patrol watched, another whaler sought safety alongside the naval vessel. The pilot did a long wide turn out to sea at Stad before returning to the coast. Gainard was still on course.

As the ship prepared for Christmas, the American consulate in Bergen was busy dispatching telegrams on behalf of the captain and several of his crew. Gainard hoped to reach Narvik, the shipping port of for the famous high-grade Swedish iron ore before the end of the year. The cargo would take a couple of days to load, but according to Dunlap in Bergen, Gainard hoped to be under sail very early in the New Year, reaching Baltimore early in February.

Before he left Bergen, Gainard had received so many offers of lecture tours, radio interviews and written articles that he had discussed his future with Dunlap, who in turn passed on his plans to Cordell Hull and his employers the U.S. Maritime Commission. In the event, Gainard did go ashore that spring and his book describing the episode was published later that year. Dunlap was concerned for Gainard's health, advising that unless he strictly curtailed his activities, he would collapse.

Ambassador Harriman was also concerned for Gainard's future. She had been impressed with his ability to handle a very difficult and delicate situation. He had, she pointed out to the Maritime Commission, been particularly careful to follow all her briefings and all her advice. Harriman felt that the situation could have been far more difficult to handle had the captain not been such a man of tact and diplomacy.[3] Unaware of her compliments, Gainard heaped praise on Mrs. Harriman when back in Baltimore, arguing that no man could have acted as a better U.S. envoy than her!

Ship's steward Joe Freer turned out to be up to the challenge of providing a proper feast for them that Christmas Day. In his book, Gainard later described the dinner as "grand," claiming that the entire crew had time to enjoy both caviar and turkey before weighing anchor and continuing north towards Narvik.

Still under Norwegian escort the *City of Flint* anchored at Narvik on Friday, 28 December, during a spell of particularly severe weather. The ship was swinging on its anchor chains in the strong gale while the heavy snow was building drifts on deck. The locals claimed not to have seen the like of it for twenty years.

Finally, on Sunday, December 30, Gainard weighed anchor and moved up to the terminal. Fully laden, they moved off again a day later, just as the weather closed in once more. Storm and a heavy snowfall were forecast as they anchored and prepared to welcome the New Year. Unfortunately, any thought of an easy start to the year was quickly blown away. Another ship, riding high without any cargo, caught the full force of the wind and the anchor, clearly not sufficiently secure in the sandy fjord bottom, dragged. British

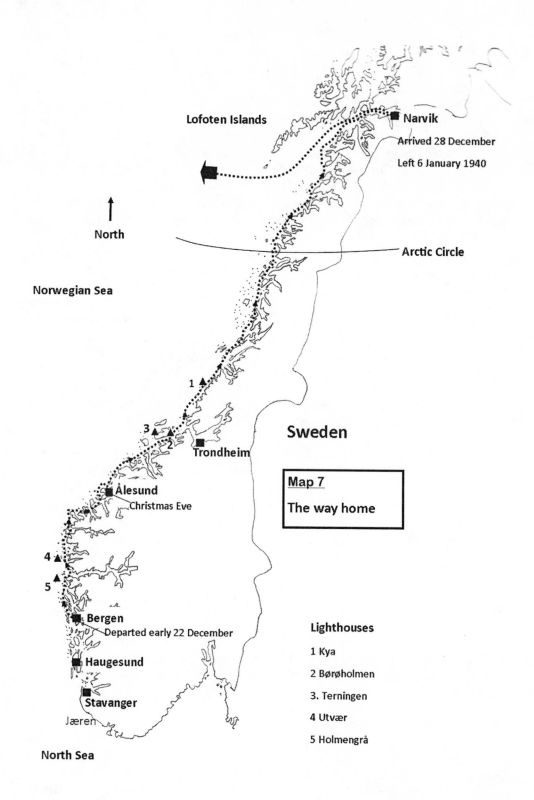

Lofoten Islands

■ Narvik

Arrived 28 December

Left 6 January 1940

↑

North

Arctic Circle

Norwegian Sea

1 ▲

Sweden

3 ▲ ▲
2 ■ Trondheim

■ Ålesund
Christmas Eve

Map 7

The way home

4 ▲

5 ▲

■ Bergen
Departed early 22 December

Lighthouses

1 Kya

2 Børøholmen

3. Terningen

4 Utvær

5 Holmengrå

■ Haugesund

■ Stavanger

Jæren

North Sea

freighter *Baron Blythswood* came around with such force that her stern slammed into the *City of Flint* just in front of the No. 1 hatch. She cracked one of the plates in the side of the American ship. As the stern swept along the side of the *City of Flint*, several supports were broken or bent, all the way back to the No. 2 lifeboat, which was dented by the force.

Although the damage was far from serious, it was decided to remain at Narvik while a Norwegian repair crew was brought out. They worked hard to make good the damage and finally late in the evening the following Saturday, 5 January, the job was done. Gainard, however, wanted to make sure the plate was watertight. He knew that a wet iron ore cargo could shift suddenly and relentlessly. Now, although late on the Saturday night, he turned out a crew with a high-pressure hose to literally blast the repairs with powerful water jets. Satisfied that there were no leaks, he ordered them to prepare for an early departure the following morning.

They were being watched. German Vice-Consul Wussov later reported that the *City of Flint* had arrived in the port empty and left laden with a cargo of ore. There was therefore no question that Narvik was being used as a transit port for the U.S. original cargo intended for British customers.[4]

Just as Pusback ordered, they went to the north of Iceland, heading south down the Denmark Strait with the Greenland pack ice to their right. The weather was as bad as before and storms and heavy seas were still the order of the day. The British Northern Patrol was monitoring shipping and this time the *City of Flint* was spotted. On Friday, 12 January a British warship challenged them by blinker, but the *City of Flint* was no longer topping the British navy's "most wanted" list and was permitted to continue its journey.

The Atlantic demands respect at any time of the year, but in January, it is a particularly uncompromising and hostile place to be. During their crossing, the weather deteriorated again. At times, the mountainous seas would wash right over the fo'c'sle, making the deck totally inaccessible, even rigged with safety lines. For up to four days at a time, the breaking waves and flying foam prevented them from accessing the forward hatches to check that no water was reaching the cargo.

A good week later they were back to the area where the *Deutschland* had spotted them early in October. This time, they met a homebound convoy, most probably HX17, which had left Halifax 22 January.

Twenty days after leaving Narvik, the *City of Flint* was finally spotted sailing past the Virginia Capes on the last lap of her long journey. Even the return to America was not that simple. In the evening of Friday, 26 January the ship was boarded by a small group of government officials. The State Department wanted to ensure that they heard the story first and could advise Gainard on how to handle the media storm they knew awaited him on the quayside. A debriefing was of great importance to Washington, so much so that the officials insisted the ship anchor in the bay over night before going to quay. After all they had been through, the crew still had to endure more questioning and waiting, and this time, even within sight of home. The case had taken on such serious political overtones. The officials now wanted to learn the actual experiences of those at the center of it all, and they needed to be sure that Gainard and his officers were aware of the wider ramifications of what they were about to recount to the assembled forces of international media. Harriman had been advised to stay well clear of Gainard's interview in Bergen, it would not be as easy to dissociate the State Department from any statements made over the next few hours at home.

In fact, two officials from the shipping line's local office had boarded the ship already the day before as she entered American waters at Cape Henry around 0730 in the morning.[5] Their task was to start working out the crew's backlog of salary—worth an estimated $20,000. To make the calculations even more complicated, new legislation came into play as Social Security status was introduced for sailors from 1 January 1940.

On Saturday morning, January 27, 1940, 114 days after she had set sail from New York, the *City of Flint* was finally safely back home in Baltimore. By now the ship was a real celebrity. Journalists and broadcasters on two continents had been competing for the best story on the ship since the news of its capture first broke. As they rode at anchor in Chesapeake Bay, the revenue cutter *Calumet* full of journalists and cameramen came out to meet them.

The news-hungry members of the press corps had begun their tour down the bay at 0800 on that blistering cold Saturday morning. America was in the middle of a wave of abnormally cold weather. The revenue cutter was moving through sheets of drifting ice. Joining this trip had been no easy task that morning. Without a pass issued by the customs authorities they would not have been allowed to go, and the passes were actually collected again by another customs officer as they came up the gangway of the cutter.

It became clear when the *City of Flint* came into view, riding at anchor in the morning sun, that she was not particularly well turned out. Sides caked with ice, rust showing through her chipped paint work, her black sided hull still read "*City of Flint*, United States Lines" in white between two huge flags. These had been re-painted for the home journey. The original Stars and Stripes had been painted out by German mariners hanging over the sides on ropes as the ship was steaming eastwards in the icy waters of the North Atlantic.

The first journalist to get the story out was the radio reporter David Goldin from the local Maryland station WFBR, who actually transmitted a live interview with the captain as the ship sailed up the bay.[6] Gainard was guarded in his response to the questioning, he would not name the German ship that had captured them. The reason for them heading north to Murmansk, he explained, was mainly due to the weather and "other things." The journalist did not pursue it; instead he switched the topic. When it was Rhoads' turn, it became clear that only Gainard and none of the rest of the crew actually ever knew where they were or where they were going—apart from the general knowledge of heading towards Germany—but on a very northerly course.

According to WFBR's Goldin the ship had been referred to as "a piece of junk" by someone in a radio program that Friday night. The crass comment stung the captain, who had been listening at the time. In his live interview from the ship as it sailed in, Gainard made a point of referring to this derogatory remark. His voice during this interview was lively, and his explanations lucid. This was the voice of a successful seafarer returning home with his ship and crew safe and sound.

Having cut their way through the packed harbor ice, they finally docked at Pier 10. It was not a pretty place; it could hardly be described as anything but an industrial setting for the homecoming. The pier was located on the Canton railhead. As the ship closed on the quay the crew could see a long line of rail freight wagons having pride of place on the narrow stretch of concrete between the icy waters and the empty cargo hall, from the days of the old Baltimore Mail Line.

Not only reporters had gathered that morning. Around 200 people waited eagerly for the ship to appear. They included many of the wives and families of the crew. The first had arrived at 0730 that morning. They too had endured. It had been an anxious time

Home again: The *City of Flint* at Pier 10 at the Canton Railhead in Baltimore, Saturday, 27 January 1940. It was a very cold morning, hence the ice (The Mariners' Museum and Park).

since the ship left port last October. Now, braving the freezing wind off the Patapsco River basin, they could easily be reminded of their menfolk's endurance in Murmansk. Waiting with them was Mrs. Ethel Gainard, accompanied by 23-year-old Miss Cathleen Schurr of Brooklyn, New York, a survivor of the *Athenia* disaster, who owed her life to the *City of Flint*. Numerous other *Athenia* passengers had sent telegrams to congratulate the crew on their successful return.

It was noon before the ship finally came to a slow rest along the frozen pier and as the formalities were settled, the gangway was finally put in place. First to board that lunchtime was the captain's wife. As she started up the gangway in double quick time, her husband was waiting, meeting her half way before taking her off for a more private few minutes in his cabin to escape the glare of the media. Mrs. Gainard had travelled down from their home in Melrose, Massachusetts, by train. They reappeared to read telegrams congratulating the ship on their successful return and to answer questions from the assembled press, who by now swarmed all over the ship, taking pictures and interviewing members of the crew. Gainard and other of the ship's officers were sporting Norwegian sweaters to help keep out the cold.

Once secured alongside the dock, he turned to his radio crew to send off two brief but very significant telegrams. The first one was to his great supporter and friend in Oslo, the formidable Mrs. Harriman: "Acey Ducey docked Baltimore. Love Gainard." They had spent hours playing the old seafaring game while at Consul Dunlap's residence in Bergen and at the Ambassador's home in Oslo. The informal tone of the telegram told the story of the friendship that had developed between them.

The second telegram was for the man who took the initiative to liberate the ship, regardless of personal consequences, the Norwegian Admiral Carsten Tank-Nielsen: "Docked at Baltimore. Takk for alt. Gainard."[7]

It is interesting to note the difference in the tenor of Gainard's voice in the interview he gave the local radio station once docked. The reality of it all must suddenly have hit home. Now came uncertainty and new challenges. Spending days, working cheek by jowl with the German Pusback, knowing that in the soldier's pocket was a hand grenade powerful enough to kill them both, would have been draining in itself, without having the responsibility for the lives of the crew and the well-being of the ship.

It was quite clear from the tone of his voice—that flat, monotone diction, a manner of speech totally void of emotion—that when Captain Gainard had taken the *City of Flint* to the quay in Baltimore that January morning, he was exhausted.[8] The job was done. He had successfully overcome Nazi pirates, Stalin's intransigence, explosives and storms to take his ship and his crew home without a single loss of life. The adrenaline rush was over, he was no longer needed. It is tempting to argue that the brilliant captain, who had seen the end of his natural usefulness loom large since the customs cutter met them the previous night, was now slipping into dark days of depression. The journey had taken a very heavy toll on the 50-year-old officer from the Navy Reserve.

The homecoming was granted a banner headline spanning the entire front page of Baltimore's *Evening Sun*—"Flint Officers tell first story of capture" it read. A photograph of a menacingly silhouetted ship, the *Deutschland*, held center stage.

So far, it had been Gainard who had handled the press on his own, exercising control of the information release, but from now on that would not be the case. The difference started to show immediately. Gainard avoided naming the ship that captured them, referring merely to a ship of the "*Deutschland* class." For reasons known only to himself, he did not want to identify the ship. Warren Rhoads, the first mate, merely referred to "The *Deutschland*" in his interview. Neither did Gainard refer to Pusback by name, even seeming to have tried to protect him, but others were not so careful, because the German was named in the article.

At this stage it turned out that several of the members of the crew had kept diaries of the journey. Amo Garnet had even managed to secure photographs of the *Deutschland* and of the *Olav Tryggvason*—the *Baltimore Evening Sun* used them both in their presentation of the story.

Even when Gainard left the ship the press pursued him. It was noted in one of the papers Monday morning that although Mrs. Gainard had booked them into a local hotel, they were in fact not at that address, but were thought to be staying with friends in the city. Gainard had won another round, this time earning some peace and quiet.

Robert McColl, water tender, had not seen his sister for several years. Now Mrs. Catherine Anderson had made the long trip from Detroit to welcome him home.

The youngest member of the crew, who had just celebrated his 19th birthday, Raymond Trump, was met by his mother Cyvilla and Raymond's younger brother Phillip who lived in Baltimore. Cyvilla was also Joe Freer's landlady so they had a double celebration in that house.[9]

By Sunday, 28 January, Pier 10 was drawing in greater crowds than nearby historic sites like Fort Henry. Cars with New York, New Jersey and Delaware plates joined the locals who filled the snow covered streets to Canton. The flow of cars was unrelenting from early morning until sunset. The local police had to place two of its officers on traffic duty, directing traffic on a road which normally was completely deserted.

To the Canton railroad police the volume of people walking over their railway tracks was a real hazard. They closed the pier itself to sightseers by stretching a rope across the access, but as the volume of people grew, the Chief of Police relented. By late afternoon he had opened the pier for people to walk along. The ship itself, however, remained out of bounds.

The story of the ship had captured the imagination and the sympathy of the American people. David Goldin signed off his broadcast as coming from "America's Adventure Ship, the *City of Flint*." But not all those who dealt with the story had the same perspective. In a proud, but somber editorial in its Monday edition, *The Baltimore Sun* praised the restraint and the discipline of the captain and his crew. The editor went on to recognize that the capture could have led to a serious international incident. He took comfort from the fact that the U.S. neutrality laws subsequently barred such journeys, which might end in similar captures.

The following Monday, 29 January, the ship was moved to the Sparrow Points Docks at the Bethlehem Steel Company where the cargo of Swedish ore was to be discharged. The crew could finally go home. On Thursday, 1 February, Gainard was expected at a lunch in his honor at the Advertising Club of New York. The famous mayor of New York, Fiorello La Guardia, was to preside at the lunch.

Several of the crew members hailed from Baltimore and as they found their way to various local watering holes, another dimension of the story of the *City of Flint* started to emerge. There was something of a sneaking admiration for the German soldiers they had encountered. They were "damned good sailors" and all polite and very restrained in their behavior.

When the ship was finally unloaded, Gainard headed for a safe port of his own, most likely without any plans for returning to sea. Later, in September 1940, the book of his experiences was published and with it, perhaps, he had exorcised the demons left by the tense sailing in northern waters.

On Wednesday, 7 February, Gainard was back in New York. He was the guest of honor at the British Luncheon Club. It was a private affair with no press allowed in, and no record exists of his speech. Most of the members of the Prize Crew were very young, he told the audience. The Germans had hired a large hall at Stettin on the Baltic. They had planned a huge propaganda event where the American crew was to have spoken to the world over the ether. Radio was to have been Hitler's international propaganda tool.[10]

Sadly, Gainard's successful return of the ship was not to be allowed to rest without a less savory aftermath. Both Harriman and Pusback had warned Gainard of resentment and hostility against him personally from some of the members of the crew, who had felt that his handling of the German takeover had not been as decisive as they would have liked. On 10 February, the National Maritime Union announced that it was filing charges of neglect of duty against Captain Gainard. The charges, which were laid before the U.S. Department of Commerce in Washington, demanded Gainard's license be revoked.

The charges were brought on behalf of Peter Walding, the chief cook, and Henry Androvett, the mess boy. According to their affidavits, Gainard had repeatedly rejected suggestions from his crew members of ways to regain control from the German Prize Crew. A mere six days later, the Department threw out the charges as groundless. They would not give serious attention, they argued, to "Statements made by a mess boy and a cook to the effect that they were not satisfied with the way the captain handled his job." Gainard's journey was finally over.

The Neutrality Act effectively barred U.S.-borne trade with Europe. The *City of Flint* was unloaded, and on 14 February 1940 laid up. U.S. merchant ships could not sail into the European war zone.

The Hog Islanders design made the *City of Flint* very useful to the Maritime Commission and the companies that had chartered their ships. She had been launched with an efficient oil-fired turbine for power and with very good cargo capacity for her size. She was a no-nonsense freighter, well-built and very economical to run, although by 1940, she was a bit long in the tooth. Hog Islanders were built as a "short-term fix" to the shortage of ships in 1918.

Early in 1940, the Moore-McCormack Lines took over the Pacific Brazil Argentine Line. Their original plan had been to service South America with brand new ships. As tension in Europe continued to escalate, the U.S. navy requisitioned all these new contracted vessels before they were ever delivered. To Moore-McCormack, the only viable alternative, in the short term, was to quickly charter three older ships. Hog Islanders would be attractive to such a plan and although they were regarded as virtually outdated by 1940, both in terms of speed and design; the *City of Flint* was one of the ships introduced to this service.

In September 1940, the Canadian Government formally recognized the gallantry displayed by the personnel of the *City of Flint* in rescuing survivors from the sinking of the *Athenia*. Canadian Minister Loring C. Christie presented the chairman of the U.S. Maritime Commission, Rear Admiral Emory S. Land, with a silver plaque. The *City of Flint* was one of the Commission's ships, but her Master Joseph Gainard was, as an officer of the U.S. Naval Reserve, prohibited from accepting an award of this kind without approval from the U.S. Congress. A similar plaque was awarded to the crew of the Swedish yacht *Southern Cross* early in September 1940.[11]

From the fall of 1939, Moore-McCormack started to experience the demands of the war in Europe, initially through the near loss of the *City of Flint*, but within a few months, another freighter the *Mormac Sea* was caught by the German invasion of Norway. She only escaped from Trondheim by permission of the occupying forces.

During this intervening period the *City of Flint* repeatedly circled South America, passing through the Panama Canal eastwards on the southbound leg, heading first for ports in Columbia and Venezuela. The next part of the journey took them along the coasts of Brazil and Argentina. The journeys saw them sail east to west through the notorious Straits of Magellan before heading north again. Each journey would have taken around 35 days to complete.

The northernmost port of call on the new route was Vancouver, where the *City of Flint* turned up in 1940.[12] She again appeared on the East Coast at the end of 1941 ready to revisit her old haunts. The role of the *City of Flint* was about to change once more.

There had been concern over the possibility of German forces occupying Iceland and Churchill decided to move first, establishing British bases there in May 1940. A good year later, the hard-pressed British needed every soldier they had at the front. Iceland, technically not a combatant nation but one seeking protection, was to be helped by the U.S. Marine Corps. They were transferred to Iceland in July. Concurrently, as Roosevelt was expanding the U.S. Navy to assert their influence in the vast part of the Atlantic, the navy was calling up their reserves; one of them was Gainard, who was recalled to active duty 30 July 1941.

SECTION III

Convoys

12

Convoy—to Murmansk

Britain had introduced the World War I concept of convoy already in the fall of 1939 and the Royal Navy regarded the experience developed since then as vital to its own survival and to keeping maritime trade and supply routes open. By January 1942, the Arctic convoys were changing both in content and in character. Since the U.S. entry into the war, goods were sent on Allied ships as well as on American ones, from U.S. ports on the East Coast directly to the Soviet Union.

It was not until 3 February 1942 that the Allies worked out a convoy escort strategy for the Atlantic that was acceptable to both the Americans and the British. U.S. Admiral Ernest J. King, the officer in charge of American naval forces in the Atlantic finally relented to having convoys being established in American waters and being escorted by U.S. Navy ships from March 1942 on, at least between Boston and Halifax. It was the beginning, running a protective screen around defenseless merchant ships at least for part of the voyage along the Eastern Seaboard. Further south were the coastal sections most prone to U-boat attacks. Here merchant shipping would remain undefended for nearly another year. Said Samuel Morrison, the official U.S. Navy historian, "it was a massacre." Naval historian Peter Padfield even argued that the loss of shipping in U.S. and Central American waters at that time amounted to a worse disaster, in terms of ships lost, than the strategic impact of the loss of battleships at Pearl Harbor.[1]

It cost America dearly in terms of ships lost, but it also cost valuable lives and tonnage from countries like Britain and Norway, whose merchant fleets were sailing these waters. The first few months of 1942 proved to be particularly disastrous for Allied shipping in the North Atlantic. U-boats sank 1.14 million tons of shipping in the first quarter of the year—1.06 million tons of that were sunk in waters under the responsibility of the U.S. Navy.

Once the U.S. production capacity for shipbuilding was gathering momentum during the spring of 1942, the situation improved. Already in May convoys were introduced, between Guantanamo, Cuba, and Key West in Florida, and between Guantanamo and Halifax. By August 1942, an impressive continuous flow of escort switching merchant shipping was in motion and an "interlocking system" of controlled shipping was in place.

The *City of Flint* had been dry-docked in a Maryland shipyard since Sunday, 23 November 1941 for repairs. By the time Lieutenant J.E. Lee of the U.S. Navy met with L.M. Long, her new Master in New York, she had had guns installed. It was Wednesday, 17 December. The USA was at war.

The purpose of Long seeing Lee was to complete a very detailed questionnaire on the ship and her facilities. The American Congress had altered the Neutrality Act to allow the arming of merchant ships on Tuesday, 17 November and the Navy had presented the

President with a plan the day after. This was a mere five days before the *City of Flint* reached the shipyard. The freighter was very high on the list of ships to be armed; she was scheduled to join a convoy to Europe.

Within a week of the American entry into the war in December 1941, British Premier Winston Churchill met President Roosevelt. At this stage, Stalin was the only leader to successfully halt the German onslaught. Thus it was very important to keep Stalin in the war with enough might to pin down the attacking German forces as this would help drain valuable German resources from other battlefields. Consequently Britain had started a regular run of Arctic convoys earlier that fall in order to supply Soviet forces.

The new Soviet-American protocols governing aid to the Soviet Union were like no other nation's Lend-Lease agreements. They contained actual commitments, which Roosevelt was keen to stick to. This meant working with the British navy on the transport of the equipment and ammunition across the Atlantic and onwards to the northern port of Murmansk.

A 4"/.50 caliber Mark IX cannon on the poop deck and four Browning machine guns, 0.50 caliber, and four Lewis machine guns 0.30 caliber were now part of the standard equipment on the ship. The bridge and the 0.50 caliber guns had been fitted with splinter protection, and separate splinter protection was installed for the radio room. Each external door was provided with a blackout switch to ensure that night sailing really could be done with the confidence of not providing any traces of light to U-boats.

The ship was now subject to U.S. Navy equipment requirements, which meant certain types of kit had to be issued for use aboard. They took on board 35 new steel helmets, for a total civilian crew of 37. They were not issued gas masks.

They were going back to the Soviet Union. This time as friends, bringing desperately needed supplies for the war. Gainard was no longer in charge and the *City of Flint* had a different crew. The memories of the Murmansk trip two years earlier were fading.

According to the Ship's Log, the destination was, at that stage, given as "Archangel via Halifax N.S."[2]

With guns came responsibility and expectations of new skills. The merchant seamen had no such skills. Those who did came from the ranks of the U.S. Armed Guard. There is no record of when the Armed Guard personnel joined the ship, but it is likely to have been around the middle of December as the armaments had been installed at that stage. These specially trained U.S. Navy personnel were now posted on all ships sailing into a warzone. Their job was to crew the guns and make sure they could be deployed as effectively as possible in any attack. Before leaving, the Armed Guard unit drew nine sets of special winter equipment, including some described as "special submarine clothing"; these were coats and trousers made of "balloon cloth" with more woolen coats and trousers to go with them. Bearing in mind the long journey, the tension and the dangers they were all to be exposed to, the final note on the form on "Welfare and Recreational Equipment" was telling. They had nothing apart from some games provided by the Red Cross to stave off the boredom and reduce the tension.

The *City of Flint* had four lifeboats, each capable of carrying 40 people. There were four rafts, each with a capacity of 18. The lifeboats were located two on either side of the bridge deck, immediately aft of the bridge. The life rafts were positioned two in the forward rigging and two in the aft rigging. They carried 50 lifebelts—but of the old type. Navy-type life jackets were only issued for the Armed Guard and for those of the Merchant crew who would assist at the guns. The log entry noted that the bridge had now been reinforced to provide protection against enemy fire. On board also was a full set of international code flags and semaphore flags; the ship was also fitted with a blinker. Until then she had not even had a Very pistol for firing flares into the air. The ship was still owned by the Maritime Commission, but was operated by Moore-McCormack Lines. In December 1941, the Baltimore Port Director recorded the ship as requiring nine officers and a crew of 28. The ship had changed its familiar black hull to the standard-issue navy grey.

The antimagnetic systems had been installed and tested, degaussed, to ensure that magnetic mines or torpedoes would not detonate by the large metal hull.[3]

The gun installation was so new that no ammunition had yet been provided. The U.S. was a mere two weeks into the war, but the ship's Master, Long, actually had convoy experience from the last war. The peace after the First World War was a mere 23 years old. The captain held the rank of Lieutenant Commander in the U.S. Navy Reserve. He had several other USNRs in the crew.[4]

With all her paperwork and repairs completed, the *City of Flint* finally sailed out of Baltimore on the last Saturday before Christmas, 20 December 1941. The orders were to pick up cargo at Boston bound for Northern Russia. They were moving down Chesapeake Bay when they received a telegram advising them to pick up ammunition at the navy base in Norfolk, Virginia. In charge of the Armed Guard was Ensign Robert J. Ahern. He and eight of his men were transferred on board at Baltimore; Frank Smith (USN) and David E. Rouse (USNR) joined them within the next few days. Their quarters were on the port side of the amidships house. Their commander, Ahern, was quartered the below the bridge. They had their own separate mess, which was located next to their quarters. As a result, they did not mix much with the civilian crew.

No time was wasted. On the way north to Boston they were sailing along the U.S. coast and here, on Christmas Day, they took the opportunity to test fire the new 4" 0.50 caliber gun. The test firing was quite important and Ensign Ahern had to produce a written report describing it. He inspected the gun mountings, the foundation, all bolts and found, fortunately, that the firing had not caused any damage.

The next day, they arrived at the Army base in Boston to load the cargo. The loading took its time and they saw in the New Year while there. Very early on Wednesday, 7 January they sailed for Halifax, Nova Scotia, to join the first convoy of the long journey. They sailed alone, with no escort or protection. Not even the declaration of war on Germany had prompted American Admiral King to accept the need for convoy measures, yet.

From the captain's point of view, there seemed to have been little to report on the crossing to Scotland. According to his log they reached Gourock, near Glasgow, on February 3 and continued north to Loch Ewe, where they anchored three days later. It was at this sheltered sea loch that so many of the Arctic convoys formed up. The narrow opening and the wide loch made it far easier to protect against U-boats than most other UK ports.

The Armed Guard commander produced a very detailed report of the journey.[5] It took them two days to sail north from Boston to Halifax. They arrived at Halifax in the afternoon and dropped anchor. The plan was to join the next convoy to Britain. Over the following few days the convoy started to form. It was to become Convoy HX-170. At the pre-sailing briefing, Captain Long, like all Masters of merchant ships about to embark on a journey in convoy, received his envelope containing a unique convoy call sign, his position in the convoy, the name of the convoy commodore and the ship where he was located.

By the time they all sailed down the narrow Bedford basin on Tuesday, 13 January 1942 and out past Halifax into the building waves of yet another North Atlantic storm, they were 25 merchantmen being escorted by six warships from the Canadian navy: two destroyers and four corvettes. Twenty-nine ships had notified the Canadian authorities of their intentions to join the convoy, but for reasons unknown, four of them did not show up.

The Befehlshaber der U-boote, the BdU (commander-in-chief) of the German U-boats, Karl Dönitz, had a total of 12 of his U-boats along the U.S. East Coast at that time. This was the beginning of Operation Paukenschlag ("Drumbeat"). By the end of January 1942 they had sunk 35 ships. Korvettenkapitän Ernest Kals in *U-130*, close to Halifax, sank two ships in the morning of 13 January, Norwegian *Frisco*, and the Panamanian registered *Friar Rock*. It was his first war patrol. Neither ship was part of the departing convoy, they were single ships moving cargo. The *City of Flint* was not touched. It was not her turn.

In the convoy, the crews were constantly on guard. For the U.S. ship, this guard duty caused problems. They had not yet seen the significance of it all. U.S. merchant ships had at that time provided for only one lookout to be on duty at any one time. Ahern clearly felt this was inadequate, but he acknowledged that any increase in the number of guards would have a real impact on the cost of the journey, it would mean paying someone overtime for all the guard duty. The labor issue also arose when members of the ship's company were on duty at the guns, working in support of the Armed Guard unit. This was part of their duties, but the merchant sailors objected to taking their meals at the guns, when on duty. Judging from his report, this turned out to be quite a problem, but somehow Ahern managed to secure the working routines he needed, although he later suggested that a representative from Naval Operations should discuss this problem with the relevant union officials.

It did not take many survivors from sunken U.S. merchant ships to talk about their experiences in the hiring halls when they returned, to convince fellow sailors of the importance of the role of the Armed Guard and their own support for them. Similarly, the Armed Guard contingents gradually learned to respect the seamanship and the competencies of their civilian compatriots.

An official history of U.S. naval operations during the Second World War, by Morison, noted this "attitude problem." He argued that apart from the lamentable U.S. shortfall in appropriate ships for anti–U-boat warfare, they were also far from prepared mentally for what was about to hit them and for the delivery of the appropriate response.

As Convoy HX-170 left Halifax, the convoy they would "pair" with was being assembled in Scotland. This was still in the early days of Atlantic convoys. At the formal level, escort roles, duties and responsibilities for the Atlantic convoys were not clear, nor agreed at the time when the *City of Flint* reached Halifax.

In charge of the convoy escort as they were about to sail, was the senior officer of the escort (SOE), Lieutenant-Commander H.S. Rayner of the Canadian Navy. His ship was the destroyer *St. Laurent* and the minesweepers *Clayaquot*, *Goderich* and *Quinte* and the corvette *Weyburn* supported him.[6] This was a critical phase for the convoy; they were just moving out of a location where ships had been seen gathering. Rayner immediately ordered a quick anti-submarine (A/S) sweep across the approaches. Over the next two hours he allowed the convoy's participants to find their stations—their locations in the nine columns which made up HX170.

If any of the Paukenschlag boats had spotted the convoy, they would have transmitted its position back to base for distribution to other U-boats in their next pre-arranged broadcast. It was standard procedure for convoys to listen for such transmissions. Several ships, ideally well-spaced out in the corners of the convoy, would be requested to carry out high frequency/direction finding (HF/DF, popularly known as "Huff-Duff") duties. Their alert radio operators would try to secure a "fix"—that is, attempt to plot the direction from which they received such a suspected radio signal. By plotting several of these directions, all from different positions in the convoy, Rayner would order one or more of his escorts to race down the plot line, hoping to spot a surfaced U-boat at the end of it. They had to reach the U-boat before the radioman could complete his message and they disappeared back below the surface. In HX-170 the ships ordered to carry out HF/DF duties were in position 41, 51 and 81, far too close to be ideal. But not all ships had the relevant radio equipment.

The weather was deteriorating rapidly and heavy seas and strong winds would come to plague the convoy during the entire crossing. The sky was blanketed in heavy clouds and a gale was building from the southwest. In London, the Air Ministry's Meteorological Office presented its daily weather report. It was, as usual, a large hand-colored set of maps, one of the British Isles and the North Sea, and the other covered the area of the Northern Atlantic and Europe. The focal point on the Atlantic weather chart that morning was a particularly deep low-pressure with an epicenter off the Southeast coast of Greenland. A high-pressure ridge from Madeira to Bermuda matched this single low-pressure area, which took in the entire North Atlantic. Transatlantic shipping was in for some very bad weather indeed. In the Minches off western Scotland, the wind was already blowing a gale from the southeast.[7]

So far their luck was holding as no U-boats had spotted them. At dusk, Rayner decided to confuse any possible watching U-boats even more. He ordered the convoy to alter course to port. The convoy steamed on this course for just over two hours in the darkness before he brought them around to starboard as part of an exercise in evasive steering.

At daybreak on Thursday, 15 January, he still had all the ships, but one of the escorts had lost touch. The *Clayaquot* never re-joined the convoy after the night's escort maneuvers. The bad weather had prevented any visual contact and they were not allowed to use radio to request help. The HF/DF trick could just as easily be turned back on them—or on the convoy.

Throughout the day, visibility was bad and the sea very heavy. They were coming close to the agreed escort hand-over point for this convoy—the West Ocean Meeting Point—WOMP, which was off Cape Race. Here they would be handed over to an escort group from the U.S. Navy that evening.[8] Rayner had sent them half-hourly DF bearings and he also used radio transmission at one stage just to ensure contact. At midnight, the destroyer *Niblack* assumed responsibility for the escorts.[9] This was Task Unit 4.1.3, comprising *Niblack* together with three old four-stack destroyers *Ellis*, *Greer*, and *Tarbell* of 1918/19 vintage, together with the Coast Guard cutter *Alexander Hamilton*. The Canadians' job was done.

Even so, as they left the convoy, Rayner was on his guard. It was not until he had been steaming westwards for a full four hours, at midnight, that he finally broke radio silence to send his report of the convoy to Convoy Operations at St. Johns in Newfoundland.

Meanwhile, the battered ships of HX-170 fought their way eastwards across a stormy Atlantic Ocean. Their escorts were working in a relay system on a convoy-by-convoy basis. For this convoy, the next hand-over point was not specified; it was merely referred to as "MOMP." Towards this point, approaching from the east sailed an outward North America–bound convoy (ON). As its participating ships were old, they could not maintain the minimum speed for a normal convoy of 9 knots. This earned the convoy the suffix "S," making the number for this convoy ONS-57. The civilian ships would continue west to America, but at MOMP the escorts would turn back, now escorting eastbound HX-170 into British waters. The theory was fine, but the problem was the weather. Rayner had struggled as long as he was responsible. The U.S. Navy fared no better. From the east came *Chelsea*—and ONS-57—with great difficulties.

For the British destroyer, it was as if she was meeting friends. She was in fact an old American "four stacker" of the same design as the U.S. escorts. Churchill received 50 old destroyers (this one was of the Class of 1918/19) from Roosevelt in the fall of 1940 and the name was changed from USS *Crownshield* to HMS *Chelsea*.

They had set out from Loch Ewe on the west coast of Scotland, Sunday, 18 January. The *Chelsea* was in charge of an escort group that comprised the Flower Class corvettes *Arbutus, Camellia, Columbine, Eglantine, Mignonette, Pimpernel* and *Snowdrop*. *Eglantine* had a Norwegian crew under Lieutenant Commander Harald Voltersvik, and flew the Norwegian three-split naval flag.

During the night, the west-bound convoy was totally broken up by the weather. The ships were scattered along the route, most had hove to as the weather worsened. There was little point in attempting to reform the convoy until the wind slackened off and the visibility improved. Finally, by the evening, when it was virtually too late, the weather lifted sufficiently for them to attempt to reform.

Tuesday night was a long one for the corvettes—their notorious sensitivity to weather and waves made the next message to them from HX-170 very unpopular. During the night the eastbound convoy had actually hove to and, therefore, they would also be late at MOMP, the Mid Ocean Meeting Point.

Neither side was too clear of their position. The high wind and the drift that it caused, together with the low visibility, made navigation difficult. Star sightings were hard to find. Fortunately, in the evening of Friday, 23 January, the weather broke and the clear skies allowed westbound *Chelsea's* navigators to achieve a firm fix on stars. During the evening they steered a southerly course and proceeded at slow speed, hoping to learn where Convoy HX-170 actually was.

It was after midnight when they heard that HX-170 was going to be an estimated 14 hours late at MOMP. The weather had been so bad that the convoy, according to Ahern, had to ride the weather for about 20 hours. The plan was to meet the convoy after daybreak in order to reduce the dangers of collision. Neither side really knew where the other was. Half an hour after altering the course, *Chelsea* located them using her "271," the shortwave, type 271, radio direction finder. Convoy HX-170 was at that stage about 15 km out from them.

The British ships now altered course and basically tracked the eastbound convoy until daybreak. Only then did they finally close on the nine columns of heavily laden vessels. It now consisted of 23 ships; two more had straggled during the storm. The very strong westerly gales had not turned and were now at least working in their favor, pushing them, but the gale was also building a very big swell. Nevertheless, the merchant navy was keeping its ships on station in the convoy. The *Chelsea* noted that considering the severe weather, they were doing extremely well.

The ON convoys would sometimes include ships bound from Britain for Iceland. These would be handed over to an American escort at the Iceland Ocean Meeting Point, ICOMP, for the onward journey. Similarly, ships from Iceland, or from Russia, would join westbound convoys at this point. The convoys were routed farther north than normal trans–Atlantic shipping in peacetime. A more northerly route kept the convoys away from U-boat bases in France and it also ran closer to Iceland, which in some cases provided extra fuel for the escorts.

On Monday, 19 January, the Convoy commodore informed the *City of Flint* by blinker that her destination was the Clyde, near Glasgow. They nevertheless continued with the rest of the ships until about a week later. The original sailing plan had the *City of Flint's* destination as Iceland.[10] The main body of ships was bound for Liverpool, and as they were heading south down the North Channel into the Irish Sea, at 0300 that final morning, the *City of Flint* left the safety of the escorts and headed for Scotland, where they anchored around 1800, on Tuesday, 27 January. None of the ships were lost during the crossing.

Convoy HX-170: The Sailing Grid[11]

Col. 1	Col. 2	Col. 3	Col. 4	Col. 5	Col. 6	Col. 7	Col. 8	Col. 9
1.1	2.1	3.1	4.1	5.1	6.1	7.1	8.1	9.1
Dagestan	Voco	Hindustan	Athelsultan	Christales	Peshawur	Empire Steel	Clan Macpherson	Empire Spray
1.2	2.2	3.2	4.2	5.2	6.2	7.2	8.2	9.2
Empire Shearwater	Anna Knudsen	Evita	Kaaparen	Rapana	Delphi-nula	Otina	Neuva Granada	Stuart Prince
1.3	2.3	3.3	4.3	5.3	6.3	7.3	8.3	9.3
Ville Marie	Idefjord	Athelqueen	Hammaren	Egda	Amastra	Laurits Svenson	Eidanger	Ulysses
1.4	2.4	3.4	4.4	5.4	6.4	7.4	8.4	9.4
City of Flint	Rapidan			Vinland				

The table refers to the actual layout of the sailing positions in the convoy. The convoy had several columns numbered 1-2-3-4-5-6-7-8-9. 1.1 is the first ship in column 1; 2.1 refers to the first ship in column; 1.2 is the second ship in column 1; 2.2 is the second ship in column 2, etc. The ships had to stay in their positions throughout the convoy and the convoy was always wider than it was long to limit targets to the U-boats.

The *City of Flint* was the first American merchant ship to visit the British Isles since Roosevelt had declared Europe a war zone in the fall of 1939 and therefore out of bounds for ships from the neutral U.S.[12] Yet, perhaps ironically, they brought no aid of any kind; it was all earmarked for Stalin's war effort. All they did was ride at anchor waiting for the signal to continue the journey. Finally a week later, on Wednesday, 4 February they could weigh anchor and under the cover of darkness sail north along the western coast of Scotland to the convoy assembly point at Loch Ewe, arriving around 0800 the following morning. The group was building quickly and early Friday the 13th convoy PQ-11 departed, bound for Murmansk.

The journey was to be a short one. After only a day at sea, they were ordered into

Kirkwall in the Orkneys for a stop of around a week. The weather was just too bad to sail. It was during this period that one of the members of the merchant crew was sent ashore to a hospital for an operation.

During the trip, it became increasingly obvious that the merchant navy's relationship with alcohol was not always as the Armed Guard unit would have wanted it. Ahern noted in his report that it had tended "to flow very liberally." Because of this, the conduct of individual members of the crew appeared at times questionable. Seen in a wider context, a drunken man in a lifeboat would be a liability to himself and his shipmates. On duty on a gun or as a lookout, he would most likely prove to be totally ineffective.

Finally on Saturday, 14 February they weighed anchor and left, bound for Arctic waters. The *City of Flint* was the only American ship in the convoy and only the second U.S. ship of the war to visit the Soviet Union. The only previous American merchantman to have made the journey was the *Larranaga*, under the command of Norwegian Master Cornelius Ree that sailed in convoy PQ-8.

The other merchantmen sailing in PQ-11 were *Ashkhabad, Barrwhin, Daldorch, Empire Baffin, Empire Magpie, Hartlebury, Kingswood, Lowther Castle, Makawao, Marylyn, North King* and *Stepan Khalturin*. The Master of *Kingswood*, owned by Constantines of Middlesbrough, was the designated Convoy Commodore. They all carried general war cargoes, apart from *Daldorch*, which also had 300 tons of platinum in her hold. Platinum gauze was used to create a particular chemical reaction during the manufacture of explosives.

The man responsible for the escort was Commander A.J. Cubison in the minesweeper *Niger*. Together with a second minesweeper *Hussar*, two Hunt class destroyers, the *Airedale* and the *Middleton*, and three anti-submarine trawlers, the *Blackfly, Cape Argona* and *Cape Mariato*, made up the escort. One day out, they met with the Flower class corvette *Oxslip* on her way back from Iceland, she had been ordered to join. Rear-Admiral Robert Burnett at Home Fleet, who organized all the convoy escorts, now removed the destroyers *Airedale* and *Middleton* and the three trawlers.

The journey north was by no means a direct one. In order to stay as far away from German patrols—both sea and air—from bases in occupied Norway, they sailed northwest to Iceland, but in winter they did not use the Denmark Strait. The sea ice on the Greenland side reached too far, at times reducing the passage to a 60-nautical mile channel. The dangers of drift ice to a thin-skinned freighter were all too real in such waters. Even in summer there were dangers from ice, but the shorter nights provided German bombers operating from Norwegian airfields with too much of an opportunity to spot the ships. They had to stay as close to the far edge of the bombers' range as possible.

The convoys skirted around the eastern side of Iceland and continued to the north of Bear Island, following the limits for the drifting ice. Unfortunately, the southernmost point of the West Spitzbergen Island pushed the ice boundary so far south that in order to avoid it, convoys had to sail within 350 nautical miles of North Cape—only a good hour's flying time for a German Ju88. The escort for the convoy would have been well aware of the added threats from *Tirpitz* and her support vessels. In fact, as the *City of Flint* was drawing closer to Murmansk, the *Tirpitz* was away from her base, on a training cruise.

Closer to the Soviet coast, the British cruiser *Nigeria* joined and on the last day the Soviets sent out two of their own destroyers, *Gromki* and *Grozni*, to meet them, together with the minesweepers *Harrier, Hazard* and *Salamander*. The convoy arrived at the inlet on 23 February 1942. It was the first one to have had an escort comprising both (for a while) new Hunt class destroyers and the new Flower Class corvettes equipped with early Model 271 Radio Direction Finders. It was probably just as well that the convoys became more self-reliant at this stage in the war; German Intelligence had cracked the general naval cipher used between the British, American and Canadian navies in the Atlantic. Whatever went out on the general broadcast frequency, the Germans would read it too.

The convoy headed through the anti-submarine nets, into the safety of Kola Bay. They were entering the most desolate port they were ever likely to visit. If Scapa Flow seemed as bad to British sailors as the Argentia base at Newfoundland to the U.S. navy, they had nothing on the original Soviet naval base at Polyarnoe. It played host to the "Senior British Naval Officer, North Russia," SBNO-NR. The person dealing with merchant shipping, SBNO-Murmansk, was based at Murmansk.

They passed the entrance to the narrow inlet into Polyarnoe to starboard, as the ships moved further up the fjord. So far, access was still easy. It was around 13 km across the water to Vaenga, where the Royal Navy had its hospital facility, close to the Soviet airfield. That area was too exposed and had too few quays to accommodate a convoy. Crucially, it was not connected to the vast Soviet railway network. The convoy was bound for Murmansk, 30 km further in. Its location provided for the intermodal transport facilities required to move all the convoyed war materials as quickly as possible to Stalin's eagerly waiting forces. Although the railway had been finished during the First World War, it was only in the 1930s that a carefully planned expansion of the port with associated rail tracks was commenced. Early on Monday, 23 February, the convoy arrived in the harbor at Murmansk. Ahern, clearly not familiar with the narrow fjords, referred to their anchorage as "in the river."[13]

Little had changed in the two years since the previous visit: the host had changed sides, the Americans were expected and none of the ships in port were German. The Soviet bureaucracy appeared as before. The Customs Office still insisted on collecting all their navy identification cards, which were only returned before departure.

The quays at Murmansk were far from adequate for all the freight being landed there and the *City of Flint* had to wait its turn to move up to a free berth. They had to anchor further out. Murmansk in 1942 was very much a port under siege. It has been argued that in all of Europe, perhaps only the Maltese port of Valetta received more enemy bombs than Murmansk that year. Now, at anchor, the Senior British Naval Officer ordered all the visiting ships not to fire at night unless directly targeted. They should rely on local air defenses. The tracer streams were too much of a giveaway as to the locations of ships in the port.

Thursday, 26 February saw the *City of Flint* at anchor, still fully laden. Late that afternoon, around 1640, four German reconnaissance planes appeared above the port, flying at around 3000 meters. As soon as the planes were spotted, they came under fire from Soviet shore batteries and from ships with heavy anti-aircraft guns. The planes came nearer and shore-based machine gun positions joined the firing and around 1650 the *City of Flint*'s guns opened fire. Two of the machine guns, no. 1 and no. 4, did not function during the action. The ships at anchor in the port tried to coordinate the firing as best they could, but none of the planes were seen to sustain any damage. Within ten minutes they had disappeared.

The following day, as the *City of Flint* finally took its place alongside berth no. 10, there was no enemy action to slow down the unloading. This quay was made of concrete, with a timber deck, and had railway access. The berths here were even served with a travelling crane. So far, the bombing had not damaged the large concrete shed (shed no. 47) opposite berths 10 and 11. An air raid shelter was located next to berth 11. Unfortunately, access to these berths was very difficult. They could only be reached via a narrow channel and, as a result, any ship berthed there had to be moved out again without being turned as there was not enough open water for such a maneuver until back in the open fjord. If they were attacked here, there was little they could do to avoid the bombs.

By the end of February, daylight in Murmansk was still limited to only a few hours. Extra lights were required to keep the unloading operation going—yet this was wartime. Britain had been living with blackouts for over two years. In the case of Murmansk, only around 50 km of extremely empty tundra and rock formations separated the Germans from the port. Here the American crew was virtually on the front line in the war, yet they had to work with lights to help them do their jobs and hope they would not aid the German bombardiers at the same time. They had a seemingly never-ending run of air raid warnings and none of them could be ignored.

Unloading under such conditions was slower and more cumbersome than normal. Work was still underway the following day. They had already been interrupted by one air raid alarm that morning, but had not seen any action while at the quay. Although the planes could be used for dive-bombing, this had been a horizontal attack with the planes flying at an altitude of 3000 meters. The port itself was not the target in this raid—they were after the ships at anchor, waiting to be unloaded, or in ballast waiting for the return convoy to be formed. The planes aimed their bombing run at the stretch of open water between Cape Sharapov and Cape Teriberka. This was actually on the coast, but when Soviet air raid wardens first spotted the planes, they would not have known what the German targets were. According to Soviet reports, the attack came at 1334 local time and lasted 32 minutes.[14] The mountains around the fjord and the harbor made early target acquisition impossible. Often the gunners had to wait until the planes were virtually overhead. Six twin-engine Ju88's from KG30, a bomber group then based at Banak in Finnmark in northern Norway, carried out the attack. Although the air defenses on and around the ships opened fire on the planes, none was brought down.

It was a classic demonstration of the type of attack that could not have been done by a flight of Stuka (Sturzkampfbombers) dive-bombers: a high altitude attack by planes flying in formation. For those who were targeted, however, good fortune was on their side. All the bombs landed harmlessly in the water. Experiences from the civil war in Spain indicated that what was then regarded as "high altitude bombing," around 6–7000 m, could be very effective if the crew was well trained. They would be expected to manage to place 90 percent of the bomb load within a square of 200 m by 150 m.[15]

The gun crews were by now on station by their guns ready for action. The second time the air raid siren sounded, the reality of it all became very clear. The enemy planes came into vision quite fast. This time it was no reconnaissance mission. It was a far larger attack, concentrated on the port area of Murmansk.[16] Soviet sources reported the attack as starting at 1739. Eleven deadly minutes sufficed for the planes to disgorge their lethal cargoes.

The Germans had assembled a larger group of aircraft for the dusk raid; five He111's from KG26, the Löwen Group based at Banak, had joined nine Stuka Ju87's from StG5 flown up from Rovaniemi. They shared the escort of six ME110's from JG5's destroyer squadron. As with the earlier attack, the bombers had been airborne for some time prior to the actual bombing. Both KG30 and KG26 would have used an airfield closer to

Murmansk as a refueling stop, normally Kirkenes or Petsamo. In fact, the closest German airstrip was only 60 km, a mere 10 minutes flying away. Once over the target area, they split up to target a wider range of ships.

Ahern counted nine planes heading their way. The three nearest were being watched, higher up in the sky and further behind, by another six. All of them came towards the *City of Flint* from the stern port quarter—the left rear flank. Again, the Germans had developed these open formations on the basis of their experiences in the Spanish Civil War while flying for Franco. Greater distances between groups and formations, combined with different heights, provided more security and greater air coverage without loss of the combined strength of the attacking force. They had tested the actual dive bomb approach in Spain. The ideal dive angle was 70°. Dive-bombing was thought to be ideal for hitting narrow or small targets; it was possible to hit a circle with a 50 m diameter.

The lower group of three planes circled round behind the ship to approximately 90 degrees off the starboard side. At that stage a plane peeled off and commenced its attack dive. The remaining two continued to circle until directly ahead, then a second plane peeled off and commenced its attack. The final one continued to circle until directly off the ship's port quarter before starting its attack. The ship was under attack by planes from StG5, the newly formed dive bomb group.

They now had three Stuka dive-bombers in steep dives coming hurtling towards the ship from different directions. Sinking ships was what this aircraft was made for. The pilot merely had to align the diving aircraft towards the target in order to score a hit, release the bombs and pull back as the bombs continued their deadly flight towards those waiting down below. This targeting mechanism was thus entirely dependent upon the skill and nerves of the pilots as they went in to their near vertical dives.

As the planes separated, gun crew commander Ahern allocated his defenses accordingly, apportioning his guns very strictly. They were all firing at their allotted targets. The guns to starboard poured fire on the first Stuka, the three forward guns faced the second plane and guns 4 and 4–1 were to take care of the last plane. Each of the German pilots would have seen the streams of tracer coming up at them, provided by gunners determined to bring the planes out of the dives before the lethal ordance was released. Each fourth of fifth round would be lighting up as it left the barrel of the guns, streaking heavenwards as an aid to zero in the gun for the coup de grace.

It was at this stage that two of the most powerful Browning 0.50" caliber machine guns malfunctioned, putting them totally out of the firefight. Mercifully, the ship was lucky again. All three bombing runs failed to land any bombs on the *City of Flint*. Whether this merely bore out the fact that the pilots came from a former training unit, or that concentrated firing was sufficient to distract their aim, is uncertain. Between them they dropped five bombs on the ship, four exploded to starboard, on the dock itself, showering the ship and the gun crews with shrapnel and splinters. The fifth bomb came across the ship itself, only to land in the water about 30 meters off the port side. None of the Armed Guard unit sustained any injuries during the attack and the ship was not damaged. Elsewhere, the concentrated firing of the ships in the port brought down two German planes.[17]

In his report of the incident, the Armed Guard commander, Ensign Ahern, praised his gunners. They had remained focused and calm during the attack. Even the personnel at the guns that had malfunctioned remained at their stations throughout, desperately working to pull the jammed rounds out of the breeches of their guns. He noted in amazement that the actual attack had lasted less than a minute. Soviet reports later claimed that their fighters had been responsible for shooting down two enemy aircraft. The Vaenga airbase was only 16 miles from Murmansk, but none of the Soviet planes were scrambled in time to head off the bombers.

This was to be the only time the *City of Flint*'s Armed Guard ever fired their guns to defend the ship. The subsequent stock report confirmed that they had used 460 rounds of 0.50 caliber and another 400 rounds of 0.30 caliber ammunition.

The machine guns, which malfunctioned at that crucial moment, were examined very carefully. They found that in these guns, both the driving rod springs and the firing pin sear springs had lost a considerable amount of tension. Ahern's astute observation on this was quite interesting. Those particular springs had been very lightly oiled, as per instructions. He found that guns with more generously oiled parts actually fared far better under the extreme weather conditions north of the Arctic Circle.

The U.S. had installed a permanent naval presence at Murmansk. The Assistant Naval Attaché had been instrumental in persuading the Soviet authorities to permit the Armed Guard unit to test fire their guns. Now, he wanted to see how their performance measured up. He came aboard on an inspection visit. He found little to complain about and deemed their battle organization, the way the watches were organized, and their training and instructions program to be excellent. In terms of their Arctic clothing, he noted that what had been issued was woefully inadequate. In fact, he pointed out that additional clothes had to be purchased at the ship's expense.[18] The lack of prior knowledge on behalf of the U.S. Navy stores, although perhaps understandable, could so easily have been fatal in the ongoing battle with mountainous icy seas and enemy submarines.

Once unloaded, the *City of Flint* returned to an anchorage away from the quay to await the departure of the return convoy. In the twilight of the morning on Saturday, 7 March a ship that had dragged her moorings again hit her. This time the Soviet freighter *Shelon* drifted down on them and a particularly proud part of her superstructure slammed into the *City of Flint*'s number 4 machine gun, damaging it beyond repair. The Detroit Shipbuilding Company of Michigan built the *Shelon* in 1918 for the U.S. Shipping Board. Fortunately they saw no further action during the return journey where the guns were required.

A huge naval operation in the Norwegian Sea to lure the German naval units, especially the *Tirpitz,* to leave port was still ongoing when Convoy QP-9 was being assembled for departure from Murmansk. This was postponed twice due to suspected enemy U-boat activity in the area.[19] They finally received the signal to "commence weighing" late in the afternoon of Saturday, 21 March. Fifteen minutes later came the crucial signal "weight and proceed." They were underway. By the time they finally sailed down the Kola inlet at 1900, it was dark. Visibility was very bad from the moment they set sail. They stayed as far away from the Norwegian coast as possible, hoping to avoid detection and possible attack by planes at least, but it also meant that they were far closer to drifting ice than if on a course further south. The course, once out into the open Barents Sea was a north-easterly one for the first 24 hours. Only then did they feel safe in turning to a general course towards the south-west and Iceland.

Until 0400 Monday, 23 March, they had the benefit of an extra local escort: the four minesweepers *Gossamer, Harrier, Hussar, Niger* and *Speedwell* from 1st and 6th MS Flotillas, based at Kola. The Soviet destroyer *Gremyaschi* should have escorted them until dusk that evening, but the bad weather meant that she never found the convoy. The destroyer *Offa* together with the minesweepers *Britomart* and *Sharpshooter* provided ocean cover until they reached the safety of Iceland. The cruiser *Kenya*, with ten tons of Russian gold bullion on board, was to have joined the convoy from 22 to 27 March, but because of the bad weather, she did not find them. The gold, however, reached the safety of British vaults.

That Monday, as they were underway from Murmansk, the port was once again under attack by bombers. This time the German aim was better: the freighter *Lancaster Castle* was sunk at pier 9.[20]

In the end, the convoy left with 18 ships in five columns, the Commodore was H.T. Hudson RD, RNR. *Hartlebury* was the first ship in the first column to the left, known as position 11. At the front of the second column, in position 21, was Kingswood; leading the third column in position 31 was *Trevoran*; column four was led by *Daldorch* in position 41. The *City of Flint* (51) was the lead ship in the fifth and last column, sailing in the convoy's front starboard corner. At this stage of the war, the columns were three cables (600 yards) apart during the day and five cables apart at night. When in column, each ship was to maintain a distance of no more than two cables behind the one in front. It was seen as safer for ships to sail in parallel than in a long line one behind the other as the latter would offer one continuous long target for enemy U-boats. In QP-9, the other ships were: *Ashkhabad* (position 34), *Barrwhin* (12), *Earlston* (24), *Empire Baffin* (44), *Empire Magpie* (13), *Llandaff* (14), *Lowther Castle* (32), *Makawao* (53), *Marylyn* (22), *North King* (52), *Pravda* (23), *Shelon* (33), and *Stepan Khalturin* (43).

The convoy arrived in Reykjavik in the evening of Tuesday, 31 March 1942, ten days after leaving Murmansk. The *City of Flint* now had to wait for a group of ships to build for the west-bound Atlantic convoy. While in port, the U.S. Port Director ordered the *City of Flint* to hand over the ship's four Lewis machine guns. Ahern had to arrange for the guns, complete with their tripod mounts and ammunition, to be delivered to the Port Director's office before they sailed.

Nearly two weeks later, at dusk, the new convoy left Reykjavik on a southerly course. These convoys that joined westbound shipping from Liverpool to Halifax, did not have unique designations of their own. They were bound for a meeting place in the middle of the Atlantic, the "Iceland Ocean Meeting Point." They reached this position after three days, according to Ahern. Judging from the departure dates, it is likely that the convoy they joined was the westbound to Halifax ON-82 that had left Liverpool Thursday, 2 April and reached Halifax on Saturday, 18 April, which fitted with Ahern's account where he noted that they reached New York at 0700 Monday, 20 April.

As the war continued, the volume of ships that experienced the mortal dangers of the Barents Sea grew. The men who served in the ships clearly felt that their service should be accorded the same recognition as those who served in other theaters of war. Other actions earned the right to wear specific campaign ribbons. By the middle of 1944, the Arctic convoys had not yet earned the sailors that right.

The Armed Guard unit of the *City of Flint* during PQ-11/QP-9 applied for such a right. When they had met at the Arcadia Conference in December 1941, President Roosevelt and Prime Minister Churchill stressed the significance of needing to help the Soviet Union continue to fight on their side in the war. This commitment made the U.S. Navy's reason for the rejection of the request staggering. The submission from the *City of Flint* had clearly been argued on the basis of their experiences in Murmansk. Although their ship was only the second U.S. ship to unload there, they were followed during the course of only the next year, by an astonishing 120 U.S. ships.

The navy chose to treat the request as a "one off." Regardless of the intensity of the actions endured, Mr. R.S. Edwards, the deputy commander-in-chief, who was Deputy Commander of Naval Operations, argued that, "because of the small number of United States units involved, their significance, based on the overall war effort, is not deemed adequate to merit award of an operation or engagement star."[21]

Edwards had clearly not attended the Arcadia Conference with Roosevelt and Churchill. Fortunately his decision was overtaken by events and within a month the U.S. Navy commander-in-chief instituted the Russian Convoy Operations Star on 22 December 1944. It covered, specifically, convoys between 16 December 1941 and 27 February 1943. The *City of Flint* was second on the list of those ships whose Armed Guard members would be eligible to wear the Star and the ship was in fact specifically mentioned in the memorandum announcing the new award.[22]

Far from all of the participants in subsequent Arctic convoys were as lucky as the *City of Flint* in returning safely to the U.S. Twenty-four hours of daylight, the easy reach of German planes based in Northern Norway and the increased U-boat menace extracted a heavy toll from the convoys. This finally persuaded Churchill and Roosevelt to inform Stalin of their reluctant decision to cease, at least temporarily, operations of Arctic Convoys for the duration of the bright summer nights. Stalin received the telegram 15 July 1942. By this time even U.S. Admiral Ernest J. King acknowledged the high level of loss on Arctic convoys and agreed that convoys to the Persian Gulf were likely to suffer less damage.

The suspension of the Arctic convoys could hardly have come at a worse time for Stalin. In his reply to Churchill of 23 July 1942, Stalin certainly made it clear how urgent he saw the situation. He also claimed that convoys to the Persian Gulf could never make up for the stopped Arctic convoys.

The U.S. view, however, was that only via the Persian Gulf could Soviet supplies actually be sustained at a time of such seasonal dangers from Arctic 24-hour daylight. But distances were so great for Persian destinations that each ship on this route would only manage a maximum of three round-trips per year.[23] This level of commitment would only be possible if the Soviet aid was given the same level of priority as the preparations for the TORCH project to invade French northwest Africa. Murmansk convoys would at the same time be downgraded in priority.

Convoy QP-9 Murmansk to Iceland
21–31 March 1942: Sailing Grid[24]

Col. 1	Col. 2	Col. 3	Col. 4	Col. 5
1.1	2.1	3.1	4.1	5.1
Hartlebury	Kingswood	Trevoran	Daldorch	City of Flint
1.2	2.2	3.2	4.2	5.2
Barrwhin	Marylyn	Lowther Castle	North King	
1.3	2.3	3.3	4.3	5.3
Empire Magpie	Pravda	Shelon	Stephan Kalthurin	Makawao
1.4	2.4	3.4	4.4	5.4
Llandaff	Earlston	Askhabad	Empire Baffin	

The timing for the new priority given to the Persian Gulf convoys was a perfect fit for the City of Flint. *Once the engine maintenance had been carried out and the guns replaced, she was ready for action.*

13

Basra

In May 1942, the *City of Flint* was destined to be one of the early U.S. ships to make her way to the Persian Gulf. By now a convoy system had finally been introduced all along the U.S. East Coast, but even so, the U-boat threat could not be eliminated. The ship was ordered across Upper New York Bay over to Bayonne on the New Jersey side in early May to check the anti-magnetic protection system.[1] Only then was the Armed Guard crew from the Murmansk trip rotated off the ship. In their place came an eight-man group under the leadership of the new coxswain, Frank Camillo. All but one (a USNR) were regular U.S. Navy personnel. They were now all issued with individual sets of foul weather clothing: overalls, short jackets and sou'westers. The equipment list was extensive. Preparations for this convoy seemed far more thorough than for the previous trip. The navy was obviously learning. The instructions now issued to Camillo included a set of safety regulations and most importantly, two sets of silhouettes, both for surface raiders and for aircraft. As the ship was likely to sail long distances on her own during the next assignment, the gun crew would have only themselves to rely on. Early recognition of any danger might make the difference between survival and sinking. More interesting perhaps is the fact that for this journey, unlike the last one, the ship took on 50 gas masks. No detail of the actual cargo is available, however.

Along with the change in Armed Guards, the *City of Flint* changed virtually the entire civilian crew after each journey. The ship's master, L.M. Long, however, remained in charge.

On Friday, 15 May Camillo carried out a thorough inspection of all the naval supplies already aboard ship. Then he went over all the guns and the equipment to satisfy himself that it was all in good condition. The only thing missing was the ammunition.

On the Sunday, while still at anchor in New York harbor, Camillo received his ammunition. They had 95 rounds for the 4"/.50 gun. For the 4" gun, eight cases of 20 mm, seven boxes 0.30 cal. Browning and 17 boxes of 0.50 cal. Browning. This is the only indication that the armaments had been changed. The four original 0.50 cal. Browning machine guns, installed on the ship in December 1941, appeared to remain on board. The four Lewis 0.30 cal. light machine guns, which had been left behind in Iceland, had been replaced with more of the same ineffective weapons. The good news was that they now had a 20 mm machine gun added to their defenses, this was the heaviest rapid firing weapon on board.

Early the following morning, they weighed anchor and moved out of New York harbor. Once underway, Camillo organized his men in a pattern of watches that provided continuous cover. They were heading south as part of a feeder convoy to Hampton Roads, Virginia, where they stayed at anchor in Chesapeake Bay overnight.[2] At the time, there was only one U-boat patrolling off New York, but the German skipper did not spot the new convoy coming south. The convoy route was completely new. In fact, the very first KS (Key West South) convoy had only sailed from Hampton Roads the previous Wednesday. They continued in convoy KS-503 to Key West.

Once at Key West, they hove to for two days, waiting for an escort. The ship's record card, noting all its destinations since October 1941, places the *City of Flint* at Key West Thursday, 28 May. When they left three days later, with the protection of a destroyer, the merchantman was only afforded escort southwards until 15° N.[3] They had sailed in convoy continuously until that point, there had been no opportunity to test fire the ship's guns. In the *City of Flint* papers from this period, there is no reference to any form of handover briefing between the previous Armed Guard team and the next one to be assigned to the ship. None of the current members of the gun crew knew that some of the guns had failed during the attack at Murmansk a few months ago. Yet the guns remained silent, Camillo did not take the early opportunity to test fire any of them.

On the assumption that they took the shortest route south, sailing between Cuba and Haiti, the escort would have left them somewhere in the middle of the Caribbean Sea, several days' sailing away from their Trinidad destination. During 1942, this was a dangerous place to be. The Allies had not yet tackled the U-boat problem and here, in an area supplying two prime war commodities—oil and bauxite (for aluminum for aircraft production)—plenty of Atlantic convoys converged. Admiral Dönitz still had rich pickings; a staggering 350 ships were sunk in this area during 1942. That summer he moved virtually all the available U-boats away from the American coast and into the Caribbean. In May and June, the Germans actually had 10 to 12 U-boats actively hunting for targets in the Gulf of Mexico and the Caribbean. As Dönitz saw it, without convoys, the potential for sinkings was extremely high.

After five days of sailing independently, they finally arrived at Trinidad on Sunday, June 7. There they rested, refueled and topped up the fresh water supplies before leaving early on Tuesday morning. Over the next few weeks they would be continuing to sail in tropical waters, crossing the equator on their way to Cape Town. Ten days into the journey, they sighted a U.S. naval patrol of two destroyers and a cruiser. Three days later, on Monday, 22 June Camillo finally decided to test fire his guns.

The *City of Flint* had a lucky break. She was not spotted by any of the patrolling U-boats and arrived safely at Cape Town only a day late according to the navy's tracking card. They moored on Monday, 5 July, refueled, topped up the water and left the following day. Captain Long kept his crew alert and ready for action. Twice weekly throughout the journey he held lifeboat drills and emergency drills.[4] Camillo kept to a similar regime with gun drills.

July was not a good month for the U-boats in the Indian Ocean. A few Japanese submarines were normally on patrol there, and during July 1942, seven ships were sunk, but fortunately the *City of Flint* saw no enemy shipping. As they sailed north through the Arabian Sea, on Friday, 17 July they spotted several ships from the British navy, who approached the *City of Flint* to verify her identification. They knew all too well that German surface raiders, disguised as civilian merchant ships, were preying on Allied shipping in the Indian Ocean.

They sailed up the Shat al Arab waterway to Abadan on Tuesday, 28 July at 2130 hrs. and immediately started to unload the cargo in order to minimize the hold-up for the valuable wharf space. Later that night they cast off again to move further up the river to Basra.

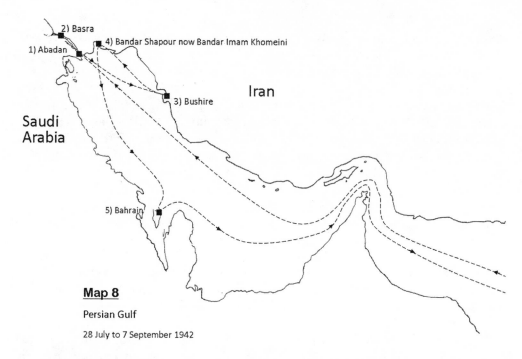

Map 8

Persian Gulf

28 July to 7 September 1942

Unloading proved to be difficult and fragmented, with the ship being sent to a number of different ports in the region. All were challenging to reach and very inefficient.

By the end of the week, they had finished discharging at Basra and left, heading back down the river and into the Persian Gulf to Bushire where most cargoes had to be unloaded seven miles out to sea into smaller native craft. The waters were just too shallow for large freighters. The isolation and the shallow draft permitted when landing cargoes made this port the least useful of all the Gulf ports for the Soviet war effort. It took them a full six days to unload the part of the cargo destined for this port. Then back up the Gulf, to Bandar Shapour on Monday for yet another discharge operation. It was a terrible place to be. The climate was extreme and the first Americans to arrive had been provided with accommodation in mud huts. Next door was a local camp full of refuse and crawling with vermin.[5] Fortunately the *City of Flint* did not stay long, before moving back up to Khorramsharh to discharge the final cargo.

The journey was slow; it was Saturday, 1 August when they finally arrived, only to find that all berths were filled. The volume of the support operation was proving too much for the small port facility. As a result the *City of Flint* had to anchor in the river to await space to discharge. The port was a real bottleneck. The unloading capacity for the entire port was a mere 700 tons per day. One single ship of the size deployed by the Allies for this purpose would normally carry at least 4000 tons of cargo. None of the berths in the Persian Gulf offered adequate facilities at the time when the *City of Flint* arrived there, but as the American construction operation gradually gathered momentum, the situation improved significantly.

The climate was particularly bad at Bandar Shapour. The afternoon temperatures would range between 110°F (43°C) and 125°F (52°C) and some would exceed 140°F (60°C). The extremely high humidity and dust storms made it all far worse to endure for the crews and the locally based personnel struggling to unload the cargoes. The crew on the *City of Flint* was no different. The heat started to take its toll on them. Every one that fell ill meant more work for those who remained fit. Even if they were fit enough to work, they struggled with morale and motivation to turn out for each watch. It was a spiral of attrition, which no one seemed able to break. The captain had to get the cargo off the ship as quickly as possible.

On Saturday, 5 September they slipped their moorings and headed back out into the Gulf. By now they had spent around 40 days discharging their cargo and moving between the ports in the area.

The Senior British Naval Officer Persian Gulf noted in his report for this period that they were struggling with a high level of seasonal sickness, entirely due to the extreme weather conditions of the area.[6]

On Monday they called in to Bahrain Island to bunker. The day after, they departed the island and shaped a course out of the Persian Gulf. The vast cargo holds were empty; for the first leg of the homeward journey the ship would be riding the ocean like a cork. They were again about to enter the hunting ground of the Japanese submariners.

During the month of August the Japanese had managed to sink only one ship, and in September, five. By that summer, however, the Germans had become increasingly aware of what the Americans could achieve if they managed to open another transport corridor to the Soviet Union. They routed some of their own U-boats into the Indian Ocean to bolster the Japanese effort—in October 1942 a total of 29 ships were sunk in the Indian Ocean, 23 by German boats, 6 by Japanese. The Japanese submarine effort was very modest indeed. They were worried about the possibility of reprisals from the Soviet Union if they attacked the U.S. supply lines.

For the next two weeks the *City of Flint* sailed independently, constantly on guard, constantly watching the horizon for the low telltale profile of a U-boat conning tower. Finally, on Sunday, 27 September they reached Durban, where they were scheduled to pick up some cargo. They had been at sea for around three weeks without any opportunity to relax, or to escape from the threat of a sudden explosion, which could so easily have shattered their fragile metal shell.

Three days later they were off again. On their own they were bound for Port of Spain, Trinidad.

The next four weeks were spent on the journey north, across the Atlantic, up along the coast of Brazil, before they sailed into Port of Spain on Monday, 26 October. Ulrich Thilo in *U-174* was on patrol in Brazilian waters from the end of October until the middle of December, sinking four ships in the process. By the time he had arrived from his unsuccessful time in the Atlantic, the *City of Flint* had just slipped past his new beat.

In Trinidad they actually had time to relax and unwind a little before joining a northbound convoy. The local U.S. Navy representative inspected the gun crew, their quarters, the guns and the ammunition stores. Again, the Armed Guard came through; everything was found to be in good order. The strain of all was beginning to tell however. One of the members of the Armed Guard suddenly broke down. The pressure of such a lonely voyage, the knowledge of the silent hunter waiting somewhere out there was too much. The reminders of the likelihood of a violent demise were all too frequent through the regular lifeboat drills, gun drills, fire drills, etc. It could become too much to bear for anyone.

The following Tuesday, 10 November, they departed, bound for Guantanamo Bay in convoy TAG-20. According to the U.S. Navy tracking card for the ship, TAG-20 was a slow convoy. U.S. naval units escorted it.

Late Thursday afternoon, as they were arriving off Curaçao, one of the escorts exploded. The convoy was skirting the Caribbean before striking out on a northerly course directly toward Cuba.[7] *Erie*, a U.S. Treasury class Coast Guard cutter, had been hit by a torpedo fired by Engelmann in *U-163*. Sadly, the fires ignited her ammunition store, which exploded, killing seven men and wounding 11, making the crew abandon ship. At the time she was less than half a mile directly ahead of the *City of Flint*. According to Camillo, there was nothing but open sea between them. Engelmann must have watched them both before deciding that the Erie was a more rewarding target than the merchantman, which would have been riding high in the water, indicating the absence of any valuable cargo. The destruction of an escort vessel would leave the rest of the convoy more vulnerable and open to further attacks.

On the *City of Flint* the Armed Guard went into action. As the Master maintained the course, the gun crew opened fire on a sector where one of the other escorts, a destroyer, dropped depth charges. They hit nothing and the journey simply continued without any interruptions. Stopping would leave the ships in the convoy even more exposed to the U-boat danger. The *Erie* was left behind. Then at 1930, the alarm called them to General Quarters again. All the guns were quickly crewed and ready. Camillo was told from the bridge that a destroyer had spotted a U-boat ahead of them off the port bow. Again, they saw nothing and this time did not discharge their guns. The gun crews were eventually allowed to stand down when the all clear signal was given.

By sheer quirk of fate, the torpedoing of the *Erie* was being watched by Captain Gainard, the *City of Flint*'s skipper at the time of the 1939 German prize incident. Unbeknownst to any of the merchantmen in the convoy, they had been joined by one of the U.S. Navy's "mystery ships," the *Big Horn,* Gainard's latest ship. Although looking like a slow, old oiler, she was in reality a well-armed trap for U-boats, made virtually unsinkable by a cargo comprising thousands of empty, sealed oil drums packed in her holds. Gainard went ashore in January 1940, only to find his "shore leave" cancelled by the U.S. Navy a year and a half later. This time his ship carried far more punch. Hidden behind false walls were no fewer than five 4"/.50 caliber guns. The Americans were determined to stop the sinking of freighters so close to their shores. It was a very dangerous type of ship to be in. The first of these so-called Q-ships, *Carolyn*, commissioned as *Atik*, was torpedoed on 25 March 1942; no one survived.

Gainard was pretending to straggle from TAG-20, hoping to offer an attractive target to the discerning Engelmann. In reality they were too far away to take any action but it could all too easily have ended with him watching his own former command disappear below the waves. During all of November Gainard was looking for unsuspecting U-boats without any luck. December 1 saw them back in New York at the Todd Shipyard in Hoboken to have hedgehog antisubmarine weapons installed. At this stage Gainard was rotated off the ship.

Dönitz had three U-boats in the area at the time. Yet the *City of Flint* had survived once more. In fact, the German count stood at ten ships sunk between Trinidad and Aruba during the first week of November 1942 alone. The area was at the time regarded as the most rewarding area of operations in the entire Atlantic theater. Within six months *U-163* was depth-charged and sunk with all hands.

Two nights later on Saturday, roughly at the same time, again as the light was fading, General Quarters was sounded. The Armed Guards rushed to crew up the guns and scan the horizon for any signs of a U-boat spying on them. Eventually the All Clear was sounded and they could relax. No shots had been fired.

Soon they reached the safety of Guantanamo Bay where they joined the final convoy for the journey home—GN-20. From there on the journey was uneventful. The convoy escorts along the Eastern Seaboard of the USA offered the U-boats too much opposition. Merchant shipping was by now far more secure moving along the coast than during any period since the U.S. joined the war. The *City of Flint* finally arrived back at New York around 2100 on Monday, 23 November 1942.

November 1942 proved to be a particularly ominous month for Hitler. Operation TORCH landed Allied soldiers on Moroccan beaches, determined to convince Vichy French troops of the value of changing their loyalties. At the same time Rommel, by good fortune, managed to evade capture in North Africa. Within days, Marshall Shukov launched his massive counterattack in the Caucasus and at Stalingrad. Giving the two initiatives equal priority was paying off for the Allies, but the effort needed to be sustained. This meant maintaining a series of long and still very vulnerable supply lines to North Africa.

SECTION IV

Torpedoed

14

The Prey

Charles City, Iowa, was in 1942 a town of around 20,000 people. It was part of the American agricultural belt, making a living on cattle, hogs, and vast corn crops. In September that year, the charitable organization, the Charles City Elks Lodge, no. 418, under its then leader, sporting the title of Exalted Ruler, Mr. Jack P. Henry, decided to help the war effort. They arranged a big recruitment drive.

Cub journalist Al Becker and his friends knew about this and one day during the campaign they skipped work, went into town and joined up. All 26 of them opted for the Navy. That Saturday the Elks Lodge organized a big banquet for them in at the park in the center of town. Part of that celebration was the actual swearing-in ceremony of the 26 new volunteers to the United States Navy. There was no time to change their minds. At the end of the celebrations, the recruits boarded a bus for the training camp. Al, the youngest of the three Becker boys, was the first to join the forces. His parents had a large farm. About two years later, his oldest brother was drafted, leaving his father with only one son to help him run the vast farm. The U.S. Government regarded such work as essential to the war effort and granted the third young Becker a deferment. His three sisters, who were still living at home, also helped with all the work.

After a long and grueling journey, travelling through the night, the new recruits arrived at the Great Lakes Camp near Chicago on Sunday, 27 September 1942. This was to be home for the next four weeks. It was to be a fairly quick conversion from a civilian to a naval way of life. At "boot camp" no trades were taught, only basic skills, drill etc. Using an old whaling boat off the pier, which was just down the road from the station, they were taught survival skills and boat drill.

At this stage, Al Becker had never seen the ocean. He had only read about the navy and hoped that he would get to see a lot of countries. He just liked it; besides he felt that there, he'd be safer than down a foxhole. It was a clean life, with a lot less danger on a battleship.

After the boot camp Al was transferred for more specialized training at Gulf Port, Mississippi. This town, on the Gulf of Mexico, and not far from New Orleans, played host to the U.S. Navy's gunnery school. Unlike the Great Lakes Camp, Gulf Port was focused on turning out well-trained gunners who could be placed aboard any U.S. merchant navy ship and handle their armaments. Six weeks it took to turn Al into such a versatile and skilled combatant. Armed Guards saw active service in every theater of the war where ships sailed. They protected their ships and their cargoes against enemy attacks by air or by sea or by land. Unlike their fellow sailors on the merchant navy ships where they served, their duties were not over when the ship arrived in foreign ports. Their ships were far more easily hit from the air when waiting at anchor or while moored at a pier somewhere, waiting to discharge their valuable cargo.

A very young Al Becker trained and ready to go to war, fall of 1942. He was 19 and had volunteered to serve his country (courtesy John Becker).

After completion of his training in mid–December 1942, Al was sent to the huge Armed Guard Center in Brooklyn, New York.

The main accommodation building at the Center was like an enormous aircraft hangar. Three-tiered stacks of bunks were spread across the main deck in the hundreds. Yet it was still large enough to accommodate an area for concerts, prize-giving ceremonies, etc. In Al's words, sleeping at the top bunk was "like sleeping up in the hayloft."[1] This was his staging post before he was assigned to a ship. He did not wait long. The U.S. merchant navy was becoming increasingly active in convoys to various parts of the world. There was not much of a chance to take in the sights of pre–Christmas New York, very disappointing to a young man who had never had the chance to see the city before.

As Al was completing his training, the crew of the *City of Flint* tidied up the ship after the long voyage to Basra and back. Captain Long went ashore. At this stage he had done two long treks in the *City of Flint*. The discharge date for his latest journey was Wednesday, November 25, 1942. On that date the responsibility for the ship passed to Master John B. MacKenzie. MacKenzie lived in New York, at 2001 McGraw Avenue, the Bronx, approximately halfway between Bronx Park and Westchester Creek. On that Wednesday he had to travel downtown to provide a signed acknowledgment that he had received the U.S. Navy's instruction for scuttling his new command.

The U.S. Government did not want a repeat of the events of October 1939 when the ship ended up as a German prize. By now they had a policy in place, which confidentially ordered the masters of U.S. flagged merchants to prevent them from falling into enemy hands. When defense was no longer an option, the Master was ordered to "open sea valves, to flood holds and compartments adjacent to machinery spaces, start numerous fires and employ any additional measures available to ensure certain scuttling of the vessel."[2]

MacKenzie's first voyage in the *City of Flint* was a short and uneventful one; on 27 November 1942 he departed New York, bound for Baltimore to complete an engine overhaul, armaments changes and a crew rotation. He knew most of them might take some time ashore after such a long tour as the previous voyage. Once at the shipyard, only a skeleton crew would be required. Those of the original crew who wanted to return, would take a few days leave and be back on board in early December. In the meantime, the Armed Guard crew stood aboard until replacements arrived and they were relieved.

Within a few days, Al and a handful of his fellow Guards were on the train, heading down the coast to Baltimore. Their orders were cut 15 December 1942. It looked like a Christmas at sea that year. The new coxswain, Melvin J. Schad, came with Al's group; 11 of them were covered by the order to join the *City of Flint* at this stage. Once on board, they joined a small group of Guards already assigned to the ship. Ensign Lewis Z. Carey, the officer in charge of the Armed Guard unit on the ship, together with seven other Armed Guards had been ordered on board a week earlier. Together they became the nucleus of the ship's Armed Guard detachment.

The next day MacKenzie received the confidential documents required for his job as the captain of a merchant vessel in wartime.[3] One of these was the BAMS Instructions: Broadcast to Allied Merchant Ships was the regular information service to Allied merchant ships at sea. The information broadcast covered news to convoys all over the Atlantic or Indian oceans, on minefields, U-boat locations, re-routings, etc.

The broadcast was transmitted at regular intervals, in code. They used Naval Cypher No. 3, which had been altered the day before MacKenzie received his new code book for MERSIGS, as the code was known. Thus B-Dienst, the German navy's own decryption operation, temporarily lost access to a very useful source of information, which often had been crucial to their operations.

Like the rest of the members of the Armed Guard, Al had no choice in the ship he should join. They were just picked. He was assigned to the *City of Flint*. It was a big seven-hold cargo ship. Al did not then know about the 1939 capture. The first impression of the ship was that she was old; she had had numerous coats of paint. She looked solid though. To Al she was a massive structure.

The ship, owned by the U.S. Maritime Commission, was still operated by the Moore-McCormack Lines of New York. It was a merchant navy ship, operated entirely by civilian merchant navy personnel; they controlled the ship. The U.S. Navy assigned a unit from the U.S. Navy Armed Guard to each U.S. merchant navy ship; they protected it. MacKenzie had known nothing about the Armed Guard until then. He did know about the U-boats, knew that they had been plaguing the East Coast all along since the U.S. joined the war.

Bethlehem Key Highway Shipyard at Baltimore, Maryland, was allocated the job to change virtually all the armaments on the *City of Flint* early in December 1942. Not until now was the 0.50 cal. Browning machine gun replaced. The weapon in 1942 was basically the same gun as the one originally introduced to the U.S. Navy in 1925. Unfortunately it had two fundamental shortcomings: its lack of effective range and the lack of stopping power due to the small projectile. A 0.50 caliber projectile is only 12.7 mm in diameter. The 0.30 caliber Lewis machine guns were even more inferior, with a caliber far smaller than that of the Armed Guard handguns, the Colt 1911's, which were 0.45 caliber. The Lewis gun was basically an automated gun firing regular rifle caliber ammunition.

City of Flint, 5 January 1943, just before leaving on her last convoy. Note all the gun platforms now protecting the ship. The torpedo hit the ship just in front of the bridge (The Mariners' Museum and Park).

The original idea was that the guns would be effective in strafing attacking planes that came within its short range. As seen from the bomb attack in Murmansk earlier in the year, the weapons were totally ineffective. The U.S. Bureau of Ordnance had agreed as early as 1928 that a heavier weapon was needed. Nevertheless, it had still taken the terrible toll of the Arctic convoy PQ-17 in July 1942, where 14 of 21 American merchantmen were lost, to make the U.S. Navy start changing anti-aircraft guns. While 0.30 caliber bullets had too short a range to be useful, the 0.50 caliber may have reached the targets, but these bullets merely tapped the sides of the incoming planes with the velocity of hailstones. Heavier 20 mm and 3-inch anti-aircraft guns were installed, although initially only on U.S. merchant ships sailing in the arctic convoys.

The new weapon, the 20 mm Oerlikon, was a popular choice. The main attraction to any navy was that the weapon required no external power supply; it was entirely self-contained. The British Navy, and a year later, in 1941, the U.S. Navy started to introduce the Oerlikon as merchant ship armaments. It could be placed anywhere on a ship's deck and if required, could be operated by nonspecialized personnel. The weapon gained a reputation as a ready and responsive gun, which, due to its short range, was most effective when the action came up close. These guns often became the hands of revenge that reached out and brought down the enemy planes—after they had come close enough to drop the bomb load.

In direct comparison of ammunition too, the Oerlikon proved a vast improvement. The 20 mm round was more than 50 percent greater than a 0.50 caliber round and thus had far greater potential for damaging incoming enemy aircraft. The ammunition offered a far more effective choice of projectiles from armor piercing rounds to high explosive or tracer.

They were also very reliable, offering qualities which were particularly significant in a midwinter storm in the Atlantic. They worked from a far greater gas pressure than did comparable weapons. As a result, potential problems such as friction, cold weather or rain, etc., were simply overcome by the brute force of the operating mechanism. Stoppages were therefore relatively rare.

On the *City of Flint*, only the 4"/.50 caliber gun on the poop deck, and Mk IX Model 5 remained on board, together with two 20 mm machine guns Mk IV. The two 0.50 caliber Browning machine guns and the 0.30 Lewis guns were removed.[4] Now the ship received five new 20 mm Oerlikons. These new guns required a change of barrel at regular intervals and they were delivered with five spare barrels. These were stored in cooling tanks next to each of the guns. The barrels were to be changed after prolonged periods of firing (around 240 rounds), normally regarded as four magazines (each holding 60 rounds). The loader, wearing asbestos gloves, would carry out the change.

The 20 mm guns were mounted in critical locations across the ship. The one on the forecastle remained, only to be swapped a week later at the Beth Yard at Hoboken for a 3"/.50 caliber gun.[5] The other of the original 20 mm guns, on the poop deck, were now complemented with a new Oerlikon. Two further Oerlikons were placed on each bridge wing with the final pair placed each side of the boat deck. The boat deck was immediately above the Armed Guard quarters and the guns were placed to the rear of the lifeboats.

The long barrels on the 4" and the 3" contributed to the guns' accuracy. Al felt that if the Range and Scale dials on either gun were set correctly, the grenade would find its target. The 3" was far more maneuverable, and being an anti-aircraft gun, the elevation of the barrel was far better than the 4", which would fire on any U-boat given a chance.[6] Both guns had "radius limiters" built in. When being wheeled around during the heat of an attack, they had to be prevented from blowing the bridge off the ship.

At the massive U-boat bunkers at Lorient, *U-575* was being overhauled before its next patrol. Lorient was an ideal location for the U-boats, it was a harbor on the Brittany peninsula, facing the Bay of Biscay.

The *U-575* was a relatively new boat. It was laid down 1 August 1940 at Blohm & Voss in Hamburg and was commissioned 19 June 1941 to Kapitänleutnant Günther Heydemann. It was his first command. The spring of 1941 had been propitious for Heydemann. After nearly three years as an Oberleutnant zur See, he was finally promoted to Kapitänleutnant at the beginning of April.

Now he was preparing for his last of seven war patrols in *U-575* before transferring to become a training officer in July 1943.

More than 700 U-boats of the VIIC design were built. The 500-ton boat had a total length of 67 meters—equivalent to a row of a dozen average sized family cars. On the surface, the twin diesel engines would give it a maximum cruising speed of 17 knots; submerged, the electrical battery-operated motors would provide 7.6 knots. The armaments comprised four forward torpedo tubes and one rear facing tube. On deck they had an 88 mm cannon and on the rear part of the conning tower a single 20 mm anti-aircraft machine gun. At the optimal surface cruising speed of 12 knots, they would have a range of 6,500 miles. The normal complement was a crew of 44. The boat's tight turning circle

All of the crew of *U-575* parading, probably at St. Nazaire in spring 1943. Note the regular military salute. The German navy did not introduce the "German Salute" until after the 1944 assassination attempt on Hitler (courtesy Michael Elstermann).

and relatively high surface speed made the VIIC a very dangerous opponent. In theory, a VIIC could outrun escorting corvettes, but she would remain vulnerable to their guns in the process.

As the *City of Flint* was re-armed, *U-575* was undergoing slight alterations to allow them to use the brand new FAT's "Flächenabsuchender" or area searching torpedoes. They could "search" an area. They could be pre-set to turn sharply to a pre-arranged side once launched and then later start turning back and forth in a zigzag pattern. This was thought to increase the chance of striking ships sailing in convoy lines, which a correctly aimed FAT would cross repeatedly.

The FAT was basically a traditional G7a torpedo with some improvements for the course alterations. The letter "G" meant that the torpedo had a diameter of 53.3 cm and "7" indicated that it was 7.16 m long. The final letter "a" indicated that this was a torpedo propelled by air and alcohol, which left a clear trail of bubbles in its wake and which pointed directly back to the U-boat. Consequently it was best used at night.

Before they moved the U-boat out to a regular quay for supplies, the torpedoes were loaded. The *U-575's* rear-facing tube had internal storage for one single reload. The one loaded in the tube, ready to be launched, was a FAT. Stored internally for the next firing, was a regular G7e—an electrically powered torpedo. The first four to go into the bow tubes were FATs. The next four were stored below the deck in the bow section, below hammocks and kit belonging to some of the crew. Swinging in the torpedo tube loading gear above them were a further two 1600 kg G7e's. This was not strictly according to regulations, but it provided another two valuable chances to hit enemy ships. Finally, outside

U-575 skipper Heydemann receiving his knight's cross. He is being congratulated by Hans-Rudolf Rösing, who was head of U-Boats West, while the medal ribbon is placed around his neck by the head of the 7th U-boat Flotilla, Herbert Sohler, on 3 July 1943 (courtesy Michael Elstermann).

the pressure hull, in front of the conning tower, were stored two extra torpedoes which could be transferred to the internal tubes in calm seas.

The next day, Tuesday, 8 December, the U-boat was degaussed and tested before finally being declared battle-ready. By Sunday, 13 December, the ship was nearly ready to sail. All non-perishable provisions and all kit was already on board and stowed. That morning, as the sign of imminent departure; the fresh provisions arrived, always as late as possible.

They departed with an escort, as they had to remain surfaced during the initial part of the exit. Furthermore, their best speed was while surfaced and they now wanted to cross the busy shipping lanes as quickly as possible. The weather was good, although a south-westerly wind at around 30 knots had started to whip up fairly frequent white horses, foam trails, on the waves.

Suddenly, an unexpectedly large wave washed over the boat, sending water crashing down on the crew below the open conning tower hatch. More seriously, it snapped the primitive radar antennae mast for the FuMB—the Funkmessbeobachtung, the Metox radar. The time had just passed 2200. They were only six hours into the patrol and blind to anything beyond the eyesight of the lookouts.

Throughout the night and the following day, Heydemann took his boat down for several long dives. It was early Monday evening before he finally ordered them to surface. Then he realized there was a serious problem. The attack periscope was malfunctioning. Visibility was gone. The header section of the periscope tube had flooded. It was full of seawater. They simply could not continue the patrol unable to attack. For offensive purposes, *U-575* was blind.

The attack periscope was operated from within the conning tower. This periscope was known as the "Standsehrohr," and the operator simply stood upright when operating it. Directly below the conning tower was the U-boat's central operations room, the "Zentrale," the nerve center of the U-boat. A second periscope was operated from here. This was by far the better of the two periscopes, as the lenses in the top section, in the "bottle," were larger. The attack periscope was as narrow as possible to avoid detection by vigilant enemy lookouts, but as a result, it was more demanding of natural light. At night the navigational periscope was a far better option, given the choice.

Even the angle of view could be altered on the navigational periscope. By tilting the lenses, the view could be changed from merely surveying the sea to allowing a view of the airspace above. This flexibility gave the periscope its nickname—it was known as the "knee bend scope." The viewing angle was changed by the operator bending and straightening his knees, while pulling or pushing on the vertical periscope column.

The attack periscope was operated from the same section of the U-boat as the machine used to calculate and set the angle and course of the torpedoes. Both were in the conning tower. The readings from the attack periscope optics were those required as input into the calculation machine, the Torpedo Vorhalt-Rechner, the advance course calculator for targeting enemy ships. They used this to plan their attacks. Against the wall in the tower were the communications tubes to the torpedo rooms in the bow and the stern as well as down to the Zentrale on the deck below. Now, the "T. Vorhaltr" was blinded. Adjusting the torpedo settings manually throughout the entire patrol was not an option. The T. Vorhaltr reduced the chance of firing the torpedo in front of or behind the ship at which it was aimed.

"Periscope must be changed," read the entry in his war diary. There was nothing to ponder over. Ten minutes later he fired off a telegram to base, informing them of his return. They were 24 hours into the patrol before they turned back to base.

Fortunately, the periscope repairs were quickly concluded. In the morning of Thursday, 17 December they topped up the provisions of fresh and perishable food and as light started to drop in the afternoon, they were escorted out. Visibility was bad as they left for the second time.

During the night they surfaced for a couple of hours, waiting to receive the U-boat broadcast from BdU, the U–Boat Command, when the FuMB radar mast rail broke again. The reinforcements had been ineffective.

Around Friday lunchtime, they surfaced to recharge the main batteries and air the boat. Using the diesel engines, they could double the speed and U-boats therefore spent most of their time at sea surfaced. This time, they were only allowed an hour's peace before one of the sharp-eyed lookouts raised the alarm. Planes were approaching. Although they dived quickly, Heydemann waited for the sound of detonating depth charges around them. None came, and after a few minutes they concluded that the planes must have been their own long-range Ju88's. Being cautious, Heydemann kept them submerged for a further six hours before resurfacing.

Only a couple of practice alarms broke the routine over the next few days. Heydemann knew where he wanted to be, namely in quadrant B45 on the German naval grid chart of the Atlantic.[7] The location was approximately half way between Lorient and Newfoundland, directly to the west of the base. Surface conditions were bad that night. The westerly wind was pushing a gale towards them, waves were building, and white

A rare photo of a U-boat flying the British Royal Navy ensign to signal that it is surrendering. The U-boat is on the way in to Derry/Londonderry, one of the official surrender ports for the German U-boats in May 1945 (author's collection).

streaks of foam were flying over the crests, making the time on look-out duty miserable and wet.

At ten that night Dönitz started to organize his forces in that part of the Atlantic. Heydemann received new orders to head south towards quadrant CF78. This would place them directly between the Azores and Madeira, in waters frequently used by Allied convoys. They were to be part of a group of U-boats operating together, as a Wolfpack code-named Delphin.

When the new complement of Armed Guardsmen joined the American *City of Flint*, the degaussing system had just been checked and calibrated and the engines had been overhauled while at the Bethlehem Shipyard.

On board the ship, the Guards discovered that they actually had their own quarters. They were amidships, behind the bridge house. Al thought it was a nice spot. They even had their own galley, but the merchant crew cooked the food in the main galley and sent it over to them. They ate in their own mess. Even at sea, they were two crews living separately. The Armed Guard did not really associate much with the merchant navy crew. None of them had actually been on the ship that long. They were, however, all very sociable and they did occasionally go to each other's quarters.

Once the skeleton merchant crew was on board, they sailed the ship north to New York, where the rest of the crew joined them. The ship arrived only three days before Christmas. Al discovered that they docked at the huge Bush Terminal in Brooklyn, then known as the Military Ocean Terminal. They were within walking distance of the Naval Guard Center where he had spent a few nights a week earlier. The area had its own railway access, making freight movements easy. The tracks cut through the Bay Ridge, looped back across Queens and across the river and north through the Bronx. The site itself stretched from 58th Street south to 64th Street.

At least being so close to the Armed Guard Center meant that they could have their Christmas dinner ashore, which was more pleasant. Regardless, the setting, the lack of festive decorations and the near blackout all contributed to Al's lack of Christmas spirit that year.

In the middle of the Atlantic, Christmas Eve was a good day for sailing—a slight westerly wind, a long gentle swell and good visibility. Nevertheless, in order to be sure of peace during their Christmas celebrations, just after 1700 Heydemann ordered them to take the U-boat down below the waves, out of sight from enemy eyes. For the next two hours the sea provided shelter as the warriors celebrated the Holy Night. An hour after resurfacing, they received Dönitz's Christmas message to all his U-boat crews: "I wish you and yours a Happy Christmas. I think of you with my best wishes to each of you. Your Commanding Officer."[8]

Christmas Day was quiet, but early the next morning, before daybreak, in bright moonlight, the lookouts spotted a corvette around 5–6 km off their stern. They were only a good 200 km off the eastern islands in the Azores. Heydemann decided to remain on the surface. It was just as well that he did; by lunchtime another route change came in. They were to continue south to the Cap Verde Islands.

By New Year's Eve, they were a day's sailing south of the Azores. At midnight they dived to be in peace for their own private celebrations, only to surface 45 minutes later to another message from BdU, he was determined to keep their fighting spirits up:

U-boat men!
The New Year sees us as during the previous three years uninterrupted in battle. Where we are, is the

enemy; from the North Cape to the Cape the Good Hope; from the American coast to the Mediterranean. New U-boats are prepared and crews are trained, we all have but one goal! To beat the enemy. This goal fills us totally. In this new year, with our hearts and with patience, not with bitterness, we will achieve it. It is all for our German homes. Live the Führer.—Dönitz, Admiral and Officer Commanding the U-boats.[9]

Two days later he ordered them further west and Sunday, 3 January, on a day with no wind and virtually no swell, with brilliant visibility, Heydemann was at the middle of the Atlantic. At three minutes to five, it all started. Auffermann in *U-514*, operating independently to the south and west of the Delphin Wolf Pack, had spotted a tanker convoy, TM-1, just five days out from Trinidad; they were half way to the Cape Verde Islands. He now transmitted the location and the course to the others. The convoy was heading towards Africa.

Immediately, Dönitz took charge. Only he knew where all his boats were located, and now he moved them in for the kill. The convoy was about to enter a part of the Atlantic where they were out of range for any air cover, exactly the area where the Delphin boats had established their beat lines, between the Azores and Madeira. Several tankers were sunk, others were left as burning hulks.

Fortunately for his prey, Heydemann hit nothing with any of his five torpedoes. Some explosions have been put down to depth charges, which by then were exploding all around. For all his maneuvers and struggle to avoid depth charges, he had no results. Others did, and several ships were drifting in the area, abandoned.

Before *U-575* moved away from the carnage of burning ships and exploding oil tankers, Heydemann returned to the scene, surfacing carefully in what must have been a surreal environment. Ahead was the towering hull of a burning, deserted tanker, her davits swinging empty, the lifeboats long since lowered by a crew anxious to get away before she exploded under them. Now the lifeboats were left empty, drifting helplessly like ducklings, around the stricken mother ship as the convoy rescue ship had abandoned them.[10] Heydemann, obviously knowing what to look for, surfaced to pick over the remains. He might be accused of scavenging, while on the other hand, he could arguably claim to merely be practical in his actions. The crew went over some lifeboats, the stores on tanker lifeboats being particularly valuable. They contained supplies the crew valued—like dried milk and vitamin pills, even clothes like pullovers and American-made oilskins and waterproof maps. Most of these were not stores found on lifeboats from other merchant ships.

Finally, at 0635, still under cover of darkness, but with good visibility, Heydemann spotted three tankers in front of him. From his position he felt it was impossible to miss; the three overlapped each other in one long continuous line of opportunity. He fired all his four bow torpedoes in one salvo, before spotting yet another ship straggling about two km away. He scored two hits this time, the Panamanian-registered *Nordvik* and the Norwegian *Minister Wedel*, crippled and set afire. Neither ship sank, however, and they awaited their fate.

Heydemann now had two electric torpedoes left for his front tubes. His bow torpedo store could hold four, which he had used. As he ordered the loading of the final two battery powered torpedoes, the engine crew reported they wanted to stop the starboard diesel engine due to piston wear.

During the night, Heydemann dived to be able to carry out the engine repairs undisturbed. The next morning he was determined to be ready for more action as soon as

A German Type VII U-boat caught on the surface (author's collection).

possible. Outside the pressure hull, below the deck plates in front of the conning tower, the U-boat had storage for another two torpedoes. By rigging up his loading hoist, Heydemann's men struggled to manhandle the two heavy torpedoes out onto deck and down the narrow loading ramp to the front torpedo room below. He was lucky; the weather remained calm with only a slow swell running throughout this operation.

One of the first of the new personnel to join the *City of Flint* at quay in New York was an army officer. He was the security officer in charge of the delivery of the cargo. The loading operation was handled by the U.S. Army. They took on board cargo only at one location, namely the Bush Terminals in Brooklyn. Al Becker and his friends in the Armed Guard Unit did not know what the cargo contained.[11] The ship was carrying ammunition, aircraft fuel, etc. It really was a "full war cargo" as Captain Moore put it: gasoline in cans, planes, tanks, jeeps and telegraph poles. In fact, she even loaded poison gas.[12] The Allies did not use gas in Africa nor anywhere else, but the fact that it was included in the cargo of a ship after the initial landings had long taken place, is interesting. Hitler did have chemical weapons, but for reasons never explained, he did not deploy them. The Allied kept stocks of chemical weapons ready in several theaters of war.

When the *City of Flint* was being loaded and they were not on guard duty, the Armed Guards would often walk back to the base to pick up mail, buy cigarettes or the like.

Just before they left New York, four of the Armed Guards who had been placed on board just before Christmas were transferred off the ship, and six new Guardsmen together with two communications crew arrived.

Once the cargo was stowed, the ship pulled out of the U.S. Military terminal, across the Bay Ridge Channel and out across the Upper New York Bay to Staten Island to pick up ammunition. The ammunition came in boxes of loose rounds. The Armed Guards had to load all of the 40 empty magazines supplied with the guns. Each gun placement had its own small ammunition store. A magazine held 60 rounds. Each round had to be lightly greased before being slid into the links of the magazine. The main ammunition stores were at the bottom of the ship, near the stem and the stern, closest to the guns using the heaviest ammunition.

The anti-aircraft guns were all loaded with a mix of tracer ammunition and regular rounds. The tracer rounds streaked through the air like lightning darts. The gunner could watch their trajectories as the projectiles neared their targets. Thus the tracer would help the gunner zero in the firing on the desired target. The actual mounted gun sight there-fore became just an aid for accuracy. In their case, they had loaded every fourth round a tracer. Al felt that these guns were very accurate and once trained, the gunner was always very much in command of the firing. The downside of using tracer ammunition was that it also gave away the exact position of the gun that was firing.

With the ammunition finally loaded, the *City of Flint* was ready for another journey. They eased slowly away from the quay and moved sluggishly out into the channel, head-ing south down into the Brooklyn Narrows, only to hear the roar of the anchor chain. Minutes later they felt the ship shudder gently as the anchor bit into the bottom below them. Part of the convoy had been "parked" here to await the final ships joining them. Loading and moving a large number of ships and cargoes in the massive, but extremely busy New York harbor was a logistical challenge to any planner.

The pressures on those whose job it was to deliver the ship were even worse and have hardly been acknowledged even two generations later. On Al's ship, the early turnover of merchant navy crew was noticeable. He gradually found out that the ship did not have a very good name and that sailors seemed to be very superstitious. As the Narrows filled up with fully laden ships, maneuvering became increasingly difficult. During the two-day wait, a ship nearby dragged anchor. Fortunately, as she slammed into the side of the *City of Flint*, the only damage was to the lowered gangway they used when at anchor. It was destroyed; the only normal exit route from the *City of Flint* had been denied her crew. The symbolism was not lost on them. It caused a massive exodus of superstitious sailors.

Tuesday, 12 January 1943, there was a Masters' conference for the skippers of the ships due to leave in the convoy. Each of them received a sealed envelope with orders specific to their own ship. Only in an emergency were they allowed to open the package. Forty-eight ships were due to leave berths and anchorages all around New York harbor the following morning. To avoid chaos they had to leave in strict order. In a separate envelope they were given their departure schedule. They had to sail out Ambrose Channel and then from buoy to buoy past the light vessel until they reached the assembly point for the convoy itself. They had to be there by 1330 Wednesday.[13]

Finally, Al could hear the heavy anchor chain being brought back up. They were underway. Slowly the ship slipped under the bridge across the sound, which for so long had been watched over by Fort Wadsworth and Fort Hamilton. On any evening in peacetime, the lights of Coney Island would now start to come into view on the left, but then, the dark blacked-out front was not going to help U-boat commanders with their navigation.

In charge of all the merchant ships was Captain L.F. Welch, USN, the Convoy Commodore, sailing in the *Housatonic*. He was responsible for the order of the actual group of merchantmen, he was not the Master of the *Housatonic*. Most importantly, for identification purposes once under sail, the codename for the convoy was DUNNOCK.

Once at sea, Welch would be working with Commander George L. Menocal, USN, the senior officer in charge of the escort and in overall command of the convoy. Menocal's ship was the destroyer *Plunkett*. Together with *Kendrick*, and Destroyer Squadron 13 comprising *Niblack*, *Benson*, *Gleaves* and *Mayo*, they made up Convoy Task Force 38 (CTF-38).

The convoy, UGS-4, routed from the USA to provide supplies to Operation TORCH, the invasion of North Africa, was a slow convoy, sailing at a predetermined speed of 9 knots. This made them particularly vulnerable to U-boats that could outrun them with a surface speed of around 15 knots. Once across the Atlantic, the convoy would split into two parts. Captain Welch would head for Casablanca on the coast of Morocco, while Commander Jay L. Kerley USN, the Vice Commodore, sailing in the Norwegian tanker *Thorsholm*, would continue past Gibraltar and in to the Mediterranean to the Algerian port of Oran. In fact, six of the ten tankers in the convoy were bound for Oran.[14]

Six of the 48 ships were Norwegian, five of them tankers; three were British, one, the *Empire Ridley*, forced to return to port Thursday afternoon. The remaining 39 ships were all American, four of them tankers.

Al Becker was on his first voyage in the *City of Flint*. None of them knew their destination. They left the Ambrose Channel early Wednesday, 13 January.[15] He was not excited, but he knew that from now on he was in danger. He felt it, saw only protection around him in destroyers etc. You were not by yourself. Once they were out of New York harbor and saw the convoy forming, he knew that "what's out there with us needs to be protected." He was not afraid.

That very same Wednesday, *U-575* was re-supplied with the deadliest tools of its trade. In the middle of the Atlantic, *U-109* and *U-575* met for the transfer of torpedoes from the homebound boat. They worked into darkness and evening to effect the transfer for Heydemann. It was a race against time as the weather deteriorated. A south-westerly wind was building, whipping up the waves. They transferred four torpedoes before giving up. Each 1600 kg torpedo had to be floated across from one U-boat to the other, suspended between a group of large flotation aids. Pulling them across were crew members rowing an inflatable rubber dinghy. It was hard work even on a calm day. The day after, as the *City of Flint* left the U.S. as part of her convoy, the tanker U-boat U-463 provided refueling for *U-575*.

Heydemann remained with the Delphin Group on patrol in the Azores area for another week. They knew and Dönitz knew that Allied convoys would normally use this route. All they had to do was to wait for the next one. The Germans had even noted that convoys routed this far south were very rarely re-routed. Such stability in routing had long been avoided in the North Atlantic. The British, American and Canadian navies all used the British Naval Cipher No. 3 for their ship to shore communication.

Within three days of the convoy leaving New York, Dönitz's people had picked up a crucial radio transmission, one of the daily U-boat situation reports, sent in the normal code, via BAMS (Broadcast to Allied Merchant Ships). Once decoded, the message confirmed that a slow convoy, Gibraltar bound from New York, was at sea. The lethal Delphin group was ordered to intercept.[16]

In a large office block on the Tirpitzufer in Berlin on the bank of the Landwehr canal, were the offices of Kapitän zur See, Heinrich Bonatz and his staff. Bonatz was in charge of the German navy's code breaking operation, the B-Dienst. Not only was he familiar with the BAMS broadcast, he had been reading the decoded messages for the last 12 months.

According to the Germans, the BAMS broadcast carried daily convoy reports, course directions for stragglers, navigational chart reference points and U-boat locations etc. Small wonder then that Bonatz deployed all available resources to cracking the new version in December 1942. After a huge effort, they had the code broken by February 1943 and continued to read it until 10 June 1943, when the Allies replaced it.[17] Bonatz's operation was so efficient that during the time when they read the code, the decoding was so fast that the BdU could actually move his U-boats to cover the new convoy courses set to avoid the wolf packs' original locations.

At its peak the B-Dienst decoding operation had up to 360 cipher clerks. At night, the daytime output was processed by up to 200 staff members using Hollerith data equipment.[18] Hut 7 at Bletchley Park also used Hollerith machines supplied by American IBM's British license holder. That Bonatz read the BAMS message concerning UGS-4 already in January 1943 underlines the efficiency of his operation and the vulnerability of the code, which regardless of cryptographic embellishments, was compromised. For the *City of Flint*, it would prove to be fatal.

On Wednesday, 20 January 1943, the Admiralty in London was told that the assumption was that as many as 95 U-boats could still be on station in the Atlantic. As the anti–U-boat campaigns and the convoys in the Caribbean and along the U.S. East Coast were becoming increasingly effective, Dönitz was thought to be concentrating on three main hunting grounds: northeast of Newfoundland, southeast of Iceland, and around the Azores.[19]

The path of Al's convoy would cut right across one of these areas, the Azores.

The weather was bad. Soon the fresh Armed Guards experienced the first of many fierce storms. It was very, very rough. By Thursday, 21 January the violent northwesterly storms had started to dislodge the *City of Flint's* forward deck cargo of telegraph poles. They disappeared overboard one by one, leaving a trail of poles. The Convoy Commodore ordered them to leave the convoy, slow down, change course, secure the cargo and then head in such a direction as to pick up the convoy three days later. They simply could not secure the cargo without "riding the weather" which meant they had to heave to, facing into the storm. Harnessing dozens of bucking telegraph poles was a dangerous job in a pitching sea and it meant leaving the safety of the convoy and its escorts. This they did, and within hours the cargo was safe. Captain MacKenzie and Ensign Carey (in charge of the Armed Guard unit) now had to open their sealed orders and they discovered that their destination was Casablanca in North Africa. From now on, the captain set a zigzag course, hoping to re-join the convoy before any U-boats located them. They were sailing to the south of the Azores, right into the trap.

The following Sunday, 24 January, Dönitz was starting to apply pressure on his U-boat commanders again. He expected two convoys to pass that evening, he told them via telegram. One convoy was going west; the other, Al's convoy UGS-4, fully laden, was going east. Dönitz did not, however, know that the eastbound convoy had turned to a more northerly course. In order to avoid the wolf pack they were sailing around the Azores on the northern side. There was no way of warning the stragglers.

The total devastation of TM-1 certainly confirmed to the Allied convoy route planners the presence of Group Delphin south of the Azores from around the 8 January 1943, less than a week prior to the UGS-4 departure. The significance of the TORCH support convoys cannot be underestimated. The dramatic damage inflicted on TM-1 in terms of lost fuel for the Allied land offensive across North Africa was even noted by General von Armin, the commander-in-chief for the German Forces in North Africa. He actually sent Dönitz a telegram to thank him.

The previous evening, UGS-4's Convoy Commander Menocal had been taking

Smoke from burning tankers from convoy TM-1, taken from the deck of *U-575* in January 1943, just before they were ordered to search for ships from Al Becker's convoy (courtesy Michael Elstermann).

stock. The toll of the fierce storms was that eight ships had lost touch. He sent a message to base, reporting the problem. As well as the *City of Flint*, he was also missing *American Press, Julia Ward Howe, Daniel Boone, Hawaiian, Charles C. Pinckney, William C. Claiborne* and *Alcoa Banner*.

Sunday morning, Menocal was ordered to come up with rendezvous points for noon Monday and for noon Tuesday. Once received by the U.S. Admiralty, they would send the message out on the regular shipping broadcast, BAMS, which the Germans could read.

That evening, U.S. naval command informed Menocal of a D/F—Direction Finding intercept. It meant that a series of radio listening stations had, between them, pinpointed the location of a U-boat to within a circle with a 60 km radius. The center of the circle was a map reference northwest of the Azores. It had been there at 1650 that afternoon.[20]

From the moment convoy USG-4 steamed away, aboard the *City of Flint*, they were very alert, watching for U-boats. The watches were four hours on, eight hours off. Then every 12 hours they "dogged" them so that they never came back to the same four hours. Until now they had never test-fired their new guns. They could not have done so as they were in the convoy all the time. Since they last saw the convoy, they had now been on their own for 4 days. During this time, they certainly had gunnery practice. They fired the 20 mm, the 4" and the 3"—all of them. Sailing alone made them feel far more vulnerable to U-boat attacks, all because of a stack of telegraph poles, but this was what they had been ordered to do.

The Armed Guards were constantly either on watch or resting. If on watch, their eyes were glued to the water, looking for the enemy. At sea they were more exposed, and now abandoned, without any escort. It was even more dangerous. "It was a different world out there," as Al put it later. At sun-up and sundown they were all on duty for General Quarters, as those times were the most dangerous for U-boat attacks. It was very hard to spot a surfaced submarine in the changing light.

Sadly, they had already been spotted. Unknowingly, the *City of Flint* had become the prey. Somewhere out there, Heydemann was stalking them.

15

The Target

Heydemann first saw the *City of Flint* in the afternoon of Monday, 25 January 1943. He had been at sea since Wednesday, 16 December, around six weeks. The crew was exhausted. As Kurt Lück saw it; they could sleep upright, or at least behind the diesel engines with cotton wool in their ears.[1] In their bow section, extra torpedoes meant that the bunks were stowed for parts of the journey. Regardless of alarms or Action Stations some routine tasks stayed with them; they still had their beaker of fresh water for brushing teeth, and their obligatory lemon to provide vitamin C; lemon often ended doubling up as toothpaste. Convenience was important at that stage of the journey.

Finally, Monday, at a quarter to five in the afternoon, convoy time, Menocal replied to the Admiralty request. The Convoy Commander had provided two meeting points for the stragglers to be brought back in behind the safety screen of the convoy escorts, Tuesday and Wednesday lunchtimes. The danger in such messages was obvious, if read by the BdU, the convoy would be met by a wolf pack rather than by merchantmen. Alternatively, stragglers could be picked off en route to the meeting points. The Admiralty presumed that the stragglers would listen to the BAMS broadcast.[2]

By sundown, at around 1730 hrs. ship's time, the German U-boat had already been tracking the *City of Flint* for over two hours. They had been spotted by the lookout on *U-575*, earlier in the afternoon.[3] The U-boat was surfaced well ahead, far out to port of the unsuspecting merchantman. First the lookout had seen only the tops of the two masts, but shortly after, they could see the ship itself. Described as "the opponent" they saw the *City of Flint* as a fast independent traveler. Visibility was good that afternoon. According to the War Diary, they were in position, map reference CE8771. Sea state 2, with a long north-westerly swell.

Now it became imperative to keep touch, "Fühlung gehalten," yet keep a respectful distance. Then as the attack was mounted, the signal to go "Auf Gefechtsstation," to Battle Stations, made them all rush through the boat. Submerged attacks using the attack optics were rare and if they happened, it would be by night and only if there was bright moonshine or if morning was breaking. For them, the fading light was ideal for a surface attack.

As was normal for new U-boats, the crew was assembled in stages as the boat took shape in the shipyard. The familiarization, popularly known as the "Baubelehrung" was an integrated part of the Work-Up (Shakedown) period. In the evenings, the crew would often find themselves at loose ends; in a city with as strong a maritime tradition as Hamburg, they had plenty of alternatives to choose from. The notorious Reeperbahn, immortalized by Marlene Dietrich in the film *Blue Angel*, was just up the hill from the Blohm & Voss shipyard. Inevitably, they would end up in the same place every night, a bar called Liliput. In recognition of the hospitality, they had enjoyed there, when the

U-575 was launched, they named her *Liliput*. They even wore the name on their tunics when in port.[4]

Heydemann was trying to maneuver *U-575* into position to attack. Repeatedly the *City of Flint*'s frequent course alterations thwarted his attempts. Every ten minutes they changed their zigzag course while maintaining a general course of 110 degrees. It worked well. They did not maintain any course long enough for the U-boat to launch a torpedo strike.

At 1840 Heydemann thought he was ready to fire, but again the Americans executed a sharp course change and the Germans were suddenly looking at the starboard side of the ship. Within ten minutes he was ready to try again. Then, as before the *City of Flint* changed course, but this time directly into the line of fire, steaming directly towards the U-boat. Heydemann had to order his boat to turn sharply to starboard, he then ran at high speed past the merchantman's bow. This maneuver placed the U-boat in a position for another torpedo run, a bit ahead and to the left of the American ship.

Aboard the *City of Flint* all eyes were on the water. Lights were blacked out and the radio was silent. It was Monday, 25 January. They had just secured from General Quarters, time was coming towards 1915, ship's time. It was going into darkness. There was no moon. The weather was clear, the sea choppy and the wind a moderate south-westerly, force 3 to 4. They were doing around 11 knots. They had 12 lookouts in place; two on the forward gun platform, two aft, one either side on the Boat Deck machine guns, and six on the bridge. Everything was done correctly, yet there was nothing they could do to avoid what happened next.

On the open bridge, at the top of the conning tower of the U-boat, they were watching the trap snap shut on the unsuspecting prey. Heydemann would have been up there, in command, lining up the shot, ensuring that the best possible firing angle could be achieved, second-guessing when the helmsman on the *City of Flint* would next alter their zigzag course. Beside him would have been his senior navigator, Obersteuermann Kurt Klotzsche. Kurt was the senior non-commissioned officer on board. Right at that moment he was bent over the "surface targeting optics," the "Überwasser Ziel Optik," the aiming mechanism for the torpedo. It was known as the UZO in the Schussreport, the Firing Report, which they completed for each torpedo they launched. The UZO comprised a set of large binoculars, which looked a bit like a sturdy-looking theodolite mounted on a solid metal base with a dial indicating the angle at which the target deviated from the longitudinal axis of the U-boat.

It is likely that Heydemann's First Officer, his Erste Wacht Offizier (IWO) Oberleutnant zur See Walter Zeplien, was in the conning tower with them, shouting his instructions down to the ratings tending to the "T. Vohaltr," and actually ordering the firing. The machine automatically used a mechanical transmission via universal joints and adjusting spindles to adjust the run angle, the depth and the speed on the torpedo once the advance angle or the compensation factor had been calculated. Zeplien had the overall responsibility for the torpedoes, their firing mechanism and the aiming mechanism. His name even went on the Firing Report along with the name of the skipper. Scoring a hit on a moving target from 1.7 km away, in a pitching sea was not easy. It was a tense moment when everything needed to be ready, even the preparations to compensate for the sudden weight change when the torpedo launched. Each torpedo weighed around 1.6 tons and carried a warhead of 280 kg of explosives.

Heydemann fired his no. V torpedo tube. This was the stern-facing tube. The torpedo, an Ato, with a speed of 40 knots, set to a depth of 3 meters, ran for 1 minute and 22 seconds before hitting the side of the ship. According to Heydemann's own "Schuss-meldung," his report of the firing, the torpedo ran for 1680 meters.[5] Aboard the U-boat, they could hear the explosion clearly. Since the torpedo left a bubble track, the American lookouts might have seen the torpedo. Even so, they would probably be too late to take evasive action. As the Germans in the conning tower watched from afar, a violent fireball suddenly enveloped the ship.

Al and the other rear lookout were on the poop deck (on the stern) on the 4" gun when the guards up front spotted it. An incoming torpedo. Al heard the shouted warning through the headphones, before he could see it (the phosphorous light of the wake of the torpedo, not the torpedo). The U-boat had to be to the north of them; the torpedo was coming in from the portside.

Carey, the guard commander, who was on the bridge, heard it too. At that stage the torpedo was a mere 200 feet off the port bow. He yelled to Wladyslaw Myszkowski, the helmsman, to turn hard right in an attempt to avoid the torpedo, as he dived off the left bridge wing and in towards the safety of the sheltered wheelhouse, Carey heard Harold Rosengren, the second mate, repeat his order. Sadly it was far too late to avoid the lethal "eel" rushing towards them, but the dive saved his life.

All they could do was to brace for the explosion, or would the torpedo miss? With only seconds to go, Al felt the ship lurch to one side, desperately trying to move out of the path of the lethal projectile, but it was too slow. Right then, Al's mind seemed to go blank. He knew the ship was going to get hit. He was becoming mentally prepared. The body was preparing for trouble. It had to take care of people, of things. Then the noise of the explosion blocked out everything else. The massive force of the blast caused the ship to roll hard to starboard. The flames were instantaneous, engulfing the entire front of the ship. They were hit at the No. 1 and No. 2 holds, where the barreled gasoline was stored. As the fireball burned above them, the momentum carried the ship forward, right into it. The fireball suspended above them quickly engulfed the whole ship.

On the bridge, Carey tried in vain to contact the various gun crews. The explosion had destroyed the communication system. All the bridge windows were shattered, but most seriously, the bridge wing had been ripped right off the ship. One of the Armed Guards, James Charles Lichtenstein, USN, was killed in the process. Rosengren later remembered seeing Myszkowski leaving the bridge; he too had survived the initial explosion.[6] According to Bill Maynard, it may have been Lichtenstein who spotted the U-boat. Bill thought he had seen the incoming torpedo literally seconds before the impact.[7]

From the shattered bridge, Carey could still see the two men in the 3" gun turret on the forecastle. Louis Marcus Bozada, USNR was there together with Donald E. Quillen, USN. They were totally surrounded by burning aircraft fuel. Carey even tried shouting to them using a megaphone. He desperately wanted to prevent them from jumping overboard until the ship was stationary in the water; otherwise they would be left so far behind in its wake that their chances of rescue would be minimal in the dark night. Unable to intervene, and perhaps due to the intense heat around them, Carey could only watch as they disappeared over the bow, never to be seen again. Watching from the U-boat, Heydemann noted in his report that the bow section sank down fast, but then steadied and remained afloat. The ship quickly developed a list to port and the fo'c'sle sank deeper in the water.

It could have been virtually any of the Armed Guard on duty up front on the bow gun as lookouts. At least half of them, Al included, had been trained on all these weapons while at Gunnery School. At sea they rotated positions, taking turns to cover all the different guns.

All the remaining guns were still crewed, but they could not see the U–Boat. The radioman William Bohn attempted to transmit distress signals from the ship's radio, but the explosion had either put it out of commission or brought down the aerials; they heard no replies to their messages. Much later, Al learned that two ships in the area, *Julia Ward Howe* and *Charles C. Pinckney*, had heard the message and were heading their way.[8]

Al could see nothing but smoke and fire from where he was on the stern. The gun crews from the bow of the ship were in the water shouting for help as the ship was sliding past them. The explosion felt like hitting a stone wall, before the ship continued forward. There was a big mass of flames that mushroomed up and out, covering everything in front of him. The spray of kerosene drops filled the air, but fortunately most of it seemed to be burned out before landing. As the ship settled after the explosion, the bow seemed to go down very quickly, thus lifting the stern to a point where the 4" gun could no longer used; it did not have enough elevation if aimed forwards, and too much if aimed astern. Then the first rapid forward flooding seemed to stop and the ship seemed to settle.[9]

The 4"/.50 Caliber was a popular gun with the Armed Guard. Although it was regarded as not much use against aircraft, they knew it could be deadly if trained on a U-boat. In fact, the gun crew on the *Charles C. Pinckney* actually drove off their assailants, at least temporarily, using their 4" gun.[10] It required a six-man crew to keep the gun firing, including the ammunition handlers, the hot shell handler and the loader at the breech.

On board the *City of Flint*, as the drama continued to unfold in front of them; Al and his colleagues waited. They hoped for an order from the gunnery officer on the bridge, Ensign Carey. No order came, and from where Al was standing by the poop gun, the entire bridge seemed to be a mass of flames. Carey's report makes it clear that he did indeed order a man aft to the 4" gun crew.[11] In the chaos and smoke, the messenger never arrived. They were on their own.

It looked like it was going to be every man for himself, but at that very moment the signal to "Abandon Ship" was sounded on the horn; a long series of short blasts. The poop deck messenger may have felt that the horn signals relieved him of his duties; he never turned up. To the gun crew on the stern, the signal meant trouble. The lifeboats were amidships. This was the area covered by smoke and flames. They proceeded to "secure life jackets," a very sobering procedure at night in the middle of the Atlantic. They all had the same type of life jackets; all came out of the same box. Now, they had to rely on them until they found something in the water to hold on to, until, "please God, a lifeboat came along to pick them up."[12] Others, who had not been on duty, were less lucky. Many left the ship not wearing life jackets.

They could not see 10 feet in front of them. They heard men in the water holler for help as the ship slid past—"Save me, save me." Al threw lifesaving rings, "doughnuts," anything that would float, to help his mates struggling in the water below.

The fireball seemed to be suspended in the air above the ship. The engines were only just secured; the momentum of the ship was still a forward motion—into the fireball. As the flames came towards him, Al realized that in order to save himself he too had to jump. He got down from the gun turret, down from the elevated poop deck to the lower main deck and jumped from the left side of the ship. Large, heavy telegraph poles were raining down in the water, going under, and then bouncing back up. He did not know where to jump due to the flames and the debris that was still flying. Where should he go? Nowhere was safe. The timber thrown up in the air by the explosion came down, sank until buoyancy pushed it back up with a violent shove. Being hit by timber in this manner was nearly as bad as if it landed on you. They were being bruised everywhere.[13] Before he jumped, Al did not think the ship would last very long before sinking. It had been such a powerful explosion.

They jumped. The smoke was so dense that from the stern they could not see if any of the lifeboats had been launched. The ship had four lifeboats and four rafts, Carey Floats, but two of them were located on the fo'c'sle where the violent fire was raging. Nobody could reach them.

The Captain and Carey had by now met. MacKenzie confirmed that as the ship was doomed, he wanted everybody off as fast as possible. Carey made his way amidships and down to the Guards' quarters in the Shelter Deck. He wanted to check that none of his men, out of shock, were left in their bunks. Fortunately he found none, but by the time he left, the corridor was waist deep in water.

The ship's routine at sea also meant that at least half the crew would be off duty at any one time. Plenty of them would be in their bunks catching up on sleep. One of these was Third Officer William Mills from Milltown, Massachusetts.[14] His lifeboat station was by the No. 4 lifeboat. William knew instinctively what was about to happen once he heard the alarm. It was his job to help lower the lifeboat.

In the officers' mess, Cadet-Midshipman John Corrigan[15] was busy, using some of his spare time for studying when the torpedo exploded. Grabbing his lifejacket, which as luck would have it, was lying next to him, Corrigan quickly made his way to his mustering station, the No. 2 lifeboat. As the signal to "Abandon Ship" rang out, the lifeboat was lowered with him and another 12 men. The boat could hold nearly 50. Corrigan felt that some of the men had lowered away other lifeboats with far too few men in them. The intense fire in the high-octane gasoline barrels brought some of the crew members near to panic. Several of them had rope burns on their hands. They had slid too quickly down the ropes rather than climbed down. One was even injured jumping directly down into a lifeboat.[16]

Busy studying, Cadet-Midshipman Donald W. Summerhayes was thrown right across the room by the explosion. As he headed for his mustering station, Summerhayes grabbed some extra clothes in case others had had less time to get dressed before abandoning ship. He helped lower his boat, the No. 1 lifeboat, only to find that he could not climb down to join them once the job was done. The ropes were burned off and the boat had quickly drifted astern.[17]

Once lowered, the No. 4 lifeboat had to be cast off immediately or the waves would have smashed it up, throwing it against the ship's side with ferocious force. One of the Armed Guards was very badly bruised across the chest as he was crushed between a lifeboat and the ship's side as he tried to climb into the boat from the wrong side.[18] Like Donald, William now had to watch his boat drift off, this one with only three men in it. Instead William had to run aft where he jumped off the ship's stern to get clear.

Fortunately, luck was on William's side. Within a few minutes the men in the No. 4 lifeboat, which had drifted aft, spotted the sailor and dragged him into the lifeboat. Myszkowski's fate was unknown. William later felt confident the sailor had jumped off the ship, but in the darkness, no one had seen what had happened to him. Fortunately, Wladyslaw was saved; he joined Al in the No. 3 boat.

Carey meanwhile, returned to his own quarters where he picked up his personal sidearm—a Colt 0.45 pistol—and a first aid kit which he later had to abandon, as he could not swim with it. In according with regulations, he also threw all the ship's confidential papers overboard, using the special weighted box he had been issued.

Things were now moving very quickly all over the ship. By the time Carey again appeared on the boat deck, the lifeboats had already been lowered and were away from the ship. He continued aft to the poop deck, where he found MacKenzie and a few other crew members sheltering from the raging fire, Donald too joined them there. Carey and the captain now ordered them all to jump off the ship before they themselves followed them into the sea. That was the last time that anyone saw Albert Persson. One of his officers, Assistant Engineer Oliver P. Cote, remembered seeing Persson prepare to jump. He was one of the older members of the crew.[19]

The waves scattered them immediately. Carey was in the water for around 45 minutes before the No. 4 lifeboat picked him up. Fortunately, Donald and MacKenzie had in the meantime been picked up the by the No. 1 boat. Summerhayes spotted the U-boat only around 200 m away. No markings could be seen during the brief moment before the U-boat disappeared. Shortly after, the No. 4 boat located the No. 1 boat and tied up to them.

These two boats had located each other and were tied together right after the ship sustained the second shattering explosion, placing it within 45 minutes of them abandoning the ship.[20] They remained together throughout the night. They did not attempt to row away from the area; they stayed put, drifting. The radioman, William Bohn, had the presence of mind to bring with him a small portable radio transmitter, when he went over the side and into the water. He was swimming while also keeping the radio afloat, fortunately it took only around half an hour before he was located and picked up by the No. 1 boat.

According to his report, MacKenzie would not have survived the time he had to spend in the water, had he been alone.[21] His Second Officer, Harold Rosengren from Philadelphia was cited in the report as having saved the captain's life by supporting him. Carey and Bohn were also named for having performed beyond the call of duty. Carey for checking the crew's quarters, and Bohn for bringing the radio transmitter.

The boats had been launched quite quickly while Al was in the water. The lifeboats were large, heavy, metal affairs, thickly covered in layer after layer of grey paint, stained in places by spots of red anti-rust lead-oxide. The boats were placed two either side of the housing amidships on the Boat deck. Boats No. 1, 2 and 4 went in easy. Launching boat No. 3 caused problems. It is likely that the explosion must have jammed part of the launch mechanism and the men struggled desperately to free it. One of the men, Bill Maynard of the Armed Guard unit, sustained serious internal injuries in the struggle. Sadly, these injuries caused him to suffer the rest of his life. In the lifeboat, nobody knew. Bill suffered in silence.[22]

The lifeboats were away from the ship in what seems like record time. The fierce fire raging before them, underlined the urgency of the evacuation. Another eyewitness account suggests that the severity of the explosion and the subsequent fire caused a brief moment of panic.[23] The injuries would seem to confirm this. The combination of the heavy swell running at the time and the somewhat uncontrolled evacuation may have proved lethal. Some of those who jumped early were more than likely never spotted from the lifeboats as they were moving away from the sinking ship. "There were flames on the water—not solid, in patches. You pushed it out of the way as you swam, otherwise the flames would stick to you. If it did you rubbed it off, or moved your hands below—the flames remained on the water."[24]

Once in the water, Al could see nothing but telegraph poles, no life, none of his mates. At this stage he was not yet past the ship. He saw a rope ladder and scrambled back on board. Al wanted something to help him stay afloat, something better than a telegraph pole, and he wanted some respite from the treacherous resurfacing wood. As he reached the ladder he met Steve Kubick—one of his colleagues. They saw nobody else on board at that stage. They were the last ones to abandon ship. They were alone. Both had hoped the ship could provide something to hang on to, ideally to climb on to. The ship ought to be able to give them with something before disappearing. They were very lucky, however, not to be torpedoed for a second time. It was not for the lack of trying. Heydemann was determined to sink the ship.

Around this time, at 1928 hrs. according to Heydemann, he fired another torpedo, but he misjudged the speed of the ship. The torpedo went too far ahead. Fortunately for Al and Steve, it missed as they were actually back on board at the time; the ship seemed to suddenly move backwards thought Heydemann.[25] This was to have been the final shot, but the ship still had not lost her will to survive.

Back on the sinking ship, they remembered the plank rafts. Al had walked past the aft ones several times a day every day since he came on board. They were set on raised platforms either side of the ship as he went past to the 4" gun. Nobody had gone for the rafts; they all seemed to have been abandoned. Looking at the closest one, it was a strong looking 20-foot square thing, placed up a sloped ramp on the starboard side, secured with by an easy-release mechanism. They hit the pelican hook with a big hammer, which was hanging there and as the raft dropped free from the ship the two mates were determined to get quickly down into the water after it. The raft went in on the right side, with Steve and Al following closely behind, desperate not to lose track of it in the darkness and the smoke.

So far Al had escaped virtually unharmed, with very few light burns and with no open wounds. He had no deep-wound burns as he had plunged his hands under water. His hands and arms had sustained some superficial cuts. He had been sliced and ripped due to pushing away much debris as he was swimming.

The aft part of the ship never burned; it was only the burning spray from the forward explosion that reached them. This meant that only ropes or canvas, etc., caught fire, but there was no massive ship's fire beyond amidships. This may well have been the saving grace for all of them. Had the loading been different, placing another part of the cargo along the flammable aircraft fuel, the kerosene, the clouds of smoke could so easily have been the more dangerous than the flames themselves. The *City of Flint* carried poison gas in her cargo.[26] She also carried planes, tanks and jeeps in addition to the kerosene and the oil.

Eyewitness accounts are clear that the only location where cargo was loaded was at Brooklyn. American authorities must have moved the poison through one of the most densely populated areas in the world in order to place the consignment in the ship. There is no reason to believe that this particular cargo should be seen as unique, thus raising the question, was something as dangerous as poison gas moved into and stored in Brooklyn on a regular basis? As luck would have it, the *City of Flint*'s share of it seemed to have been untouched, probably in another hold at the rear of the ship. The poison gas was part of

Churchill's insurance; should Hitler resort to the use of gas, the Allies wanted to be ready to respond in kind. The British Government had worried about gas attacks since the outbreak of war in 1939.

As Al and Steve abandoned the ship for the second time, the bow was under and the screw was out of the water. When Al had returned on board, the ship was still burning, but it was level; otherwise the afterdeck would have been raised too high for them to climb up. It was fairly stable when they got back on board.

As soon as they had the raft in the water, it was moved away from the ship. Now, they swam carefully around it searching for ropes attaching it to the hull. They did not want it being pulled down from under them when the ship sank, as they knew she would all too soon. By now Heydemann must have been growing increasingly impatient. Just then, less than ten minutes after they jumped off the ship for the second time, the German fired a third torpedo, which caused a huge explosion that seemed to rip the heart out of the ship. According to Heydemann, the time was now 1945. He hit the target, according to his report, below the forward mast. According to the American eyewitnesses, the torpedo hit below the rear mast.

The German version is likely to be correct. Had the torpedo hit the ship astern, the explosion would have opened the ship's side, released the air pocket and made the ship sink very quickly. In this case, the only result was that although the fo'c'sle sank deeper in the water, she remained afloat.

Heydemann had brought his U-boat in to a distance of only 750 meters—the last torpedo ran at maximum speed for only 36 seconds.[27] They were close enough to see the giant column of water thrown up by the explosion, but far enough away for the torpedo to arm itself. It required a run of 300 meters to become self-armed. Instead of sinking, much to Heydemann's annoyance, the ship slipped noticeably lower at the stem, but settled and remained afloat. All the air trapped in the stern section acted as a giant flotation aid.

Included in the Firing Report for the final torpedo is a one-liner stating that "ship was finally sunk with artillery fire." The reality was that the German U-boat waited another 45 minutes, on the surface, cloaked by darkness. Heydemann must have been very confident that the "independent traveler," as a ship sailing alone was called, really was independent. In this case, two other stragglers from the same convoy had heard the emergency signals transmitted from the *City of Flint* and changed course to steam to their aid. Sadly they were two days away. Disastrously the emergency signals had drawn them right into the path of the wolf pack and they too were about to be torpedoed and sunk.

Fortunately, the smoke and the darkness parted to allow the No. 3 lifeboat to appear. They had spotted the raft and asked if Al and Steve wanted to join them. It was not a loaded boat, holding nine before Al and Steve climbed aboard. The raft had a compartment in the middle for food and water. Al held the raft against the side of the lifeboat as Steve rummaged in the little compartment at the center of the raft. All there was to be had was a couple of canisters of provisions and a pair of work gloves.[28] Unfortunately, the raft's water container was secured to the frame. Steve could not dislodge it and the extra water had to be abandoned. But they were not out of danger yet. As they were transferring the provisions from the raft, they came under fire from an unseen machine gun.

At this point there is a significant difference between the German War Diary and the American eyewitness accounts. According to Heydemann, the ship was still not sinking fast enough for his liking.[29] He did not want to waste any more of his valuable torpedoes.

Block-Nr. 868 Anlag. 3 zu **Schußmeldung** 5 264 16. März 1943 Seite OKM
"575" **für Überwasserstreitkräfte und U-Boote** Obit.z.f. Zeplien,IWO.to.
(Schießendes Fahrzeug) **Geheim!** (Dienstgrad, Name und Dienststellung des Schützen)

Datum: 25.1.43. Ort:☐ DG 1326 Uhrzeit des Schusses: 2205

Wassertiefe: 3500 m Wetter:O 2 Sicht: gute Nicht Wind: SW 2

Seegang: 2 Dünung: Richtung u. Stärke lang, flach

Ziel: Frachter (City of Flint) 10 000 BRT 160 m 7 m
(Name) (Größe) (Länge) (Tiefgang)

Beladezustand u. Ladung: voll beladen Kriegsmaterial, Tanks

Erfolg: 1. *Treffer/* *Fehlschuß* *Angriffsschuß* *Fangschuß (auf gestoppt liegendes Ziel*

Lfd. Nr.	Einzelschuß		1	2	3	4
1		Zeittakt in sec und Streuwinkel in Graden				
2	Torpedo	Art, Nummer, Aptierung G 7 a	6674			
3		V_t und eingestellte Laufstrecke	40 sm	größte	Laufstr.	
4		Eingestellte Tiefe	3 m			
5	Pi	Nummer, Art der Aptierung PI H	28644			
6		Z-Einstellring				
7		S-Einstellring				
8	Rohr	Bezeichnung	V			
9		Ausstoßart	U.W.			
10	Beim Schuß	Eigene Fahrt	60	stopp		
11		Eigener Kurs	180			
12		Schiffspeilung	160,7			
13		Schußwinkel				
14		Zielstelle, Ziel- und Rechengerät Brücke –UZO–T. Vorhaltr.				
15		Abkommpunkt	Mitte			
16		Torpedokurs	220,3			
17		Eingestellt Schußunterlagen $V_g = 14$ sm	$\gamma = 80$	$\beta = 20$		
18		Tauchtiefe beim Schuß (nur bei U-Booten)				
19		Lastigkeit beim Schuß (bei Schiffen usw. Krängung beim Schuß)				
20		Entfernung. a)geschätzt, b)eingest, c)Laufzeit Torp	a+b) 15 hm c) 1 Min.22 sec. = 1680 m			
21		Torpedoniedergang und Lauf				
22		Schuß im Abdrehen oder auf geraden Kurs	g.K.			
23		Eingestellter Winkel nach Farbe u. Graden				
24	TVA	Bei G7e und Schußweite über 3000 m: a) letzte Nachladung vor dem Schuß b) letzte Heizung vor dem Schuß				

The torpedo firing report. For each torpedo fired, the U-boat had to file a report. This is the report for the torpedo that hit the *City of Flint* (Bundesarchiv-Militaerarchiv).

Finally at 2330, Berlin time,[30] Heydemann went for the final move. He ordered his artillery crew on deck. The ship would provide some target practice for his gunners. From the deck gun they fired 30 rounds, explosive and incendiary, into the side of the ship. The plan was to "bleed" the air pocket in the stern section of the stricken ship in order to accelerate the sinking. Time was dragging on, it was by now one and a quarter hour since the first devastating explosion and Heydemann was still in the area and on the surface.

Amazingly, none of the American eyewitness accounts refer to Heydemann's use of the artillery to sink the ship. In the confusion, the shelling would have been mistaken for continued explosions on board the burning freighter. As the U-boat moved in close, they were spotted by Corrigan in the No. 2 boat.[31] Corrigan first heard the sound of the diesel engines before the survivors gradually managed to make out the silhouette of the dark hull against the black night backdrop. Although a mere 200 meters away they saw nothing that could help identify the U-boat. Within minutes, the black silhouette of the menacing nemesis again merged with the night-time horizon, never to be seen again by any of them.

This was the stage when the lifeboats allegedly came under machine gun fire. The U-boat's 20 mm anti-air gun would not have been sufficient to penetrate the thick steel hull of the *City of Flint*. There was no real reason for wasting any rounds of AA ammunition on the ship—other than providing gunnery practice. Readying the AA guns quickly might one day save their lives. A surfaced U-boat was very vulnerable to air attacks, a fact which was about to be brought home to many of them within a year.[32] There is no record of any such firing, but if this happened it would have provided the effect described from the lifeboats. The trajectory would have brought the firing arching over the heads of the

The gun crew on *U-575* being put through their paces. An efficient crew could fire 15 to 18 rounds a minute from their 88mm deck gun (courtesy Michael Elstermann).

people in the No. 3 lifeboat, perhaps spraying the sea around any other lifeboats further away from the scene. The burning ship was at that stage located between the U-boat and the No. 3 lifeboat, thus making it very difficult for the German AA gun crew to see the small boat in the darkness.

To their right, the ship was sinking, albeit too slowly for Heydemann. The firing came from somewhere behind the smoke screen directly ahead. It had to be the U-boat, they thought. All the men from the No. 3 boat could hear the U-boat's diesel engine chugging but they never saw it. Judging by the sound, they knew the general direction of it. The engine noise was so clear. The distance between them could not have been more than a few hundred meters. Only the darkness, combined with the clouds of black smoke from the burning oil provided cover.

Fortunately the firing did not last long. The arc of tracers went right over their heads. They were convinced they were the targets. They could hear, as well as see that they were being fired at. Quickly several of them got back into the water and hung on, below the edge of the boat, but stayed with it. They thought they were going to be wiped out at this stage. They were helpless, why shoot at them? The shooting came from face on. Even in retrospect, Al was convinced that it was not from the *City of Flint* itself. Some of the men in the boat claimed that somebody had been shooting from the ship earlier, but Al had not seen that. As they discussed the firing, they compared it to the earlier arc of tracer fire, which had reached out from their right to their left, as if pointing out the direction of the wake of the ship. It had been well in front of them, they could watch it without any danger of themselves being the targets. This fire could have come from the ship, due to a "cook off," i.e., ammunition exploding in the heat of the fire.

Heydemann's own War Diary records the time lag between the first and second hit as around 40 minutes.[33] The fire in the front portion of the ship was still burning, but it had not spread and the intensity of the initial fireball had diminished. The greatest likelihood of any cook-off occurring would have been immediately after the first explosion, not after the second one, which reportedly did not cause a new fire.

The intense heat of the raging fires could simply have detonated the ammunition. We know the Oerlikons were crewed and ready for action after the first explosion, but the enemy offered no targets. The guns' safety mechanisms would have been switched off, in readiness for the briefest opportunity to hit back. None were provided, which meant each gun would have had a full magazine at the time the ship was abandoned.

The first round therefore, already chambered, could if detonated by heat, cause a chain reaction. Each successive round could also self-ignite through this process. In fact, the increasingly hot chamber would make every new "cook off" even more likely than the previous one. Furthermore, the Oerlikon was an automatic weapon, designed to operate with sustained automatic firing. At the Oerlikon's rate of fire at between 250 and 320 rounds per minute, a magazine holding 60 rounds would be emptied in 12 to 15 seconds. There was nobody to reload for any further bursts of firing, but other forward guns could have overheated later, as the fire continued to burn in the front hold, although with far less intensity.[34]

The timing of the second explosion is significant in the reconstruction of what must have been a terrifying and confusing set of events. Carey stated in his report that during the three-quarters of an hour he was in the water, he witnessed the second explosion rocking the ship. He too reported the tracer fire. He corroborated the view from the No. 3 lifeboat in that the explosion occurred before the shooting. It is interesting to note that Carey reported the firing as being sprayed on the water around them in the No. 4 boat, which thus placed them further away from the ship—behind Al and Steve who were located below the trajectory of the firing.

Two independent accounts, by Carey and by Bill Maynard, two navy personnel who had been trained to handle such guns, one of them the Guard contingent's commanding officer, claimed to have seen tracer fire while in the lifeboats. But if they could not see the U-boat, how could the U-boat see them to aim the fire?

Two formal reports of the sinking referred to the firing, but without being too sure of its origin. The eyewitnesses had not had the opportunity to talk to each other since they abandoned ship. They ended in separate lifeboats, were rescued separately and arrived back in the U.S. on different ships at different times.

Steve and Al were around 150–200 yards from the ship when she sank. She just rolled over and—bow first—disappeared below the surface. They were afraid of the suction pulling them down. They looked skywards to see the screw, which was still turning, there was a hissing sound, but the mass of flames was gone. "Suddenly, no more ship, and we were alone," as Al later put it.

The actual sinking still left a huge patch of burning oil on the surface, the black smoke lingering over the waves, blocking the view from the lifeboats. At this stage all four of them were relatively close to the ship. The two lowered from the same side of the ship had managed to stay together.

The U-boat was sufficiently close to the sunken ship to spot one of the survivors in the water. The impression from the War Diary is that it was not for reasons related to operational intelligence that the sailor was picked up by the Germans. It was noted that he was a man in distress. That man was 62-year-old Robert Daigle, the chief cook, who like so many of the other crew members had felt they were forced to jump into the dark sea to get away from the sinking ship. Heydemann now took his boat back out to a safe distance further away from site of the sinking, but no record exists as to how much longer he remained on the scene.

When the U-boat disappeared, they rowed all night to get out of the area (according to Al, they had two oars in the boat). This was a mistake. They went in the opposite direction to the other three boats. The others hung together and were picked up within three days. They rowed; they were terrified of the U-boat. "When the ship had sunk we saw no more shelling and we were moving out of the area with every ounce of strength we could put on the oars, and we took turns to row and we maintained that rowing throughout the night."[35]

Aboard the U-boat, Daigle was interrogated. Judging from the account of the event in the War Diary, Daigle did a good job. The account, which was sent back to the U-boat Command by radio man Werner Popp, may not have been entirely in line with the facts as the Americans saw them. They had, apparently become separated from the convoy around 22 January. The convoy was completely dissolved due to the storm, with all the ships proceeding independently. The cargo included 30 tanks, 15 of which had been on deck. The ship was being described as being "heavily armed" and fast, capable of 15 knots. The armaments stem and stern were heavy artillery with complete protection, caliber around 12.5 cm (ca. 5"), with a smaller gun of around 88 mm further back on the fo'c'sle. This "secondary armament" was the size of the U-boat's main gun; no wonder the Germans were impressed with their kill. In addition the ship had eight anti-aircraft positions with probably 20 mm guns. The bridge wings had an additional AA gun of around

Members of the crew of *U-575* posing with their "Liliput Jumpers." Liliput was the name of the Hamburg bar they used to frequent between patrols. Behind them, on the wall of the conning tower, is a painting of a ship with a broken back. This was symbolizing the *City of Flint*, their largest target. The skipper, Heydemann, is sitting on top of the conning tower on the right; he was the only one with a white cap (courtesy Michael Elstermann).

37 to 40 mm with total protection in addition to the two machine guns they had located there.[36] As Al later put it, "Daigle must have been as good at bluffing as cooking."[37]

Heydemann's radio message to base was relayed over the broadcast to all the U-boats, informing them that the convoy, which had left New York on the 13th, had been completely broken up by the bad weather around ten days later. It helped save them.

Eight hours later, Dönitz decided to act on Daigle's information. He ordered two boats, Werner Hartenstein in *U-156* and Karl Neitzel in *U-510*, to remain on station to look for more individual ships from the same convoy.[38] Others were drawn in to extend the beat lines in order to reduce the chances that other individual ships from the scattered convoy could reach port safely. They remained in the wrong place for several days thanks to Daigle's inspired debriefing.

Sadly, it was an Allied situation report on the locations of German U-boats which gave the game away. The convoy UGS-4 had not been scattered, it was still sailing on towards its African destination. The signal confirmed to Dönitz that Daigle's statement had in fact been false, or at best erroneous, based on wrong assumptions due to the storm. The fact that German intelligence was decrypting and reading Allied convoy radio traffic so readily could have cost Daigle dearly. As he had exaggerated the extent of the armaments on an average American freighter, the shrewd cook also dramatized the fate of the convoy as he imagined it to be detrimental to the German effort to do so. He hoped the wolf pack would stop looking for a convoy if he could throw them off the scent. Daigle undoubtedly bought the convoy time. It was probably just as well that he did not know his own side destroyed his achievements.

The sloppy use of code routines by the Allied naval units not only risked Daigle's life, it also confirmed to Dönitz that the Allies were aware of the locations of his Delphin boats as the convoy had been re-routed on a more northerly course. What Dönitz never grasped throughout the entire war was that someone, somewhere, was reading his signals even better than he was reading the Allied ones.

In the U-boat, they were initially unsure of how to behave towards Daigle. One of them, Hannes, had learned some English in school and from his time on a Christian sailing ship. He learned that Daigle had been in his cabin at the time of the first explosion; in fact he was in the middle of shaving when it happened. As they talked, it came out that Daigle's sister would like to run a restaurant in San Francisco and that he had not wanted to sail any more. According to the German crew, after the initial suspicions, "something developed, which one would describe as friendship."[39] Daigle was 62; he could have been their granddad. Daigle must have had a fair amount of freedom of movement aboard the U-boat. He even cooked for them "something resembling Plum pudding." But perhaps even more important was a trick from his long experience of life at sea, namely how to wrap one of the bunk's straps around your thigh to prevent being thrown around from side to side in heavy seas. As they docked, two soldiers with rifles arrived to take Daigle away; at that stage, some of the U-boat crew even wondered if the guns were really necessary. Daigle was subsequently transferred to a prison camp and survived the war.

When dawn broke, the men in No. 3 lifeboat did an inventory of kit and food, etc., and checked the boat for damage. The water tank was located at the middle of the boat, underneath one of the thwarts. Regardless of this protection, the tank was damaged. In a top corner, it had two deep dents and one had caused a fracture. The tank was perforated. Fortunately the damage was so high up, near the very top of the tank, that the storage capacity was not too badly reduced. The total capacity was 30 gallons. Although they

Members of the crew from *U-575* on shore leave in St. Nazaire after the sinking of the *City of Flint*. Posing with the life saver probably used by Robert Daigle, the man they saved. At right, Funk Gefreiter Werner Popp; the rest are unknown (courtesy Michael Elstermann).

tried to seal it with wooden plugs, by the time of the rescue, the water was starting to taste salty. The damage was most probably sustained as they were struggling to launch the boat.

They had no rudder; the mast was difficult to get to work. They did have some canvas and some rope. There was one sheath knife in the boat and best of all, a sailmaker's kit. Al remembers Rohmar Johansen, a young Norwegian, smile when he saw it. During the stay in the boat he used all of it. The kit included some thread, which was like thin rope to Al, but there was also a spike, some smaller tools as well as a large hatchet knife. It was all part of the lifeboat gear and was stored in a metal container under the rear seat, which due to the shape of the boat was particularly deep. The gear also included a Very pistol, used to fire colored flares into the air to attract the attention of passing ships. They also found a sail in there, and a sextant, which proved not to be working.

First Rohmar fixed the wooden mast. The humidity in the lifeboat had warped and expanded the wood. Now it would no longer fit the metal mountings. In his report, Bill later suggested the base of the mast be made of metal to avoid this problem.[40] But hoisting a sail was not much use without a rudder. Again, the Norwegian's sailing experience helped them. He rigged up a rudder using one of the two oars. He had to lash it to the end of the boat using some of their ropes. That rudder was always in the hands of one of them from that moment onwards. They wanted to be in control. Next they set an easterly course, which they hoped would take them towards the Canary Islands.[41]

The sail was not much good either. Rohmar took one look at it and told them that, as it was, the sail would not be able to withstand the gale force winds he expected them to experience. Instead he fashioned a new sail from canvas in the sailmaker's kit. Sewing together stiff canvas using the equally stiff thread and the curved needle was not easy. He probably worked for at least three days on the new sail before he declared it ready. The new sail was bigger than the old one. Once in place against the mast, Rohmar's sail never came down again. No repairs were ever needed.[42]

From the canvas, the stiff thread in the sailmaker's kit, and using some more of the rope, Rohmar proceeded to make a sea anchor, which drifted behind them steadying progress in heavy seas and storms. It took him a couple of days to make it. The wooden frame was fashioned from parts of the bilge slats in the lifeboat. Around this he sewed the canvas funnel or cone. Once dropped over the side, the sea anchor served its purpose throughout. Rohmar had served the early apprenticeship on his first ship well and now his basic skills contributed to saving them all.

The food locker was located next to the water tank, below the same seat at the middle of the boat. In Al's boat, they had quite a bit of food—two to three dozen food tins of pemmican and malted milk tablets. These were about "the size of a nickel and as thick as a lifesaver." They were chewable. The men were very conservative with all their rations and even when they finally were rescued, they still had a small amount left due to catching fish for extra food.

During the initial confusing time after the sinking, the four lifeboats all actually remained around the burning freighter. As the U-boat sightings and soundings illustrated, they were all very close to but without spotting each other. It was therefore perhaps not surprising that the U-boat did not see any of them. Had the firing not occurred, there was every likelihood that they all would have remained in the area until morning. They would have been able to join each other as the new dawn afforded their first sight of the terrifyingly vast, empty ocean before them, wherever they looked.

Some of the men in the captain's lifeboat, No. 1, also searched through the compartments of two rafts for extra supplies.[43] They did this less than 12 hours after Steve and Al had emptied theirs. The final two rafts located at the front of the ship were never launched. They all thought these had been destroyed in the explosion or the subsequent fire.

At daybreak Tuesday, 26 January, the two lifeboats, No. 1 and No. 4, located the No. 2 boat about a mile off and tied up to this one too. The skipper, MacKenzie, did a roll call that morning. Together the boats held 48 survivors from the ship's original crew of 65; of these, 32 were merchant navy men, one was from the U.S. Army and 15 were Armed Guards.

During the day radio operator Bohn transmitted an SOS distress signal every two hours. Fortunately, the sea-state was moderate and there was at that stage only a light wind blowing from the southwest. These three boats, each equipped for 40 passengers, could easily sustain the survivors for a few days. Nevertheless, they started to ration the food to 4 oz. of water and two biscuits each, per day.

By Wednesday, 27 January, MacKenzie's boats had remained at the site of the sinking for two days without being picked up, or even spotted; now they decided to set sail for the Azores. According to the Third Officer, William Mills, they were around 450 km (280 miles) southwest of the island of San Miguel. This meant separating the boats, but they hoped to stay in touch. Unfortunately this proved to be impossible. Sailing the lifeboats individually meant that they very quickly moved apart. They were so low in the water as to make it literally impossible to spot the other boats as they moved between the rolling waves.

Like the *City of Flint*, two other stragglers from the original convoy proceeded independently towards Casablanca. They did not know the convoy had been diverted to the north of the Azores. Independently and in total ignorance of the danger, they sailed one after the other, directly into the Delphin patrol zone to the south of the islands.

The two other unfortunate ships, *Charles C. Pinckney* and *Julia Ward Howe*, were both torpedoed that Wednesday. Only one lifeboat with 14 men was rescued from the *Charles C. Pinckney*, which was sunk by *U-514*. The crew of the *Julia Ward Howe* was more fortunate, although they lost the captain, Andrew Hammond, and Thomas L. Haley, the chief engineer, who died later aboard the *Lima*. The rest of the crew survived. Their nemesis came in the form of *U-442*. Within six months, both U-boats had been sunk with all hands.

Fortunately the Portuguese destroyer *Lima* was already looking for survivors. The Portuguese navy actually informed the British navy at Gibraltar that the *Lima* had set to sea the previous Tuesday, the day before the two ships were torpedoed. She was headed directly towards the location where the *City of Flint* had reported being sunk.[44]

The commander-in-chief of the Portuguese navy sent a telegram in the morning of Thursday, 28 January advising U.S. Naval Operations that the *Lima* had just picked up 62 survivors from the *Julia Ward Howe*, but had not yet located any from the *City of Flint*.[45] The survivors were picked up from a position virtually halfway between the location where their own ship had been torpedoed and where the *City of Flint* went down. At the same time, the *City of Flint* survivors in the No. 1, 2 and 4 boats were by now sailing their boats independently towards them.

Luckily, by nightfall, the *Lima* had also rescued the *City of Flint* survivors in the three lifeboats.[46] The Portuguese sank all the lifeboats once emptied. The weather was by now deteriorating rapidly. That night, the storm was so severe that the Portuguese destroyer was badly damaged on her way to port with the survivors. Out to the southwest, the men in No. 3 lifeboat were fighting for their lives.

Three days later, all those rescued were landed at Ponta Delgada in the Azores. Once ashore, a new problem faced the survivors. They had no money and no forms of identification. They had known that German U-boat commanders would seek out officers from sunken vessels for interrogation and even for shipment back to Germany if thought to be particularly useful. In fact, the Captain of the *U-442*, that sank the *Julia Ward Howe*, had surfaced to question the crew. He even brought the second mate on board the U-boat for further questioning. Fortunately he was later released. Crews were advised to destroy all proof of their identity. This was causing the U.S. consulate in the Azores problems. They had neither money for around 100 stranded mariners, nor the authorization to hand out funding. They had to send an urgent telegram to Washington for assistance.[47]

William Mills, from Milton, Massachusetts, was one of the survivors rescued from the first group. He described the sinking as having happened one evening without warning. Due to the volatility of her cargo, he explained, the ship was abandoned within ten minutes due to the intensity of the fire. William had still had the presence of mind to bring all his money when he left the ship. Now he put some of it to good use. On 5 March, William paid $245 cash, for a one-way ticket on the *Serpa Pinta*, bound for Philadelphia where he arrived ten days later. On the 17th he reported for duty again in New York. Such was the commitment of the merchant navy.[48] As he arrived back in the U.S. as the first survivor, the U.S. Navy announced the fate of the once so famous ship. *The New York Times* even featured a photograph from her proud homecoming 3 years earlier.

The Navy actually broke its normal procedure for reporting losses at sea when the *City of Flint* was lost. They did not normally name the ships they lost, but due to her fame, the famous Hog Islander was identified. They did so, however, only two months after the tragedy actually took place, probably to minimize the operational value to the enemy of making such an announcement. As submarine commanders' claims of "wins" were notoriously unreliable, the navy was not going to help them. All those Americans who had loved ones sailing in the *City of Flint*, however, had not seen the survivors yet. None of them arrived home until the month after the articles appeared in the press.

All the 117 survivors from the torpedoed three ships, *Julia Ward Howe, Charles C. Pinckney* and the *City of Flint*, had to endure some very crowded conditions during their enforced stay in the Azores. The Portuguese authorities, on behalf of a neutral country, would not permit a warship to pick up known combatants from their territory. The shipwrecked sailors had to wait for the arrival of a civilian vessel.

Finally they were all repatriated to the U.S. in the Portuguese steamer *Nyassa*, which took ten days to cross the Atlantic, arriving in Philadelphia April 26, 1943. The day after, they were back in New York.

In the No. 3 boat, life was far more dramatic. First they had to fight just to survive the storm that nearly sank the *Lima*. They decided to push the food to last 3 weeks—thinking that was a pessimistic estimate. They just did not know how careful they had to be. They really could not know how long they would be in the lifeboat. As Al saw it, it was a big puddle out there, and no grocer's store down on the corner. Their concern was making the food last until the last day, no matter when that day would be. They were determined to see beyond their time in the lifeboat. Everybody thought three weeks was a crazy guess for the time they would be in the boat. There had to be ships, they were in the shipping lanes.

The tins of food contained pemmican—fruit, meat, coconut oil pressed into tins looking like sardine cans. The cans did not have a ring pull; one needed to cut the lid off. It was about half the size of an 8-ounce water glass. According to Al, it got to be really tasty, but was not that good per se.[49]

The Armed Guards did not even know any of the merchant navy men. Until then, they had all done their own things and had their own quarters. They had not been together that long to even get to know one another. They were disassociated from the crew. When they were loading the ship, the Armed Guard unit provided guards at the gangplank and deployed 2 men at each gun. Once at sea, they stood their own watches, separate from most of the merchant seamen.

As they pulled desperately on the oars that first night to get out of the area away from the U-boat, they were 11 in the boat. Six of them were from the Armed Guard crew; the other five were merchant navy. None of them had been on board for even two months. The merchant seamen were Norwegian Rohmar Johansen, Walter Kielek, Carlos Lusisall, William Myszkowski and Walter Vanderhorst. The two Walters would have known each other, Kielek was galley man, Vanderhorst mess man. There was no clear date for when the civilians joined the ship, but early December 1942 is the likely time, when the ship was being readied to sail north to New York to take on the cargo.

Apart from Rohmar, the other merchant crew members were probably twice as old as the Guardsmen. The navy personnel were all less than 25 years old. In fact, Pennsylvanian Arthur Voorheis had apparently bluffed his way into the navy; he was only a teenager and the youngest man in the boat.[50]

The two first Armed Guards to meet on the ship seem to have been Stephen Kubick from Flint, Michigan, and William Maynard from Council, North Carolina, who were ordered on board 7 December 1942. Albert Becker, Iowa; Thomas Leoni Blanton, Georgia; Elmer H. Brandal, Sandusky, Ohio; and Arthur F. Voorheis were all ordered to join the ship 12 December 1942. All six would have trained together on the ship, shared watches and exercises. They all felt more of a team than the civilians did.

Al knew the Armed Guard men well—he had lived with them for over a month; one of them was his friend Bill Maynard. Initially there seemed to be some tension in the boat. Bill outranked them all and the Armed Guards placed him in charge. A couple of merchant seamen had words with the other civilians—they did not like how the Armed Guards took the initiative to run the boat. And the Armed Guards did not like the attitude of these two. They were in one end of the boat, at the front. The Armed Guards stayed at the back, around the rudder. This was also where the kit locker was. The navy men had a Government Issue 0.45 Colt pistol. It was a persuasive measure. They all knew where it was; in the locker, wrapped in waterproof cloth. As long as they were in the boat, the gun was never picked up, there was no need, it was never out in the open.

During the first few days, the merchant fleet men kept counting up how much money they were making. Their salaries were all far higher than what the navy men were paid and in addition, the civilians now knew they would be paid their "torpedo bonus." All the money talk irked the Armed Guards who were, after all, sitting in the same lifeboat all too well aware of having volunteered to fight this war and of the meager rewards for their dedication. But as a week followed another monotonous week of rain, sunshine, storms and heavy seas, the money-angle gradually faded. Survival was the only target worth the candle.[51]

Some of the merchant sailors only got into line when a storm blew up. In the storms they all helped. There was never a refusal. The Armed Guard got respect from most of them, even if some of them were hard to understand. Al admitted that he could certainly not understand all of what the merchant sailors said. They were all of different nationalities, Norwegian, Spanish, and Polish—a real mixture. Still, there was never any animosity between the two groups although it often became clear that they had very different outlook on things.

Frequent storms made it a struggle to keep afloat. The waves would spill into the boat virtually on a continuous basis. They had two army helmets. These were used for bailing water. There were always two men bailing; during storms they bailed like crazy. The rest would be taking turns holding the rudder. They would need to change every 15–20 minutes. "The rudder could nearly tear your arms off. Then you'd go rest awhile before taking your turn bailing water." Al felt that if they were to die, he would have bet the storms would take them.[52]

The Norwegian, Rohmar S. Johansen, was born in Bergen in Western Norway 3 October 1919. He was only 23 years old. His parents were Karen (nee Kolstad) and Konrad Johansen. Rohmar had three brothers; two of them were also in the merchant navy. Rohmar first registered as a sailor 12 June 1937, His merchant navy registration number was 8131.[53] His first ship was Stamer Shipping's *Heimgar*, built in 1921. He switched ships and by April 1940, when Germany overran Norway, he was working deep-sea routes, sailing in *Nordvangen*, which he left in October 1940. Virtually the entire Norwegian merchant navy was handed over to the Allied nations at that time and they spend all of the war moving supplies for the Allies. Sadly, as one of the many merchant vessels to suffer this fate, Clausen in *U-129* sank *Nordvangen* in the Caribbean in February 1942, with all hands.

During the first three weeks they spotted only one ship, but the ship did not see them even if they fired the Very pistol in the air, discharging a red flare. When at sea level, it is often difficult to see even a flare. On the other hand, it is perfectly reasonable to think that even if the officer of the watch on the freighter did see something, he chose to look the other way, to preserve his own life. If Al had been the skipper, he would have disregarded what he had seen. Even if the ship did see the lifeboat, it would have been dangerous to stop to pick up the survivors. To any submarine using the lifeboat as a decoy, the ship would be a sitting duck. It was heartbreaking—they knew there was help, but how could they get to it? All they could do was to watch the ship sail out of sight. They were all waving and fired the pistol 2–3 times. All were very depressed after this, and some cried. Al's view of life after the episode was the only one viable. He did not allow himself to give up hope. If there was one ship, there was bound to be another.

On Thursday, 18 February 1943, when Heydemann returned to St. Nazaire after the patrol, his crew was proud of their kills, most of all of the *City of Flint*. In an apparently rare display of achievement, the profile of the *City of Flint* was painted on the barrel of the U-boat's gun. It inspired the boat's unknown artist to reproduce the profile of a sinking ship with its "back broken"; i.e., with the stern and stem sections pointing upward in the shape of a V, with a pirate's insignia of skull and crossbones superimposed. This was painted on the front of the conning tower, beside it, the "Snorting Bull" insignia of the 7th U-boat Flotilla.[54]

Each kill was claimed in inflated tonnage for each ship. This was displayed on triangular pennants—one per ship—flown on the signal line when returning to port. In the case of the *City of Flint*, Heydemann had doubled her size to 10,000 tons, thus boosting the significance of his victory.

When Daigle was picked up, he may have been kept afloat by one of *City of Flint's* rescue rings, a "doughnut." Judging from Heydemann's War Diary, they only stopped the once, to "rescue a man in need."[55] Only then were they close enough to the actual debris field as it was still covered in parts in burning oil. Once back at St. Nazaire, fellow crew member Kurt Lück photographed the radioman, Werner Popp and three of his mates as they posed outside a bar with their trophy, the rescue ring, and wearing their Liliput tops.[56] What they did not know was that as the young Germans celebrated their own perceived success, the equally young Americans in the No. 3 lifeboat had been adrift for 23 days. They were still determined to be rescued.

Al was in charge of rations. They could not afford to be overfed. The rations meant that each day they each had a quarter of a can of pemmican and two milk tablets. The pemmican came out in one piece, then Al would use a knife to quarter it. They had water twice every day. It was shared out in a small container on a chain about the size of a shotgun shell. There was never any invasion of the food store. All took what was theirs. They ate twice a day, mid-morning and late in the afternoon. It was the same routine every day.

When they had fish, it was a banquet. Within three weeks they had thought of fishing. They realized they were in trouble and the food was going down. Their intake had to be reduced to make it all go further. Fishing would help the food last longer.

They saw fish swimming close to the boat. They were swimming with sharks. It seemed so easy, they were just so close. The Norwegian and some of the others fixed up a line and a hook. Only the first fish they ever caught was caught on a line, but that was a barracuda.

Although it was a big fish, they eventually managed to haul it into the boat. The trouble was, they could not kill it. They were afraid to go close enough to cut it with a knife because of its teeth. They had to keep out of his way; he had some teeth! A wound could have had fatal consequences under those conditions. It took all day to die. They could not use the machete, as they were afraid of cutting through the thin metal skin of the boat.

Once skinned and cut up into pieces, the fish was eaten raw. They each had a goodly sized piece of fish. They really felt they feasted on that fish, which tasted like steak. Then they felt guilty having wasted it. After that they rationed what was left. They cured it in the sun and again Rohmar knew what to do. In the evening when they had fish, the Norwegian wrapped it up and put it away, "to keep it from the moonlight," which would have rotted it he claimed.[57] During the day he dried it and preserved if for them.

All the other fish was caught with a sheath knife. These were pilot fish. They swam with the sharks and would come really close to the boat. They would spear the fish in the belly from underneath and throw them into the boat. They managed perhaps one fish per 50 attempts. It took lots of patience and skill. They learned to wait until the afternoon, when they would sit on the shady side of the boat with a hand in the water—below the fish. They had to get under them to flick the fish into the boat. It could be 3–4 days with no sight of any fish. If they saw Porpoises there were no sharks and therefore no fish. When they saw sharks, there was fish to be had. Sometimes they never left the sides of the boat. They were actually pleased to see sharks. They were beautiful, and treacherous. They rubbed up against the sides of the boat and the men petted them. Al petted them like a puppy dog, until they would roll over and you would see the teeth. Other times it was far more scary as the sharks would rub against them from underneath and the floorboards of the boat moved, then the men would take the remaining oar and gingerly push them away. They were worried the force of a large shark could crack open a seam or something. The boat was about 18 feet, the sharks about half that size.

In the boat, it could be claustrophobic, and one did not move about. You got to know your neighbor. The men just sat in the morning where they had been sitting the night before. Or they might get up to stretch or to crawl over to talk to some of the others. They had no duties. There was nothing to do but to wait. They had far too much time to think.

Early on, they started to have informal prayer sessions. Virtually all the members of the Armed Guard had copies of a small prayer book, a 3" by 5" volume which included Psalms, Bible passages, prayers and various types of verses to support and encourage those who required help. Most of them did not carry the book on their person. Fortunately Steve Kubick had brought his copy when they left the ship.

They read 2–3 times a day. It seemed to be a great comfort. Every day, weather permitting they would have a reading. Gradually they all became involved in this; it was a set thing for them to do, which seemed to help to keep their spirits up and as a morale booster, they all felt that it worked.[58] It settled their minds. They seemed to have realized this as they all took turns and the book was passed around. Al had religion, but was not religious. He remembered their readings well. They would all start with the 23 Psalm:

The Lord is my shepherd. I shall not want, He maketh me lie down in green pastures, He leadeth me beside the still waters.

After that opening, each would then pick a passage of his own choice to read.

All the navy personnel and the Norwegian, Rohmar would read. The Norwegian was the 7th man of the group. He was part of the in-crowd from the very beginning.

Rohmar would come over and say something like "let me help" or "we need to do this, we need to do that." They did not need the navy, they needed help and more often than not, it was Rohmar's seamanship that saved the day. He often did not have much to say for himself; he was more interested in listening to the others.

They always sailed to the east, when they could. The sail was not down for 46 days, storms or not. They knew where they were, and where they had to go. Rohmar could navigate, knew what to do. He was a great relief to them all. He was not all that easy-going. Although young, he was very mature, and calm with it. He had a "developed mind," as Al put it. Rohmar knew what he had to do and when he had to do it. Everybody in the navy crew would try things, never expected any help and the merchant sailors did little, but when they were needed, they were there to be called upon and then they pitched in too. Rohmar was often busy making and fixing things, even studying the charts they found in the boat.

They had a lot of bad weather. It was possible to see it coming—the clouds would start forming, the sea would get choppy, next you would see big waves, 30 to 40 feet, huge waves from crest to bottom; they could be terrifying. Once Al sat in the boat, looking straight down, and saw nothing under the boat. They were right at the crest of a huge wave. Next they would fall and when he looked up, he'd see sky between the two huge swells. That was the most terrifying sight of all.

Dönitz noted in his memoirs that the weather was particularly bad in the Atlantic that winter and that once January came, conditions deteriorated even further. The U.S. Coast Guard noted that the winter storms in the Atlantic that year became the yardstick against which future storms were measured. At the time, it was recorded as the worst winter in the Atlantic for 50 years, 116 days out of 140 saw winds of gale force or greater.

They would never give up hope, as long as the boat was the right way up. But not all of them found it equally easy to remain optimistic and sane.

During the first three weeks they were in and out of some really bad storms. Rohmar knew that one of the merchant seamen, Vanderhorst, had been torpedoed 2 or 3 times before. This time it had affected him very badly; mentally he would "come and go." Sometimes he would be rational, but he had started to behave strangely after only a few days in the boat, then a week or so later, he seemed to have recovered. He had quite a bit of money with him; occasionally he would lay it out to dry. Then he would give somebody some and ask them to get a water taxi so he could go ashore or to get him a bucket of crab.

The equipment in the boat included a rubber survival suit called a Vaco Suit. It had been designed by Norwegian Carl Dybberg a few years earlier to help prevent sailors dying from exposure if they ended in the water. It even had lead in the boots of the suit to keep the person wearing it floating upright, when using the lifejacket as a flotation aid. Now they thought that if they kept Vanderhorst dry, he might not suffer so much. They helped him put on the suit, a big one-piece affair with a yellow hood.[59] As if the trouble fitting him into the suit was not bad enough, he also carried a huge, menacing hatchet. Vanderhorst never once let go of the hatchet, which he had picked up from the lifeboat tools. Had he used it, it would easily have damaged the boat. They did not mess with him. Fortunately, he did not want to fight, but he still kept hold of the hatchet. Then one night around 20 February, in the middle of a terrible storm while the others were bailing, he just stood up and literally walked right overboard.[60] He had never permitted any of them to close the drawstrings in the suit. As the top was open, water filled the suit like a bucket. Sure, he did not know what he was doing, but it was heart-breaking to the others to see it happen, he had been through so much. Now he was too quick for any of them to save him from himself or his private demons.

Virtually none of those in the boat had their life jackets on at the time of the attack, perhaps only 1 or 2. Most did not even take time to slip them on when the ship went down. The explosion had seemed to be so violent. Only those on watch duty wore the appropriate gear. If the life jackets were not in their immediate possession, they did not have one.

A storm could go all night, and they had to keep working in order to survive. If you gave up you were done. Moving to and fro the rudder they were crawling to relieve each other. When their arms got too tired it was difficult to even hold on to the rudder, let alone control it. In the pitching seas you would be crawling over anybody to get there to help the person fighting to control the boat.

For nearly a third of the time in the boat they had to endure stormy or bad weather. A lot of the time, the sea was like a mirror. Then two or three days later storm and rain would envelop them, but never really thunder and lightning, just storms with huge waves. Waves could quickly grow from just 10 feet to a towering 30–40 feet. The boat was riding like a cork. When there was a storm, they would be heading into the wind; the direction was not important, staying alive was. The rest of the time they could control the course.

Towards the end, they moved away from that kind of weather. They sailed into better waters, the color changed and it was warmer. The Norwegian knew the boat was close to a coast or to land; he could tell, and they saw seagulls for the first time. By now they were always exhausted. The small rations were far from adequate to provide sufficient nutrition, but so far they had survived. They were so determined to stay alive.

Towards the end they spotted seaweed. During calm days the Norwegian showed them how to "pick berries," small blisters from seaweed drifting past. They contained tiny amounts fresh water, which was what they needed. They could sit all day squeezing these, drop for drop. The two most common species of seaweed drifting in the Atlantic are both of the Sargassum family. It is thought that the nightly "cell respiration," normally only associated with carbon-dioxide, together with condensation would create these minute quantities of water.[61]

The seaweed was pulled into the boat by the armful and all would sit plucking it like monkeys, according to Al. They had nothing else to do; it hung on the side of the boat, to be picked at. When they were picked up, the boat looked like a hay wagon as they had recently come into a lot of this seaweed. The men did not let it go by. They would throw the old off and get new on board.

They never actually ran out of provisions or water. If they had a decent storm, not too rugged, they would catch rainwater off the sail and replenish the tank. They would try to keep it at the level of the holes. They caught what they could, they never thought of the water running out. They had surplus fish and they still had some of the original provisions left at day 46. After around 3 weeks in the boat Al noticed that the food supply was starting to go down. They kept cutting back, changing from 4 to 5 guys on a can of pemmican. The slices were cut a little bit thinner. But without fish or water they would not have survived. It was the Norwegian's idea. He knew how to preserve the fish. In Al's words, he was a Godsend.[62] They would not have lasted as long without fish.

The monotony was terrible. There was nothing to do, or to decide or discuss. If something required a decision, they would decide on the spot, as they needed to. Everything was so repetitive; nothing ever changed.

The sun was another problem. All were very dark when they were picked up, but they were not burned, only very tanned by the wind and the sun. In the other extreme, it could be terribly cold. Each storm drenched them all and could last for what seemed to be an eternity. Even if they bailed, they were quickly soaked, sea spray would drift over them, and waves would crash into the boat. They only had the clothes they had on their backs when the torpedo exploded and they lasted. All had shoes and socks; none had boots. Al had no jacket, only a khaki shirt and navy blue jeans, and he shivered a lot. They huddled back to back. And in exhaustion they slept. It was sad to watch the others when they were sleeping; their mouths were going "100 miles an hour." Guys were dreaming of eating, and drooling in their sleep.

When awake they would talk about home, about crazy things they had done as kids. They were all young. There was a lot of humor. Somebody would always think up something that would get a cackle, until the very end.

Three times they saw whales about ½ mile away. The first time they spotted one, they initially thought it was an island, it was that big. When the Norwegian saw them he knew what to do. He ordered utter silence: "Don't make a move." If they got wind of them, the whales would go under the boat and capsize it. Whenever they saw one, silence.

They had scratched lines on the side of the boat, one for each day they spent there. First four and then one to cross them out to make five, then another group, and another. By the time they were rescued they had filled a whole panel. The new mark for each day was always made in the morning. Whoever had the rudder did the marking. They knew what month it was.

What kept Al going was first and foremost that he was determined to survive: "you need to have the 'will to life.' You don't quit if there is still an ounce of strength." They were all pulling together, then nothing bad could come of it. It was bound to work. They were a good crew. Al could live with them any day. None would ever really talk too openly about home. They did though, privately, but they did not share all. Any of them could think about things for hours, but it would not come out. Each had his own problems, concerns and worries about not making it home and the effect that would have on those waiting, hoping.

They first spotted the plane early one morning, shortly after sun-up. They had seen a lot of seagulls. Thought it was a seagull that came at them, but then it grew too large! As the plane circled the boat, they waved at it and it disappeared. Now, they felt absolutely certain they were going to be picked up that day. From then on they relaxed; they simply knew, just waited for help to come.

As the men looked forward to the rescue they so desperately wanted to happen, the day passed. At dusk, finally, they saw smoke on the horizon. Gradually they could see the smoke get bolder. Then they saw the actual ship coming towards the boat; she bore right down on them.

Tuesday, 16 March 1943, it was 46 days after the sinking.[63] There was euphoria in the boat.

All held their places, all were too weak. They knew others would do it for them. Mentally they felt fine. Physically, they had not much power. But it was very emotional for them.

The warship had initially been worried they were being used as a decoy for a U-boat. The metal hull of the lifeboat confused the Asdic (sonar), which was continuously searching for U-boats. When they first spotted the lifeboat, the ship came slowly past, then one guy jumped in to the boat, and he tied ropes around them. Then the ship came by again, moving slowly. The ship backed up, the British sailor threw the ropes up and the crew pulled Al and the others up like sacks of potatoes, then immediately aimed a gun on the lifeboat and sank it, and with it the Colt .45, never once lifted in anger. The ship never really stopped. It was British—*Quadrant*, a brand new "Q" Class destroyer, launched the previous year.

The *Quadrant* crew had picked up survivors before, but even their attitude changed when the crew learned how long the people in the lifeboat had actually been at sea. They could not believe it.

They looked a mess, had not shaved. The shirts were stiff and white from salt. All they had been able to do in the lifeboat had been to wring them out and hang them to dry. Their hair was a foot long. They were all in the same fix. But this didn't last long. Then came their first meal, plain bread and butter. To Al, it was the best food in his life. And then the cup of rum, quite a bit, but not too much. But the ship's doctor quickly stopped the party when he heard they'd been in the lifeboat that long. He said their stomachs would be bone dry. He would not let them have solids until they reached Gibraltar. They had very coarse skin from all the salt water. Al had no open sores, none of them did, but Steve Kubick, Al learned later, had very bad feet as a result of all the seawater. He did not know that in the lifeboat, for not once had Steve ever complained.

On the *Quadrant*, "it was nice." It seemed like luxury to have their own individual hammocks. The six Armed Guard crew stayed together. Late Wednesday they were safe in Gibraltar harbor.[64] It was St. Patrick's Day, Al recalled. The arrival itself was a strange experience after not seeing land for so long. Gibraltar immediately sent a coded message to U.S. Naval Operations informing them of the rescue.[65] Sadly, there were still 7 men unaccounted for. Five of them perished in the explosion; three Armed Guards, Louis M. Bozada, James C. Lichtenstein and Donald E. Quillen, together with merchant navy men, Barila and Person. Lichtenstein and Quillen were among the 6 Armed Guards who had joined the ship just before they set sail from New York. Regrettably Walter Vanderhorst had jumped overboard after nearly 30 days in lifeboat No. 3. Unbeknownst to them all, the final man, the cook, Robert Daigle, had actually survived too, but he was in Germany, as a POW.

In port, they were transferred to an American ship, the *Almack,* where they stayed for 3 days prior to the transfer for the journey back to America. They saw little of life in Gibraltar. Only once did the group actually go ashore. They had no money anyway. This was quite normal for survivors from any sinking and the sailors around them probably knew all too well that it could easily be their turn next. Between them, they collected a few dollars for Al and his friends, $5-$10 Al thought. Now they did their one trip ashore and spent the entire collection on a huge pile of oranges. In reality it would probably have taken them months to consume them all, but right then, to the men from the lifeboat, this seemed an important thing to buy. Oranges were a potent symbol for life on land where choices were made routinely, where food could be colorful and fresh tasting.

They received no money of their own, which apparently was standard procedure; the U.S. authorities would not give any survivors any money until they had verified their true identity. The U.S. authorities were, however, prepared to get them all home quickly.

Access to Spain itself was limited to daytime only. Al noticed that the big gates across the access road were closed at night.[66] The aftermath of the civil war was still all too real. Sadly the Americans saw many of the Spanish going through the rubbish looking for salvage. The waste from all the ships at anchor was piled up daily for disposal and every day locals would go through it.

For the trip back to the U.S. they were put aboard the British twin-screw troop-transporter *Tamaroa*, built for Shaw, Saville & Albion at Harland & Wolf in Belfast in 1922. This was a huge ship, a 12,405 ton steamer with room for nearly 2000 passengers after its conversion to troop carrier. As the convoy was being assembled, a U-boat attacked. The ship took off like a shot on her own and zigzagged all the way to New York. During the entire journey, none of the survivors from the No. 3 lifeboat went below deck to their assigned quarters. They stayed in a sheltered area, on deck.

Friday the 13th of April, they arrived in New York, nearly two weeks earlier than the rest of the crew who had been rescued long before Al and his friends. Once through the questioning and debriefing sessions, the civilians were free to seek a new job, to ship out on a new journey in a new convoy, facing the same threats all over again. The Armed Guard group from the No. 3 lifeboat went directly to the Armed Guard Receiving Station in Brooklyn. They were back at the Bush Terminal, where the journey had started four months earlier. From here they too were reassigned new duties on ships facing the same dangers all over the world.

Al Becker at the *Red Barber Show,* being broadcast live from the huge Bush Terminal at New York, probably autumn 1943. The show supported the sale of war bonds. Al's uniform is now decorated with three medal ribbons, two of which have been identified: The American Defense ribbon and the American Campaign ribbon (courtesy John Becker).

At that stage Al, like the others who had been in the lifeboat, were listed as "missing in action." His folks had had a telegram when it happened, and they had heard no more. Now, he was sent home on leave without any prior notification to the family. When he reached Chicago, Al phoned home to Charles City to get them to meet him off the train. When she answered the phone, all his mother managed to say was "Oh my God, no, we'll be there!"[67] In Charles City they had had church services to get him back, not services "in memory of"; now their prayers were answered.

Against all odds, Al returned. He arrived at the rail depot at 0100. It was party time. Like the men in the boat, his family had not given up hope. There is always hope; they had been notified that Al was missing, not that he was dead. There was a huge difference. As it was, Al had left home in September 1942 and saw his folks again in April 1943.

Carey and the rest of the Armed Guard contingent all reported for duty at the Receiving Station on Thursday, 26 April. The entire group of Armed Guard survivors was never united after they abandoned the *City of Flint* in January 1943. Emotional needs were never factored into warfighting as early as 1943.

When Al returned to New York from leave, he never went back to sea. Instead he was stationed at the large Armed Guard Center in Brooklyn. The vast facility became home for the next year. The Center was a hive of activity as the war in Europe was expanding. Fortunately for Al, he no longer had to share his quarters with hundreds of others on the Main Deck. Instead, as ship's company, he was quartered on a small ship berthed permanently at the rear of the base.

During this time, the Center played host to many great shows, by a range of famous names. They all came to entertain the troops: Benny Goodman, Tommy Dorsey, Harry

Double date. On the right, Catherine and Al Becker; the other couple is unknown. Probably at the Bush Terminal in late 1943 (courtesy John Becker).

James, Judy Garland and many, many others. They had two shows every month to help to liven up the base, boost morale and make all those shipping out in between shows really jealous. It was during this time that Al met Catherine, his wife-to-be. Her mother ran a shop only a few blocks away on the corner of 79th Street and 3rd Avenue. In September 1944 Al was discharged from the Navy and returned to Iowa to help prepare the farmland for the spring planting. By Christmas, however, he was to be found back in New York, but this time to prepare for a wedding. On Sunday, 21 January 1945, Catherine became his wife.

The effect of it all "makes a believer out of you." Al truly believed that. There has to be something beyond this life or you wouldn't have made it. Any person who has the will to live can do it. But you need certain things—even if it nearly kills you to get them, but never give up hope. It's just there. You dare not give up hope.[68]

Living through this experience took them all to the edge. It is harder to believe today, and perhaps easier to rationalize now. Al knew, he was there. He could never leave it behind, not entirely. It was just there. "If things go wrong all you have to do is think about it and things will straighten out." Even much later, there could be flashes of memories—triggered by seeing something disastrous, something way beyond the normal:

> If you have a little faith, things will straighten out. Have a lot of faith in life, it will be straightened out. No matter what it is, if you have life in you, it will straighten out.

In retirement, Al explained that he did not dream much about the time in the boat anymore. It was so far away, although some episode may occasionally come back. He used to relive some of it, mostly the rough weather, and the storms. He was scared then, it was truly terrifying. "The storms scared the living hell out of you. They were bad. Thank God for that Norwegian. He knew how to keep that boat right way up."[69]

Postscript

16

Still Waters Once Again

Gainard's new command, equipped with even more anti-submarine weaponry and supported by two smaller craft, deliberately straggled from convoy UGS-7 near the Azores. This was a mere month after Al and his friends in the final lifeboat had been picked up. Again, no German U-boat was tricked into attacking them. They tried once more, as part of UGS-13 in July, but they were equally unsuccessful this time.

As Gainard took his ship back to New York, he was ordered to move on to another re-commissioned ship. He was to take over command of the troop carrier *Bolivar* (AP-79). They left New York in the *Bolivar* towards the end of October bound for California and Gainard took his new command into San Pedro Naval base Monday, 1 November 1943.

The U.S. Ambassador in Norway, Mrs. Harriman, had expressed concern for his health already before the ship left Bergen. Nearly four years later, in December 1943 Mrs. Gainard was to rush to California to join her husband at his bedside. Unfortunately he had fallen ill at sea and had been transferred from his ship to the large U.S. Naval Hospital in San Diego, only a week after arrival. By then Gainard was suffering from severe heart problems and pleurisy.[1] Six weeks later, hospital staff was so concerned that they decided to contact his wife. Sadly Joseph Gainard passed away shortly after his wife's arrival as if he had been waiting to see her just once more, before slipping the moorings of life with his wife by his side 23 December 1943.

The *Bolivar* remained at the base, participating in the training program to prepare soldiers for amphibious landings in the Pacific until January. Less than a year later, in November 1944, the destroyer *Gainard* (DD-706) was commissioned in his memory in New York. His widow sponsored the ship.

In January 1944 two articles appeared in the press describing the sinking of the *City of Flint*—one in America about the victims, the other describing the perpetrators, in Germany.

Hamburg was proud of its links with *U-575* and keen to show its support for the boat. In January 1944, local weekly magazine *Hamburger Illustrierte* featured three of the U-boat's ratings on the front cover. They were posing over the gun barrel, which still displayed the trophy painting of their proudest sinking, American *City of Flint*.[2] The inside double-page spread set out the story in detail, suitably written to boost Nazi morale, "of the ship that would not sink, and how they sank her." The one vital clue missing from the published story was the actual identity of the ship. Fearful of reprisals, the name, which was clearly visible on the original photograph, had been blanked out prior to publication.[3] The article contributed little to the luck of *U-575*; the boat was sunk two months later with the loss of 17 men, one of whom was MaschinenObergefreiter Kurt Lück, who had recorded the story of his boat until its demise.

Crew members from *U-575* posing over the U-boat gun. An edited version of this photo was published in a propaganda magazine in Hamburg during the war, but with the name of the *City of Flint* erased (courtesy Michael Elstermann).

In America, Al's story equally embellished to boost morale, told the story of their survival and rescue after 46 miraculous days at sea.[4] Unlike the German story, this article named names, but sadly omitted the name of the man who did most to save them, Norwegian Rohmar Johansen. It has taken 80 years before his contribution would be placed on record.

On his return to New York after the *City of Flint* rescue, Rohmar too provided a sworn statement where he briefly described the sinking as he had experienced it all. At the time, he was living at the Norwegian Seamen's Church in South Brooklyn, at the hostel located on the corner of Carrol Street and Clinton Street. It was not far from the quays at Red Hook, or from the Armed Guard Centre where Al was based for the next year. Al never knew how close he had been to his friend for all that time.

Regrettably, very little is known about this very private man or about his life after the war. He seemed to lead a restless life, spending most of it at sea. Nor is it known what he did during the rest of the war. June 21, 1948, Rohmar re-joined the Norwegian merchant navy register as he joined the crew of *Ingertre*. He remained in deep-sea traffic until his death. From 1960 to 1968 he had a base of sorts in New York, but as the shipping routes altered, he moved his base to Genoa in 1968, where he left his last ship, *Concordia Fjord* on 17 August 1974.

For many years the Norwegian Concordia Line sailed between New Orleans and Genoa. Staff from the Norwegian Seamen's Mission in New Orleans at the time, remembered the ships well, but could not remember Rohmar. Because of these routes, Rohmar was not the only Norwegian with a base in the North-Italian city and it was probably one of them who discovered that he had passed away 29 October 1974, a mere two months after coming ashore and just over three weeks after his 55th birthday.

His had been a lonely life. Like so many living or working abroad, Rohmar sadly missed his mother's death 20 September 1957, although he did come home to see his father and visit her grave later that fall. He had left his ship in Gent, probably as soon as it returned to a European port, and he was in Bergen over Christmas that year. New Year's Day he jumped on a train to Oslo, where he had his medical check-up 2 January. After three months, 25 March 1958, he joined a ship in Copenhagen, only to miss his father's death in Bergen less than a month later. Unmarried and with most of his siblings in similar circumstances, away in the merchant navy, dry land seemingly held no attractions for him. According to his merchant navy record, he spent only a minimal amount of time ashore between ships. Perhaps the price for his wartime survival continued to be extracted, like for countless other war sailors, "peace of mind" was all too often far less achievable than "peace in our time."

When Robert Daigle was escorted off the U–Boat in France, he was transferred to the MILAG—Marine Internierten Lager—the prisoner of war camp for merchant sailors, located at Tarmstedt, 20 kilometers northeast of Bremen in northern Germany. His POW no. was 1030. Daigle was actually repatriated on 15 January 1945, in a swap of POWs arranged by the Swiss Red Cross.[5]

Together with another 40 merchant sailors he arrived in New York on the Swedish liner *Gripsholm*.

It could perhaps be argued that Pusback's personal strategy for surviving the war started as soon as he was ordered aboard the *Deutschland*. He would have remembered the might of the Royal Navy from the battle of Jutland, and regardless of the size of the guns of the *Deutschland*, they would be alone against the enemy's scores of ships. Pusback would be far better off on the deck of a prize on its way back to Germany. Chances are that he actually volunteered to take the first prize home. On such a ship he would be back among the familiar routines of a merchant ship and even if the British stopped him, he could watch the futility of the remainder of the war from behind British barbed wire. If he reached the shores of neutral Norway, that would offer its own possibilities for a skilled and careful strategist. The detour to Murmansk was a "blind alley" for him, but once back in Norwegian waters, his chances for a successful end of the Prize Command grew.

Haugesund was his last chance, and he took it. He anchored, as he had been ordered, knowing full well that in so doing he again violated Norwegian Neutrality Regulations. He had been in the navy long enough to recognize the movements of the two Norwegian ships, but he posted no guards. Internment kept him out of reach of the war for a further five months. He even had the opportunity to see his family for a week that Christmas. This visit to Germany, with a week reporting in Berlin, brought him into direct contact with the team of Admiral Canaris, the head of Abwehr, the German military intelligence organization. A future association with Abwehr would help protect Pusback from the challenges of front-line duty and continue to ensure that at the end of it all, he was alive to reunite with his family at Bremerhaven.

As Germany invaded Norway 9 April 1940, Pusback became attached to the German embassy staff as soon as he reached Oslo. He worked as a support officer to the Naval Attaché. From here his career becomes less certain. His service record from the First War is very detailed, covering a total of 21 postings, each with specific start and end dates, all of them consistent, with no gaps. Pusback's time on the *Deutschland* and on the *City of Flint* appears on his record as a single vague entry:

15.08.1939–03.11.1939 Kommando nicht vermerkt—post not known

His internment fills the time until he took up the position in Oslo. There is, however, no end date for this engagement. Sometime later, he transferred away from Oslo. At the end of May 1944, less than a week before the invasion, Pusback ended a period as an Abewhr officer, working in Rouen in Normandy. Whatever he did during the intervening years, he did well. By the end of 1940, he had been promoted to Oberleutnant zur See; on 1 January 1941 he became Kapitänleutnant and a year later, Korvettenkapitän. Two months later, on 20 April 1943, he was awarded the War Service Cross second class. The official German records from Deutsche Dienststelle in Berlin cannot offer any extra information on Pusback's service record.[6]

As the fall 1944 came to a close, Pusback was working with the man in charge of all Abwehr activities in France. He would have seen the intelligence reports on the progress of the war. France was by then a lost cause to Germany. At the same time Abwehr's influence was in rapid decline. Canaris had been arrested in the aftermath after the failed 20 July 1944 assassination attempt on Hitler and his organization was being absorbed into Himmler's Central Security Department, the Reichssicherheitshauptamt, RSHA. With his boss in jail and the organization being dismantled, Pusback managed yet another change.

On Friday, 24 November 1944, Pusback took up a new post back in Germany, in the defense of Dresden. It is not known if he was in the city at the time of the violent bombing in February 1945, nor how he saw out the end of the war, but his service record ended on 8 May 1945. Together with his son he established a successful business in Bremerhaven and he entered local politics, where he was equally successful. Pusback died in October 1965, a popular and successful man.

Rudolf Gahler was posted to a coastal defense craft flotilla, a Vorpostenflottille, after the internment in Norway. Initially he was back in Bergen, but later he was transferred to France. He met Pusback once during his time in France, probably at Rouen, and again, once in Bremerhaven during the 1950s when Rudi was there on duty in the German Federal navy. Later Rudi joined the new naval border guards, the Bundesgrenzschutz-See. He retired Fregattenkapitan and lived to a ripe old age. In November 2009, in his 97th year Rudi stepped down from his last watch.

Heydemann was a naval officer who had started his career as a sea cadet in 1933, before Hitler gained control of Germany. During his time in *U-575* he sank 12 ships. His only command, *U-575* was transferred to Oberleutnant zur See Wolfgang Boehme. Together with 36 of his crew Boehme survived when his U-boat was sunk 13 March 1944. Günther Heydemann left *U-575* at the end of July 1943. For the rest of the war he was an instructor for new U-boat crews. He survived the war and was interned briefly at Neustadt barracks in May 1945 before spending a few months with the German Mine Sweeping Administration. He was discharged 1 October 1945. He died in Hamburg early in 1986.

Al helped bring the story of their incredible survival out into the open. After the war, Al worked for IBM until he retired to the beautiful countryside of upstate New York. Together with Catherine, his warm and happy wife, they have travelled the length and the breadth of America, often visiting old mates from the Armed Guard, some from the *City of Flint*. Many times they would head south towards Florida as winter gripped the northern states. As Al put it, "not a rusty nail" did any of them ever get in compensation for the endurance they tackled so well during all those stormy days in the spring of 1943.[7] Al and his wife Catherine passed away during the summer of 2017. Al was buried with full military honors.

Donald W. Summerhayes went back to the U.S. Merchant Marine Academy to complete his 4 year course before going on to college. He always loved the sea and ships.

APPENDIX 1

The Prize Command

Surname	First name	Rating/rank	Designation	Occupation	Date of birth	Home address
Pusback	Hans	Leutnant zur See	Prize Comm.		13/02/1891	Gruensstr. 37, Bermerhaven
Grasshoff	Alfred	Leutnant zur See	Deputy Prize Comm.		15/10/1896	G. Elbestr. 68, Wesermuende
Futterlieb	Frits	Ob. Maschinist	NCO	Engineer	24/09/1911	Middelsfaehr bei Wilhelmshaven 103
Gahler	Rudolf	Ob. Steuemannmaat	Senior NCO	Navigator	04/08/1913	Zacnorlauerstr. 24, Aue in Sachsen
Pieper	Richard	Machine Maat	Junior NCO	Engine staff	16/04/1915	Heidmuelen in Holstein
Struck	Paul	Ob. Gefreiter	Leading Seam.	Seaman	31/10/1915	Jaegerstr. 44, Hamburg Wandsbeck
Muschwik	Helmuth	Ob. Gefreiter	Leading Seam.	Seaman	06/08/1913	Bobersbergstr. 2, Grossenhain in Sachsen
Gutheil	Karl	Signal Ob. Gefreiter	Leading Seam.	Signals	17/08/1917	Zimmern. Under Dhaun
Jaekle	Reinold	Masch. Gefreiter	Able Seaman	Engine staff	09/09/1914	Wasenstr. 52, Schwenningen am Neckar
Sackmann	Karl	Masch. Gefreiter	Able Seaman	Engine staff	12/01/1914	Schellenbergstr. 11, Osnabrueck
Langwenues	Frantz	Matrosen-Gefreiter	Able Seaman	Seaman	30/07/1916	Markstr. 13, Altona, Hamburg
Wahlich	Rudi	Matrosen-Gefreiter	Able Seaman	Seaman	22/11/1916	Hebrechtstr. 5, Neu Koeln, Berlin
Muellensiefen	Kurt	Matrosen-Gefreiter	Able Seaman	Seaman	02/03/1920	Saarlandstr. 74, Dortmund
Sander	Heinrich	Matrosen-Gefreiter	Able Seaman	Seaman	05/05/1915	L. Fressenstr. 17, Wesermuende
Pawlowsky	Otto	Matrosen-Gefreiter	Able Seaman	Signals	16/10/1917	Kries Leobschutz, Alstedt o.s.
Stoehr	Cornelius	Matrosen-Gefreiter	Able Seaman	Radio staff	17/08/1914	Weenhuser Colonie, Kreis Leer, Ostfriesland

City of Flint Crew in Norway, 1939

Surname	First name	Designation	Home address
Allen	Maurice	Oiler	Chance, VA
Androvett	Henry	Messboy	1141 Kelder Ave. The Bronx, NY
Codoner	Manuel	Deck Cadett Off.	Point Delgado, Azores
Cook	John T.	Watertender	Massachusetts
Dorman	William	Messboy	Ohio
Ellis	Carl C.	Junior Third Mate	Newtonville, MA
Faust	Clarence	Second Radio Officer	Orangeburg, PA
Freer	Joseph	Steward	Baltimore, MD
Gainard	Joseph A.	Master	43 Marvin Road, Melrose, MA
Garnet	Amo C.	Carpenter	Lansdowne, PA. NYT 25.10.39
Haddock	Herman D.	Ordinary Seaman	Norfolk, VA
Kebler	Fritz T. (Ferd)	First Asst. Eng.	83 Standard St. Mattapan, Boston, MA
Keeling	Martin C.	Messman	Baltimore, MD
Kimmelmann	Isadore	Eng. Cadet Off.	Philadelphia, PA
Landric	Walter H.	Able-Bodied Seaman	St. Louis, MO
Lane	Marter	Second Cook	Pittsburgh, PA
Langston	Jesse	Watertender	Philadelphia, PA
Lewis	Ralph	Third Officer	Upper Darby, PA
Logan	William H.	Chief Engineer	Baltimore, MD
MacConnachie	James	Radio Operator	Glasgow, Scotland
MacDonald	Richard R.	Second Asst. Eng.	Monterey, CA
Massy	George B.	Able-Bodied Seaman	Dade City, FL
McColl	Robert	Watertender	Detroit, MI
McFarlane	William S.	Second Officer	6900 Fenway Road, Dundalk, MD
McHaffie	Percy W.	Oiler	New Orleans, LA
Meehan	James	Ordinary Seaman	Mathews, VA
Neher	William	Able-Bodied Seaman	25 South St. New York City

Surname	First name	Designation	Home address
Parker	Dallas	Able-Bodied Seaman	Manteo, NC
Reynolds	Dwight	Wiper	965 Amsterdam Ave. New York City
Rhoads	Warren W.	First Mate	704 Wallace St. York, PA
Roberson	Jesse V.	Third Asst. Ang.	531-W Olney Road, Norfolk, VA
Schuss	William	Radio Officer	Norfolk, VA
Sellars	Alison	Wiper	Wilmington, NC
Shelling	Wesley	Able-Bodied Seaman	Rialto, CA
Sourwine	Abraham	Ordinary Seaman	Erie, PA
Spicer	Harry J.	Able-Bodied Seaman	Oriental, NC
Swain	Robert B.	Oiler	Norfolk, VA
Taylor	William	Wiper	Nashville, TN
Thistle	Harry	Jnr. Third Asst. Eng.	Lowell, MA
Trump	Raymond	Steward Utility	1403 Covington St. Baltimore, MD.
Walding	Peter	Chief Cook	Midland City, AL
Webb	John E.	Boatswain	Norfolk, VA

APPENDIX 3

City of Flint Crew at Murmansk in 1942

Surname	First name	Date put aboard	Branch	Designation	Occupation
Ahern	Robert J.	17/12/1941	USNR	D-V(G)	AG
Baranski	Edward	17/12/1941	Merchant	Wiper	merchant navy
Barker	Edward	17/12/1941	Merchant	Wiper	merchant navy
Blume	Harry	17/12/1941	Merchant	Messboy	merchant navy
Buchacy	Adam C.	17/12/1941	Merchant	OS	merchant navy
Ceppi	William J.	17/12/1941	Merchant	Second Officer	merchant navy
Chlebus	Tosarck	17/12/1941	Merchant	Oiler	merchant navy
Clark	William B.	17/12/1941	Merchant	Jnr. 3rd Asst. Eng.	merchant navy
Cole	Francis J.	17/12/1941	Merchant	AB	merchant navy
Corrin	Chester D.	17/12/1941	Merchant	1st Asst. Eng.	merchant navy
Dewey	William T.	17/12/1941	Merchant	3rd Asst. Eng.	merchant navy
Dunbar	Leroy	17/12/1941	Merchant	2nd Cook	merchant navy
Frankish	James A.	17/12/1941	Merchant	AB	merchant navy
Freitas	Joseph	17/12/1941	Merchant	Fireman	merchant navy
Johnson	Clarence J.	17/12/1941	Merchant	Jnr. Third Mate	merchant navy
Jones	Fred L.	17/12/1941	Merchant	Messman	merchant navy
Klu	John C.	17/12/1941	Merchant	Steward	merchant navy
Kuling	Henry E.	17/12/1941	Merchant	AB	merchant navy
Litvin	Samuel	17/12/1941	Merchant	OS	merchant navy
Long	Lawrence M.	17/12/1941	Merchant	Master	merchant navy
Marman	Edward C.	17/12/1941	USNR	0–1	AG
Mattson	Kenneth	17/12/1941	Merchant	Radio	merchant navy
Mazzci	Edmund B.	17/12/1941	USNR	0–1	AG
McCale	Kinsey	17/12/1941	Merchant	Oiler	merchant navy
McClure	Earl	17/12/1941	Merchant	Second Mate	merchant navy
McConaty	Walter Leo	17/12/1941	Merchant	Oiler	merchant navy
Medlock	Robert A.	17/12/1941	Merchant	Messman	merchant navy

Surname	First name	Date put aboard	Branch	Designation	Occupation
Miller	Albert	17/12/1941	Merchant	Cook	merchant navy
Moran	Arthur.	17/12/1941	USNR	0–1	AG
Neubauer	James F.	17/12/1941	USNR	0–1	AG
Nevin	John I..	17/12/1941	USNR	0–1	AG
Nigvo	Adrian A.	17/12/1941	USNR	0–1	AG
O'Leary	John M.	17/12/1941	Merchant	Messman	merchant navy
Robesson	Georg D.	17/12/1941	Merchant	AB	merchant navy
Robinson	Lawrence C.	17/12/1941	Merchant	Std. Util.	merchant navy
Rouse	David Euge	17/12/1941	USNR	V-6	AG
Sanley	Herbert E.	17/12/1941	Merchant	AB	merchant navy
Shea	Thomas F.	17/12/1941	Merchant	Third Mate	merchant navy
Shuttlewort	Harvey	17/12/1941	Merchant	Fireman	merchant navy
Smith	Frank	17/12/1941	USN	AS	AG
Spollen	Joseph P.	17/12/1941	USNR	0–1	AG
Stefanr	Ionis James	17/12/1941	Merchant	Bos'n	merchant navy
Streger	James E.	17/12/1941	Merchant	Chief Eng.	merchant navy
Strickland	Ernest L.	17/12/1941	Merchant	OS	merchant navy
Stuty	Granaford	17/12/1941	Merchant	AB	merchant navy
Upton	Frank N.	17/12/1941	Merchant	Chief Mate	merchant navy
Wargols	Alexander	17/12/1941	Merchant	Fireman	merchant navy
Williamson	Edward S.	17/12/1941	Merchant	2nd Asst. Eng.	merchant navy
Zenner	William J.	17/12/1941	USNR	M-2	AG

APPENDIX 4

City of Flint Crew at Persian Gulf in 1942

Surname	First name	Rating/rank	Date put aboard	Occupation
Aurillio	Louis	OS	12/05/1942	Merchant
Barillo	Marcello	Wiper	12/05/1942	Merchant
Bassett	Thomas	Messman	12/05/1942	Merchant
Bjornsen	Bjorn	Radio	12/05/1942	Merchant
Bohn	Alexander	AB	12/05/1942	Merchant
Buck	George Jnr.	Third Mate	12/05/1942	Merchant
Camillo	Frank Jr.	Cox	20/05/1942	USNAG
Campbell	William	1st Asst. Eng.	12/05/1942	Merchant
Campeau	Theodore J.	A.S.	20/05/1942	USNAG
Ceppi	William J.	Ensign, USNR	17/12/1941	Merchant
Cyerniak	Morris	Third Mate	12/05/1942	Merchant
Daigle	Robert	2ndCook	12/05/1942	Merchant
Daniels	Ferdinando	OS	12/05/1942	Merchant
Desrey	William	3rd Asst. Eng.	12/05/1942	Merchant
Dewey	William	Ensign, USNR	17/12/1941	merchant navy
Doran	James	Std. Util.	12/05/1942	Merchant
Gardner	John	Oiler	12/05/1942	Merchant
Gresser	Samuel	2nd Asst. Eng.	12/05/1942	Merchant
Hamsick	Robert	Wiper	12/05/1942	Merchant
Harvey	James Henry	Sea2c	20/05/1942	USNAG
Haselden	Charles Alfo	Sea2c	20/05/1942	USNAG
Hoon	Peter	AB	12/05/1942	Merchant
Johnson	Clarence J.	Ensign, USNR	17/12/1941	merchant navy
Jones	Grant Pusey	Sea2c	20/05/1942	USNAG
Jones	Fred	Messman	12/05/1942	Merchant
Juba	Peter Harry	Sea2c	20/05/1942	USNAG
Karciauckas	Edward J.	Sea2c	20/05/1942	USNAG
Klu	John C.	Steward/ChiefStwd	17/12/1941	merchant navy

Surname	First name	Rating/rank	Date put aboard	Occupation
Kundlya	John	Sea2c	20/05/1942	USNAG
Larson	Alfred	Fireman	12/05/1942	Merchant
Lawrence	Joseph	Cadet	12/05/1942	Merchant
Little	James E.	Sea2c	20/05/1942	USNR Comm. Liaison
Long	Lawrence M.	Lieut. Com., USNR	17/12/1941	merchant navy
Macarintso	Abraham	Chief Eng.	12/05/1942	Merchant
Martin	Israel	Chief Cook	12/05/1942	Merchant
McFarlane	James J.	Sea2c	20/05/1942	USNAG
McKnight	Timothy	Messman	12/05/1942	Merchant
McMurray	Jack	Oiler	12/05/1942	Merchant
Meacham	George A.	SM3c2		USNR Comm. Liaison
Moran	John	Fireman	12/05/1942	Merchant
Nabongy	Frank	Fireman	12/05/1942	Merchant
Nordstrand	Gustave	Bos'n	12/05/1942	Merchant
Petersen	Ernest	Eng. Cadet	12/05/1942	Merchant
Poerschne	Herm.	3rd Asst. Eng.	12/05/1942	Merchant
Prado	Jorge	Std. Util.	12/05/1942	Merchant
Roberts	Lee	OS	12/05/1942	Merchant
Seiler	Mathew	AB	12/05/1942	Merchant
Shea	Thomas F.	Lieutenant, USNR	17/12/1941	merchant navy
Siiro	George	Oiler	12/05/1942	Merchant
Sorensen	Carl G	AB	12/05/1942	Merchant
Steen	Harry	AB	12/05/1942	Merchant
Stevens	Edwin Lore	Sea2c	20/05/1942	USN Comm. Liaison
Sturdy	Richard O	Second Mate	12/05/1942	Merchant
Upton	Frank N.	Ensign, USNR	17/12/1941	merchant navy
Wilson	Clarence	AB	12/05/1942	Merchant

City of Flint Crew on the Final Convoy, January 1943

Surname	First name	Military number	Rating/rank	Date rescued	Occupation
Abrams				28/01/1943	merchant navy
Alcoba				28/01/1943	merchant navy
Andrews				28/01/1943	merchant navy
Barela Alonso	Alonso			**Perished**	merchant navy
Beck	Wesley Hudson	651-36-74	Sea2c 2	28/01/1943	AG
Becker	Albert	621-15-99	Sea1c 2	16/03/1943	AG
Benton				28/01/1943	Merchant
Blanton	Thos. Leonidas	269-78-52	Sea1c 3	16/03/1943	AG
Bohn	William			28/01/1943	Radio
Bovio	Antony Norman	725-17-56	Sea1c 2	28/01/1943	AG
Bozada	Louis Marcus	669-57-24	Sea1c 2	**Perished**	AG
Brandal	Elmer Hearson	615-15-94	Sea1c 2	16/03/1943	AG
Brennan	M			28/01/1943	Merchant
Brennan	Vincent Edw.	642-52-35	Sea2c 3	28/01/1943	AG
Campadlo				28/01/1943	Merchant
Campanello	Louis M.	224-95-03	Sea2c 2	28/01/1943	AG
Carey	Lewis Z.		Ensign 2	28/01/1943	AG
Cavannaugh				28/01/1943	Merchant
Corrigan	John		Cadet Midshipm. 2. c	28/01/1943	Merchant
Cote	Oliver P		2nd Ass. Eng	28/01/1943	Merchant
Daigle	Robert	POW	Chief Cook 2	25/01/1943	POW
Demartin				28/01/1943	Merchant
Derosa				28/01/1943	Merchant
Evans				28/01/1943	Merchant
Fila	Marion Richard	646-19-47	Sea1c 2	28/01/1943	AG
Gabel				28/01/1943	Merchant

Surname	First name	Military number	Rating/rank	Date rescued	Occupation
Gaines				28/01/1943	Merchant
Gaskill				28/01/1943	Merchant
Golen	James	607-21-90	Sea1c 2	28/01/1943	AG
Gutierrez	Stacey Milton	637-07-84	Sea1c 3	28/01/1943	Comm. Liaison
Hatch				28/01/1943	Merchant
Hays				28/01/1943	Merchant
Heinmizell				28/01/19433	Merchant
Henderson				28/01/19433	Merchant
Henson	Talmage Dwight	560-26-88	Sea1c 3	28/01/1943	Comm. Liaison
Johansen	B			28/01/1943	Merchant
Johansen	Rohmar			16/03/1943	merchant navy
Kielek	Walter L			16/03/1943	merchant navy
Kruppski				28/01/1943	Merchant
Kubick	Stephen	622-56-58	Sea1c 2	16/03/1943	AG
Lichtenstein	James Charles	300-74-36	Sea1c	**Perished**	AG
Loankozicik				8/01/1943	Merchant
Lund	Norman Peter	413-43-38	Sea1c 2	28/01/1943	AG
Lusisall	Carlos			16/03/1943	merchant navy
MacKensie	M.			28/01/1943	Merchant
MacKenzie	John		B 2	28/01/1943	merchant navy
Maynard	William Gethro	656-33-15	GM3c 2	16/03/1943	AG
Mills	William N.		Third Officer 2	28/01/1943	Merchant
Myszkowski	Wladyslaw		Able-bodied seaman	16/03/1943	merchant navy
Nelson				28/01/1943	Merchant
Niland				28/01/1943	Merchant
Paradise				28/01/1943	Merchant
Persson	Albert		Oiler	**Perished**	
Poisson	Leo Arthur	204-90-10	AS. S1c 3	28/01/1943	AG
Pucci				28/01/1943	Merchant
Quillen	Donald Eugene	244-02-74	Sea1c 3	**Perished**	AG
Rosengren	Harold		Second Officer	28/01/1943	merchant navy
Shepard				28/01/19433	Merchant
Stevenson	S.E.	616-18-09	Sea1c 2	28/01/1943	AG
Summerhayes	Donald W.		Cadet midshipman	28/01/1943	Merchant

Surname	First name	Military number	Rating/rank	Date rescued	Occupation
Vanderhorst	Walter			**Perished/** fm lifeboat	merchant navy
Voorheis	Arthur Frank	608-50-75	Sea1c 2	16/03/1943	AG
Winkles	Ernest Lee	604-47-73	Sea1c 3	28/01/1943	AG
Young				28/01/1943	Merchant
Zucconi	Domenick Josep	256-43-37	SM3c 2	28/01/1943	Comm. Liaison

Final Convoy: The Final Lifeboat

Becker	Albert	.AG
Blanton	Thos. Leonidas	AG
Brandal	Elmer Hearson	AG
Johansen	Rohmar	merchant navy
Kielek	Walter	merchant navy
Kubick	Stephen	AG
Lusisall		merchant navy
Maynard	William Gethro	AG
Myszkowski	Wladyslaw	merchant navy
Vanderhorst	Walter	merchant navy
Voorheis	Arthur Frank	AG

It is quite interesting that the telegram which was transmitted from *Quadrant*, on the way to Gibraltar, listing the names of the men in the lifeboat, included only nine names.[1] The telegram contained several spelling errors of the names of the survivors, but most importantly one of the merchant crew, Wladyslaw Myszkowski, was omitted altogether.[2]

Chapter Notes

Chapter 1

1. Showell, p. 62.
2. Gemzell (1965).
3. Postan (1952), p. 58.
4. Hinsley, Vol. 1, p. 55.
5. OKM (1940).
6. Prager (1981).
7. Henderson, p. 303.
8. Hull, Vol. 1, p. 663.
9. BAMA, RM 92/5226.
10. I.G. Farben (1940).
11. KTB, SKL, Teil A, Band 1, p. 16.
12. Dinklage (2001) describes this mess in detail.
13. KTB, SKL Teil A, Band 1, p. 93.
14. Meltyukhov.
15. Medlicott, p. 152.
16. KTB, SKL Teil A, Band 1, p. 67.
17. KTB, SKL, Teil A, Band 2, p. 61.
18. KTB, SKL, Teil A, Band 1, p. 111.
19. KTB, SKL, Teil A, Band 1, p. 74 and p. 135.
20. PRO, GFM 33/1045, D576698.

Chapter 2

1. Several published accounts have dealt with the details of the sinking of the *Athenia*. This chapter will focus only on the role of the *City of Flint* in the actual rescue and beyond.
2. The *Southern Cross* was a luxury yacht. She had originally been built as the *Rover*, in Glasgow in 1930, but after the owner's death on board while at Monte Carlo, Howard Hughes purchased the ship in 1932 and changed her name to *Southern Cross*. Hughes tired of the ship and in 1937 sold her to his Swedish friend Axel Wenner-Gren, who had built his vast wealth on Electrolux and armaments. The new owner installed a Swedish crew, and by summer 1939, Karl A. Sjödahl was her captain.
3. Telegram from McClelland Archive.
4. Pedersen, Arne Stein: Senkingen av Athenia. Populærhistorisk Magasin, No. 4, 2001.
5. *Hamilton Spectator*, 21 Nov. 1939.
6. *Hamilton Spectator*, 6 Sept. 1939.
7. *The Times*, 8 Sept. 1939.
8. *New York Times*, 6 Sept. 1939.
9. Lulu E Scweigard had just been awarded her Ph.D before going to Europe to celebrate. She was Head of Department at New York University's Department of Physical Education, a psychiatrist and a leading authority on posture and movement and an early convert to the use of Pilates. Cf. Leena Rouhainen in *Nordic Journal of Dance*, Vol.2, 2010, p.59.
10. PRO, FO371/23096.
11. Gainard (1940), p. 134.
12. Gainard (1940), p. 115.
13. Winnipeg Tribune 14 Sept. 1939, accessed 13 July 2017.

Chapter 3

1. Marine Rundschau (1959), No. 6, p. 336.
2. Bidlingmaier, Vol. 35.
3. Rudi, 30 Jan. 2004.
4. BAMA, RM 92/5226.
5. BAMA, RM 92/5226.
6. Urkunden, No. 253 and 254.
7. PRO, FO 952/3.
8. NARA, *City of Flint* Bridge Log.
9. PRO, FO 371/23702.
10. BAMA, RM 92/5226.
11. PRO, ADM 199/2130.
12. Jim Miller, *The Flint Journal*, 14 Feb. 2005.
13. NARA, *City of Flint* log.
14. PRO, ADM 199/2130.
15. BAMA, RM 92/5226.
16. *North Eastern Gazette*, 25 Oct. 1939.
17. PRO, FO 371/23702.
18. PRO, CAB, 65/1 War Cab. 57(39).
19. Confirmed by Roskill, p. 114.
20. BAMA, RM 92/5226, p. 13b.
21. PRO, GFM 33/1067.
22. PRO, FO 371/23702.
23. *New York Times*, 28 Jan. 1940.
24. Kristiansson (1950), Vol. II, p. 760.
25. BAMA, RM 92/5226
26. PRO, ADM 199/2126.
27. Prisenordnung (1940), Article 28 and Urkunden No. 490.
28. NARA, 300.115(39) *City of Flint* /52.
29. BBC Written Archives, Interview with James MacConnachie, 1 Nov. 1939.
30. NARA, *City of Flint* log.
31. Einwohnerbuch Bremerhaven und Wesermünde, 1934.

32. *Stadtarchiv Bremerhaven*, 28 Nov. 2003.

33. The company was owned 2/3 by German interests and 1/3 by the American United Fruit Company. It had been created purely to comply with the new German trading laws.

34. Dinklage (2001), Vol. II, p. 137.

35. www.theshipslist.com.

36. PRO, ADM 199/2130.

37. Rudi, 30 Jan. 2004.

38. *Whitby Gazette*, 3 Nov. 1939.

39. OKM (1940). Art. 65

40. GB, 30 Jan. 2004.

41. BAMA, RM 92/5226.

42. BBC, MacConnachie interview, 1 Nov. 1939

43. NARA, 300.115(39) *City of Flint*/172, Box 1195, 7 Nov. 1939.

44. PRO, GFM 33/1067.

45. UK Meteorological Office weather map.

46. PRO, ADM 199/390.

47. PRO, ADM 53/110556.

48. NARA, *City of Flint* log.

49. PRO, GFM 33/1067.

50. PRO, ADM 199/390.

51. NARA, *City of Flint* log.

52. NARA, *City of Flint* log.

53. *Stavanger Aftenblad*, 10 Nov. 1939. Gainard later argued that he had embarked on this journey with 6 U.S. flags onboard. He had purchased none, and he still had six onboard.

54. PRO, ADM 53/110556.

55. Dinklage, p. 524.

56. PRO, ADM 199–390.

57. BAMA, RM 92/5226.

58. BBC, Written Archive Centre, MacConnachie interview Dec. 1939

59. *Evening Sun* (Baltimore), 27 Jan. 1940.

60. PRO, GFM 33/1067.

61. PRO, FO 371/23702.

62. PRO, FO 952/8.

63. BBC, 22 Oct. 1939.

64. Dinklage (2001), p. 79.

65. KTB SKL, Teil A, Band B-1, p. 216.

Chapter 4

1. NARA, *City of Flint* log.

2. PRO, GFM 33/1067.

3. Rudi, 30 Jan. 2004.

4. The Captain's affidavit signed 9 November 1939 by Gainard. Washington National Record Centre, Consular Post Records, Bergen 1939, Box 17, Vol. Part VII.

5. BBC, Written Archive Centre, MacConnachie interview Dec. 1939

6. PRO, FO 371/23702.

7. KTB SKL, Teil A, band B-2, p. 180.

8. NARA, *City of Flint* log.

9. RA KA file 1256.3/10 Box 1599.

10. PRO, GFM 33/1067.

11. RA, file KA 1256.3/10 box 1599.

12. PRO, GFM 33/1067.

13. PRO, GFM 33/1067 D587797.

14. German Foreign Office Archive, file R40392.

15. RA, Box 38, Box no. 9052; incl. KA note 21 Oct. 1939.

16. PRO, CAB, 65/1 War Cab. No.55(39); CAB, 100/1 no. 48, 21 Oct.39.

17. RA, File Adm. 1599, 5 Nov. 1939.

18. PRO, 371/23702.

19. PRO, GFM 33/1067.

20. Urkunden no. 485.

21. Harriman note to Secretary of State, 8 Nov. 1939. Library of Congress, Harriman Papers, Container no. 4.

22. PRO, GFM 33/1067.

23. NARA, *City of Flint* log.

24. SKL KTB Oct. 1939, p.28

25. *Evening Sun* (Baltimore), 27 Jan. 1940.

26. PRO, FO 371/23702.

27. Rutebok for Norge (1939).

28. PRO, GFM 33/1067.

29. PRO, ADM 199/2130.

30. Norwegian National Library, Rutebok for Norge, Autumn 1939.

31. PRO, GFM 33/1050 no. 579489–593.

32. RA, File Adm. 1599, 22 Oct. 1939.

33. PRO, ADM 199/293.

34. RA, File Adm. 1599, Aide-memoire of 30 Oct. 1939, quoting Reg. of 13 May 1938.

35. Lovtid.1938, p. 615, 19 Aug. 1938.

36. PRO, FO 371/23701.

37. PRO, GFM 33/1047.

38. Even the German Prize Regulations of 1940 excluded details on the Soviet Union's acceptance of the Hague Conventions of 1907

39. KTB der SKL Teil A, Band 1 and 2; Sept.–Oct. 1939.

40. PRO, GFM 33/1067.

41. NARA, *City of Flint* log.

42. NARA, *City of Flint* log.

43. Ahrens, p. 127.

44. Ahrens, p. 127.

Chapter 5

1. *Bergen Arbeiderblad* 25 Oct. 1939.

2. NARA *City of Flint* log.

3. PRO, GFM 33/1067.

4. *Marine-Rundschau* No.2 (1960), Knacksted, p. 79.

5. *New York Times*, 24 Oct. 1939.

6. BBC Written Archives, 24 Oct. 1939.

7. PRO, GFM 33.1045.

8. BBC Written Archives, 24 Oct. 1939.

9. *Bergens Arbeiderblad*, 24 Oct. 1939.

10. Urkunden, n. 491.

11. KTB SKL, Teil A, Band B-2 p. 197.

12. PRO, GFM 33/1045.

13. NARA 300.115(39) *City of Flint*/5.

14. NARA, 300.115(39) *City of Flint*/7.

15. BAMA RM92/5226.

16. KTB SKL Teil A, Band B-2, p. 124.

17. www.us-botschaft.de, 9 Nov. 2004.

18. Today this building, the Bendlerblock, is a memorial site for the German resistance. The street itself has been renamed in honor of the man who

perhaps came closest to assassinate Hitler, namely Colonel von Stauffenberg, who was executed in July 1944. www. kulturplannung.de, 9 Nov. 2004.

19. PRO, GFM 33/1045.

20. NARA 24 Oct. 1939, 300.115(39) *City of Flint/*8.

21. *Stavanger Aftenblad*, 24 Oct. 1939.

22. NARA, 24 Oct. 1939 300.115(39) *City of Flint/9.*

23. NARA *City of Flint* log.

24. PRO, CAB, 65/1 War Cab. 59(39).

25. BBC, Written Archives, 25 Oct. 1939, 4pm.

26. NARA *City of Flint* log.

27. NARA 25 Oct. 1939 300.115(39) *City of Flint/*25.

28. PRO, GFM 33/1067.

29. Molotov was both the Premier and the Commissar for Foreign Affairs.

30. German Foreign Office Archive, R40392, telegram 26 Oct. 1939.

31. NARA 300.115(39) *City of Flint* /13.

32. KTB SKL, Teil A, Band B-2, p. 210.

33. PRO, FO 371/23702.

34. Supplementary Affidavit, signed 9 November 1939 by Gainard. Washington National Record Centre, Consular Post Records, Bergen 1939, Box 17, Vol. Part VII.

35. German Foreign Office Archive, R26453.

36. Supplementary Affidavit signed 9 November 1939 by Gainard. Washington National Record Centre, Consular Post Records, Bergen 1939, Box 17, Vol. Part VII.

37. NARA *City of Flint* log.

38. NARA 300.115(39) *City of Flint* /29.

39. PRO, ADM 199/2130.

40. PRO. FO 371/23702.

41. NARA, recording 200-G-1288.

42. NARA, 27.10.39 300.115(39) *City of Flint* /52.

43. Supplementary Affidavit signed 9 November 1939 by Gainard. Washington National Record Centre, Consular Post Records, Bergen 1939, Box 17, Vol. Part VII.

44. PRO, GFM 33/1045.

45. NARA, *City of Flint* log.

46. NARA, recording 200-G-1288.

47. *Lübecker General-Anzeiger*, 27 Oct. 39.

48. NARA *City of Flint* log.

49. PRO, ADM 199/293.

50. Urkunden, quoting U.S. State Dept. Bull as no. 492.

51. See the UN Convention on the Law of the Sea (UNCLOS). It is seen as customary law with general principles accepted even by countries (e.g., The USA) who have not formally ratified it.

52. T.A. Taracouzio; The Soviet Union and International Law, New York 1939, page 339. As quoted in Ginsburgs p.133.

53. NARA, recording 200-G-1288.

54. RA Box file 38, Box no. 9052.

55. NARA *City of Flint* log.

56. German Foreign Office Archive, File R 26409.

57. PRO, FO 371 23701. 28.10.39. In reality this was simply not the case.

58. NARA *City of Flint* log.

59. PRO, FO 371/23701.

60. NARA report from Cloyce K. Huston, Oslo to Secretary of State 30 April 1947.
No. 946,857.00/4–3047, RG59, Box 6310.

61. PRO, GFM 33/1067.

62. NARA, recording 200-G-1288.

63. NARA, *City of Flint* log's final entry.

64. PRO, FO 371/23702.

65. *Lübecker General-Anzeiger*, 28 Oct. 1939.

66. PRO, FO 371/2370 1445/28.10.39.

67. *Deutsche Dienststelle*, 15 Mar. 2005.

68. KTB SKL, Teil A, Band B-2, p. 247.

69. PRO, GFM 33/1067.

70. OKM 1940, p. 11.

71. Dahl, p. 7.

Chapter 6

1. PRO, GFM 33/1067.

2. Urkunden no. 487.

3. PRO, GFM 33/1045.

4. RA, FA3020 Y094/0277.

5. PRO, GFM 33/1067 D587799.

6. RA, FA 3020 Y094/0277.

7. RA, Box file 38, Box 9052.

8. PRO, GFM 33/1067 D 587796.

9. RA, KA Box file 38, Box 9052.

10. PRO, FO 371/23701, 30 Oct. 1939.

11. RA, Admiralstaben ref 1256.3/10 Box 1599, note dated 30 Oct. 1939.

12. RA, KA Box file 38, Box no. 9052.

13. Steen (1954), p. 39.

14. RA, KA ,ref 1256.3/10 Box 1599.

15. RA, KA Box file 38, Box 9052.

16. RA KA Box file 38 Box 9052.

17. BBC Written Archive, 30 Oct. 1939.

18. RA, file Utenriksdept. Box file 38, Box 90542 no. 1/39–3/39.

19. RA, KA ref 1256.3/10 Box 1599.

20. PRO, FO 371/23701 30 Oct. 1939.

21. KTB SKL Teil A, Band B-2 p. 254.

22. PRO, GFM 33/1045 D576701.

23. Affidavit signed 9 November 1939 by Gainard. Washington National Record Centre, Consular Post Records, Bergen 1939, Box 17, Vol. Part VII.

24. PRO, GFM 33/1045 D576698.

25. PRO, ADM 199/293.

26. Conventions and Declarations between the Powers. The Hague 1915. Martinus Nijhoff (no page nos.)

27. PRO, ADM 199/293.

28. PRO, ADM 199/293.

29. Ziegler (1985), p.126. They had the same great-grandmother, Queen Victoria, which made them second cousins.

30. PRO, FO 952/9, 1521/29 Oct. 1939.

Chapter 7

1. PRO, CAB, 65/1, War Cab. 66(39).

2. PRO, ADM 199/293 31 Oct. 1939.

3. PRO, ADM 199/293.
4. PRO, ADM 199/293.
5. PRO, FO 371/23702, 1 Nov. 1939. and CAB, 65/2.
6. K.A. Jnr. 7676/1939 II: *Olav Tryggvason's* befatning med *City of Flint*.
7. Statsarkivet, Stavanger, Haugesund Havnekontor file no. 8.
8. RA, file FA 3020 Y094/0277.
9. PRO, AIR 24/370.
10. PRO, GFM 33/1045.
11. PRO, FO 952/9 30 Oct. 1939.
12. PRO, FO 952/8.
13. PRO, GFM 33/1067 and Berlin Foreign Office file R 26409.
14. PRO, ADM 53/108896 HMS *Glasgow*, Log, November 1939.
15. PRO, FO371/23702 3 Nov. 1939.
16. PRO, ref. AIR 24/370 and AIR 27/1458.
17. PRO, AIR 27/1412.
18. PRO, File ref. ADM 53/108896 HMS *Glasgow* Log, November 1939.
19. PRO, File ref. ADM 199/293.
20. RA, file FA 3020 Y094/0277.
21. K.A. Jnr. 7676/1939 II: *Olav Tryggvason's* befatning med *City of Flint*.
22. RA, KAref 1256.3/10 Box 1599.
23. PRO, GFM 33/1045.
24. RA K.A. Jnr. 7676/1939 II: *Olav Tryggvason's* befatning med *City of Flint*.
25. RA, KA, ref 1256.3/10 Box 1599.
26. PRO, GFM 33/1067.
27. RA, File Admiralstab, 1599.
28. PRO, GFM 33/1067.
29. K.A. Jnr. 7676/1939 II: *Olav Tryggvason's* befatning med *City of Flint*. and PRO File ref. ADM 199/293.
30. RA, File Admiralstab 1599 and PRO, GFM 33/1067.
31. The stern x-turret was not removed until several years later.
32. K.A. Jnr. 7676/1939 II: *Olav Tryggvason's* befatning med *City of Flint*.
33. BBC Written Archives, 3 Nov. 1939.
34. PRO, FO371/23702.
35. NARA, file 300.115(39), *City of Flint*, 3 Nov. 1939 No. 2261.
36. PRO, File FO 371/23702.
37. PRO, ADM 199/293.
38. Located right below the new, large Sotra Bridge just to the south of Bergen.
39. PRO, GFM 33/1067.
40. RA, Box file 38, Box no. 9052.
41. PRO, GFM 33/1067 D576700.
42. BBC, file E1/1115.
43. PRO, GFM 33/1067 D 576700.
44. Statsarkivet Stavanger, Fyrvesenet—Kvitsøy File 58.

Chapter 8

1. PRO, GFM 33/1067.
2. PRO, FO952/9.

3. PRO, GFM 33/1067.
4. Affidavit signed 9 November 1939 by Gainard. Washington National Record Centre, Consular Post Records, Bergen 1939, Box 17, Vol. Part VII.
5. PRO, GFM 33/1067.
6. Harriman Papers, 8 Nov 1939; note to Cordell Hull, Library of Congress, container no 4.
7. PRO, GFM 33/1045 D576701.
8. PRO, GFM 33/1067.
9. KTB, SKL, Teil A, Band B-3, p. 7.
10. KTB, SKL, Teil A, Band B-3, p. 9.
11. PRO, GFM 33/1045 D576703.
12. Prize Regulations OKM 1940, paras 76–77.
13. PRO, GFM 33/1045 D576703.
14. Affidavit signed 9 November 1939 by Gainard. Washington National Record Centre, Consular Post Records, Bergen 1939, Box 17, Vol. Part VII.
15. Hull (1948), Vol. I, p. 705.
16. BBC Written Archive, 3 Nov. 1939.
17. Harriman Papers, Container no. 6, section M, Library of Congress.
18. RA, box file 38, Box no. 9052.
19. *Bergens Tidende*, 4 Nov. 1939.
20. PRO, GFM 33/1045.
21. RA, Box file 38, Box no. 9052.
22. RA, KA ref. 1256.3/10 box 1599.
23. RA, KA ref 1256.3/10 box 1599.
24. PRO, GFM 33/1067.
25. PRO, ADM 199/293.
26. Harriman papers, Container no. 6, section M. Library of Congress.
27. Scheen (1947), p. 49.
28. Source withheld 23 Apr. 2006.
29. RA, KA ref 1256.3/10 Box 1599.
30. Library of Congress, Harriman Papers, Report from Dunlap to Hull, 25 November 1939, no. 211 Container #4.
31. RA, Box file 38, Box no. 9052.
32. PRO, GFM 33/1067.
33. *Bergens Tidende*, 4 Nov. 1939.
34. NARA file 300.115(39) City of Flint 137, 4 Nov. 1939.
35. PRO, ADM 199/293.
36. *New York Daily News*, 4 Nov. 1939.
37. KTB, SKL, Teil A, Band B-3 p. 25.
38. KTB, SKL, Teil A, Band B-3, p. 26.
39. KTB, SKL, Teil A, Band B-3, p. 32.

Chapter 9

1. RA, Box file 38, Box no. 9052.
2. NARA file 300.115(39) City of Flint /137/138/139/141.
3. PRO, GFM 33/1067.
4. NARA 4 Nov. 1939 No.6, 711, RG84.
5. The record of what he had to say by way of explanation ran to just over two typewritten pages.
6. RA, Box file 38, Box no. 9052.
7. SKL KTB Teil A. Nov. 1939, p. 26.
8. Dinklage (2001), Vol. 1, p. 472.
9. PRO,. ADM 199/293.
10. Harriman (1941), p. 167.

11. RA Adm. Box 1599, file note dated 4 Nov. 1939.

12. RA, Box File 38, Box no. 9052, note in Koht's hand.

13. PRO, GFM 33/1045 and OKW Bericht, 5 Nov. 1939. 0800.

14. He was wrong, as shown by Wenneker's War Diary, he may have reached 69°N, BAMA file RM 92/5226.

15. RA, KA, ref 1256.3/10 Box 1599 Koht file note 5 Nov. 1939.

16. NARA file 300.115(39) *City of Flint*/151, dated 5 Nov. 1939.

17. Øivind Ask, *Bergens Tidende* 2002.

18. *Gula Tidend*, 6 Nov. 1939.

19. NARA file 300.115(39) *City of Flint*/151.

20. PRO, FO 371/23702.

21. PRO, ADM 199/293.

22. Miles Tollemache to author, September 2002.

23. *Bergens Tidende* 7 Dec. 1946.

24. PRO, GFM 33/1067.

25. Harriman Papers, Container #24, Library of Congress, Interview Tuesday, 3 June 1941.

26. NARA file 300.115(39) *City of Flint* /267.

27. Max Jordan had no chance of actually reaching the western side of Norway in time. But only astute listeners would have picked up the fact that just Gainard was actually in Bergen on one side of Norway while Max Jordan, the interviewer, was talking to him from Oslo, a ten-hour train journey away. In terms of sound or quality there were no differences between the two when they spoke.

28. They even made an unofficial recording of the interview: Norwegian Broadcasting Archives no. 53684. NBC reporter Max Jordan 6 Nov. 1939.

29. The signal went via a cable through Germany to Switzerland and from there on a shortwave transmission to the East Coast of America.

30. NARA file 300.115(39) *City of Flint* /267.

31. RA, KA ref. 1256.3/10 box 1599.

32. RA, KA ref. 1256.3/10 Box 1599.

33. Prize Instructions para 65, note 1. OKM 1940.

34. RA, KA file 1256.3/10 box 1599.

35. PRO, GFM 33/1067 and GFM 33/1045.

36. RA, FA 3020 Y094/0277.

Chapter 10

1. PRO, ADM 199/293 and FO 371/23702.

2. NARA file 300.115(39) *City of Flint* /267.

3. NARA file 300.115(39) *City of Flint*/165.

4. PRO, GFM 33/1045 D576698–702.

5. KTB SKL, Teil A, Band B-3, p. 54.

6. NARA file 300.115(39) *City of Flint*/169, Telegram to Hull, 8 Nov. 1939.

7. PRO, File ref. FO 371/23702.

8. PRO, ADM 199/2126.

9. Lagevorträge, 10 Nov. 1939.

10. NARA, 11 Nov. 1939, 300.115(39) *City of Flint*/191.

11. RA, KA ref. 1256.3/10 Box 1599.

12. Berlin, Foreign Office Archive file R 26409.

13. Statsarkivet Stavanger, Haugesund Havnekontor, file 61.

14. Astrid Riddervoll, 1 Apr. 2004, and *Kongsvinger Arbeiderblad*, 27 Nov. 1939; currency: *Bergen Arbeiderblad*, 4 Nov. 1939.

15. Statsarkivet Stavanger, Haugesund Havnekontor, file 8.

16. RA, KA ref. 1256.3/10 Box 1599.

17. Harriman, 29 Dec. 1939, Harriman Papers, Container no. 6, section M.

18. Dunlap to Secretary of State, 30 Nov. 1939, Washington National Record Centre, No. 212, 711, RG84, Consular Records, Bergen, Box 17.

19. Astrid Riddervoll, 1 Apr. 2004.

20. Sivert Alne, 4 Aug. 2003.

21. Dunlap to Secretary of State, 30 Nov. 1939, No. 212.

22. *Haugseunds Avis*, 12 Dec. 1939.

23. Sivert Alme, 4 Aug. 2003.

24. Astrid Riddervoll, 1 Apr. 2004.

25. One of these radios was even taken to Oslo to provide a young student with her entertainment. When Astrid Riddervoll went off to University after the war, so did one of the American radios.

26. Statsarkivet, Stavanger, Haugesund Havnekontor, file 61.

27. Hildebrand, Röhr and Steinmetz, Vol. 9, p. 232.

Chapter 11

1. Statsarkivet Bergen; Marinens Flyvestasjon, Flatøy.

2. Launched 1910.

3. NARA 300.115(39) *City of Flint*/227 Harriman.

4. Berlin, Foreign Office File Ref. R 26409.

5. NARA, recording 200-G-790.

6. NARA Recording code 200-G-790.

7. Translation: "Thanks for everything."

8. NARA recording, code: 200-G-1288.

9. In 1989 Raymond donated his collection of material related to the *City of Flint* to the Nimiz Library at Annapolis. The inventory refers to a scrapbook on the *City of Flint* and the *Athenia* rescue. Cyvilla Freer had compiled it. Raymond's mother had subsequently married his much older mate Joe.

10. PRO, ADM 199/293.

11. Leifland (1989).

12. Heal (2002).

Chapter 12

1. Padfield p. 223.

2. NARA-NY. *City of Flint*—Official Log Book, dated 22 Apr. 1942.

3. The process would neutralize a ship's natural magnetic field by moving the ship along an electric cable carrying a very high electric current. This

altered the magnetic signature of the ship, making it the same as that of the earth's magnetic field. The Germans measured magnetism in Gauss. A certain value of Gauss present near a magnetic mine would detonate it. Reducing its magnetic value, its Gauss value, was referred to as degaussing.

4. The Chief Engineer, James E. Streger (Lieutenant); the First Officer Frank M. Upton (Ensign); Third Officer Thomas F. Shea (Lieutenant); Junior Third Officer Clarence J. Johnson (Ensign) and the Third Assistant Engineer William T. Dewey (Ensign).

5. NARA, *City of Flint* file, report endorsed 22 Apr. 1942.

6. NAC file 8280 HX170, part 1.

7. The Met. Office.

8. PRO, ADM 199/684.

9. PRO, ADM 199/1145.

10. PRO, ADM 199/684.

11. The *Diniera* or *Dimeria*, was part of the convoy although not included in the pre-sailing chart. In some cases ships would join or leave last minute. PRO: ADM 199/684.

12. NARA *City of Flint* file, 16 Nov. 1944.

13. NARA, *City of Flint* file, Armed Guard Report.

14. Rune.

15. Christensen (ed.) (1939), p. 130.

16. Rune.

17. NARA, *City of Flint*, file 16.11.44.

18. NARA, *City of Flint* file, S.B. Frankel letter, dated 3 Mar. 1942.

19. PRO, ADM 234/369.

20. PRO, ADM 199/2140.

21. NARA, *City of Flint* file, Memo dated 22 Nov. 1944.

22. NARA, *City of Flint* file, Memo dated 22 Dec. 1944.

23. Vail Motter, p. 17.

24. Ruegg and Hague (1992).

Chapter 13

1. NARA, *City of Flint* file, memo 23 May 1942.

2. NARA, *City of Flint* file, signal dated 16 May 1942.

3. NARA, *City of Flint* file, Camillo 30 July 1942.

4. NARA, *City of Flint* file, Camillo 30 July 1942.

5. Motter, p. 394.

6. PRO, ADM 199/428.

7. NARA, *City of Flint* file, Camillo's report.

Chapter 14

1. Al Becker, 22 Oct. 2002.

2. NARA, *City of Flint* file: Op-23L-JH (SC) S76–3.

3. NARA, *City of Flint*, file 16.12.42.

4. NARA, *City of Flint* file.

5. The barrel lengths on U.S. guns were related to their designations. A 3"/50 therefore had a barrel which was 3x50 calibers long=150 inches or 12ft 6".

Similarly the 4"/50 had a barrel length of 200 inches or 16ft 6".

6. Al Becker, 20 Aug. 2004.

7. Rohwer Appendix, Karte 3.

8. BAMA, U-575, KTB.

9. BAMA U-575, KTB.

10. U-575 Das Luk zur Freiheit. Crew memoirs, un-published.

11. Al Becker, 8 July 2004.

12. NARA, RG38, *City of Flint*, dated 25 Mar. 1943 and Moore p. 56.

13. NARA, *City of Flint* file, 01.43.

14. NARA *City of Flint*, file, Record Group 38, UGS-4 convoy and routing file.

15. One ship returned to port.

16. MOD 1989, Ch. VI, p. 81.

17. Bonatz, p. 40.

18. Bontaz, p. 32.

19. PRO, AIR 24/364.

20. NARA, *City of Flint* file, 01.43.

Chapter 15

1. U-575 Das Luk zur Freiheit. Crew memoir, unpublished.

2. NARA, *City of Flint*, file.

3. BAMA, U-575 KTB.

4. U-575 Liliput, Die Geschichte unseres Bootes. Unpublished crew story.

5. BAMA, U-575 KTB, Schussmeldung 25 Jan. 1943.

6. NARA, *City of Flint*, file 18 Mar. 1943.

7. Al Becker, 14 Feb. 2002.

8. Al Becker, 6 Mar. 2003.

9. Al Becker, 11 Mar. 2002.

10. U.S. Coast Guard, Historian's records.

11. NARA, *City of Flint* File, Carey, 28 Apr. 1943.

12. Al Becker, 11 Mar. 2002.

13. Al Becker, 20 Nov. 2011.

14. NARA *City of Flint* file, 18.03.43.

15. Cadet Midshipmen Corrigan and Summerhayes were both on placement from the U.S. Merchant Marine Academy at King's Point, Long Island. The Academy had only been founded the year before.

16. NARA, *City of Flint*, file 25.04.43 and King's Point Enemy Action Report dated 29 April 1943.

17. NARA, *City of Flint* file, 30.04.43 and Kings Point Enemy Action Report dated 30 April 1943.

18. NARA, *City of Flint*, file 25.04.43.

19. NARA, *City of Flint* file 18.03.43.

20. NARA, *City of Flint* file, Carey, 28 Apr 1943.

21. NARA, *City of Flint* file, Captain's intelligence report, 25 Apr. 1943.

22. Al Becker, 07 Jan. 2003.

23. NARA, *City of Flint* file, report 15.4.43.

24. Al Becker 16 Mar. 2001.

25. BAMA U-575 KTB, Schussmeldung 25 Jan. 1943.

26. NARA, *City of Flint* file—Confidential memorandum, Office of the Chief of Naval Operations, 25 March 1943.

27. BAMA, U-575 War Diary.

28. Al Becker, 31 Dec. 2004.

29. BAMA, U-575 War Diary.

30. Central European Time, the Time Zone all German U-boats set their clocks to.

31. NARA *City of Flint* file.

32. It was an aircraft, which located U-575 on its final voyage a year later (Kemp (1999), 2, p. 177).

33. BAMA U-575, KTB.

34. The Oerlikon had a mechanical trigger. The trigger itself was a rod sticking out from the left side of the weapon. Pulling the rod back would release the sear and start the breechblock's forward movement. This would take a round from the magazine and drive it into the firing chamber where the hammer and firing pin, travelling with the breechblock, fired the cartridge. There was no spring in this mechanism. Instead it relied on a set of "hammer toes," which rammed the firing pin into the cartridge's detonator once the round was chambered. If the sear was fractured, if it had snapped or had developed a fault as caused by an explosion, the gun could have fired on its own; on automatic fire.

35. Al Becker, 03 Jan. 2003.

36. BAMA, U-575 War Diary.

37. Daigle's bluff has gone down in the British Official Record of the Uboat War. In his account, written for the British Ministry of the Defense, Hessler referred to U-575, which "sank a large transport." In reality, this was the *City of Flint*, a mid-sized Hog Islander of around 4500 tons.

38. BAMA, U-575 War Diary.

39. U-575 Das Luk zur Freiheit. Crew memoir, unpublished.

40. NARA, *City of Flint* file, intelligence report, 24.4.43.

41. NARA, *City of Flint* file 16.03.43.

42. Al Becker, 20 Aug. 2004.

43. NARA, *City of Flint* file 18.03.43.

44. PRO, ADM 199/767.

45. NARA, *City of Flint* file, telegram dated 28.1.43.

46. NARA, *City of Flint* file, telegram dated 1.2.43.

47. NARA, *City of Flint* file, telegram, dated 9.2.43.

48. NARA *City of Flint* file 13.3.43.

49. Al Becker, 16 Mar. 2001.

50. Al Becker, 21 May 2004.

51. Al Becker, 21 May 2004.

52. Al Becker, 21 May 2004.

53. Merchant navy database, Norwegian State Archives, Bergen.

54. Michael Ellsner.

55. BAMA, U-575 War Diary.

56. Michael Ellsner.

57. Al Becker, 16 Mar. 2001.

58. Al Becker, 29 Aug. 2004. Al still remembered the 23 Psalm well.

59. Hjeltnes (1995), p. 131.

60. NARA *City of Flint* file 16.04.43.

61. Marine Botany, Univ. of Oslo, 5 June 2003.

62. Al Becker, 21 May 2004.

63. They survived one of the longest periods ever recorded in a lifeboat.

64. PRO, ADM 199/767.

65. NARA, *City of Flint* file.

66. Al Becker, 30 July 2004.

67. Al Becker, 16 Mar. 2001.

68. Al Becker, 14 Feb. 2002.

69. Al Becker, 22 Oct. 2002.

Chapter 16

1. *The Sun* (Baltimore), 14 Dec. 1943.

2. *Hamburger Illustrierte*, No.4, 22 Jan. 1944.

3. Michael Ellsner.

4. *True Magazine*, Jan. 1944.

5. Elphic letter 2001.

6. Deutsche Dienststelle, 15 Mar. 2005.

7. Al Becker, 20 Nov. 2011.

Appendix 5

1. Browning (2001), e-mail to author.

2. Moore (2001), letter to author.

Bibliography

Primary Sources

Manuscripts

ADM means a file from the Admiralty. FO a file from the Foreign Office, etc.

British

PRO files

ADM 53/108896 HMS Glasgow, Log November 1939
ADM 53/110556
ADM 173/15780 L-27 Log October 1939
ADM 199/24
ADM 199/293
ADM 199/347
ADM 199/348
ADM 199/362
ADM 199/390
Adm 199/428
ADM 199/684
ADM 199/767
ADM 199/1145
ADM 199/1147
ADM 199/2126
ADM 199/2130
ADM 199/2140
ADM 234/369
AIR 24/370
AIR 27/1298
AIR 27/1458
CAB 65/1 (War Cabinet minutes)
CAB 65/2
CAB 66/3
CAB 1001/1
FO 371/22841
FO 371/22842
FO 371/23096
FO 371/2370
FO 371/23701
FO 371/23702 (CAB 69(39))
FO 952/3
FO 952/8
FO 952/9
GFM 33/1045 German Foreign Ministry
GFM 33/1067 German Foreign Ministry

Imperial War Museum

File 9309, Misc. 15 (337)
File 10896, Box P284
File 11420, Box P284
File 591367, Box 289/1

BBC Written Archives

File E1/1107
File E1/1114/1
File E1/1115

Norwegian

Riksarkivet (The Norwegian State Archive):
Adm.ref KA 1256.3/10 Box 1599, Admiralstaben.
FA 3020 Y094/0277.
KA, Box File 38, Box 9052.
Utenriksdept. Box file 38, Box 90542, no. 1/39–3/39.

Statsarkiv Bergen

Losoldermannen i Bergen, Losoppgjørsbok, file 60.
Marinens Flyvestasjon, Flatøy.
Merchant Navy database.
Statsarkiv, Stavanger:
Haugesund Havnekontor, files no. 8, no. 23, no. 58, no. 61 and no. 152.
Fyrvesenet, Kvitsøy file no. 58.
Fyrvesenet, Utsira file no. 29.

Norwegian Broadcasting Archives

No. 53684. Sound recording: NBC reporter Max Jordan 6 November 1939.

Norwegian Nobel Institute

Harriman notes to US Secretary of State, at Library of Congress.
NARA NWDNM references.
Washington National Record Centre.
NARA report from C.K. Huston.
NARA Record Group 57: File ref 857.00/313.

German

http://ubootwaffe.net holds the U-boat Command's war diaries.

BAMA RM98/1053 *U-575* Kriegstagebuch, 1 December 1942–31 January 1943.
BAMA RM 92/5226 Kriegstagebuch Panzerschiff *Deutschland* 24 August 1939–31 October 1939. Deutsche Dienststelle.

American

Record Group 24, Records of Bureau of Naval Personnel, Casualty reports on Naval Armed Guard, SS *City of Flint.*
Record Group 38, Armed Guard Voyage Reports Tenth Fleet, Ship Movement Cards, SS *City of Flint.*
Record Group 178, Bridge Log Book 24, SS *City of Flint.*
NARA 300.115(39), *City of Flint* file.
City of Flint Bridge Log dates.
FDR Library files- online.
Sound recording 200-G-1288.
Sound recording 200-G-790.

Canadian

Maritime Museum of the Atlantic, Halifax: *City of Flint* file.
National Archive of Canada file 8280 HX170, part 1.

Newspapers

Aftenposten
APWirephoto
Bergen Arbeiderblad
Bergens Aftenblad
Bergens Tidende
The Connacht Tribune
Evening Sun (Baltimore)
Gefle Dagblad
Globe and Mail
Gula Tidend
Hamilton Spectator
Haugesunds Avis
Inverness Courier
Kongsvinger Arbeiderblad
Lübecker General-Anzeiger
Morgenavisen
The New York Daily News
The New York Times
Nordlys
North Eastern Gazette
The Scotsman
Stavanger Aftenblad
The Sunday Times
The Times
Toronto Daily Star
Toronto Telegram
Whitby Gazette
Winnipeg Tribune

Websites

http://ktb.ubootwaffe.net
http://uboat.net

www.ww2.dk/air/kampf/kg26.htm
www.yale.edu/lawweb/avalon
www.navyhistory.com
www.uboat.net
www.mooremccormack.htm
www.arkivverket.no/bergen (Hitler i Norge article 19/05/2005)
www.usmm.org (MARLAG MILAG POW camp information)
www.state.gov

Maps

Admiralty Chart no. 2333, Mys Nemetsky to Mys Teriberskiy.
Admiralty Chart No. 4011, North Atlantic Ocean, Northern Part.
Admiralty Chart No. 4010, Norwegian Sea and adjacent seas.
Norwegian Chart No. 307.
UK Meteorological Office, Weather maps—October 1939, January 1942, January 1943.

SECONDARY SOURCES

Books

Ahrens, Adolf. *Die Siegesfahrt der 'Bremen.'* Berlin: Verlag Ernst Steiniger, 1940.
Anttonen, Ossi. *Luftwaffe in Finland 1941–1944.* Vantaa: Finnair Ofset, 1980. Vol. II.
Anttonen, Ossi and Valtonen, Hannu. *Luftwaffe in Finland 1941–1944.* Vantaa: Finnair Ofset, 1976. Vol. 1.
Avery, Norm L. *B-25 Mitchell, The Magnificent Medium.* St. Paul, Minn.: Phalanx Publishing, 1992.
Bercuson, David J. and Holger H. Herwig, *Bismarck.* London: Pimlico, 2003.
Berntsen, Harald. *I Malstrømmen, Johan Nygaardsvold 1879–1952.* Oslo: Aschehough, 1991.
Beyer, Kenneth M. *Q-Ships versus U-Boats.* Annapolis: Naval Institute Press, 1999.
Bidlingmaier, Gerhard. *Einsatz der schweren Kriegsmarineinheiten in ozeanischen Zufuhrskrieg.* Vol. 35. Kurt Vowinchel Verlag, 1962.
Black, Conrad. *Franklin Delano Roosevelt, Champion of Freedom.* London: Weidenfeld & Nicholson, 2003.
Black, Edwin. *IBM and the Holocaust.* London: Little Brown, 2001.
Blair, Clay. *Hitlers U-Boat War, The Hunters 1939–42.* London: Cassell & Co., 2000.
Bloch, Michael. *Ribbentrop.* London: Abacus, 2003.
Bonatz, Heintz. *Seekrieg im Äther.* Herford: Verlag E.S. Mittler & Sohn, GmbH, 1981.
Bowen, Frank C. *The Flag of the Southern Cross 1939–1945.* Published privately for Shaw, Savill & Albion Co. Ltd., c. 1947.
Bullitt, Orville H. (ed.) *For the President, Personal and Secret.* London: Andre Deutsch, 1973.
Butler, J.R.M. *Grand Strategy Vol. II Sept. 1939–June 1941.* London: HMSO, 1957.

Christensen, Chr. A. R. (ed.) *Den Annen Verdenskrig* Oslo: H. Aschehoug & Co.1940. No 1 & No. 7.

Churchill, Winston S. *Andra Världskriget*. Stockholm: Skoglunds Bokförlag, 1950. Cols. 1–6.

Clowes, Wm. *The Royal Navy*. London: Chatham Publishing, [1897] 1996. Vol. I.

Collier, Basil. *The Defense of the United Kingdom*. London: HMSO, 1957.

Crecraft, Earl Willis: *Freedom of the Seas*. Freeport, New York: Books for Libraries Press. 1969 reprint of 1935 edition.

Cressmann, Robert J. *The Official Chronology of the US Navy in World War II*. Annapolis: Naval Institute Press, 1999.

Crowe, Fanning, Kennedy, Keogh and O'Halpin (eds). *Documents on Irish Foreign Policy Vol. VI 1939–1941*. Dublin: National Archives, 2008.

Dahl, A.D. *Med Alta Bataljon mot Tyskerne*. Stockholm: Bokførlaget Natur och Kultur, 1945.

Dannevig, Birger. *Skip og Menn*. Oslo: J.W. Cappelens Forlag AS, 1968.

De Kerbrech, Richard. *The Shaw Savill Line*. Norfolk: Ship Pictorial Publications, 1992.

Derry, T. K. *The Campaign in Norway*. London: HMSO, 1953.

Dinklage, Ludwig and Hans Jürgen Witthöft. *Die Deutsche Handelsflotte 1939–1945*. Hamburg: Nikol Verlagsgesellschaft mbH & Co., 2001. Vols 1 & 2.

Divine, A.D. *The Wake of the Raiders*. London: John Murray, 1941.

Dönitz, Karl. *Memoirs*. London: Cassell & Co., 2000.

Dybvig, O. *SIG Luftwaffe Documents*. Norway: Private issue, 2003. Vol. 1.

Elphic, Peter. *Liberty, The Ship That Won the War*. London: Chatham Publishing, 2001.

Furre, Berge. *Norsk Historie 1905–1940*. Oslo: Det Norske Samlaget, 1971.

Gabler, Ulrich. *Unterseebootbau*. Bonn: Bernard & Graefe Verlag, 1997.

Gainard, Joseph A. *Yankee Skipper*. New York: Frederick A Stokes Company, 1940.

Galland Adolf. *The First and The Last*. Bristol: Cerberus, 2001.

Goldberg, Mark H. *The "Hog Islanders": The Story of 122 American Ships*. New York: The American Merchant Marine Museum, 1991.

Grenfell, Russell. *Jakten på Bismarck*. Oslo: Essforlagene, 1953.

Hadfield, Charles. *World Canals, Inland Navigation Past and Present*. London: David & Charles, 1986.

Hague, Arnold. *The Allied Convoy System 1939–1945*. Ontario: Vanwell Publishing Ltd., 2000.

Hamburg: Koehlers Verlagsgesellschaft, 2001.

Harriman, Florence Jaffray. *Mission to the North*. London: George G. Harrap & Co., 1941.

Hart, B.H.Liddel. *Den annen verdenskrig*. Oslo: J.W. Cappelens Forlag, 1971.

Hauge, Andreas. *Kampene i Norge 1940*. Sandefjord: Krigshistorisk Forlag, 1995. Vol. 2.

Heal, Sid C. 'The Hog Island Steamer *City of Flint*,' *Nautical Magazine* (Fall 2002).

Helgesen, Jan-Petter. *Kampen om Sola*. Stavanger: Dreyer Bok, 1999.

Hildebrand, Hans H., Albert Röhr, and Hans-Otto Steinmetz. *Die deutschen Kriegsschiffe*. 7 vols. Herford: Koehler, 1979–83.

Hilger, Gustav and Alfred G. Meyer, Alfred G. *The Incompatible Allies*. New York: Hafner Publishing, 1971.

Hinsley, F. H. *British Intelligence in the Second World War*. London: HMSO, 1979. Vol. 1.

_____. *British Intelligence in the Second World War*. London: HMSO, 1981. Vol. 2.

Hjeltnes, Guri. *Handelsflåten i krig*. Vol. 3: Sjømann—Lang Vakt. Oslo: Grøndahl Dreyer, 1995.

Hodges, Peter, and Norman Friedman, *Destroyer Weapons of World War 2*. Greenwich: Conway Maritime Press, 1979.

Holmestrand, Størmer et al (eds). *Aschehough's Konversasjonsleksikon*. Oslo: H. Aschehoug &Co., 1969.

Hull, Cordell. *The Memoirs of Cordell Hull*. London: Hodder & Stoughton, 1948. Vol. 1.

IG Farben, 'Wichtige Unternehmen der Chemischen Industrie in Grossbritannien und Nord-Irland.' 21 Nov. 1940. In-house publication.

Internationalen Militärgerichtshof. *Der Prozess gegen die Hauptkriegsverbrecher*. Vols 1–23. 1947–48. New ed. by Frechen: Komet [undated reprint].

Jacobsen, Hans-Adolf (ed.). *Generaloberst Halder, Kriegstagebuch*. Stuttgart: W. Kohlhammer Verlag, 1962. Vol. 1.

Jensen, Magnus. *Norges Historie*. Oslo: Universitetsforlaget, 1968.

Jordan, Roger. *The World's Merchant Fleets 1939*. London: Chatham Publishing, 1999.

Keegan, John (ed.) *Atlas of the Second World War*. London: HarperCollins, 2003.

Kemp, Paul. *Convoy! Drama in Arctic Waters*. London: Brockhampton Press, 1999. (1).

_____. *U-boats Destroyed*. London: Arms & Armour, 1999. (2).

Kershaw, Ian. *Hitler, 1936–45: Nemesis*. London: Allen Lane, The Penguin Press, 2000.

Knackstedt, Heinz. 'Der *City of Flint* Fall,' *Marine-Rundschau*, No.2 (1960): 79–98.

Koop, Gerhard. *Battleships of the 'Deutschland' Class*. Annapolis: Naval Institute Press, 2000.

Kraska, James. 'Prize Law,' *Max Planck Encyclopedia of Public International Law*. 10 vols. New York: Oxford University Press, 2012.

Krigshistorisk Avdeling. *Operasjonene i Glåmadalføret, Trysil og Rendalen*. Oslo: Gyldendal Norsk Forlag, 1953.

Kristiansson, Sten. *Världskriget i Bild*. Uddevalla, Sweden: Bokförlaget Hermes AB, 1950. Vol. 2.

Kunz, Josef. 'British Prize Cases 1939–1941,' *The American Journal of International Law*, Vol. 36, No.2 (April 1942): 204–228.

Lakowski, Richard. *Deutsche U-boote Geheim, 1935–1945*. Berlin: Brandeburgisches Verlagshaus, 1991.

Leifland, Leif. *Svartlistningen av Axel Wenner-Gren*. Stockholm: Askelin & Hägglund Förlag Ab, 1989.

Liversidge, Douglas. *Den tredje front*. Oslo: Ernst G. Mortensens Forlag, 1961.

Mallmann-Showell, J.P. *Das Buch der deutschen Kriegsmarine, 1935-1945*. Stuttgart: Motorbuch Verlag, 1991.

Martinus Nijhoff. *Conventions and Declarations between the powers*. The Hague, 1915.

Matishow, G. and E. Olesik, et. al. *Regional Feasibility Report (ECORA)*. Murmansk: Oblast, 2001.

Mc Sherry, James E. *Stalin, Hitler and Europe*. Cleveland and New York: The World Publishing Co. 1968. Vol. 1.

Medlicott, W. N. *The Economic Blockade*. London: HMSO, 1952. Vol. 1.

Meltyukhov, M.I. *Stalin's Missed Chance, The Soviet Union and the fight for Europe* [Russian only] Moscow: Veche, 2000.

Ministry of Defense. *The Joint Service Manual of the Law of Armed Conflict*. London: JSC 383, 2004.

Ministry of Defense (Navy). *The U-Boat War in the Atlantic, 1939–1945*. German Naval History. London: HMSO, 1989.

Mogens Victor. *Utenrikskronikk*. No 30, 5 August 1939.

Möller, Eberhard. *Kurs Atlantik*. Stuttgart, Oberkommando der Kriegsmarine: Motorbuch Verlag, 1995.

_____. *Seekriegsrechtliches Sammelheft*. Berlin: Prisenordnung mit Kommandanten-anweisungen Oberkommando der Kriegsmarine, 1940. Vol. 1.

_____. Urkunden zum Seekriegsrecht. Berlin: Zusammengestellt vom Oberkommando der Kriegsmarine, 1941.

Moore, Arthur R. *A Careless Word. A Needless Sinking*. New York: U.S. Merchant Marine Academy,1982.

Morison, Samuel Eliot. *The Battle of the Atlantic, September 1939–May 1943*. Urbana and Chicago: University of Illinois Press, 2001.

Mortensen, Sverre (ed.) *The Norway Year Book*. Oslo: Johan Grundt Tanum Forlag, 1962.

Olsen, Bjørn Gunnar. *Tranmæl og hans menn*. Oslo: Aschehough, 1991.

Owren, Nils. *Klar til å åpne ild*. Oslo: Norsk Kunstforlag, 1982.

Padfield, Peter. *Dönitz, the last Führer*. London: Cassell & Co., 2001.

Pattinson, William. *Mountbatten & the Men of the 'Kelly.'* Wellingborough: Patrick Stephens, 1986.

Pedersen, Arne Stein: 'Senkingen av Athenia,' *Populærhistorisk Magasin*, No. 4, 2001.

Peillard, Léonce. *Geschichte des U-Boot Krieges 1939–1945*. München: W. Heyne Verlag, 1985.

Phillips, Julian. *A Brief History of the Chemical Industry on Teesside*. Middlesbrough: Teesside Chemicals Initiative, 1999.

Postan, M.M. *British War Production*. London: HMSO, 1952.

Prager, Hans Georg. *Panzerschiff 'Deutschland,' Schwerer Kreuzer Lützow*.

Rankin, Nicholas. *Telegram from Guernica*. London: Faber & Faber, 2003.

Rastad, Per Erik. *Kongsvinger Festnings Historie*. Kongsvinger: Hovedkomiteen for Kongsvinger Festning, 1987.

Rohwer, Jürgen. *Die U-Boot-Erfolge der Achsenmächte 1939–1945*. München: J.F. Lehmanns Verlag, 1968.

_____. *War at Sea 1939–1945*. London: Caxton Editions, 2001.

Roskill S W. *The War at Sea 1939–1945, Vol. II: The period of balance*. London: HMSO, 1956.

_____. *The War at Sea 1939–1945. Vol. I: The Defense*. London: HMSO, 1950.

Rouhiainen, Leena: 'The Evolution of the Pilates Method and Its Relations to the Somatic Field,' *Nordic Journal of Dance*, Vol. 4, 2010.

Ruegg, Bob, and Arnold Hague. *Convoys to Russia 1941 to 1945*. Kendal: World Ship Society, 1992.

Savas, Theodore P. (ed.) *Silent Hunters, German U-Boat Commanders. of World War II*. Annapolis: Bluejacket Books, 2003.

Scheen, Rolf. *Norges Sjøkrig 1939–1940*. Bergen: John Griegs Forlag, 1947. Vol. 1.

Sebag-Montefiore, Hugh. *Enigma. The Battle for the Code*. London: Phoenix, 2001.

Seekriegsleitung. *Kriegstagebuch der Seekriegsleitung 1939–1945*. Berlin: Mittler, 1997.

Shirer, Willian L. *The Rise and Fall of the Third Reich*. London: Pan Books, 1971.

Showell, Jak P. Mallmann. *German Navy Handbook 1939–1945*. London: Sutton Publishing, 2002.

Sjøforsvaret. *Norske torpedobåter gjennom 125 år* (1998).www.mil.no/sjoforsvaret/mtb/.

Smith Amanda (ed.) *Hostage to Fortune. The letters of Joseph P. Kennedy*. New York: Viking, 2001.

Speer, Albert. *Inside the Third Reich*. London: Sphere Books, 1971.

Staveseth, Reidar. *Nordover med Hurtigruten*. Oslo: Johan Grundt Tanum, 1943.

Steen E. A. *Norges Sjøkrig 1940–1945. Bind I: Sjøforsvarets nøytralitetsvern 1939–1940*. Oslo: Krigshistorisk Avdeling, Gyldendal, 1954.

Stern, Robert C. *Type VII U-boats*. London: Brockhampton Press, 2002.

Syrett, David (ed.) *The Battle of the Atlantic and Signals Intelligence. U-Boat Tracking papers 1941–1947*. London: Ashgate for the Navy Records Society, 2002.

Talbot-Booth, E. C. *The Naval Calendar*. London: Sapson Low, Marston & Co., Ltd., 1938.

Tarrant, V.E. *The U-Boat Offensive 1914–1945*. London: Cassell & Co., 2000.

Thiel, Reinhold. *Die Geschichte des Norddeutschen Lloyd*. Bremen: Verlag H.M. Hauschild GMBH, 2004. Vol. 4.

Thompson, William. *The War at Sea 1914–1918*. London: Sidgwick & Jackson, 2005.

Vail Motter, T.H. *The Pacific Campaign*. Edinburgh: Birlinn Publishing, 2001 (2).

_____. *The Persian Corridor and Aid to Russia*. Washington: Center of Military History, United States Army, 2000.

Van Der Vat, Dan. *The Atlantic Campaign*. Edinburgh: Birlinn Ltd. 2001 (1).

Wagner, Gerhard (ed.) *Lagevorträge des Oberbefehlshabers der Kriegsmarinevor Hitler 1939–1945*. München: J.F. Lehmanns Verlag, 1972.

Wetzel, Eckard. *U995 Das U-Boot vor dem Marine-Ehrenmal in Laboe*. Erlangen: Karl Müller Verlag, 1996.

Williams, Andrew. *The Battle of the Atlantic*. London: BBC, 2002.

Williams, Anthony G. *Rapid Fire*. England: Airlife, 2000.

Woodman, Richard. *Arctic Convoys 1941–1945*. London: John Murray, 2004.

Ziegler, Philip. *Mountbatten: The Official Biography*. London: Book Club Associates, 1985.

Journals

Drei und ihre Kanone in: Hamburger Illustrierte, No. 4, 22 January 1944.

'46 Days Adrift' in *True Magazine* (January 1944), reprinted in *The Pointer* (June–Aug. 2000).

London Gazette, 4 September 1939, Supplement.

Marine Rundschau, No. 2 (1960), Knacksted p. 79.

Marine Rundschau, No. 6 (1959), p. 336.

Norsk Lovtidende 13 May and 19 August 1938, 1939.

Rutebok for Norge 1939.

Strecker, Karl Günter, in *Schaltung Küste,* Vol. 43, no. 182 (March–April 2000): 34.

Unpublished

Ellsner, Michael. *U-575 Liliput, Die Geschichte unseres Boots.*

_____. *U-575 Das Luk zur Freiheit.*

The McClelland Archive.

Norwegian State Archive, Bergen; Merchant Navy database.

Index